Memories of
Margaret Thatcher

Memories of Margaret Thatcher

A PORTRAIT, BY THOSE WHO KNEW HER BEST

Edited by Iain Dale

FOREWORD BY DAVID CAMERON

Biteback Publishing

Royalties from the sale of this book are donated to the Margaret Thatcher Foundation

Based on *Memories of Maggie: A Portrait of Margaret Thatcher* edited by Iain Dale,
published by Politico's in 2000.

First published in Great Britain in 2013 by
Biteback Publishing Ltd
Westminster Tower
3 Albert Embankment
London SE1 7SP

ISBN 978-184954-607-2

10 9 8 7 6 5 4 3 2 1

A CIP catalogue record for this book is available from the British Library.

Set in Baskerville and Bulmer

Printed and bound in Great Britain by
CPI Group (UK) Ltd, Croydon CR0 4YY

Contents

Acknowledgements

The idea for this book came on a holiday to the United States when I came across a marvellous book called *Recollections of Reagan: A Portrait of Ronald Reagan* (edited by Peter Hannaford and published by Morrow in 1997). Using the premise that if it was good enough for Ronald Reagan it was good enough for Margaret Thatcher, I stored the idea at the back of my mind and eventually decided that the book should appear to coincide with the tenth anniversary of her resignation (or, perhaps more accurately, overthrow) as Prime Minister. Just as people remember where they were when Kennedy was shot, most people in Britain remember exactly where they were when they heard Margaret Thatcher had resigned.

The first edition of this book, titled *Memories of Maggie*, was published in the autumn of 2000. On the day she died, 8 April 2013, I was inundated with emails and texts from people asking me to republish it, and garner some new contributors.

I am so grateful to all of those who agreed to write something for the book. I have also included many of the tributes to Lady Thatcher made in both Houses of Parliament on Wednesday 10 April 2013.

This book has been a pleasure to compile, edit and indeed publish. I am indebted to the contributors, whose anecdotes are entertaining, informative and, on occasion, quite moving. They all provided their contributions on the understanding that royalties from the book would be donated to a worthy cause and, as such, royalties from this edition of the book will go to the Margaret Thatcher Foundation.

The book contains anecdotes from world leaders, former Cabinet ministers, Members of Parliament, journalists, civil servants and many other people who have experienced memorable encounters with the Iron Lady. We have also received cooperation from several leading publishers which has allowed us to reprint relevant passages from the memoirs of the late Ronald Reagan, Mikhail Gorbachev and the late Alan Clark among others. We have endeavoured to gain copyright clearance from all relevant parties.

The book contains parliamentary information licensed under the Open Parliament Licence v.1.0.

Some of the original entries read as if she were still living. We decided to leave them as they were originally written.

Introduction

I became a Thatcherite at the age of sixteen. Thirty-four years later I still hold to the beliefs and values that defined Margaret Thatcher's time in office. Twenty-three years after her fall from power, Margaret Thatcher and her legacy still have an important and telling influence on British political life, in the same way that Gladstone and Disraeli did a century earlier. Even though she hadn't made a full speech for ten years by the time she died, she retained the ability to make news and influence current-day politicians in a way which no other politician could. But with her legacy come a lot of myths, myths which I hope this book can help dispel.

She is loved and hated in equal measures. The bile and venom on the internet whenever her name is mentioned has to be seen to be believed. She is often held to be responsible for all the ills of today's economy and society, even though it is more than two decades since she left Downing Street. She was inexplicably blamed for the recent banking crisis, her critics conveniently ignoring that it was the Labour government who introduced a new system of banking regulation in the late 1990s.

But those of us who remain firm adherents and defenders of the Thatcherite legacy must also recognise that times move on and that what was right for the country in the 1980s might not be the medicine that the country needs now. I think the secret is to understand how Thatcherite principles can be applied to today's politics, rather than to get hung up on individual policies.

Perhaps, though, the main lesson that today's politicians must learn from Margaret Thatcher is to look at her policy of 'sound money'. We seem to conveniently forget how much of a basket case the British economy was in 1979, when the Conservatives won the election. Only three years earlier the Labour Chancellor, Denis Healey, had humiliatingly been forced to go to the IMF. Nationalised industries were overmanned and inefficient and British industry was clinging onto the glories of an industrial past, without realising that other countries were overtaking us in an increasingly competitive international market. It wasn't the Thatcher government that destroyed British manufacturing in the 1980s. It was weak management and rampant trade unions which combined to prevent the modernisation of working practices that was proving so disastrous to the British car, steel and coal industries, among many others. Margaret Thatcher forced industrial leaders to wake up to the fact that without standing up to the trade unions they might as well give up.

She also woke up a nation which had got used to its decline in world influence, and had never really recovered from Suez. It wasn't just the Falklands War that put the 'Great' back into Great Britain, it was the strong diplomacy deployed in her dealings with the European Community and the Soviet bloc that restored a pride and self-respect to Britain which had been missing for decades. And it brought a new respect from other countries and world leaders. We were no longer regarded as a soft touch in international negotiations. All this came as a deep shock to the Foreign Office mandarins, who were in the business of 'managing decline'.

In the introduction to a previous book on Margaret Thatcher, *As I Said to Denis: The Margaret Thatcher Book of Quotations*, I said that an aim of the book was to give the reader insight into the character of Margaret Thatcher and her political views. It is even more the case with this book and I hope it goes some way to destroying the myth of a hard, uncaring and ill-meaning politician. I hope that you, the reader, will enjoy the anecdotes in this book and will forgive me for getting the ball rolling with my own!

Margaret Thatcher is the reason I became actively involved in politics. She inspired me, as a sixteen-year-old, to join the Conservative Party and do my bit to help revive Britain. One of the tasks of today's political leaders is to provide a lead, to inspire, to motivate. Margaret Thatcher was able to do that in a way few politicians in this country have been able to emulate. My first tentative footstep into the political arena was to set up a Conservative organisation in 1982 at the very left-wing University of East Anglia. Only a few months later followed my first encounter with Margaret Thatcher when she invited the chairmen of the various University Conservative Associations to a reception at No. 10.

For a country boy like me, it was unbelievable to have been invited and it was something I had been looking forward to for months. Just to climb those stairs, with the portraits of all past Prime Ministers on the walls was worth the trip on its own. And there at the top of the stairs was the Prime Minister. She had obviously perfected the art of welcoming people to receptions and as she shook you by the hand and wished you a good evening, she moved you on into the room without you even knowing she was doing it. Most of the Cabinet were there – I remember discussing with Cecil Parkinson the number of free running shoes he had been sent after a recent profile had announced to the world that he was a keen runner. He offered me a pair but it turned out his feet were much smaller than mine! We were constantly plied with wine and I made a mental note to stop at two glasses. But after the second glass was emptied I felt rather self-conscious without a glass in my hand so grabbed another. Just as the Prime Minister walked by I took a sip. All I remember is my stomach heaving and me thinking that I was about to throw up at the Prime Minister's feet, thus ending a glorious political career which had hardly got off the ground. Luckily I managed to control my stomach and all was well. It turned out that it was whisky in the glass, rather than white wine.

Later in the evening, as I was talking to my local MP, Alan Haselhurst, the division bell sounded. Although there were at least forty MPs there, none made a move to leave to go and vote over the road in the House of Commons. Mrs Thatcher started to look rather irritated and was obviously none too impressed. In the end she walked to the middle of the room, took off one of her shoes and banged it on the floor. There was instant silence. The Prime Minister then spoke. 'Would all Conservative MPs kindly leave the building immediately,' she instructed. 'And the rest of us will stay and enjoy ourselves!' Naturally we all laughed uproariously, enjoying the sight of the MPs trooping out of the room in a somewhat sheepish manner.

After I graduated I went to work at the House of Commons as a researcher for a Norfolk Member of Parliament, Patrick Thompson. He was not a particularly well-known MP and never courted public-ity. He had a marginal seat and devoted himself to his constituency rather than join the rent-a-quote mob. It served him well as he held his seat for the next two elections. If ever there was an MP less likely to be involved in sleaze it was him. But one day, a careless error by me left him open to charges of dirty dealing. We ran a businessmen's club in the constituency, called The Westminster Circle. It served two purposes – firstly to keep the MP in touch with local businesses and secondly to raise a little money for the very poor constituency association. For £100 a year, business people joined and were given a dinner in the House of Commons, usually addressed by a Cabinet minister, and another dinner in the constituency, addressed by a more junior minister. These clubs were common in all parties up and down the country. But in a publicity leaflet designed to attract new members I had used the phrase 'with direct access to government ministers'. By this I had meant that they would be able to meet and speak to a government minister at the dinner. In those pre-'cash for questions' days we were all rather innocent. But it proved to be my undoing – and very nearly my employer's.

Early one Tuesday afternoon Patrick found out that at that day's Prime Minister's Questions, the Liberal leader, David Steel, would raise this subject with the Prime Minister. He immediately went to see her in her office behind the Speaker's Chair. He must have been quaking in his boots but he later told me she had been brilliant. She sat him down, offered him a coffee and heard him out. She did not disguise her dislike for Steel and thought it typical of him to operate in this manner. She told him she would let Steel have both barrels, and of course she did! He returned to the office after PM's Questions and related the events of the day to me. I had been completely oblivious, which was just as well as I would no doubt have been having a premonition of what a P45 looks like.

A few months later I was having lunch with a couple of Tory MPs in the Members' cafeteria. We had just finished our lunch when in walked Mrs T. and her entourage. She grabbed a tray and chose a light lunch of Welsh rarebit. Unfortunately, as we had finished, I did not have cause to hang around too much longer so left the room, cursing that we had decided to have an early lunch. A few minutes later I realised I had left some papers and magazines on the table in the cafeteria and returned to retrieve them. As luck would have it, the Thatcher group had sat themselves at the table we had been sitting at and Mrs T. had her elbow plonked on my papers. I decided to summon up the courage and interrupt them to ask for my papers. Just as I had started I looked down at the pile of papers and to my horror saw that my copy of the new issue of *Private Eye* was on the top of them and the front cover had a particularly nasty photo of Denis Thatcher. Mrs Thatcher cottoned on to what I wanted, removed her elbow and gazed down at the offending magazine. My heart stopped. 'Oh, *Private Eye*, Denis loves it,' she gushed. To my eternal shame, I just picked it up, along with the rest of the papers, made my excuses and left. What a wimp.

In 1995 I took an American friend, Daniel Forrester, to the T. E. Utley Young Journalist of the Year awards at the Reform Club. Lady Thatcher had been invited to present the awards. She treated us to a half-hour impromptu speech on political issues of the moment, which seemed to go by in about five minutes – quite an achievement as her entire audience had to remain standing throughout. After she had finished Daniel whispered to me: 'I have to meet her, what should I do?' Knowing of her penchant for strapping, 6-ft-tall, dark-haired American men, I encouraged him to go and introduce himself. He suddenly got cold feet so eventually I dragged him over to where she was talking to several of the award winners. In typically American style he launched into a sycophantic introduction which immediately attracted her attention. 'Mrs Thatcher,' he began. I kicked him. 'Er, Lady Thatcher,' he hurriedly corrected himself. 'May I say how much our country misses your leadership...' and he continued in that vein for a few seconds. While he was speaking, the diminutive figure of the Iron Lady (for she was much smaller in height than most people imagine) stared up at him, her eyes never leaving his. When he had finally finished having his say, Lady Thatcher hardly paused for breath. 'Your President, President Clinton.' She paused, heightening the drama for our American friend. 'He is a great communicator.' Up came the forefinger, almost prodding Daniel's chest. Then in a particularly contemptuous tone, came the pièce de résistance. 'The trouble is, he has absolutely nothing to communicate.' With that she was away. It was almost a flounce. Daniel eventually came down from whichever cloud he had been on – probably nine – and said, 'I'll remember that for the rest of my life' – and as a well-known critic of Bill Clinton, has been dining out on it ever since.

Another encounter came at a retirement party for ITN's much-missed Political Editor Michael Brunson. My friend Alan Duncan, the Tory MP for Rutland, started a conversation with her and she suddenly asked where Denis had disappeared off to as they had to leave for a dinner. Being of diminutive stature, and me being over 6 ft tall, he asked me to scan the room. Both of them looked at me expectantly.

To my horror I spied Denis on the other side of the room talking to Michael Heseltine. I summoned up all the courage at my disposal and explained where he was. Lady Thatcher's eyes became even bluer than normal and she exclaimed: 'Denis and I are having dinner with Cap Weinberger tonight. I think he's rather more important than THAT man, don't you? If Denis isn't over here within one minute I shall go over and stare at them.' Luckily for Michael Heseltine, she didn't have to.

Early in 2005 I invited Lady Thatcher to come to a fundraising party to raise money for my campaign as Conservative candidate in North Norfolk. To my delight she accepted and on a cold March evening turned up on time to work a room of fifty friends and political acquaintances. And boy did she work! She was particularly pleased to meet the teenagers present, including one with a particularly eye-catching piece of metal face jewellery. My task for the evening was to guide Lady T. around the room so she could meet everyone. It was a thankless task. The Iron Lady decided where she was going and no amount of me tugging at her elbow was going to persuade her otherwise!

And then, in November 2005, I launched my book *Margaret Thatcher: A Tribute in Words and Pictures* at a function in the City of London, kindly hosted by the Corporation of London. Lady Thatcher agreed to attend and made a point of speaking to everyone in the room while she was there. Especially poignant for me was the sight of her having a protracted chat with my two nieces, Isabella and Ophelia Hunter, who were then aged ten and six, and my parents. It was a very touching moment as they posed for pictures. It brought back a memory from 1988, when my cousin Nicola's daughter Emma – then an infant – asked her mother: 'Mummy, can a man be Prime Minister?' She soon found out that the answer was no.

The last time I spoke to Lady Thatcher was in January 2009 when I went to the Carlton Club for a drinks party hosted by Liam Fox. I was delighted to see Lady Thatcher arrive and looking absolutely fantastic. For a woman of eighty-three and supposedly in frail health, she looked absolutely stunning. I had a couple of minutes talking to her and told her it was twenty-six years to the day that I first met her at a reception for Conservative students at 10 Downing Street. 'I think I remember that,' she said. 'It was so nice to see so many young people in the building. That didn't happen very often.' We talked a little about newspapers and she said: 'I never read them. I had Bernard to do it for me.' Everyone needs a Bernard...

As I left the Carlton Club, a thought struck me. If Lady T. were in her heyday and had to take over as Prime Minister now, what would she do? If I had asked her, I know exactly what her reply would have been. 'Restore sound money, dear,' she would have said. And you know what? She'd have been dead right.

Like others I'm devastated by her death. On the lunchtime of the day she died, I was wandering through Charing Cross Station when I got a call from my LBC producer, Matt Harris. 'There are rumours that Margaret Thatcher has died,' he said. 'It'll be another of those Twitter hoaxes,' I said. But instinct kicked in and I wondered if this time it might be for real. Three minutes later the news was officially confirmed. For a moment time stood still. I can be a little lachrymose on occasion but journalistic professionalism kicked in and not a tear was shed, and I headed straight for LBC to prepare to go on air three hours later. As a broadcaster you want to be on air when these massive news stories break, but there was a part of me which wondered whether I could really do four hours and not become at all emotional. Well, I did and as I write this a few days later, I hope I did her memory justice.

What memories! What a woman! What a Prime Minister!

Iain Dale
Tunbridge Wells
April 2013

Foreword

By the Prime Minister, Rt Hon. David Cameron MP

I was fifteen when the Falklands War began. I remember listening to the radio for the latest news from Mount Tumbledown and Goose Green; that calm, unflappable voice of the MoD spokesman; the pictures of those bleak brown battlegrounds; and above all I remember Margaret Thatcher – her utter conviction and belief that freedom and sovereignty would win out in the end.

The thing about Lady Thatcher is that everyone has powerful memories of her whether they met her or not. She was not just part of the backdrop to people's lives for a decade or more, but a prominent figure in them.

My strong sense growing up as a teenager was that, on the big arguments, she was absolutely right. I felt particularly strongly about standing up to communism and keeping our nuclear deterrent. We lived near Greenham Common and it was something we all talked about. My views were strengthened when I travelled across the Soviet Union and parts of Eastern Europe between school and university.

She was no less formidable in person than she had been in that picture of her in a Challenger tank. Our first encounter was at a Christmas party in Conservative Central Office. Some of the people working there called her 'Mother' affectionately – as in 'Mother's on the line' – and about halfway through the party, word got around that Mother was going to drop in.

I remember her walking towards me at one point, the crowd parting. She must have been told that I was working on the trade and industry brief at the time as, without much in the way of introduction, she fixed me with blue-eyed intensity and asked me what I thought of the trade figures that week. Horror: I didn't know them. It's at this point in my memory that the music stops and the tumbleweed blows across the floor. She expected us all to be absolutely on top of our brief – quite rightly – and believe me, I never made the same mistake again.

Our meetings went uphill from there. Whenever I met Mrs Thatcher – as a candidate, as Leader of the Opposition and Prime

Minister – she was faultlessly courteous and kind. That kindness is the thread running through a lot of these anecdotes. She could be incredibly stern in public but wonderfully kind in private, which is why when we held a special parliamentary session to pay tribute to Mrs Thatcher, the affection was palpable (and let's be honest, for the House of Commons – unusual).

As history is written it is important to remember that icons are people too. A character as strong as Mrs Thatcher is easily cast as a caricature, but that's far from the whole story. She was a woman of immense belief, conviction, even stridency – but as these memories record, she could be a woman of wit and warmth and subtlety too.

Margaret Thatcher
1925–2013

With the passing of Baroness Margaret Thatcher, the world has lost one of the great champions of freedom and liberty, and America has lost a true friend. Here in America, many of us will never forget her standing shoulder to shoulder with President Reagan, reminding the world that we are not simply carried along by the currents of history – we can shape them with moral conviction, unyielding courage and iron will.
– Barack Obama, President of the United States of America 2009–

The world has lost a true champion of freedom and democracy. Ronnie and Margaret were political soulmates, committed to freedom and resolved to end communism. The United States knew Margaret as a spirited and courageous ally, and the world owes her a debt of gratitude.
– Nancy Reagan, First Lady of the United States of America 1981–89

Mrs Thatcher was a political leader whose words carried great weight. Margaret Thatcher was a great political leader and an extraordinary personality. She will remain in our memory and in history.
– Mikhail Gorbachev, President of the Soviet Union 1990–91

Margaret was, to be sure, one of the twentieth century's fiercest advocates of freedom and free markets – a leader of rare character who carried high the banner of her convictions, and whose principles in the end helped shape a better, freer world.
– George H. W. Bush, President of the United States 1989–93

She was an inspirational leader who stood on principle and guided her nation with confidence and clarity. Prime Minister Thatcher is a great example of strength and character, and a great ally who strengthened the special relationship between the United Kingdom and the United States.
– George W. Bush, President of the United States 2001–09

Today we lost a great leader, a great Prime Minister and a great Briton. Margaret Thatcher didn't just lead our country – she saved our country. For that she has her well-earned place in history – and the enduring respect and gratitude of the British people.
– David Cameron, British Prime Minister 2010–

Margaret Thatcher was a towering political figure. Very few leaders get to change not only the political landscape of their country but of the world. Margaret was such a leader. She will be sadly missed.
– Tony Blair, British Prime Minister 1997–2007

Margaret Thatcher was a true force of nature, and political phenomenon. Her outstanding characteristics will always be remembered by those who worked closely with her: courage and determination in politics; and humanity and generosity of spirit in private.
– John Major, British Prime Minister 1990–97

She was a great lady, she had very strong opinions. And to those of us who knew her over the decades, she was a very warm person, which is not the public image that is often given. For the United States, it was her staunch loyalty and commitment to the Atlantic alliance – she was a reliable and steady ally.
– Henry Kissinger, United States Secretary of State 1973–77

She gave Britain's presence in the world a formidable reach. I was witness to the fact that in the European Union, she was by far the most popular politician. She had strong convictions. She served them, and now I think everyone must bow respectfully and affectionately before her memory.
– Valéry Giscard d'Estaing, President of France 1974–81

I think she was a remarkable leader and I pay tribute to the strength of her conservative convictions and the strength of the leadership she displayed in so many areas.
– John Howard, Australian Prime Minister 1996–2007

The world today has lost one of its giants. Margaret Thatcher was the most transformative leader of her country since Churchill. She played a crucial role in the successful navigation of the end of the Cold War and the launch of a new era.
– Brian Mulroney, Canadian Prime Minister 1984–93

Her beliefs – in thrift, hard work and proper reward for merit – were not always popular. But her legacy is colossal. This country is deeply in her debt. Her memory will live long after the world has forgotten the grey suits of today's politics.
– Boris Johnson, Mayor of London 2008–

The United Kingdom has lost its first woman Prime Minister, an iconic states-woman and a fearless leader. The United States has lost one of its dearest friends and most valued ally.
– Bill Clinton, President of the United States 1993–2001

Thatcher was certainly one of the most colourful political figures of the modern world. With her political wisdom and extraordinary will-power, she devoted her life to serving Britain's interests.
– Vladimir Putin, President of Russia 2000–08, 2012–

I greatly valued Margaret Thatcher for her love of freedom, her incomparable openness, honesty and straightforwardness. She was a great woman and there was no substitute for her. She was one of the most exceptionally gifted Prime Ministers there ever was.
– Helmut Kohl, Chancellor of Germany 1982–98

She was an extraordinary leader in the global politics of her time. I will never forget her part in surmounting the division of Europe and at the end of the Cold War. As she took the highest democratic offices as a woman before that was common, she set an example for many.
– Angela Merkel, Chancellor of Germany 2005–

She was a great person. She did a great deal for the world, along with Ronald Reagan, Pope John Paul II and Solidarity; she contributed to the demise of communism in Poland and Central Europe.
– Lech Wałęsa, President of Poland 1990–95

Thatcher was one of the greatest politicians of our time, in the Czech Republic she was our hero. She was one of the most outstanding political personalities of the last quarter of the twentieth century and I believe that with the passing of time, her name will not lose importance.
– Václav Klaus, President of the Czech Republic 2003–13

There are people, there are ideas. Occasionally those two come together to create vision. Lady Thatcher was an exceptional leader. She showed how far a person can go with strength of character, determination and a clear vision.
– Shimon Peres, President of Israel 2007–

Boris Johnson
Mayor of London

Boris Johnson was Conservative MP for Henley from 2005 until 2007. He has been Mayor of London since 2008. He writes a weekly column for the Daily Telegraph.

The flags are at half-mast across London; even, they say, at the offices of the European Commission. The tributes are pouring in from around the world. The BBC is still running wall-to-wall coverage. On the blogosphere and in the Twittiverse there is vicious hand-to-hand conflict between her partisans and those who thought she was a divisive old termagant – and worse. In a few days' time her funeral will be attended by all the public honour and dignity that this nation accorded the late Queen Mother or the Princess of Wales.

It is impossible to imagine that the death of any other British politician could produce such a reaction. I mean no disrespect to the memory of these worthy servants of the people, but do you remember anything much about the passing of Edward Heath? Of Harold Wilson? Of Jim Callaghan? I rest my case.

It is now almost a quarter of a century since she was deposed by yellow-bellied members of her own party, and there must be people under-25 who can't understand, frankly, what all the fuss is about. So I want to explain what Margaret Hilda Thatcher meant for people of my generation, and what we mean when we say that she changed this country and the world.

She was the greatest Prime Minister since Winston Churchill, we say – and the comparison is apt, because she was as brave as Churchill; indeed, you could argue that she was even more combative than the wartime leader, more willing to pick a fight on a matter of principle.

First I remember the horror of the IRA hunger strikes, and my teenage disbelief that the government of this country would actually let people starve themselves to death. But I also remember thinking that there was a principle at stake – that peace-loving people should not give in to terrorists – and whatever you thought of Margaret Thatcher's handling of the tragedy, you could not fault her for consistency.

Then I remember watching that Task Force head for the Falklands, when I was doing my A levels, and thinking the whole thing looked mad. The islands were thousands of miles away and seemed to be mainly occupied by sheep. The Americans weren't backing us with any particular enthusiasm, and the BBC was endlessly burbling on about some 'Peruvian' peace plan, under which we would basically accede to the larceny of Argentina.

I could see that the Prime Minister's position was desperate; and yet I could also see that she was right. She was sticking up for a principle – the self-determination of the Falkland Islanders and I remember a sudden surge of admiration.

And when Arthur Scargill and the miners tried to unseat her in her second term, I remember the other students passing the bucket round in the Junior Common Room. I thought about it, since I could imagine that things were tough for communities where coal had been a way of life for generations. I could see how it would eat away at your self-esteem to be told that your labour was no longer necessary.

Then I reflected on what was really going on, and the way Scargill was holding a strike without a proper ballot, and the fundamental dishonesty of pretending that there was an economic future for coal. I suddenly got irritated with my right-on student colleagues, and was conscious that some kind of line had been crossed.

I was now a Thatcherite, in the sense that I believed she was right and the 'wets' were wrong, and I could see that there was no middle way. You either stuck by your principles or you didn't. You either gave in to the hunger strikers, or you showed a grim and ultimately brutal resolve. You either accepted an Argentine victory or else you defeated Galtieri.

You either took on the miners or else you surrendered to Marxist agitators who wanted to bring down the elected government of the country. You either stuck by America, and allowed the stationing of missiles in Europe, or else you gave in to the blackmail of a sinister and tyrannical Soviet regime.

That was what was so electric about Margaret Thatcher, and that was why I found myself backing her in her last great battle, over Europe. Once again, it was a matter of principle.

The first time I found myself in her presence was at the Madrid EEC summit in 1989, which I reported on for this paper. I remember distinctly how she bustled into a packed and steaming press room – brushing right past me. 'Phwof,' she said, or something like that, as if to express her general view of the Spanish arrangements.

It struck me then that she was much prettier than I had expected, in an English rose kind of way. I also thought she seemed in a bad mood. She was. As we were later to discover, she had just been ambushed by two very clever men – Nigel Lawson and Geoffrey Howe – and told that she must join some European currency project called the exchange rate mechanism. She resisted, and they had threatened to resign.

She objected to their proposals because she didn't believe you could solve the country's economic problems by trying to align sterling with other currencies in a kind of semi-straitjacket. 'You can't buck the market,' she said, and she was proved resoundingly right. The ERM turned out to be a disaster, and the British economy only started to recover when the pound crashed out on 16 September 1992.

She was right not just about the ERM, but about the euro itself. She was virtually alone among all European leaders in having the guts to say publicly what many of them privately agreed – that it was courting disaster to try to jam different economies into a currency union, when there was no political union to take the strain.

Look at the unemployment rates in Greece and Spain, look at what is happening in Cyprus and the sputtering growth of the eurozone. It is impossible to deny that she has been vindicated – and she was right because she took a stand on principle: that it was deeply anti-democratic to try to take crucial economic decisions without proper popular consent.

I cannot think of any other modern leader who has been so fierce in sticking up for her core beliefs, and that is why she speaks so power-fully to every politician in Britain today, and why we are all in her shade. In the end she was martyred by lesser men who were fearful for their seats.

But by the time she left office she had inspired millions of people – and especially women – to believe you could genuinely change things; that no matter where you came from you could kick down the door of the stuffy, male-dominated club and bring new ideas. She mobilised millions of people to take charge of their economic destiny, and unleashed confidence and a spirit of enterprise.

She changed this country's view of itself, and exploded the myth of decline. She changed the Tory Party, she changed the Labour Party, and she transformed the country she led: not by compromise, but by an iron resolve.

Lord Biffen
Cabinet Minister 1979–87

John Biffen served as a Cabinet minister under Margaret Thatcher from 1979 until 1987, initially as Chief Secretary to the Treasury then later as Secretary of State for Trade, Lord President of the Council and Leader of the House of Commons and finally as Lord Privy Seal. He died in 2007.

The career and character of Margaret Thatcher will fascinate historians for decades to come. Her achievements and limitations will bear constant reinterpretation. This short piece would not seek such an academic task, but only offer a personal recollection.

Her actions never betrayed the trivial or banal. She was puritanical and committed to the work ethic. She despised the worldly and cynical politics of many Tories. I suspect she looked upon the Macmillan period with some unease and felt that his sunset years, from Profumo onwards, showed the consequence of a lack of political purpose. Her decision to stand against Edward Heath for the Conservative leadership in 1975 was an example of cool courage. No member of Heath's Cabinet, and more particularly William Whitelaw, was prepared to stand against him. She, alone, broke rank, although Keith Joseph might have done so had he possessed the suitable temperament. Margaret Thatcher was not foolhardy in her venture. She had self-confidence and a deep sense that the Conservative politics of the Heath government needed reversing. Thirty years later it is difficult to recapture how demoralised the Tories had become by U-turns and ineffective trade union legislation.

Doubtless this inspired Margaret Thatcher to convert a defeated party into a government in exile. Rarely have policy groups worked so assiduously to propose measures 'proof against U-turn'. The trade union plans were recast to avoid the ignominy of the unenforceable Industrial Relations Act of Geoffrey Howe and Robert Carr. A host of City executives and academics, and notably Arthur Cockfield, toiled to produce a fiscal and monetary policy that would restore liberal economics and escape the thraldom of price, income and exchange control. The technical financial skills accumulated in opposition fully matched the resources of the Treasury under Denis Healey.

Margaret Thatcher was not a commanding Commons speaker, certainly not equal to James Callaghan, but she was a formidable party leader. For her, politics was not a game for amateurs: everything was played in earnest. This austere drive inspired the parliamentary party, and even more raised the morale of the Conservative activists in the country. Her rhetoric became sharper and more effective as she was able to tone down her natural shrillness. The Soviets dismissed her as 'the Iron Lady'. She grasped the epithet and turned it into a compliment. The irony was that in many ways her commitment to firm government was reminiscent of her predecessor whom she had toppled. 'Ted Heath in drag' observed Denis Healey; but she was determined to succeed in economic and trade union policies where he had been ill served by fortune.

The redoubtable character of Margaret Thatcher became increasingly apparent in the early years of her premiership. Britain had a premier in a hurry. She was calculating and determined, placing her known supporters in the key Treasury and economic posts. The relative isolation of the pragmatists – later derided as 'wets' – was a high-risk strategy; but it paid off. There were no resignations on account of policy, and the Cabinet was gradually reshaped with younger and more sympathetic members. Her Chancellor, Geoffrey Howe, loyally carried out the essential tenets of the new liberal economics. Exchange controls were abolished along with regulated prices and incomes. Public spending was stabilised and taxation was changed to enable income tax reductions to be financed by increases in value added tax. It is no disparagement of Howe to say that he could not have achieved such major changes without the full-hearted support and prodding of his Prime Minister. No Cabinet cabal of spenders could prise apart the Downing Street partners. Alas it was not always to be the case.

Margaret Thatcher's single-mindedness was best demonstrated in the latter half of 1981. Unemployment had risen sharply; there were the usual government 'mid-term blues'; the academic world was almost unanimous in calling for 'moderation' and a return to some kind of Keynesian economic policy. She persisted with her plans despite her growing adverse reputation for stubbornness. The sobriquet coined by Ronnie Millar, surely the decade's most elegant spinner, was 'the lady's not for turning'.

This view of her determined courage was emphasised by the Falklands dispute with Argentina. That conflict has been well documented. The task of recapturing the islands was a logistic nightmare. Success has subsequently created the false impression of comparative ease. Margaret Thatcher knew only too well the hazards of distance to the South Atlantic and the ambivalence of some of our NATO allies. Politically the campaign was conducted by a small inner Cabinet. There was general domestic political support for the venture but it would have been dissipated if there had been defeat or misfortune. Margaret Thatcher knew this and kept her nerve. There was no shortage of those who vainly sought a compromise settlement. If victory goes to the brave she certainly deserved her triumph.

There can be a nemesis which may mock the quality of determination and courage. Self-confidence becomes self-righteousness, and commitment becomes stubbornness and a vision becomes an obsession. Furthermore, as Churchill discovered, the British electorate is often short on gratitude. It was an experience that Margaret Thatcher suffered unhappily in her premiership between 1987–90. One particular measure focused growing hostility: the community charge, popularly described as the 'poll tax'. The radical agitators took to the streets and incensed members of the middle classes bombarded Tory MPs with hostile correspondence. Undeterred, Margaret Thatcher pronounced the tax as the 'flagship' of government policy and planned that it should raise more revenue than the rating system it was scheduled to replace. Such a reaction had panache but little electoral guile; ostensibly it was firm government but lacked political touch.

We live too near the events to judge properly the various factors that impelled Margaret Thatcher to lose control of the Conservative parliamentary party. My instinctive judgement is that the poll tax was the major issue, not least because it had a lightning conductor attraction for other items of lesser discontent. Of course there were also major matters including the poor relations with the Chancellor, Nigel Lawson, and their divergent economic views. Her unhappy years with Geoffrey Howe over Europe have been well chronicled, and, though important, were not decisive in balancing Tory opinion in the Commons. At any rate a Prime Minister, however iron her resolution and fearless her politics, is unwise to quarrel simultaneously with her Chancellor and Foreign Secretary. The outstanding qualities of course that Margaret Thatcher bestowed upon the Conservative Party in the 1970s–80s simply had to be adjusted to meet Britain's changing economic and social circumstances. 'Not for turning' was no longer a compelling Thatcher slogan. Of course this reluctance to bend meant a somewhat poignant epitaph to her premiership, but it can never deny the overall quality of courage and perseverance that distinguish her politics.

Adam Boulton
Political Journalist

Adam Boulton is the Political Editor of Sky News and was formerly the Political Editor of TV-am. *He has been a lobby correspondent since 1983.*

I doubt even Bill Clinton has had a British Prime Minister on hands and knees before him but it's happened to me, and it was the mighty Iron Lady as well. We were in her constituency office in Finchley preparing for an interview. When the crew moved a desk they exposed the generations of fluff and paper clips gathered in a pit in the carpet pile. It was too much for the grocer's daughter; the housewife Prime Minister was kneeling in a split second to tidy things up. Whatever you think of her, that's vintage Margaret Thatcher: she lived in her own world and honoured her own values with never a thought for the concerns or pomposities of others. At times her personal cocoon may have made her insensitive, but if you got to deal with her face-to-face it also meant she was unprejudiced, without airs and graces.

For the most part though, I had only a passing acquaintance with 'Prime Minister Thatcher', passing me on a thousand doorsteps, in planes, in corridors, always on the way to something more important.

Or was it really something more important? Certainly Margaret Thatcher always gave full value on the doorstep. The impression at least was that she would stop, think and voice a spontaneous reaction to the questions unceremoniously shouted at her by the hack pack. It's a marked contrast to Tony Blair. 'The Prime Minister doesn't do doorsteps!' is one of Alastair Campbell's proudest boasts – by which he meant that even if you asked Mr Blair what he thought about the Second Coming now underway, he'd still walk past your cries, consult with his advisers and, maybe, come back out with a carefully crafted sound bite on his lips.

Maggie wasn't like that. Indeed, the best bit of advice I ever got about her was the first I ever received, from Andy Webb, then my boss and Political Editor of *TV-am*. 'She takes everything at face value,' he said, 'so think before you speak. If you say "good morning", she's quite likely to reply "is it?" and go into a full appraisal of current mete-orological conditions.' This, of course, made her fantastic television for reporters like me. She could always take you aback, for example likening the ANC to IRA killers even as the one-day South African President Thabo Mbeki was being feted under the same roof at the 1987 Vancouver Commonwealth Conference.

At work and study in the USA from 1980 to 1982, I missed out on the rise of Thatcherism at home. I sat out the Falklands in Washington: my most vivid memory of her then is of an over-stimulated Secretary of State Alexander Haig speculating luridly with the White House corps about the precise intimate nature of the relationship between Thatcher and Reagan given their frequent one-on-one meetings. So I suppose I didn't know any better and was fair game to be sent into the Iron Lady's den as a lobby correspondent shortly after joining *TV-am* in 1983.

Thatcher's other-worldliness, or at least her determination to live in her own world, worked in my favour. She didn't read the newspa-pers and her ability to discriminate between TV networks depended entirely on who she recognised with her basilisk eyes.

Indeed, when she remembered it, she tended to get my name right. Perhaps because 'Mr Boulton' gave her the chance to exercise her elocution on the long 'o'. My more illustrious rivals John Cole and Michael Brunson usually had to settle for the not-quite-right 'Mr Brunston' and 'Mr Coles'.

Mind you, you were never quite sure she knew who you were. Sometimes she didn't seem to distinguish between journalists and her hard-pressed handbag carriers. Working on a David Frost interview during the 1987 election, I was a little bemused to find the Prime Minister's finger poking into my chest in the green room, telling me 'the message you've got to get out'.

I have no doubt that she was an instinctive 'gut' politician, what in politer circles is called 'a conviction politician'. But I still don't know what to make of one incident. In the 1987 general election campaign Labour had made much of the case of Mark Burgess, a ten-year-old boy awaiting an NHS operation for a hole in the heart. Several years later, long after Margaret Thatcher's third election victory, Mark, very sadly, died.

This coincided with the end of a European Council in Denmark, when Mrs Thatcher was due to give a series of television interviews. You would not be allowed to eavesdrop today, but in those days, with the latest deadline, I was allowed to wait my turn in the interview room itself. And so I heard four separate uneasy interviewers ask the same final question: 'I know it's got nothing to do with the summit, but my newsdesk insist... your reaction to Mark's death.' And I saw the same emotional reaction repeated four times: the hand to the heart, the catch in the throat... the 'as a mother I know how terrible this must be'.

True or bluff? I still don't know.

I do know how sensitive she was about her family. Even after her enforced retirement, the affairs of her son Mark remained the only subject absolutely off-limits in interviews tied to her memoirs. By contrast, her husband Denis was no buffoon; brief encounters left no doubt how sharp he was, and how fiercely right-wing.

Chris Moncrieff of the Press Association is rightly the reporter most associated with the Thatcher years. One day I hope he delivers on his promise to publish his memoirs. His working title is *Maggie Thatcher's Flying Circus*. It's a good one because we used to get closest to her on her numerous foreign trips. There were drawbacks because where her successors have favoured commercial charters, Mrs Thatcher insisted on using the ageing VC10s in the Queen's Flight. The acoustics were so poor that only the person bold enough to sit in the seat next to her ever heard the briefings which she gave in the soft voice reserved for social occasions.

Bernard Ingham would always ensure that the print journalists had plenty of time for sightseeing, shopping and golf, with a briefing conveniently timed for deadlines. But for those of us who had to record the visit on tape, the pace was more hectic. The day usually started with a dawn call for a wreath laying. I've visited practically every British war cemetery in the world with Maggie, including in Turkey the graves from the Crimean War (the more recent Gallipoli battlefield was held back for a visit of its own the next year). Turkey was also a first for the one and only recorded cultural stop on a Thatcher tour. I had expected the visit to the British-made Istanbul sewage works, and the gas plant where the gasometers were painted with giant portraits of PMs Ozal and Thatcher. Even the courtesy call on the general widely whispered to be the government's 'Head of Torture' was not a surprise. But I never thought I'd accompany Mrs Thatcher on a canter through St

Sofia and the Okapi Palace. A British embassy official explained: 'She struck it out of the programme but we told her there would be an international diplomatic incident if she didn't come.'

There was a real crusading spirit about those foreign trips. Downing Street did not boast a White House-style advance team, and no one seemed quite certain what was going to happen. Suspense was at its highest in her groundbreaking forays behind the Iron Curtain. Here again she not only bolstered politicians like Lech Wałęsa and Mikhail Gorbachev, she also sought out dissidents in their freezing flats. Margaret Thatcher, clad in her new Aquascutum wardrobe, careering round the outer-Moscow tenement blocks is still the most impressive exercise in political canvassing I've seen. Thatcher certainly worked hard on her foreign policy. The most shaken I ever saw her was in Brussels – ashen and near tears when the new President Bush made clear Helmut Kohl was his preferred special relation in Europe. A couple of years later, of course, she'd won Bush back, as he took up her strong line against Saddam Hussein.

With hindsight, we in the Westminster press corps were as well placed as anyone to see the end coming. Cabinet ministers complained she stopped listening. With us, she stopped engaging. The gleam faded in her eyes and the fresh response to questions was replaced by a rambling monologue. 'On and on and on' was too long as she began to believe her own publicity.

It was a splendid exit: 'We fight on, we fight to win' on the doorstep of Downing Street; the tears in the car. Transitions of power are difficult for impartial reporters to cover: it's about people you know; you can feel the elation of the victors and the desolation of the vanquished.

Finally I'd like to confess that I've returned the compliment and been on my hands and knees before Margaret Thatcher – crawling quite literally under a live camera before an interview. Ever frank she cried, 'You look like a giant mouse.'

A *Guardian* reporter once rang to ask me to nominate an icon of the twentieth century. There was an intake of breath on the line when I said, 'I assume you've already got the obvious ones like Thatcher.' I chose her anyway.

Lord Hamilton
Margaret Thatcher's PPS 1987–88

Sir Archie Hamilton was Member of Parliament for Epsom and Ewell from 1978 to 2001. After serving as a government whip and as Parliamentary Under Secretary of State for Defence Procurement he became Margaret Thatcher's Parliamentary Private Secretary (PPS) in 1987, remaining with her until 1988 when she made him a Minister of State at the Ministry of Defence.

I first met Margaret Thatcher when she came as Leader of the Opposition to support me in my by-election in 1978 when I was first elected as MP for Epsom and Ewell.

At the end of a full day of walkabouts and opportunities to meet my prospective constituents, we had a press conference. The questions from our local newspapers were not exactly challenging and the last one was particularly sycophantic.

'Mrs Thatcher, it looks very much as if you might win the forth-coming general election. If you do, will you find a place for Archie Hamilton in your government?'

I was expecting a reply that, while being non-committal, would sing the praises of the candidate hoping to enter Parliament. Not a bit of it.

'Oh no! It's much too early to consider that.'

Knowing her as I now do, I suspect that she was much more concerned about appearing to take the outcome of the forthcoming election for granted than being committed to having Archie Hamilton in her government.

I joined the whips' office in 1982. The highlight of our year was when the Prime Minister came to have dinner with us, which normally ended with a question-and-answer session when her Praetorian Guards of whips were treated rather like backsliding leftists. However, it was always a very invigorating occasion. It was a great honour for us when she then suggested that she might return the favour and that we might come with our wives to have lunch at Chequers. Unfortunately, that never happened because the Brighton bomb came in between, so instead dinner was laid on in Downing Street for both the Lords and the Commons whips.

That meal ended in the same way, with the Prime Minister saying, 'Right, does anybody have any problems or concerns they would like to raise?' I remember Lady Trumpington asked the first question, about pensions. She got slapped down pretty swiftly, and then John Major, who was the Treasury Whip, piped up and said, 'Prime Minister, there is deep concern in the country on the following issues.' She went for him such as I have never seen. A row erupted of such seriousness that it ended on a very sour note. At one stage, we thought that John Major might even walk out of the room, and we were very concerned that he may have completely destroyed his political career. As we walked from the dining room to the drawing room in Downing Street, Denis Thatcher came up to him and said, 'Don't worry, dear boy, she gets like this sometimes.' The next day, she reconciled the position with John Major, and three months later he was a junior minister in her government. That story is becoming better known and is very significant, because it indicates the sort of woman that she was. She loved the row but never had any feelings of bitterness. She respected people who stood up to her and never held it against anybody at all.

I was PPS to Margaret Thatcher as Prime Minister for the fifteen months following the 1987 election.

We were sitting one evening in her rooms in the House of Commons and she raised the question of women priests in the Church of England. Although brought up a Methodist, she had become an Anglican and was troubled that ordaining women would split the Church.

I took issue with her and argued that as a woman Prime Minister she really could not be seen to be against women entering the priesthood.

'Anyway,' I said, 'I don't know why you are so worried. I think women are capable of greater spirituality than men and also they are less inclined to succumb to sexual temptation.'

'Oh, I don't know about that,' said the Prime Minister.

As with so many arguments, she would never cede any ground and, on occasions, one was left wondering whether one had gone too far and upset her. It was a week later that I read a short excerpt in the paper headed THATCHER BACKS WOMEN PRIESTS.

I came to get to know her much better in 1987, when I was made her PPS. If I am brutally frank, I was not terribly good at the job.

I did very badly when Alan Clark came to see her as Minister of Trade, and I totally failed to tell the Prime Minister something. I do not think she was aware that Alan Clark always rather prided himself on having two attributes of Adolf Hitler, namely that he was a vegetarian and hated foxhunting. His pitch to the Prime Minister was that he considered it a very good idea if labels were to be put on furs saying, 'The fur being sold here has been caught in an extremely inhumane trap.' It would have been rather like having a health warning on cigarettes. The Prime Minister was absolutely appalled by this and said, 'Alan, what on earth makes you so concerned to do this?' He said, 'Prime Minister, didn't you know that I'm a vegetarian?' She looked at him and said, 'But Alan, you are wearing leather shoes.' He drawled, 'I do not think you expect your ministers to wear plastic shoes, Prime Minister.' Needless to say, the pleas got nowhere because the calculation that Alan Clark had not made was that because the Prime Minister was MP for Finchley, many of her Jewish constituents were furriers and the last thing she was going to do was ruin their business.

I always remember a meeting, held at Downing Street at five o'clock in the evening, to discuss a policy paper. I thought that it would all go quite calmly; I knew that the Cabinet minister who was presenting the paper was a friend and somebody she supported. He had no opportunity to present his paper as such. She launched into him and said, 'It strikes me that the problems with this are the following,' and so forth, and another furious argument took place, leaving us all looking at our feet and wondering, 'Goodness, where is all this going to go?' She always kept to the timescale, which was half an hour for the meeting. We were coming to the end, and she summed up by saying, 'Of course, I agree with absolutely everything you are trying to do here. I just thought I'd play devil's advocate and make sure that you'd thought out all the arguments.' That is just one of the reasons why she was a very great Prime Minister.

Weekdays in No. 10 started with a meeting to discuss forthcoming events and what was in the newspapers.

Staff in Bernard Ingham's press office must have got up very early to produce an extraordinarily succinct summary of all the stories in the newspapers on a couple of sides of foolscap. Closely argued articles from the broadsheets would be reduced to three lines.

I asked Margaret Thatcher one day whether she ever read the daily papers.

'Oh no!' she replied. 'They make such hurtful and damaging remarks about me and my family that if I read the papers every day I could never get on with the job I am here to do.'

Some years later, when John Major was Prime Minister and having serious problems with the press, I repeated Margaret Thatcher's remark to him. He did not respond but just gave me one of those pitying looks that people reserve for the feeble-minded.

Margaret Thatcher did not read the daily papers but she invariably studied the Sundays during her weekends at Chequers. She always took great heart from Woodrow Wyatt's articles in the *News of the World*.

Monday morning meetings with Cabinet colleagues often started with the Prime Minister saying 'Did you see Woodrow's marvellous article in the *News of the World*?' Many Cabinet ministers found that it became almost compulsory to add the *News of the World* to their Sunday morning reading.

Margaret Thatcher was always known to be an avid listener of the *Today* programme, which she had on the radio while she got up. I remember her telling me that the coverage of *Today* regularly infuriated her husband Denis, and she used to hear him shouting 'Bastards!' as he lay in bed listening to the programme.

Margaret Thatcher had a rather odd belief that it was impossible to write a speech for the party conference until the conference itself was underway and the 'atmosphere' of the gathering had been accurately assessed. The result was that most of her conference speech had to be written at the end of a series of hard days among the party faithful and would stretch on until the early hours of the morning. Contributions came in from all and sundry but invariably only small bits were selected, with the rest being torn up by the Prime Minister amid cries of 'Nothing fresh here!'

There was an occasion when one of Margaret Thatcher's Cabinet ministers had asked himself to Sunday lunch at Chequers. The Prime Minister did not want to be subjected to unremitting pressure from this man for most of her Sunday, so she asked me, as her PPS, to join the two of them, plus Denis, for lunch. I gladly accepted the invitation, although slightly worried that I was neglecting my family at home. A

few days later, the Prime Minister realised that her invitation might
have disrupted a family weekend.

'Why don't you bring your wife Anne too?' she asked.

'The problem is, Prime Minister,' I replied, 'that she has our three
teenage daughters at home that weekend.'

'Bring them all,' she said.

Later on, life was made even more complicated when it became
apparent that my youngest daughter had also invited a friend home
from school.

'I am afraid, Prime Minister, that my youngest daughter has invited
her friend Abigail for the weekend as well.'

'Bring her too!'

I admired the Secretary of State who arrived for what he imagined
was to be a *tête-à-tête* with the Prime Minister only to be confronted
with the Hamilton family and a row of teenage girls. It must have
resembled a scene out of St Trinian's. Not a flicker of emotion crossed
his face; he was charm itself.

Conversation at the ensuing meal was somewhat strained. The
minister struggled in vain for a hearing, as one daughter, in that
uncompromising teenage mode which is determined not to be overawed,
rolled up her sleeves and, putting her elbows on the table, embarked
on what seemed an interminable anecdote. The PM drummed her
fingers on the table, while another daughter, benefiting from the adult
distraction, dipped her finger in the jug of cream. Her friend Abigail
sat immobilised as if she were a rabbit caught in the headlights.

It crossed my mind that Mrs Thatcher might have regretted her
generous invitation.

To understand the exceptional qualities of Margaret Thatcher as a
politician, one should think of her as an evangelical. She was born a
woman with immense powers of concentration, a prodigious memory
and an exceptionally analytical mind. What made her one of the greatest Prime Ministers of the last century was the conviction with which
she drove her policies and the way she was prepared to risk serious
short-term unpopularity for doing things which she knew were right
in the long term. Although prepared ultimately to compromise, she
always dragged the argument further than most into her own territory.

I often wondered whether her determination to press her own point
of view could be attributed to the fact that she was a woman. All I do

know is that all the men I have met and worked with in politics have shown themselves more ready to compromise than she.

As the leader of the Conservatives she was always terribly bothered that the socialists had something called 'Socialist International'. She thought that this gave a lot of respectability to left-wing parties, and she could not quite understand why the Conservatives should not have the same thing. She was, therefore, very much party to setting up something called the European Democrat Union, which later moved on to be the International Democrat Union. Although she never took me, as her PPS, on foreign trips, this was a party political occasion, because the IDU meeting was being chaired by Chancellor Kohl. We sat in the most enormous room in the Reichstag building – this was, of course, before the wall came down – and Chancellor Kohl gave a speech to welcome everybody that I strongly suspect was written by somebody else. She just made a few short notes, and when it came to her opportunity to speak she pointed through the window and said, 'People tell me that the building that we can see over the Berlin Wall, out through this window, is the headquarters of the East German intelligence service. People also say to me that they are probably listening to every word we are saying here today, in which case I would like them to know...' and she then went into a great tirade about how freedom was what we were all fighting for, and that freedom would conquer in the end. How right she was; the wall came down not very much later.

She could survive on three or four hours' sleep. I had to spend quite a bit of my time travelling in an armour-plated Daimler, whose roof was of course lowered to make it more bombproof. It had a very inadequate air-conditioning system, and we usually had very large policemen and drivers sitting in front. The heat used to accumulate massively, and I have to say that both she and I used to nod off quite regularly. It became rather embarrassing when my wife went around saying, 'Archie spends much of his time sleeping with the Prime Minister in the back of her car.'

Margaret Thatcher first came to stay with me in the country shortly after she stood down, in January 1991. It was interesting. We were sitting there in the evening and the telephone rang. It was John Major ringing her up to say that the hostilities were about to begin in the Gulf. Needless to say, she stayed up the whole night listening to the wireless to hear what was going on. I was Minister of State for the

Armed Forces but went to bed and listened to the news the next morning. That might be one of the reasons why she was Prime Minister and I never was. It was an indication of her extraordinary determination to be involved and, of course, it was a war that she had been very much involved with in the beginning.

The Thatchers came to stay with us quite regularly from that moment. We even had them to stay twice for Christmas. Shortly after Denis died, she came to stay with us down in Devon. At that stage, she still thought that Denis was alive. There was a period of her life which was quite short, I think, when she was not really reconciled to the fact that he had died. It is regrettable that so much of that film *The Iron Lady* should have been on the period in her life when she thought that her husband was still with us. She was never really the same again after he died. It knocked her very hard. He was a great companion to her and life was extremely difficult for her from that moment on.

She was a very great lady. She was an evangelist. She was not like most modern politicians. She had a mission. But everything that she stood for will survive her. From my point of view, it has been a very great privilege to have served with her and to have served in her government.

Hugo Young
Political Journalist

Hugo Young was Political Editor of the Sunday Times *from 1973 until 1984 before becoming a columnist for* The Guardian. *His biography of Margaret Thatcher,* One of Us, *is regarded as the definitive account of her life. He died in 2003.*

Margaret Thatcher knew from the start that I wasn't likely to be 'one of us'. I worked for the *Sunday Times*, then an independent and liberal paper not under the suzerainty of an owner who was one of her cheerleaders. I had all the wrong instincts, being neither a Conservative nor someone who believed any political journalist should have other than sceptical connections with politicians. But despite these bad basics, we got on quite well, which was more to her credit than to mine.

It was partly, no doubt, a matter of prudence. The *Sunday Times* was a very big paper with a lot of politically uncommitted readers, and any interview in its pages reached an important audience. I did several of them when she was Prime Minister. The first, I well recall, was preceded by her personal search for Nescafé to get some cups of coffee together. If that happened at No. 10 today, you could be sure there had been a meeting of the spin-doctors beforehand, to assess precisely what impression should be made on this or that journalist who was coming in. Nothing happens by accident now. But the early Thatcher was a cosmetic artefact only when she appeared on television. Her personal coffee-making wasn't, I thought, done for effect. Like her obsession with turning off the Downing Street lights, it was the extension of Grantham housekeeping into the prime ministerial world.

The reason I survived for ten years as an acceptable interviewer, and occasional off-the-record conversationalist, was, I think, twofold.

First, Mrs Thatcher always liked an argument. Although argument was not what this interviewer particularly sought, it was a mode of discourse she found irresistible. Somewhere along the line, the very fact that I was so plainly not in her camp became a virtue. I was bestowed with 'convictions', and even principles. When Matthew Parris left her service as an MP, he once wrote that he was especially counselled to read my stuff as a way of keeping in touch with the world he was deserting, perhaps to know who the enemy was.

Once allotted this label, I never seemed to lose it. One of the things Mrs Thatcher said, intimidatingly, to an early civil servant was that she usually made up her mind about a man in ten seconds – 'and I rarely change it'. So, perhaps, it was with me. One of her attractive virtues was that she never, in those days, showed any side. The grandeur of the post-imperial years was nowhere to be seen. Argument could flow on almost equal terms. She was utterly convinced that, in the course of such discussion, any reasonable person was certain to be persuaded to the way she thought: which is the trait she most specifically shares with Tony Blair.

Her encompassing of me within her invincible power of persuasion was due, however, to the second feature of our relationship. I'm sure she never read a word I wrote. I retained my place in the tent of the acceptable because she never knew what I really thought, since she was a stranger to my columns. These became, as the years went by, critical to the point of savagery. I questioned her honesty as much as her wisdom (over Westland, for example). I impugned her motives, ridiculed her judgement and even cast doubt on her sanity. I remained, unread, within the pale: an ambiguous fate, but one which gave me scarcity value at my new employers, *The Guardian*, which otherwise seemed to have no contact of any kind with the Thatcher people.

One thing Mrs Thatcher certainly did not read was my biography of her, *One of Us*. This was an unofficial work in every sense. It drew on my talks with her over the years, but I never asked for a biographical interview. Members of her entourage told me, in due course, that they thought the book rather good. Perhaps because my columns were spiky, they expected a more polemical work between hard covers, and were relieved when that wasn't quite the book I wrote. But from herself – nothing. And after all, why should she? Who would want to read what purported to be a detailed account of their life and thought, when knowing that every nuance, however honestly chronicled, was bound to be not quite how it really was? Besides, by that time, I was permanently excluded from the bunker that had become her residence, the closed world that eventually produced her downfall.

The last time I met her was in what could, nonetheless, be called a biographical context. The occasion was the annual Christmas party given by the American ambassador. A long queue was lining up to shake his hand, and suddenly my wife and I found that Lady Thatcher and her husband had materialised beside us. This wasn't long after she had ceased to be Prime Minister and she could still not quite credit that she had to queue at all. A frisson of doubt on her face plainly revealed an inner impulse to march up to the front and be greeted without delay. But Denis decided against such a display of amnesia as to who they now were, and the two of them therefore faced ten minutes imprisoned in our company.

The talk, led by her, immediately turned to writing. This was a subject which used to attract little but her scorn. She once asked me in very public company when I was going to get down to some proper work – building wealth, creating jobs etc. – instead of wasting my time with journalism. It was one of the little regrets of my life that I had lacked the presence of mind to say, given such an opportunity: 'After you, Prime Minister.'

But now, she told me, she had just completed the first volume of her memoirs. Naturally, this became the sole subject of our ten-minute shuffle in the queue. She was now a writer. The book had been a great labour, she recalled. But I wouldn't know anything about that, would I? Because I was a professional journalist. I was incredibly lucky, she said with patent reproach. A note of envy was even detectable. It was all so easy for me. She, on the other hand, had had to labour at getting it all down. She had written every line of the first draft herself, she said, although that nice John O'Sullivan had helped her rearrange some of the words into a better order. But it was essentially all her own work. And there would be another volume to come, on which her researchers were already hard at work. Meanwhile, what mattered was who owned the copyright to the over-matter in her television interviews. Here Denis stepped in with a commercial reckoning as to the value of what lay, untransmitted, in David Frost's archives. This was serious author talk.

In recent years, she has taken up her life as a politician, albeit surrounded by a court rather than colleagues, and certainly not by journalists invited to give her an argument. Long ago, I resumed my original distance and she, in more exaggerated form than ever, the delusions of unchallengeable, world-correcting rightness that marked her last months in office. But I bask in the moment when, with ego pumping in a new direction, she was briefly one of us, absolving us writers, just for a year or two, from being one of them.

Lord Whitelaw
Deputy Prime Minister 1979–88

Willie Whitelaw served as Leader of the House and Secretary of State for Northern Ireland under Edward Heath and as Chairman of the Conservative Party. In Margaret Thatcher's Cabinet he was Home Secretary, Lord President of the Council and Leader of the House of Lords. He served as Deputy Prime Minister under Mrs Thatcher until his retirement in 1988. Lord Whitelaw died in 1999. This passage is taken from his book, The Whitelaw Memoirs.

I have often wondered how two such different people managed to get on so well together. Of course, as Prime Minister and party leader, it was in her hands to decide how she treated me and used me. I must therefore say at the start that it was her personal kindness and constant understanding which gave me the opportunity to help her. For my part, I hope I always remembered that she was the leader, who had to face all the ultimate pressures and take the final decisions. Life at the top is very lonely and extremely demanding. Anyone in an immediately subordinate position should never forget the exceptional pressures which a leader faces, and the personal reactions which they provoke. I believe we both started from these particular positions, and understood them.

Second, we both had a passionate belief in our party and so in its government. We probably had somewhat different perceptions of how we would like to see it react in particular circumstances. On such occasions I would certainly have the chance to argue my case, but of course I had to accept that in the final event Margaret Thatcher was the leader and had the ultimate right to decide. I do not think I ever left her in any doubt that I understood that relationship.

Third, we both knew that we were very different people with varying backgrounds, interests and thus reactions. As a result we had never been close personal friends before we were brought together in this particular political relationship.

I am often asked what it is like serving a woman leader. In general I would say it is no different from serving a man, except that it would be futile not to appreciate that women are always ready to use their feminine charms, and indeed their feminine qualities, to get their way. Margaret Thatcher is no exception, nor could anyone fail to recognise her great personal charm. Perhaps it was easy for me to work with a woman as I had been brought up by my mother and spent much time alone with her. No one who knew her could deny that my mother was a powerful character.

I was reminded the other day by the hostess who brought my mother and Margaret Thatcher together of their only meeting not long before my mother died. No one knew how it would turn out, since my mother was immensely protective of me and, naturally perhaps, proud of my performance. She was therefore very suspicious of this woman Margaret Thatcher, who had been preferred to her son as leader of the Conservative Party. In the event, I am told, for I certainly was not present, that they got on famously together. My mother subsequently became an immense fan of Margaret Thatcher, even to the extent of upbraiding me for failing to support her more effectively. Alas, she died before she could see Margaret Thatcher as Prime Minister and her son as Home Secretary. I know she would have been far more critical of the latter than the former.

On another topic, I am asked if Margaret Thatcher ever listens to points of view other than her own. This question, with its perception of her, angers me, for it is grossly unfair. I think she probably enjoys an argument more than most people, and the more vigorous it is, the better, as far as she is concerned. She is by nature a conviction politician and so has very strong views, yet she can certainly be swayed and influenced by good arguments in the final event. I wish the critics would realise that no one could have presided over such a successful team as leader unless they had been prepared to take account of internal discussions. Of course it is not easy to convert her, but that should surely be the case with a powerful leader. She is certainly the type of chairman who leads from the front and from the start of a discussion makes no secret of her own feelings and views. But all chairmen have their different methods, even if most successful ones like to get their way in the end. I know that I am totally different from Margaret Thatcher in the way that I handle meetings, and that some people regard me as too conciliatory. But I have to acknowledge the truth of the remark which Norman Tebbit alleges that I made to him: 'My image is emollient – and so I am, but only when I am getting my own way.' I suspect too that Margaret Thatcher did not always find me easy to deal with. She had to experience – which I must say she did stoically on occasions – my sudden and unexpected outbursts of rage when crossed in argument. She often accepted, although I imagine she sometimes found it irritating, my cautious approach to parliamentary difficulties and tendency towards compromise. She seldom interfered with my conduct of sensitive Home Office issues, although she must have disliked some of my decisions on the treatment of offenders, and perhaps particularly on broadcasting matters, where we have never quite seen eye to eye.

In particular we tended to have different views on the bias of BBC programmes. Naturally, Prime Ministers feel particularly sensitive to criticism which they consider unfair, since they are constantly in the firing line. My feelings about the BBC, on the other hand, were conditioned by my experience in dealing with broadcasting matters as opposition Chief Whip during the 1960s. When I argued our party's case at that time I felt that I was treated most fairly by the BBC, some-times to the intense irritation of Harold Wilson and the then Labour government.

My experience and so perhaps inevitably my views were very differ-ent from those of the Prime Minister and the overwhelming majority of my colleagues. And so when there were controversies over different television or radio programmes, I tended to come out as a defender of the BBC. In addition to my natural instincts, I also felt that as Home Secretary it was my duty to stand up for their point of view. This led to spirited discussions on occasions. As is well known, Margaret is a regular listener to the BBC *Today* programme and, waking early as she does, is extremely well-informed of every detail in the news each morning. So she naturally came to some meetings with that day's programme in the forefront of her mind. I have to say that on occa-sions I wished I had stronger grounds on which to stand up for a BBC programme. I recognise that I had some bad mornings when I aban-doned defence of the indefensible. But generally I stood my ground for I felt it was good for me and for my other colleagues, including the Prime Minister, to test our views against each other. Anyway, we prob-ably all rather enjoyed the arguments and perhaps sometimes they did affect subsequent government reactions.

I suppose the Prime Minister listened to me most on parliamentary and party matters, where I obviously had a great experience, and least on economic and foreign policy, where I did not claim any special knowledge and where other senior ministers bore the responsibility.

She was always very generous with her time in giving me opportunities privately to express my feelings on any subject. She also consulted me frequently and kept me fully informed on major issues. I therefore seldom had any reason to argue with her in wider ministerial meetings and usually intervened only if I felt I could be of general assistance.

I can only conclude with a general observation. Margaret Thatcher is a remarkable and powerful leader in every way. Of course, like everyone in her position, she has her critics and detractors. No doubt she has made mistakes, but no one can deny her incredible achievements, nor should anyone neglect the great contribution that Denis Thatcher has made to them, as the country as a whole has increasingly recognised.

Sir Alfred Sherman
Adviser to Margaret Thatcher

Sir Alfred Sherman co-founded the Centre for Policy Studies with Sir Keith Joseph and Margaret Thatcher in 1974, where he acted as a formative influence on Thatcherite political and economic thinking. He served as a speech-writer and aide to Margaret Thatcher from 1974 until 1983. Sir Alfred died in 2006.

Those who reached the top of the greasy pole this century can be counted on your fingers; identifying qualities which brought them to the top where many others failed remains infinitely challenging. I had personally identified Margaret Thatcher as a potential successor to Heath under certain circumstances back in autumn 1973, when asked by two friends, Basil (now Lord) Feldman, a leading party figure, and Barry Rose, publisher and one-time Conservative council-leader. Basil called this far-fetched. How right he was. That it came to pass does not make it any less so. That an almost unknown middle-aged lady from a lower-middle-class background whose political career had been unspectacular could within sixteen months reach the top in the Tory interest seemed inconceivable. Nor were her chances of leading her party to electoral victory, once precariously established as leader, rated highly until the Callaghan government's last few months were beset by difficulties of its own making. Yet in a short time she became one of the few twentieth-century leaders of whom it could be said that she 'bestrode our narrow world like a colossus.' But per Hegel: 'all that is real is rational'; there must have been valid reasons for her achievement.

When I forecast that Margaret might receive the mandate of Heaven, I had never met her, and only once even seen her. What struck me then was the fervour of her beliefs. The Spanish political philosopher, José Ortega y Gasset, distinguished between ideas and beliefs, complaining that historians and political writers over-emphasised the importance of the former at the expense of the latter. Current sensitivity among Conservatives about what they pejoratively dub 'ideology', by which they mean ideas or conceptual frameworks, reflects the fact that for generations Conservatives managed on the basis of implicit beliefs incorporating practices which had evolved over time and ideas derived from classical philosophy and Protestant Christianity. As Nigel Lawson was later to argue in a CPS pamphlet, Conservatives had managed quite well without a structure of explicit ideas until Liberals and Labour elaborated theirs, following which the Conservatives had no alternative but to match them. MT filled the gap with her Conservative beliefs: the puritan ethic; personal responsibility; patriotism. Conversion of these beliefs into ideas as a basis for policies was left till later, too late.

I did not meet her till the spring of 1974, under Keith Joseph's auspices, after he had accepted my outline for the 'we were wrong' Upminster speech in June, which was to become the first in his series on 'Reversing the Trend', rejecting Butskellism and advocating radical Tory counter-revolution. The speech was designed to launch his new think tank (soon to be named the Centre for Policy Studies) which Heath had suggested after Keith had declined the shadow Cabinet portfolio offered, in the hope that it would keep him busy and out of mischief expounding Butskellism and Europhilia, but which I had persuaded him – I am still not sure how – to devote to expounding radical Conservatism, which eventually became known as Thatcherism.

He decided to offer Margaret Thatcher the deputy chairmanship. She was then fifty, with grown-up children, but there was then something girlish about her: her enthusiasms, the simplicity of her beliefs, her trusting nature. She reminded me of nineteenth-century explorers, aware that their ambience was strange and dangerous but unquestioningly confident in themselves. At the time, she believed strongly that Keith should become party leader and that only Lady Joseph's reluctance to give him full support was preventing this. Since Keith had always been the antithesis of a leader, this convinced me that she was a bad judge of character.

She was unapologetically aware that her grasp of ideas, politics and economics was insufficient for the role in which she was subconsciously casting herself, and had no hesitation in casting me as a second John the Baptist after Keith.

When we first met, her chosen persona was as an upper-middle-class Tory lady in twinset and pearls. But her first reactions to

Keith's epoch-making 'we were wrong' Upminster speech, praising it for its 'economy with words', suggested to me an alternative persona, the puritan grocer's daughter, bringing faith and common sense to the convoluted world of public affairs and economic controversy: 'Economics is Greek for running a household.' Peel's dictum that a Prime Minister must be 'an uncommon common man' was relevant. Her outward demeanour as a housewife shopping at Marks & Spencer reassured many who are basically suspicious both of politicians and of political ideas, believing that politics and government ought to be much simpler.

In opposition, and to some extent in government, we worked closely for hours on end, often *à deux*, sometimes with her PPSs. During the day, we worked in the Leader of the Opposition's office, overlooking Boudicca's statue, evenings and weekends we worked at her home in Flood Street, Chelsea, in the dining room, with a typewriter on the table. When we had progressed, she would go into the kitchen to prepare food, giving instructions through the linking door, exemplifying her dual roles. In her flat at No. 10 – living over the shop – she was in and out of the kitchen, as no other premier ever was.

It is not easy for labourers in the vineyard to get into the minds of the great, who achieve greatness precisely because their mind and spirit work distinctively. I found that she possessed a razor-sharp mind and great application, but because they had been honed in natural science and the law her thinking was linear rather than lateral. But it was her will which marked her out. Though power wrought its effects on her in time, she remained free to the end from the side and self-importance which it inflicts on so many politicians. I remember an occasion when I had arranged to bring an American to see her, who ran a media-monitoring unit which I believed we should emulate. As we waited in the ground-floor reception at No. 10, she suddenly appeared in the doorway in stockinged feet and took us up to her study. Conversely, she never fully acquired the art of suffering fools gladly, so essential in democratic politics. It was her body language rather than her politics which so enraged Geoffrey Howe that he steeled himself to resign his benefice and stab her in the back.

In the course of time her enthusiasm for ideas seemed to lapse, while the ironclad self-confidence, which had been so essential when she was an outsider storming the citadel, became an impediment.

The leadership election, which she had lost by four votes, epitomised the personal dimension in her trajectory. Had she stayed and fought it, personally meeting waverers and lukewarm supporters, and impressing on enthusiastic supporters not to disqualify their vote by writing slogans on their ballot paper, and hence spoiling it, she would have come home comfortably. Instead, misled by naive canvass reports which took voting promises at face value (since many MPs, characteristically, backed themselves both ways) and hankerings after the glory of the prestigious Paris end of the Cold War summit which coincided with the leadership contest, she went to Paris and left re-election to look after itself. Her fall, like her rise, was the stuff of which cautionary fables are made.

As I argued earlier, Margaret Thatcher's rise to power had come about by the interplay of chance and 'necessity' (Hegel's rendering of the Greek *ananke*) between the accidental, incidental and inherent, per Aristotle. I had been catalyst to this process. When, after her 1983 election victory (which looked much larger than it actually was) Margaret Thatcher was persuaded to dispense with people and ideas which had brought her to power in the first place, it was not apparent to her that she might be eroding the ideal cement of her own power base, that her native hue of resolution might depend on the ideas which had fed into Thatcherism. In the event, de-Shermanisation of the CPS and its milieu, which had been the seed-bed of Thatcherism, set in motion de-Thatcherisation, leaving her bereft of a lodestar and vulnerable to her colleagues-cum-enemies. Legend and literature contain many such instances.

Lord Powell
Prime Minister's Adviser on Foreign Affairs and Defence 1984–91

Charles Powell served as a diplomat in Washington, Bonn and EC Brussels before becoming the Prime Minister's Private Secretary and adviser on foreign affairs and defence, a position that he held from 1984 until 1991.

After a previous Foreign Office career spanning twenty years during most of which Britain's standing and influence in the world steadily declined, I found working for Margaret Thatcher on foreign affairs an exhilarating if sometimes tempestuous experience. Her extraordinary will-power and leadership broke the seemingly endless and inevitable cycle of national decline, restored the nation's confidence and gave us the feeling that Britain once again counted in the world.

It was not exactly a tranquil experience. She was non-stop and so was the turbulence created by her legendary handbag. Foreign visits were invariably conducted at the double: I think our record was seven countries – Malaysia, Singapore, Brunei, Indonesia, Sri Lanka, India and Saudi Arabia – in eight days. Yet only once in twelve years did a slip of the tongue give away that she forgot which country she was in. That had been more of a problem for one of her predecessors, Sir Alec Douglas-Home, whose wife used to follow him down the aircraft steps on foreign visits chanting 'China, Alec, China' or whatever the country was.

Of course it helped being a woman: that made her more easily identifiable among world leaders. But it was the personality and the policies which counted. The strong and unyielding stand against communism, in partnership with Ronald Reagan, which led to the West's triumph in the Cold War; victory in the Falklands; getting 'our money' back from Europe; extricating Rhodesia from illegality to independence; standing by our American allies over Libya when others turned their backs; ensuring a resolute response to Saddam's invasion of Kuwait. All these turned her into a heroic figure, the Iron Lady of legend. She did not win all her battles, with German reunification the prime example. And she fought some unnecessary ones, mainly with her own colleagues in government. But she indisputably raised Britain's international profile and whatever the pained expressions and snooty comments of old-style diplomats, she advanced Britain's interests. In the simplest terms, we were taken a lot more seriously in 1990 than in 1980.

Margaret Thatcher was never a diplomat and proud not to be one. She had no time for courtly phrases and carefully drafted compromises. She was ready to go toe to toe with any world leader from Gorbachev to Deng Xiaoping. She had the huge advantage of being unembarrassable, a quality not always shared by her Private Secretary. I recall a meeting with President Mitterrand in Paris during which the President took her for a stroll in the Elysée garden. I sat down in the sun for a blissful moment of peace with my French opposite number, only to be shaken from my reverie by the sight of Mitterrand hurrying back, clutching a blood-stained handkerchief to himself. For a moment of panic I thought: 'she's gone too far this time, she's bitten him!' It turned out to have been an over-enthusiastic puppy which did the damage, but it was a nasty moment.

She was deeply suspicious of the Foreign Office as an institution, believing that its tribal culture led it to give too much weight to the foreigners and too little to Britain's interests, as well as having its own agenda on European integration. She would gleefully recount the old chestnut of the man asking a policeman in Whitehall during the Second World War black-out, which side the Foreign Office was on and being told 'the other'. There were some memorable rages, as when she demanded to inspect the gift which the Foreign Office had thoughtfully procured for her to take to Gorbachev and discovered a handsome pair of silver-backed hairbrushes.

'But he's completely bald,' she stormed, and a messenger had to be sent out from London with a replacement gift.

Fortunately the prejudice against the institution was matched by a high regard for many of its most distinguished servants, who were granted a sort of amnesty for the misdeeds – real or imagined – of their *alma mater*.

Margaret Thatcher's diplomacy was less concerned with making friends than with winning battles. That had a downside in her relationship with Chancellor Kohl, who went to great pains to win her friendship. This extended to inviting her to spend a weekend in his home town in the Rhineland, including a visit to his favourite tavern to sample his favourite dish of pig's stomach. Margaret Thatcher's appetite seemed mysteriously to fade as Chancellor Kohl went back for seconds and thirds. We moved on to the great crypt of the Romanesque Cathedral of Speyer where Margaret Thatcher was invited to inspect the tombs of Holy Roman Emperors, precursors of earlier attempts at European Union. While she undertook this task without visible enthusiasm, Chancellor Kohl took me behind a pillar. 'Now she's seen me here in my own home town, right at the heart of Europe and on the border with France,' he said, 'surely she will understand that I am not just German, I am European. You must convince her.' I accepted the assignment with trepidation. As soon as we boarded our aircraft for the return to Britain, Margaret Thatcher threw herself into her seat, kicked off her shoes and announced with the finality which was her trademark: 'My God, that man is so German.' Gutless, I aborted my mission to persuade her otherwise.

Margaret Thatcher captured the imagination of people outside Britain even more than at home. One only had to witness the rapturous welcome which she received from huge crowds in Poland, Russia, Georgia and Armenia in the late 1980s to realise that she symbolised their hope for relief from communist tyranny. Or to experience her ability to rouse an American audience with her forthright rhetoric on democracy, the rule of law and the need for strong defence. Or to be swept away by the ecstatic welcome of crowds in Africa, despite fatalistic Foreign Office warnings that she would be shunned.

A sometimes embattled but always defiant figure, she invariably stood up for Britain. And just as she galvanised Britain itself, so she galvanised other countries' view of Britain as once again a strong, dependable, worthwhile ally and a country which gives a lead in world affairs. We still benefit from that.

Margaret Thatcher was not happy about losing office and she did not hide it. An election defeat she could have handled: she invariably prepared for it by packing up all her belongings in the No. 10 tenement flat on the eve of elections. Being defenestrated by her own parliamentary party was a different matter. She made life uncomfortable for her successor by leaked complaints about 'the government'. But then she frequently complained about 'the government' when she was Prime Minister, even when I pointed out it was her government. She appeared to think they were nothing to do with her.

She was realistic enough to know that there would never be a come-back. But at the end of well-lubricated lunches with Bernard Ingham and myself in the 1990s she would declaim: 'Come on, we are going to march up Downing Street and reclaim No. 10.' Bernard and I offered to escort her as far as the Downing Street gates but no further, and were berated for our lily-livered performance.

For some years she occupied herself with frenetic travel and speech-making, sometimes startling well-intentioned questioners by pummelling them into the ground as though they were Neil Kinnock at PM's Questions. But it was the exercise of power she was built for, and without that she felt life lacked purpose. A dreadnought is out of place in a fishing fleet.

She was treated with generosity and respect by all four of her succes-sors and enjoyed her occasional return to No. 10, though it's hard not to believe it also caused pangs.

In later years she travelled less, but occasionally came to stay with my wife and me on our small farm outside Rome. We put her to work picking cherries and docked tax and national insurance from her pay just to remind her what governments do to wage-earners. She liked to visit Italy's great cathedrals and was tickled by the hordes of German and Japanese tourists who wanted to be photographed with her. 'Don't say, "we won the war",' I would admonish her. 'Just once, Charles?'

My wife took her to meet the Pope, which made me a bit uneasy as to what she might say. But my wife pointed out that Paul Johnson was going along too, so there would be no need for her to speak.

As she became more frail she was tended by her two carers, Kate and Anne, with affection and a fair bit of gentle teasing. Following an oper-ation in December, she convalesced at the Ritz thanks to the generosity of the Barclay family, *The Spectator*'s proprietors. A small circle of long-time friends would come by to satisfy her craving for information about what was going on. I timed my visits to coincide with the Ritz's famed tea, and we quarrelled briskly over who had eaten the most chocolate biscuits. It was a gentle twilight to a life of extraordinary achievement.

Andrew Tyrie
Conservative MP 1997–

Andrew Tyrie served as an adviser to Nigel Lawson at HM Treasury and was elected MP for Chichester in 1997. He chairs the Treasury Select Committee.

My first meaningful encounter with Margaret Thatcher took place at 7.15 a.m. in a windowless back room in Conservative Central Office just before a press conference during the 1984 European elections. Having been at Central Office for only a few months, I was unnerved to find myself placed opposite her. She had, it seemed, read all the extensive briefing that we had prepared for her. She fixed me with a stare. Her first question identified an apparent contradiction in the briefing. Before I had time to admit that I did not know the answer, Geoffrey Howe, who was sitting next to me and did, saved me by replying.

Margaret Thatcher was kind enough to add me to a lunch party at Chequers after those elections. No doubt identifying me as the junior man, she told me to sit next to her for lunch. Within minutes, she announced to the table that I was far too thin and insisted on overseeing my consumption of two puddings.

I met Mrs Thatcher sporadically over the following few years. I was at the Treasury, with a ringside seat for the Thatcher–Lawson row, the rights and wrongs of which – and there were both – are for another day. More generally, I had a chance to observe several of her well-known traits. At the heart of her approach was her instinctive understanding that the restoration of prosperity depended on supply-side reform: breaking down the entrenched privileges – of the professions as much as of the trade unions – simplifying and reducing taxes, cutting back the tangle of regulation, and enhancing individual opportunity and aspiration. She wanted to break with the consensus of an over-mighty state and a dependent people.

Some have been arguing recently that Mrs Thatcher's reforms are responsible for the failings of the banks today. I doubt that. Whatever the merits of the prudential regulation that came with the Big Bang in the 1980s, those rules were no longer in place when the crisis broke five years ago; they had been replaced by another set of rules put there in the 1990s in both the US and the UK. In any case, the notion that Mrs Thatcher, who cared most of all about the consumer and the taxpayer, would be an apologist for the banks, is implausible. She would have found the abuse of market power by some bank leaderships for their own gain at the expense of the rest of us every bit as deplorable as the behaviour of trade union leaders.

It has been said that Mrs Thatcher's judgement faltered at the end, and there was perhaps a touch of that hubris that always lurks in No. 10's bunker after a long stay. The pain of her reforms still lingers. Over the longer view, none of that, I think, will detract from her legacy. What will linger in the memory is the single most extraordinary achievement of any leader in the post-war era – that of turning a failing country and a basket-case economy into a country that had recovered its self-respect and had a future.

Lord MacGregor
Cabinet Minister 1983–1990

John MacGregor was Private Secretary to Edward Heath and was elected to Parliament as MP for South Norfolk in February 1974. He was a minister during the entirety of the Thatcher government, entering the Cabinet in September 1985 as Chief Secretary to the Treasury. He later served as Education Secretary, Agriculture Secretary and Leader of the House of Commons.

Shortly after I was elected to the House of Commons in 1974, I became a member of the committee on the Finance Bill, which in those days went on interminably and at great length for many days, through the night in the upper corridors of the House of Commons, going line by line through the various proposals in the Finance Bill itself. Baroness Thatcher was at that point our opposition frontbench spokesman on Economic Affairs, so led on the Finance Bill in the committee stages. On the day of her election as leader, we were meeting in committee that afternoon and evening. As some others will recollect, none of us on the committee expected her to be with us at all that evening, given the many interviews that she had to give and the many celebration drinks and so on with all of her supporters. Robert Carr, later Lord Carr, who was then her frontbench deputy on Economic Affairs, took the lead in committee. I happened to be on my feet, dealing with a very abstruse and technical point on some aspect of the Finance Bill, in full flow at about half past ten, when to my astonishment the door opened and in walked Margaret Thatcher. She proceeded to sit on the front bench for the whole of the rest of our session, through the night, leading from the front bench. I was so astonished at her arrival, and so obsessed with my technical details, that I am afraid I mumbled a rather inadequate congratulation on her victory. However, we were all absolutely amazed that she stayed to see the session through. That demonstrated in a remarkable way her dedication and very strong sense of public duty, and her commitment to her duty in the House of Commons.

Secondly, as Minister for Agriculture, I was very much involved in the first full-blown reform of the Common Agricultural Policy. We had many sessions in Brussels on that front. We had got to a point in the middle of the night where we were near to reaching agreement, but it went beyond the negotiating brief agreed for me by the Cabinet. I had to refer back to the Prime Minister for her agreement and authority to go ahead in the way that I wanted to. If I remember correctly, this was at about three o'clock in the morning, so I agonised long and hard about when I should ring her to get her approval. I rang at about 6 a.m., got straight through and heard her response in a very clear voice. Clearly she had been up for some time, working on her briefs. I got her agreement and we were able to go ahead. That demonstrated her indefatigable energy, her immense capacity for work and her decisiveness when convinced.

On one occasion in Brussels, I collapsed with a burst ulcer in the middle of the night and had to be carted away briefly to hospital. I was astonished the next morning to receive a very large bowl of flowers and a warm sympathy note from Baroness Thatcher herself. It was another example of her kindnesses in so many ways. I was greatly touched.

I very much support others who have described the way in which she absolutely tore into you if you were not a master of your brief and in full command not only of the facts but of the arguments. This was a bit disconcerting at first. You thought that she was basically disagreeing and that you would get nowhere, but if you persisted and knew the facts of your brief, she would agree. It took me some time to realise that this was her style, because I recognised that it was what I did to civil servants who put forward briefs to me. I always looked overnight for the points that I was not happy about or did not agree with, and started off with those before in the end agreeing with the conclusions that the paper had made. That was a great feature of all the negotiations that we as individuals had with Baroness Thatcher.

My last example is her final speech in the House of Commons on her resignation. As Leader of the House, I was sitting next to her during the speech. It was obviously an immensely difficult occasion and I was very nervous for her. I need not have worried. She defended her record and achievements with great clarity, power and eloquence. Halfway through she was questioned by some opposition backbenchers – in particular, if I remember correctly, Dennis Skinner – to whom she responded with great gusto, drawing a huge response from her own backbenchers. At the end of the put-down she said something like, 'Now, where was I? You know, I'm enjoying this.' It was absolutely typical of the way in which she approached these speeches. It was a remarkable speech, and a performance that displayed the qualities of great courage and conviction that have been referred to frequently today and by which I will always remember her.

Sir George Gardiner
Conservative MP 1974–97

Sir George Gardiner was the Conservative MP for Reigate from 1974 until 1997 when he joined the Referendum Party. He is the author of Margaret Thatcher: From Childhood to Leadership *and* A Bastard's Tale. *Sir George died in 2002.*

The 1975 Thatcher campaign team used to meet in a subterranean committee room below the Commons under the shrewd chairmanship of Airey Neave. Our task was to conduct a discreet canvass of how most of the 276 Conservative MPs intended to vote in the leadership ballot, all duly recorded by William Shelton. We were an odd bunch: backbench worthies like Julian Ridsdale, John Stokes and Angus Maude; hard-hitters like Norman Tebbit and Nicholas Ridley; the lovable rogue Billy Rees-Davies, severely war-wounded and minus an arm; and a few like myself, products of the previous year's elections. Airey then reported to Margaret's sponsor, Sir Keith Joseph. We were as unlikely a cell of revolutionaries as ever you could find – yet did we realise quite what a hurricane force we were about to release on the British people, a woman who would break the miserable mould of post-war politics together with its complacent and stifling corporatism? Did we hell!

Few of us then could envisage a time when the mighty union leaders could no longer aspire to dictate Cabinet policy or indeed bring down governments. In a speech nine days after her election as leader she dealt with the issue very cautiously: often when you find a solid rock blocking your path, she said, it was best not to charge it head on, but to move round or undermine it. What on earth, we asked, did she mean?

Not until we were into the following parliament did we begin to get an inkling of what we had done. The first Thatcher manifesto, after all, was a pretty cautious document – new laws to curb picketing, slight tightening of the law on the closed shop, fresh curbs on immigration, more incentives through taxation – but not much more.

At the time the leadership election was called I was on Christian-name terms with Margaret, but nothing more. Then a publisher asked me to write her biography, and she agreed to cooperate. So it was that in spring that year I went regularly on Saturdays to her flat in Chelsea's Flood Street with my tape recorder. During these sessions I came to realise just how much her roots in Grantham meant to her. She was eloquent in describing her father, Alderman Alfred Roberts, the grocers' shop run by her family over which they lived, the local Methodist Church and its culture, and how the privations and hopes of World War II made her what she was. Only years later did she amplify this in her own memoirs.

From then until her downfall in 1990 I was one of her foremost backbench supporters, and for the final six years of her premiership saw her regularly as Chairman of the '92', a group of around 100 right-of-centre Tory MPs.

If you stood by Margaret in tough times she was supportive and loyal in return. But I am always amazed by the press caricature of her as an impetuous bully, happily handbagging everyone in sight. In fact, she was immensely cautious. So anxious was she to pacify the old wets and supporters of her predecessor, Edward Heath, that after victory in 1979 she gave them preponderance in her Cabinet for eighteen months until she reshaped it more in the image of the party as a whole. Peter Walker, who ran Heath's leadership campaign, was brought into her Cabinet, and even while he was delivering coded speeches attacking her policies she kept him there. Privatisation of the public utilities was barely heard of until just before the 1983 election. When miners' leader Arthur Scargill first challenged her on pit closures she backed off; not until she was equipped to beat him did she come back fighting.

Contrary to press myth, she was tolerant of other points of view, provided they were well argued. I flouted three-line whips many times, but never did she see this as an attack upon herself, nor did it affect our trusting relationship The totalitarianism that crept into the party after her downfall had no roots in her. In opposition, when I was among those advising her twice a week in preparation for Prime Minister's Questions, I helped to organise a rebellion on the renewal of economic sanctions against what was then Rhodesia. We inflicted humiliation on the Tory whips, yet when I turned up somewhat abashed to help advise her next day (along with Geoffrey Pattie, who had rebelled too) she was in teasing mood: 'What's the matter with you two? Have you lost your tongues?' She knew our rebellion was based on principle.

Never did she allow her high office to diminish her concern for her friends. Once, during her first parliament as Prime Minister, I called one evening at Downing Street to compare notes with Ian Gow, then her PPS. I met him in her flat, where we watched the TV news. Our intention was to go on to his club for dinner – until Margaret arrived unexpectedly early. 'You two boys must be hungry.' Despite our protests she disappeared into the little kitchen, took chicken kievs, peas and carrots from the fridge – then insisted we sat at the kitchen table to join her for supper. Before we were finished Denis arrived, and he made coffee. Was there any other significant nation in the world, I asked myself, whose Prime Minister (or President, as the case may be) would insist on cooking supper for unexpected visitors?

When I was in hospital in 1992 awaiting bypass surgery she sent encouraging messages every few days. The weekend before my operation I wrote a leader-page article for the *Sunday Express*; no sooner was I out of my anaesthetic than there was a note from Margaret saying how spot-on my piece had been. When I was a lunch guest at Chequers one Sunday I watched her crouching beside Margaret Tebbit's wheelchair lifting food on a fork to her mouth. She felt it deeply that the IRA's Brighton bomb, which left Margaret Tebbit paralysed, was in fact intended for her.

It often seemed that the media were determined never to present this human side to her character. There was the time I persuaded her to perform the official opening of the new East Surrey Hospital in my constituency. It was the first hospital she had ever opened; Geoffrey Howe, Kenneth Baker and I joined her, since the hospital served our constituencies; Health Secretary Norman Fowler and Reigate's Mayor were also there. The afternoon's itinerary was way behind as Margaret spent far more time than was scheduled at bedsides, listening to individual cases and sympathising. Likewise she spent far longer with staff than had been planned, asking and answering probing questions. Cameras followed her all the way. Yet what did the BBC report? Only that some trade unionist at a tiny demonstration outside had thrown an egg at her car! Big deal.

Her final downfall could not have been more brutal. Over the preceding year I and officers of the '92' often warned her of the dangers lurking, but she always believed she could face her critics down. Then Geoffrey Howe plunged the first dagger over European policy, opening the way for Michael Heseltine's challenge; Heseltine said he had a better alternative to the poll tax, which was deeply unpopular, and as the election drew near many Tory MPs were anxious.

She had a so-called campaign team, but there was no evidence of a proper campaign; utterly complacent, they gave her totally wrong advice. Worse still, she was in Paris for the election. Not until evening the day after the first ballot (which she led, though just short of an outright win) were I and others in the '92' able to get through to her. But by then it was too late; her resolution had been broken by Cabinet colleagues pledging support while telling her she could never win – 'treachery with a smile on its face', as she put it later. I will never forget her then, on the verge of tears as we pleaded with her to stay in the race, which I am convinced to this day she would have won with a last-minute campaign worthy of the name.

I doubt whether we shall see the like of her as Prime Minister again. Yet the woman who sent packing the likes of Scargill, General Galtieri and the hooded assassins of the IRA, who restored pride to her country after years of creeping socialism, and who with President Reagan hastened the end of the evil Soviet Empire, was brought down by a clutch of her own MPs in a blue funk over a looming election, and by ministers who owed her everything.

Lord Mackay

Lord Chancellor 1987–97

After a distinguished legal career in Scotland, James Mackay was raised to the peerage in 1979. He served as Lord Advocate from 1979 until 1985 and then as Lord Chancellor from 1987 until 1997.

I had the privilege of being appointed to serve as Lord Advocate in Margaret Thatcher's first administration in May 1979. We had never met and my appointment was offered and accepted over the telephone. I was privileged to continue as Lord Advocate into her second administration when I became a Judge of the Supreme Courts of Scotland. On her recommendation I was appointed a Lord of Appeal in Ordinary, one of the two Scottish full-time judges in the House of Lords in October 1985.

In October 1987 I was listening to a debate in the House on the Criminal Justice Bill after the judicial sitting had terminated when I received a message from the secretary of the then Leader of the House, Viscount Whitelaw, to ring urgently the Prime Minister's Private Secretary. That I did and was invited immediately to come over to meet the Prime Minister.

I duly went over to No. 10 thinking the Prime Minister had an inquiry of some kind that she wished me to undertake. Whenever I arrived at No. 10 I was ushered into the Prime Minister's study. She arose to welcome me, immediately asked me to sit down and sat in the chair opposite. She informed me that Lord Havers, the Lord Chancellor, had come to see her a little earlier that day and had tendered his resignation on the grounds of ill health. She asked me to become Lord Chancellor in succession to him. As you can imagine, this was an extraordinary surprise and I answered that she knew my commitment to Sunday as a special day, to which she replied that she was also of the view that it should be a special day and that there would be no difficulty on that score. I then said that I would need to consult my wife but the Prime Minister knew better than any that when one is in an important public office there are profound effects for wife and family. She said, 'Certainly, please go and ring her up,' so I was duly presented with the telephone at the other end of the table from that at which we were sitting and I telephoned home, only to find that my wife was out. The Prime Minister said, 'We are very anxious to put the news out tonight of the new appointment along with Lord Havers' resignation and therefore I am very keen to have your answer as soon as possible.' I left promising to let her know as soon as I could.

As you can imagine, I kept ringing home to Edinburgh at frequent intervals and eventually my wife came in and when I told her my message she said, 'Oh well, you can hardly refuse that offer.' I duly telephoned to the Prime Minister's Private Secretary but he declined to take the message and put me through to the Prime Minister herself. I told her my wife's reply and in view of that reply I was happy and honoured to accept her invitation. She kindly said that she was delighted and that arrangements would be made for the intimation as soon as possible. The intimation was in fact made on the seven o'clock news that evening.

Shortly thereafter my wife was in London and we met the Prime Minister in Speakers' House. When we met I said to the Prime Minister, 'This was the lady for whose reply we were waiting the other day.' And with that charm and grace which was so characteristic of the Prime Minister she gave a very nice bow and said to my wife: 'We were very delighted with your reply.'

In the order of precedence which is established for state occasions the Lord Chancellor takes precedence immediately after the Archbishop of Canterbury, before the Archbishop of York and before the Prime Minister. I hope it is easy to imagine that I felt very embarrassed, and so did my wife, at the idea of preceding the Prime Minister. Again, her charm and grace always showed and on such occasions she would always encourage us to take our proper place in front of her, making it a lot easier for us to do so than if we had not been shown that charm. I remained as Lord Chancellor during the remainder of the tenure of Margaret Thatcher as Prime Minister and she was always most respectful and very clear about the importance of the executive, not interfering in the work and affairs of the judiciary.

Matthew Parris
Broadcaster and Columnist

After working for the Conservative Research Department and in Mrs Thatcher's private office, Matthew Parris became the MP for West Derbyshire in 1979, a position he held until 1986. Since then he has worked as a broadcaster and most famously as a parliamentary sketchwriter for The Times.

When I was a Branch Chairman of South Battersea Conservative Association we welcomed Margaret Thatcher, as Leader of the Opposition, on an official visit to our neighbourhood. I and others were deputed to guide her on a walkabout down the Northcote Road (a little market) for the local press. This was about 1978.

She spotted a council workman driving a motorised street cleaner. After speaking to him she began to climb into the driver's seat, crying: 'Show me how this thing works and I will clean the street. Only a woman knows how to get into corners men cannot reach.'

In 1978 the RSPCA asked Mrs Thatcher to present me (at the time I was her Correspondence Secretary) with their award for bravery in rescuing a dog from the River Thames.

The ceremony took place on Westminster Bridge in the presence of a number of officials, the dog (Jason) and some photographers. Privately, Mrs Thatcher thought I had been mad to rescue the dog. But she was a kindly employer and no doubt spotted a good photo opportunity too.

During the ceremony the dog began (as little male dogs too often do) to mate with her elegantly stockinged leg. She took absolutely no notice and carried on smiling for the cameras. To this day I have never been quite sure whether she realised what was going on down below, and never dared ask her.

Did she have a heart? In two years working for Margaret Thatcher in the opposition leader's office, I never reached a conclusion, yet my personal admiration for her only grew. We received from the public between 500 and (at one point) 5,000 letters every week. With three letter-openers and secretaries, I had to deal with all of them. We quickly learned her instincts towards public correspondence.

She was not greatly interested in individuals' ideas or opinions. She was interested in general movements of opinion and the overall public response to events, and to herself, and never discouraged us from bringing her adverse tidings. But it was her attitude to what we called 'the poorlies', members of the public who had turned to her in their personal troubles, that was unlike any other leader's I've known.

Mrs T. (as we all called her) insisted we show her anything we thought needed her personal touch; she was meticulous and unsparing in dealing with these, even when we ourselves felt she had better things to do than sit up late, her blue felt-tip in hand, penning sympathy, advice and reassurance.

I'll never forget one such: her reply to a lady who, grief-stricken by the loss of her husband, wanted the comfort of knowing that the Conservative leader believed in Heaven. In Mrs T.'s otherwise consoling letter, her answer to this question itself stood bleakly out as oddly tortured, almost legalistic: 'Christians believe in the Afterlife, and I am a Christian.'

I loved her for the trouble she took with people of no account, but could never quite banish a suspicion she was doing this because in childhood she had absorbed the strict lesson that this was what a nice person would do. But I took, and take, refuge in the words that Robert Bolt, screenwriter, places in the mouth of Prince Feisal in *Lawrence of Arabia*: 'With Major Lawrence, mercy is a passion. With me it is merely good manners. You may judge which motive is the more reliable.'

Lord Ashcroft KCMG PC
Conservative Peer

Michael Ashcroft is an international businessman and philanthropist. He was raised to the peerage in 2000. He is a former Conservative Party Treasurer and Deputy Chairman.

I have numerous memories of Margaret Thatcher and all of them are fond ones. To me, she was not just a colossus of British politics but also a fiercely loyal friend when I was under fire. Her death today has saddened me greatly.

I credit Margaret Hilda Thatcher with rekindling my interest in politics after I had drifted away from it for well over a decade. I had admired her from afar long before I knew her – and not just because she was Britain's first (and to date only) woman Prime Minister.

I thought that if a grammar school-educated grocer's daughter from Grantham in Lincolnshire could make it to the top in the Conservative Party (she led the party in opposition for four years before becoming Prime Minister in 1979), then there had to be room for a wider variety of people.

By the time Margaret became Prime Minister, I had been fortunate enough to make some money as an entrepreneur. I applauded her strong leadership of the country and I decided I wanted to help out the party financially.

In 1981, I made my first donation to the party: £50,000. By the time Margaret stood down as Prime Minister in 1990, I had contributed £1 million to the party and lent it £3 million. While she led the country, I – and many other like-minded people – felt proud to be British.

As a party donor and supporter, I was first introduced to her in the early 1980s when I was in my mid-thirties. It was impossible not to be impressed by her drive and leadership, together with her vision and commitment to the party and country that she loved.

Particularly after Margaret's firm handling of the Falklands crisis in 1982, I felt inclined to give British politics another go, having drifted away from the party in the mid-1970s because, although I was a natural Tory, I had felt the party was out of touch with the electorate and its core supporters. Doesn't that sound familiar!

The Conservative Party under Margaret's leadership in the 1980s was a genuine meritocracy: it allowed people to get to the top through their ability rather than where they had gone to school, or how rich and well-connected their parents were.

Margaret was single-minded and cut through the nonsense. With the Falklands War, for example, she had a direct approach. She knew that the islands belonged to Britain, the Argentinians had invaded them and therefore, unless they withdrew, Britain would send a force to eject them.

During the miners' strike she was equally decisive. Anticipating an ugly dispute marred by violent picketing, she resolved to increase the nation's coal stocks. She was determined that Britain would be in a position to survive a long dispute and finally curb the power of militant trade unionism, which had grown too strong for the good of the country.

Events in industries that I knew about had also propelled me towards her. For years, many public services were overmanned and run in the producers' interests. Some Conservative-controlled councils wanted to cut costs and raise productivity by scrapping restrictive practices and opening local government services up to private competition – so-called tendering out.

This allowed private firms to bid for work such as street cleaning and school maintenance. Although this was common in other countries, the response in Britain was extraordinary. Strikes and sabotage – refuse trucks were even set on fire – were just a few of the reactions from left-wing extremists. No country could afford to be governed in this way – and Margaret made sure her government stood up to such utter nonsense.

During the 1980s, I became friends with Margaret and, even more so, with her husband Denis, who I served with on the board of the same public company. Denis was also a founder trustee and staunch supporter of Crimestoppers, the crime-fighting charity that I launched twenty-five years ago. The Thatchers were a loving and devoted couple and were married for more than fifty years before Denis's death in 2003.

I have one abiding memory of Margaret that I will take with me to my grave. Shortly before she resigned as Prime Minister in November 1990, I had to meet Denis to discuss some business affairs.

Because he was particularly busy, he asked me to pop round to see him at 10 Downing Street. We were sitting in the Thatchers' lounge going through some papers when Margaret walked into the room.

I immediately got up to greet her but she just said: 'Sit down, sit down. Would you boys like a cup of tea?' It was a strange feeling sitting there while the Prime Minister of the day disappeared into the kitchen, boiled the kettle and poured us tea in silence so as not to disturb our meeting. Even today, I sometimes try to imagine how Britain would be without Margaret's resolve and leadership. She undoubtedly deserves to go down in history as Britain's greatest peacetime Prime Minister. It took someone with astonishing will-power and principle to change the course of history, and Margaret Thatcher was that person.

As Prime Minister, she offered people hope, opportunity and a chance to run their own lives. I have lost an old friend while Britain will be a poorer place without her. One thing is certain: we will not see her like again soon. And isn't that a pity in the world today.

Baroness Jenkin
Conservative Peer

Anne Jenkin was raised to the peerage in 2011. She is married to Conservative MP Bernard Jenkin and is the co-founder of Women2Win.

At the height of Margaret Thatcher's power, when many of my colleagues in the House of Lords were working closely with her as senior civil servants or as ministers, to the rest of the world she was a myth, to whom all triumph and disaster could be ascribed. To me, growing up as a Conservative activist, then later in 1987 a Conservative candidate and from 1992 as a young MP's wife, she was a legend and like many others, I was in awe. I was among those who cheered her at party conferences, calling for 'five more years', and worked hard for those three consecutive Conservative victories because she inspired and motivated so many of us.

But later, as I got to know her personally, she was no longer a myth. She was Mrs T. and then Lady T.

In old age she became really quite ordinary, an old lady coping as best she could with diminishing horizons. Sitting beside her in her home in Chester Square in recent years, drinking coffee, flicking through magazines about the royal family or the 1940s, and chatting away, sometimes about gossip from the party conference, sometimes about what it was she had for tea when she got home from school as a girl, it was easy to forget that this was *Margaret Thatcher* – and then when I did remember, I had to pinch myself. The younger me would have been astonished!

As co-founder, with Theresa May, of Women2Win – the pressure group set up in 2005 to get more Conservative women into Parliament – one of the things we realised when encouraging more women to come forward as Conservative candidates, was that she was at the same time a role model and a deterrent. Many women were put off from coming forward, fearing that they could not live up to her achievements and that they did not have the requisite dedication to public life. They were worried that they didn't have what it took. That they wouldn't be able to live up to the exacting standards that she had set.

She has been criticised for not doing more for women – and particularly women in the Conservative Party – but I can speak from personal experience that she was fully engaged with the new generation of women MPs, the talented group of forty-nine women who were elected in 2010. She supported many of them at fundraising events and encouraged and advised them about what attributes and characteristics they would need to be a successful MP. She came to lunch at my home to chat to candidates and Women2Win volunteers, one of whom told me this week that for twenty-four hours she was the most excited person on the planet. It may be that she wasn't focused on the feminist agenda while in power – after all she had other priorities at that stage – but she certainly made up for it later on. And now that capable group of women MPs are themselves great role models for a new generation following on behind them.

In 2005 I accompanied her to the Women of the Year lunch where she received their Lifetime Achievement award. Sitting with her handbag on my lap while she went up to the podium to a standing ovation to collect her well-deserved award was one of the proudest moments of my life. I was especially struck by the number of women who came to tell her that they had reached the top of their profession, or achieved recognition in their chosen field, because she had led the way. Whether they were Permanent Secretary, on the board of Shell, ambassador, each one told her they could not have done it without her. She was so impressed by their individual achievements, and extremely modest in accepting their words of gratitude. The organisers had been told that she could not possibly be asked to speak. I had reminded her, 'No need to say anything: just receive the award.' She stepped up to the podium to accept the award, and then my heart stopped as she made hesitatingly for the microphone. The whole room sensed a kind of crisis. She had told me several times over the past hour how as Prime Minister she had spoken in the Guildhall at the annual Lord Mayor's Banquet – and that is how she started, over dead silence. What would she say next? Everyone was holding their breath, but as if by instinct she told us how over lunch she had been studying the statue of the Duke of Wellington, opposite where she sat. Then she declared with a flare of her old style: 'All the attributes which made Britain great when he was in charge are what makes our country great today!' There was a huge and emotional outburst of cheering and applause.

I remember Shirley Williams coming up for a chat at that lunch. Just imagine if Lady T. had remained in the same robust good health as Shirley Williams what amazing debates we would have continued to enjoy in the Lords and elsewhere!

To me her lasting legacy is a combination of inspiration and aspiration. She showed others that it doesn't matter where you come from. If you have ability, drive, conviction, determination and are prepared to put in a lot of sheer old-fashioned hard work, you can get to the top. Today's generation of women and girls should remind themselves that she has given them reason to supplant fantasies of being princesses with a different dream – the real-life option of leading their nation; this is what is groundbreaking and admirable.

I shall miss her. I shall miss the very idea of her and, from the large number of friends and acquaintants who have contacted me over the past couple of days, just to share their feelings of admiration of her with someone who was privileged enough to have met her and spent time with her, I know that there are millions who feel the same.

Michael Thornton
Journalist

Michael Thornton is a journalist with the Sunday Express.

Margaret Thatcher's place in history, as the only woman leader to date of the Conservative Party and as Britain's first woman Prime Minister, is secure for all time.

Yet but for the biggest and strangest scoop of my journalistic career and a meeting between Thatcher and myself at her London home on an unforgettable October afternoon in 1974, next Wednesday's lavish military and ceremonial funeral would not be taking place.

For without my challenge to her in the form of a bet and the astonishing repercussions when my interview with her was published three days later in the *Sunday Express,* Thatcher would never have become the Conservative leader, far less gone on to win three elections as Britain's most successful peacetime Prime Minister.

This is a bold claim but she herself acknowledged the truth of it in writing and never varied from that admission for the rest of her days.

I cannot explain, even now, exactly what impelled me to write to Mrs Thatcher, as she then was, to ask for an interview. I was not a political writer. I had begun my Fleet Street career eleven years earlier at the age of twenty-two under the then Editor of the *Sunday Express,* John (later Sir John) Junor, to all of us the legendary and powerfully influential 'JJ'.

He made me the paper's film and theatre critic, at that time the youngest there had been. My age provoked one gossip columnist to lampoon me as 'the only critic in London who needs an adult to accompany him into an A-feature'.

By 1974, I was a freelance feature writer with only one previous political scoop to my credit. In 1969, I had persuaded the disgraced John Profumo to give me the first, and last, interview he gave to any journalist after the scandal of his enforced resignation as War Minister in 1963 over his affair with Christine Keeler.

So what made me write to Mrs Thatcher without even telling John Junor what I was doing? I think I kept the wily JJ in the dark out of fear that he might take the idea away from me and hand it to a political writer.

The Tories, at that point, were in political limbo, having suffered two electoral defeats in the space of eight months. The position of their unmarried leader Edward Heath was clearly under threat and there were widespread rumours of a leadership challenge.

Margaret Thatcher was not, officially, a contender. Among the list of possibles drawn up by Ladbrokes she appeared low down as a 50–1 outsider. The front runners to succeed Heath, if he could be persuaded to stand down, were Sir Keith Joseph, the former Secretary of State for Health and Social Security, and William Whitelaw, the former Lord President of the Council and Leader of the House of Commons. I had never met Thatcher. What little I knew about her suggested that she was regarded, in some political quarters, as a bit of a joke. As Education Minister her abolition of free milk for primary schoolchildren had led to chants of 'Margaret Thatcher, milk snatcher' and her genteel twinset-and-pearls image was frequently derided.

I suppose I thought that her feminine view of the situation might provide some amusing copy so I wrote and asked to meet her, never dreaming for a moment that at such a sensitive time she would agree or even respond to my letter.

To my astonishment a telephone call came almost immediately from her secretary at the House of Commons summoning me to a meeting at Thatcher's London home. 'Please try to be prompt,' advised the crisp female voice, 'she does value punctuality.'

I therefore arrived early on the afternoon of 17 October 1974, but when I rang the bell at 19 Flood Street, Chelsea, a modern Georgian-style house 50 yards off the King's Road, I had no very clear idea of how I was going to conduct the interview.

The door was opened by Thatcher's 21-year-old daughter Carol bursting out of a pair of battered jeans and plainly unimpressed by the arrival of yet another journalist. She had no idea then that one day she would become one herself. 'Mum's out,' she announced in a bored voice, 'but she won't be long. If she said four o'clock, it will be four. On the dot.'

Sure enough, as the clocks of Chelsea chimed the hour the future Iron Lady made her entrance, immaculately coiffured, without one blonde hair out of place and wearing an elegantly severe cream dress with geometric patterns in black ribbon.

For the first time I heard that measured, plummy voice, and from the moment that she sat down and turned those searching, challenging ice-blue eyes upon me I instantly revised my earlier opinion of her. This was no lightweight. She exuded power and determination.

She possessed, even then, at the age of forty-nine, a carefully rehearsed quality of infinite precision and calculation and I was soon overwhelmed by the impression that she had staged this interview for strategic purposes, though whether her object was to bid for the Tory crown, or merely to bring down Heath, seemed debatable.

Before I could ask a question she cut to the chase. 'It's an agonising time for all of us in the party,' she said, referring to the two Conservative electoral defeats. 'No one really knows what to say or do. The last thing we want is to pressure Ted but he must let us know what he intends to do. Things just cannot drift on as they are. We all feel that this present uncertainty must be resolved before Parliament sits.'

The tone was outwardly sympathetic but the criticism was obvious. Defeated chieftains fell on their swords but here was Heath stubbornly clinging to the party leadership.

Before the interview, one of Thatcher's colleagues, the former Foreign Secretary, Lord Home, whom I knew socially, had confided to me that there was little love lost between Heath and Thatcher. Heath had found Thatcher 'over-talkative' in Cabinet and frequently slapped her down in a brusque and boorish manner in front of other ministers.

Now, faced with growing discontent and criticism within the Tory ranks, Heath was being pressured by the 1922 Committee to hold a leadership election. Thatcher had recently gone on record saying: 'It will be years before a woman either leads a party or becomes Prime Minister.' In her Chelsea drawing room Thatcher's face became deeply contemplative. 'Yes, I did feel that at one point,' she conceded, 'but I'm not sure that I do any longer.'

'Why not now?' I challenged. She threw up her hands. 'No, no, no!' she insisted, in an eerie prelude to her later stance on Europe at the end of her time in power. 'I think perhaps I might be leader one day but not the next leader.'

'I disagree,' I heard myself telling her. She looked startled. 'Why?' she asked. 'What are people saying?' I smiled. 'They are saying that

Sir Keith Joseph and Mr Whitelaw will not do. Wrong image in both cases. People think it is time for a change, time perhaps for a woman to lead the Conservative Party.

'Of course,' I added, 'political leaders have normally occupied one of the three top Cabinet posts – Foreign Secretary, Home Secretary or Chancellor of the Exchequer, but you have not held any of those as yet.' A sudden surge of energy and determination illuminated Thatcher's face. 'That is true,' she admitted, 'but remember, there are notable exceptions. The present Prime Minister, Harold Wilson, occupied none of those posts before becoming leader.'

She returned to the vexed subject of Heath. 'All this is so wretched for him, coming straight after the tragedy of *Morning Cloud*.' (Heath's yacht had sunk in a force nine gale in the Channel, a portent, some thought, of his submerging political fortunes.)

'Poor Ted!' sighed Thatcher. 'And unlike me he hasn't a family around him from whom to draw strength.'

These last words, a pointed reminder of Heath's problematic bachelor status, were the daggers of the Ides of March, plunged in October, in the honeyed tones of *Mrs Dale's Diary*. She had proved, to my complete satisfaction, that she possessed the most important quality of all for political leadership: the killer instinct.

As I left the house, I played my final card. 'I'll make a bet with you that you will be the next leader of the Conservative Party,' and I held out my hand. She laughed and shook my hand. 'I'll accept your bet,' she said. 'I say I will not be the next leader.'

Despite her words, though, the gleam of aspiration had shone in her eyes. Somehow I had guided her to the realisation that the moment had come to throw her hat into the ring. 'Political dynamite' was how John Junor described the interview when he saw it. 'Are you sure you haven't exaggerated, laddie?' he asked. 'Did Maggie really say all of this?'

Sceptical, JJ sent the interview by courier to the House of Commons. To his amazement, it was returned by Thatcher, approved in every detail.

The interview was published in the *Sunday Express* three days later, under the headline I'M SO SORRY FOR TED, SAYS MARGARET THATCHER. It says much about the political clout of this newspaper that within hours of it appearing on the streets, there were a series of astonishing repercussions.

Junor was woken up by Heath apoplectic with fury, describing the article as 'the ultimate knife in the back' and denouncing Thatcher and myself as 'damned traitors'. He never forgave us. Thatcher and I were rushed on to the BBC radio programme *The World This Weekend* and the odds on her at Ladbrokes shortened dramatically from 50–1 to 6–1. On 4 February 1975, Thatcher defeated Heath decisively by 130 votes to 119. A week later she went on to defeat his preferred successor Willie Whitelaw by 146 votes to 79.

From the House of Commons, Thatcher, the new Leader of the Opposition, sent a letter to acknowledge that I had won my bet.

'I do think that you should be rather pleased with yourself for your prediction!' she wrote. 'I am amazed that it all happened.' Four years later she entered 10 Downing Street as Britain's first woman Prime Minister and remained in power for the next eleven years. Whenever we saw each other during those years she would say: 'Ah, here comes Thornton the Kingmaker!' Significantly, she did not say Queenmaker.

In 1991, a year after she was ousted from power, she wrote (of my interview): 'I well remember the article and the impact it had.'

At the Thatcher Foundation, where all aspects of her life are graded into four ranks of importance, key, major, minor and trivial, the interview is described as 'key'.

If the *Sunday Express*, in the person of myself, helped to change the course of British political history by bringing Margaret Hilda Thatcher to power, then I shall always regard it as one of the better things I have done in my life.

Lord Owen

Leader of the SDP 1983–87, 1988–92

Dr David Owen served as Foreign Secretary under James Callaghan from 1977 until 1979. In 1981 he resigned from the Labour Party to form the Social Democratic Party with Roy Jenkins, Bill Rodgers and Shirley Williams. He became leader of the SDP after the 1983 election, resigning in 1987 over the merger with the Liberal Party. He was re-elected leader of the SDP in 1988 and remained in that position until 1992 when he became Chairman of the International Conference on former Yugoslavia. Lord Owen now sits as a crossbencher in the House of Lords.

My first personal memory of Margaret Thatcher was as Secretary of State for Education in the early 1970s. A medical friend had come to dinner with her in the House of Commons to discuss a young patient and when she bumped into me in the division lobby she asked if I would go and have a drink with them. It was a revealing occasion, for as the conversation developed Margaret Thatcher's best and worst qualities were on display: consideration for a young constituent and the wish to get to the bottom of a problem coupled with a total inability to comprehend how any seventeen-year-old could be depressed.

As Foreign Secretary we met at many official functions. In April 1979 I was interviewed in the *Daily Mirror* and said, 'I saw her the other evening in the House of Commons and for the first time she looked really rather attractive. She'd had a couple of whiskies and was quite glowing, in the nicest possible way. She came over, smiling that special smile of hers, and wafted a combination of expensive scent and alcohol over me.'

This was described by an angry Conservative Party as the first dirty trick of the forthcoming election campaign. It was mild compared to President Mitterrand's remark later that 'she has the lips of Marilyn Monroe and the eyes of Caligula'. But John Junor, the Editor of the *Sunday Express*, who had lunch with her next day, found her relaxed, even flattered. It was at about this time that I had realised that we faced in her a far more formidable opponent than it was fashionable for most Labour politicians to admit.

In addressing Margaret Thatcher's leadership I believe the 1984 miners' dispute showed her at her best. She had cut her losses and settled when challenged by Joe Gormley in 1981 and had then planned ahead for the inevitable confrontation with Arthur Scargill. When the pit deputies union, NACODS, threatened sympathetic strike action at the end of October 1984 I was extremely worried that any concession to them could be used by Scargill as a face-saver. I took the opportunity of being in the same room as Margaret Thatcher to have a private talk with her. She seemed genuinely pleased to find that my worries about letting Arthur Scargill off the hook were exactly the same as hers. She made no attempt to conceal the fact that some of her colleagues wanted to settle but that she was adamantly against it. She was clear-sighted about the danger of Scargill being able to claim a spurious victory. When the end came in March 1985, fifty-one weeks after the strike had started, it was the miners who disowned their leaders by streaming back to work with their funds running low, good men with their self-respect in tatters. But for the country as a whole it was essential for our self-confidence that intimidation and violence could be resisted without tear gas or mobilising the armed services. The police, with a few exceptions, did extremely well.

Meeting with the Prime Minister at No. 10 in 1983 I raised the question of SDP representation at the Cenotaph. I was barely halfway through my case than she intervened to reject it, declaring that she was adamantly opposed to widening representation. Suddenly the atmosphere was heated. I told her bluntly that I could see absolutely no reason why a party that had attracted three and a half million voters should not be entitled to lay a wreath at the Cenotaph. Eventually I rose to go and said that I hoped that, since the decision was formally the Home Secretary's, she would give the matter renewed thought, otherwise I would have to take my case before the bar of public opinion. She became incandescent, alternating between a prim 'How could you?' to a furious 'How dare you?' The *Daily Telegraph* reported that the issue sharply divided ministers, that many senior members of the government were unhappy and that one of the service chiefs had actually objected to our exclusion. Newspapers up and down the country took our side. It was a good example of the basic fairness and decency of the British people asserting itself. Eventually Whitehall produced a formula to save the Prime Minister's face. What the whole episode showed was that though she was still totally dominant, she did not have an absolute hold on public opinion or newspaper editors and was politically deeply partisan, as she showed by taking the salute at the Falkland Victory parade instead of the Queen.

On the morning of 15 April 1986, Britain woke up to find that during the night the Americans had bombed terrorist targets in Libya using F-111 aircraft from bases in Britain. The Prime Minister was under immediate attack for authorising their use. Opposition leaders, like me, opposed the action as illegal. In government, however, decisions have to be made and the choice is often between two evils. The lesser evil in this case was to support President Reagan's request and try to pretend, as Margaret Thatcher did, that it was covered under Article 51 of the UN Charter and was an act of self-defence, whereas it was really retaliation forbidden under the UN Charter. Having been given crucial military support by President Reagan during the Falklands War, Margaret Thatcher knew that she owed him similar support. Given her personality, she would have found it impossible to refuse and it is to her credit, in such trying circumstances, that she gave permission.

When history assesses whether Margaret Thatcher was a great Prime Minister, this decision deserves to be weighed in the balance. Her refusal would have done immense damage to our relations with the Reagan administration. She showed courage and loyalty but she also demonstrated one of the distinguishing features of great leadership, the ability to turn a blind eye to instructions or to legal niceties and just to follow one's instincts.

After her 1987 election victory it was Margaret Thatcher in No. 10 on 7 July 1988 who proposed quite directly to me that I should join the Conservatives. She had given a dinner for Lord Carrington to mark his retirement from the post of NATO Secretary General and had quite deliberately taken both Debbie, my wife, and me aside as we were leaving. In her blunt way she said to Debbie, 'Your husband has a big choice to make and it can no longer be avoided. There are only two serious parties in British politics and we women understand these things; it is time he made up his mind.' Debbie bridled and I politely refused to join the Conservative Party then, as I had refused all others who had raised the issue with me.

Margaret Thatcher's downfall began on Tuesday 30 October 1990 when she came to the House of Commons to make a statement on the Rome summit. I helped wind her up by my question supporting the use of the veto. It was already clear from her earlier press conference, when she came out with her series of 'no, no, no' statements that she was on an emotional high and the adrenalin was pumping around her system as she handbagged every federalist proposal. She was taking her stand against the single currency and even beginning to backtrack from the agreed government position over the hard ecu. I watched Geoffrey Howe's face as she answered these questions; he looked miserable and unhappy. Truly, I thought, a dead sheep. How wrong I proved to be. On 1 November Howe resigned and his forthright resignation speech gave Michael Heseltine the opening he longed for to challenge her leadership. She had been brought down by hubris over the European Community, not the poll tax. Her excessive self-confidence was by then being flaunted day by day in the face of friend or foe alike. She had pitted herself against her own source of power, the Conservative MPs. She had reached a stage where she was not only not listening to her parliamentary colleagues but was contemptuous of their views. The Cabinet had been reduced in stature and in quality. Majority opinion was frequently flouted or manipulated. People of substance, who well knew that Cabinet government was a great constitutional safeguard, had allowed this to develop over the years to the detriment of us all. It was not just because she was a woman that the Cabinet had been so supine but it was a material factor. With the Cabinet too weak to act, the Conservative MPs had shown their power.

As leader of the SDP I identified with those parts of her modernising counter-revolution which would help reverse Britain's economic decline. In the late 1990s Tony Blair, as leader of New Labour, continued courageously with much the same modernising programme as, in fairness, did John Major before him. In a real sense this is a middle-class counter-revolution. It has by the start of the twenty-first century not yet achieved all its objectives, and its gains are not yet permanent. But it has made much-needed changes in Britain. Its driving force and its chief architect was Margaret Thatcher, but it has not solely been her revolution, nor that of the Conservative Party. Indeed, in terms of monetary discipline the revolution began with Denis Healey and James Callaghan in 1976. Many people in the country have supported this counter-revolution who do not consider

themselves party political. Essentially it has sought to reassert a national
self-confidence, to rediscover the commercial market-orientated prosperity of the Victorian era which had not just been the product of our
empire but owed much to British invention, design, entrepreneurship
and industrial skill. It has also been a movement to reassert the role of
the individual and to roll back the frontiers of an intrusive state. Sadly,
Margaret Thatcher did not draw sufficiently on those other middle-
class aspirations to serve the common good, to contribute to society as
a whole, and indeed at times, as over the NHS, she quite unnecessarily
upset those who held those values.

For centuries the middle class had been patronised by those with
hereditary wealth but they had found they could escape from their
backgrounds and by their own efforts create wealth. The crippling
levels of personal taxation in the 1960s and 1970s, however, began to
make it virtually impossible for the law-abiding, tax-paying, middle-
class citizen to accumulate wealth. All that has changed. Now the
middle class are the wealth creators. Britain has become the fourth
wealthiest country and we ought now to be able to progressively allevi-
ate poverty and improve our health and education services.

Margaret Thatcher was one of the four radical Prime Ministers this
century. As you walk through the door into the Members' Lobby in
the House of Commons, you face statues of Winston Churchill and
Lloyd George, guarding the entrance to the Chamber of the House
of Commons. On the right of the door is a statue of Clement Attlee
and on the left a place left empty for another statue. There is no doubt
that eventually, as the first woman Prime Minister, she will occupy that
position and deservedly so.

Lord Spicer
Conservative Peer

Sir Michael Spicer has served as the Member for South Worcestershire from 1974 until 1997 and for West Worcestershire from 1997 to 2010. He has held ministerial positions in the Department of Transport, Department of Energy and Department of the Environment. From 2001 to 2010 he chaired the 1922 Committee. His book, The Spicer Diaries, *was published in 2012.*

For a brief period, during the 1983 general election, I acted as Parliamentary Private Secretary to Margaret Thatcher. I was already Deputy Chairman of the party. As I had coordinated most of the detailed planning for the election, it was decided that I was sufficiently under the skin of what was going on to stand in as the Prime Minister's bag carrier in place of Ian Gow who, somewhat understandably, felt he needed to spend a little more time in his constituency of Eastbourne.

For me personally this was an exciting time. Margaret Thatcher was at the height of her prowess and Conservative policies were rampant. It was also for me a dangerous time. Margaret was always wary of those who had seen her at very close quarters in moments of high intensity. A few events may help to explain why my career went into somewhat of a tailspin after my spell as PPS to the PM.

In the run-up to the election I went on a practice tour with the PM around East Anglia. The trip took us to the privatised Felixstowe docks. When we were shown the highest crane in Europe, Margaret Thatcher expressed a desire to climb it. Not a single voter waited for us at the top, but the world's press stood slobbering with expectancy at the bottom; this was partly because she was dressed in a tight black skirt in which she intended to climb hundreds of feet of vertical iron laddering.

My job was to climb up so closely behind her that they never got the photo they were hoping for. Going up was a piece of cake. Coming down required me to guide the Prime Ministerial feet from rung to rung. The inevitably embarrassing (for me) picture did make the national press.

Then there was the occasion during the election itself when we were landing at Edinburgh Airport. I was chatting to Denis Thatcher in the seat behind me. Next to me was David Wolfson; beside him was the PM. Suddenly there came what were for me fatal words: 'See what Michael thinks of the last sentence of the speech.' I looked at it and said something banal like 'could do with some tightening up'. The PM exploded – she was hyping herself up for a mass rally of supporters waiting for her in the Scottish capital. 'Why am I always surrounded by so much negative unhelpfulness?'

When we landed I was put in a car with the Secretary of State for Scotland and his deputy and told to come up with a 'last sentence' before we reached the city centre. I was still fairly relaxed and told the others that this was normal before a big speech. We came up quite easily with not one but three 'last sentences' – each to be tossed back at us with contempt when through screaming crowds we finally reached the ante-room to the conference hall. The Press Secretary was going frantic. 'We've got to give something to the press.' It was Denis who found the answer. 'Don't have a last sentence,' he said, and the PM went on to make one of her best speeches of the campaign. I don't think I was ever forgiven.

Then there was the time when, returning from a BBC programme chaired by Sue Lawley, on which someone called in to be rude to the PM about the sinking of the *Belgrano*, I was asked to enquire of the Chairman of the Party (my old friend Cecil Parkinson) whether we could abolish the BBC after we had won the election. The PM was a few yards from me when I made the appropriate telephone call from her flat in No. 10. She could therefore clearly hear Cecil's expletives, and laughingly turned to Denis with the words 'I don't think the Chairman likes our little idea'. It was a good joke.

Winning that election was never much in doubt, so much so that I was asked to leave the Prime Minister's aeroplane in the last week of the campaign while it waited for me on the tarmac. I found the nearest payphone in the airport terminal. My instructions were to ask Tim Bell to 'pull' a three-page advertisement from all national newspapers attacking our rivals; the last page of this was a complete blank and was meant to represent the Liberal manifesto. 'People will think that a total waste of paper,' the Prime Minister had pronounced, 'especially as we are going to win.' She was right. The 1983 election was the high water mark of Conservative fortunes in the second half of the twentieth century.

One memory I will share goes back almost to her last day in government. I was Minister for Housing and she summoned me to the Cabinet room. It was a one-to-one meeting – I was on my own with her – and she said the words that will always be in my mind. We had had our meeting and I was packing up my papers when she said, 'Michael, you know we've failed to destroy the dependency culture.' That stuck with me. A lot has been said today about her caution. What has not been said is that she did in some cases regret that caution. That is something that has not fully come over. It was not just the dependency culture, although she did regret that she had not done anything to make sure that the welfare state was focused on those who really needed support. In the modern idiom, she would have 'done her nut' had she realised that it would be a Conservative–Lib Dem coalition government who would be the first to do something about it.

On privatisation, there were all sorts of things that she would have liked. She did not privatise coal, the railways, the nuclear industry or the Post Office. With the really difficult one, electricity – as it happened I was the minister who took the Bill through the Commons – I believe that it was very much the powers of persuasion of Cecil Parkinson, against the advice of Walter Marshall, her great friend and mentor in many ways, that created the Bill that we eventually put through Parliament. It was very much touch-and-go as to whether we went ahead with that privatisation, because of her caution.

I stress her caution only because others have emphasised her sense of direction and the wonderful things that she achieved. Her caution stretched beyond privatisation to Europe. She did, I think, regret the Single European Act and how far she pushed the Maastricht Treaty before it came into being.

All that is something of an antidote to some of the more critical things that have been said about her extremism and her desire to do things in a hurry. Far from it – I think that sometimes she felt that she had not done things in enough of a hurry. I think her impetuosity has been much misinterpreted. She was a very cautious and very wise person, and that is why she was so effective. It was a great honour to serve with her in that context.

She was the victor, a heroine of Elizabethan proportions. As at the court of the Fairy Queen, it was best to be a pace or two apart. No politician progressed very far after working intimately at her court.

Mike Freer

Conservative MP 2010–

Mike Freer was elected to Parliament in May 2010 in the seat of Finchley and Golders Green, having previously spent four years as leader of Barnet Council.

From the outset Finchley Conservatives knew they had a winner. One of my stalwarts, Derek Phillips, recounts how as a Young Conservative he went into that selection meeting saying, 'I'm not voting for a woman.' He came out having voted for that woman. He changed his mind in short order when she was clearly head and shoulders above the men, and from that day on, she remained head and shoulders above the men around her.

Much is said about Mrs Thatcher's background. She is described, often disparagingly, as the grocer's daughter and the housewife who knew the value of thrift and of living within one's means, as if there was something wrong with that. For me, Mrs Thatcher illustrates clearly and sharply what shapes our views as Members of Parliament, whether is it ideology, background or our casework. It is probably a blend of all three.

The day-to-day issues that faced Mrs Thatcher as a local constituency MP influenced her policies. Finchley was where she came to recharge her batteries. She knew that when she came to Finchley, she would leave the advisers behind and she would hear the unvarnished truth, as seen by her constituents and, equally importantly, by her supporters and her activists. One of her agents tells the story that within minutes of Mrs Thatcher returning to Downing street, the No. 10 machine would be on the phone, demanding politely to know what she had been told in Finchley, because she had returned to Downing street full of vigour, demanding to know what was going on with this or that. Finchley brought home to her what needed to be done.

There is one incident that perhaps explains her drive to abolish the rates and introduce the community charge. This is an example of how I believe her constituency work shaped her policies. The rights and wrongs of the community charge are not for today, but the casework that Mrs Thatcher came across drove home the inequality of a household with several wage earners paying the same as a pensioner. She saw at first hand the struggle that many on low and fixed incomes had with the rates. One experience I will relate. I am told that one elderly resident came to see her in a state of distress. The resident had paid her rates in cash in an envelope to the town hall. The cash went astray. Mrs Thatcher knew the hardship that having to find the rates once had caused, let alone having to find them a second time to make up the cash that had gone astray. It is not commonly known that Mrs Thatcher quietly sent a cheque and paid the rates for that resident. She was far from the heartless caricature portrayed in the media and by her opponents.

Mrs Thatcher took enormous interest in her constituents, and her ability to remember their names and their concerns, often months after first meeting them, was truly astounding. In the early 1990s when I was a local councillor in Finchley, Mrs Thatcher came to a summer fête, which was held every year on a small council estate. She arrived bang on time, for she was a stickler for punctuality. She swept in, in the Jaguar. Out she came, as immaculate as ever. She ignored the local dignitaries such as humble councillors, went straight across to the organiser of the fête, whom I will call Mrs Smith, and said, 'Now, dear, how did your daughter get on with her GCSEs? She sat them last year, didn't she? Wasn't she sitting seven?' I was completely bowled over by this. I spoke to her agent and asked if he made copious notes while no one was looking so that he could brief her before she arrived. I was firmly told, 'No, she simply remembers.' That was the measure of the woman as a constituency MP.

Mrs Thatcher had an amazing knack of being able to put anyone at ease, usually because she knew that what was important to them had to be important to her. The dripping tap that the council would not repair was the most important thing to that constituent, and so it became the most important thing to Mrs T. There are countless examples of her warmth and her compassion. The devotion of those who worked with her and stayed with her after she was no longer the Prime Minister is testament to that. Many of her close protection officers chose to stay with her, rather than move up the ranks. One of them recently told me of a Christmas time at Chequers. He came back to the police mess room to find that Mrs Thatcher had been in. She had tidied up and decorated it with Christmas decorations. She had cleaned out the hearth, laid a fire and left a flask of coffee on the table for her police officers. That is the woman few people saw.

Robert Halfon
Conservative MP 2010–

Robert Halfon is a former adviser to Oliver Letwin and Political Director of Conservative Friends of Israel. He fought Harlow twice before successfully winning the seat in May 2010.

I first came across Mrs Thatcher when I was ten years old. I remember it vividly. Reading the *Daily Express* (I think), there was a cartoon, entitled *SuperMaggie,* based on an old Harold Macmillan cartoon, *SuperMac* (so I later found out). I have genuinely been hooked on Mrs T. ever since. I started listening to her on the radio and watching the odd bit of TV. Later at school, I took part in political discussions and debates. I found myself in agreement with much of what she said, especially when it came to communism in Russia and Eastern Europe.

In 1986 at the age of seventeen, my father took me to meet her for the first time at a St John's Ambulance event. I shook her hand and felt incredibly proud.

After that time I became much involved in Conservative politics – rising through the Young Conservatives, then the student movement, the local association, as a Parliamentary Candidate and finally as an MP. I last met her in 2006, in London, where she held up a leaflet 'Harlow Matters, the Future is Conservative'.

Why did I like Mrs Thatcher in such a way? Her principled politics, her strength as the first woman PM, the clarity of her convictions, her determination and her fighting spirit.

Truly great people come along once a generation and Margaret Thatcher was one of our greatest Prime Ministers.

Lord Jenkin
Cabinet Minister 1979–85

Patrick Jenkin served in Margaret Thatcher's Cabinet from 1979 until 1985, initially as Secretary of State for Social Services, moving to the Department for Industry in 1981 and the Department of the Environment in 1983. He was raised to the peerage by Margaret Thatcher in 1987.

Let me get one thing clear from the outset: never in all the fifty odd years that I have known Margaret Thatcher have I, or any of her colleagues in the party in either House of Parliament, ever called her 'Maggie'. Indeed, we never used the word, either when speaking to each other, let alone when speaking to her. She was always 'Margaret' or, in Cabinet, 'Prime Minister'.

I mention this because it is a stark illustration of the gulf that exists between the world of politics as portrayed by the populist media and the real world in which the players actually operate. Apart from seeing the word in print, where I suppose journalists were after a snappy headline, MAGGIE SWINGS HER HANDBAG AGAIN, one remembers the left wing demos where the marchers chanted 'Maggie, Maggie, Maggie, out, out, out!' By giving a political leader a label like that, it becomes easier to build up a caricature that is further and further removed from the real person.

I once discussed this phenomenon with her, not because I myself ever had a media nickname (I was not important enough to merit that!), but I was experiencing what everyone in politics faces from time to time – a concerted press campaign of mockery and vilification which bears little or no relation to reality. Margaret's reaction was immediate and very clear: 'I never read the nasty things they write about me, because it would only upset me,' she said, 'and I strongly advise you to do the same!'

She was of course right; the press soon tire of pursuing one victim and go off to find another. I suppose that it sells newspapers but I wonder how many people who might make a real contribution to public life are put off, not because they fear becoming victims of what

I recently heard described as 'tabloid crucifixion', but because of the endless denigration of all politicians.

Yet there is another side, and this story illustrates it. I was ending an election walkabout with our candidate in Monmouth when, just as I was getting into the car, a man came up, and in that wonderful lilting Welsh accent, said: 'Excuse me, Mr Jenkin, can I have a word?'

'Of course,' I replied, 'if you can keep it short.'

'Oh, it won't take long. I just wanted to tell you,' (and his voice became very bitter) 'I hate your party, I hate your policies, I hate everything you stand for!'

I replied, with a smile, 'It doesn't sound as if we are going to get your vote!'

'Oh, yes you will!' he said. 'She's the only one who knows what she wants to do!'

The chattering classes have never understood that phenomenon. Margaret Thatcher's appeal, over the heads of the political establishment and the media, to millions of ordinary men and women in all walks of life was remarkable and was the foundation of her long spell as Conservative leader and Prime Minister. Mr Blair sees himself cast in the same mould, but spin is no substitute for character and focus groups are no substitutes for conviction. It was the force of Margaret's character and the conviction with which she pursued her goals that won her the huge support of the people, and ensured that she won every general election she fought.

I have known Margaret for nearly fifty years. We met in the early 1950s when she and I served on the executive committee of what was then the Inns of Court Conservative and Unionist Society. She had joined the same set of Chambers in the Temple as I had, though we worked with different barristers. She came with a rising reputation as a formidable politician: her election campaigns in Dartford in 1950 and 1951 had attracted the attention of senior MPs, including Iain Macleod, who had spotted a winner very early on.

I remember an early argument with Margaret over the future of the steel industry. I had spent a week campaigning in South Wales and had witnessed, in Ebbw Vale, the early effects of nationalisation on investment in new plants, and was unsure whether it would be wise to try to denationalise the industry. Instead, I argued for giving the workers a stake in the businesses through some form of co-partnership. Margaret was scornful; only the full rigour of market disciplines would ensure the industry's success, and we should not shrink from the inevitable political row. But when the next Conservative government did denationalise it, it was followed by renationalisation by the next Labour government. Thirty years after that argument with Margaret, as Industry Secretary in her first administration, I prepared British Steel for privatisation which was finally achieved during her period in office. She was of course right – but it took over thirty years for her wisdom to prevail.

Despite our long acquaintance, I was not sure that she was the right person to lead the party after Ted Heath had been defeated in the 1975 leadership election and I voted for Willie Whitelaw. She was well aware of that, and though I was in the shadow Cabinet, she asked Denis Thatcher if she could rely on my loyalty. He gave me a clean bill, and I retained my job as shadow Energy Secretary. In January 1976 she asked me to take over shadowing the Health and Social Security portfolio. 'You have been in the Treasury and understand public finance. You must now experience the pressures on a major spending department,' she told me. However, she went on to impress on me the overriding need to avoid any new spending commitments at all. Indeed, I was asked to ensure that the DHSS would find savings to contribute to the cuts in public spending needed to finance tax cuts – and thereby hangs a tale.

In the run-up to the 1979 election we had committed ourselves to just two specific pledges in my policy area: we promised that we would not cut NHS spending, and we promised to protect pensions and other long-term benefits against rising prices. On health, where we were to inherit the three-year projection of modest increases in spending (at constant prices), I realised that during the campaign I would be challenged as to what our pledge meant: did we mean no cuts but no increases, or did we mean that we would maintain the modest increases planned by our predecessors? I was able to persuade Geoffrey Howe, the shadow Chancellor, that I had to be allowed to say that it was the second of these, and I duly gave the pledge on a BBC *Newsnight* programme.

That did not stop the Treasury demanding cuts, and in Cabinet I came under pressure from other ministers to find my share of the savings to which we were all committed. I read out the very specific pledge I had given on TV and Margaret at once, with no argument, agreed that that must be honoured – and of course it was.

We then came to Social Security. The Treasury demanded that we should allow no uprating of the short-term benefits in our first year, and uprate the pension and long-term benefits by less than inflation. I had earlier warned Margaret (in private) that I would feel obliged to remind colleagues of the words she herself had used in a radio interview. 'Of course, you must; we must have all the facts whatever we decide.' She had, of course, repeated the manifesto pledge 'to protect pensioners against rising prices'. When I read this out, one colleague said, 'Well, that's it, isn't it? Next business.' Margaret made it clear that she would be willing to face the music if the Cabinet agreed with the Treasury's proposal but, very wisely, her colleagues demurred, and we held to the pledge that she had given.

It is far too soon for history to form a balanced judgement on her reign as Prime Minister. The legends and the myths abound – of her abuse of colleagues, of her taking sides against her own government, of her trying to force decisions before even hearing the minister in charge – there was an element of truth in all this but of course it would be wholly wrong to think that it was the whole truth. She often showed that she had a sharper brain than most of the rest of us, and if she got her way it was because she had an amazing eye for detail. I will end with an illustration.

As Industry Secretary, I faced pressure from Sir Ian Macgregor, Chairman of British Steel, to allow him to close the loss-making Ravenscraig plant at Motherwell. However, this works had become a touchstone of the Scots' conviction that Mrs Thatcher did not care about Scotland. I made it clear to Sir Ian that closure was not politically possible, and asked him to explore other options.

He knew the American steel industry well. He asked me to meet one of the American steel bosses and the three of us had dinner at the Waterside Restaurant at Bray, not far from Heathrow. There, they put to me a scheme which involved British Steel, then still in the public sector, buying a quoted American company, Kaiser Steel, with a big works near Los Angeles in California. Ravenscraig would manufacture steel 'semis' – large slabs of steel – for shipment to California for Kaiser to manufacture heavy pipes for the then burgeoning oil fields in Alaska. This would be a new UK export market, which was too far from the big US steel makers in Chicago and Pennsylvania for them to supply competitively. I asked them to work it up, making it clear that this would need Cabinet approval.

Although the negotiations to buy Kaiser were difficult and complex, involving as they did the technicalities of the rules of the New York Stock Exchange, a way forward was devised. I had the firm support of the Scottish Secretary, George Younger, and of several other ministers. It all came to a head at a late-night meeting in the Cabinet room at which there were present, not only Treasury and Foreign Office officials, but also our New York investment bankers and lawyers. The Prime Minister questioned these Americans minutely, asking them to spell out exactly the several different stages in the acquisition process, concentrating on the issue of the precise point at which British Steel, and therefore the British Exchequer, would become committed. One of the answers caught me by surprise, and I did not immediately react as I could not see the way round it. It appeared that we would be bound at an earlier point than I had been advised, before we had had a sight of the full documentation on Kaiser.

This was a moment of truth. Margaret had spotted a weakness in the arguments, and from that moment the discussion could lead only to a decision that we could not go ahead on the basis proposed. We broke up long after midnight, very disappointed at this outcome.

The next day I discussed the decision with her and indicated that it might be very difficult to revive the project in a way that would get round the difficulty she had identified. 'When you did not respond immediately to the lawyer's point,' she told me, 'I realised that your department had not thought of it, and that it would be too risky to go ahead on the basis you and George were proposing.'

Significantly, she had refused to allow Sir Ian to attend that meeting: 'He will bamboozle us all into supporting his scheme and I need to be certain that it would be safe to commit the Exchequer to the guarantee it would have to give.' I have no doubt that, as so often, she was right!

Most people who decide to go into politics have the perfectly laudable ambition of serving in office. I was very fortunate that six of my ten years on the government front bench were in Margaret Thatcher's Cabinets. Although she and I had several monumental rows during these years, I will always look back on those six years as the high point in my political career. When I retired to the back benches in 1985, *The Guardian* chided me for an excess of loyalty to her. All I can say in response is that she earned it, and I have no regrets!

Lord Selkirk
Conservative MP 1974–97

Lord James Douglas-Hamilton was a minister at the Scottish Office and was a government whip during the Thatcher years. He was a member of the Scottish Parliament from 2000 to 2007.

Margaret Thatcher was prepared to go the extra mile on small, non-political, non-party matters last thing at night when she returned to her office in Downing Street. I remember being told that by the late Ian Gow, who took me into her office and showed me the kinds of letters that were sent to her, as well as bottles of whisky for charity fêtes and the like. Just like an old trooper, she would settle down and sign the lot.

Being a minister in her government was challenging, interesting and never dull. In Scotland, home ownership went up from about 30 per cent to about 60 per cent under her premiership, which was a massive change. Lady Thatcher believed very strongly in expanding home ownership, and one episode is extremely vivid in my memory. The Prime Minister was in Uphall, West Lothian, for the first rent-to-mortgage sale in Scotland to former public sector tenants. As we stood in their sitting room in that small house, a girl who was the Editor of the local school magazine asked Mrs Thatcher, as she then was, what her favourite sport was. The Prime Minister immediately made the surprising revelation that it was skiing. She then went on to say that neither she nor any of her ministers would be doing any skiing at all, as none of them could afford the time off if they broke a leg. As it happened, I looked across at Michael Forsyth, who was Secretary of State for Scotland and was standing just beside her. I knew for a fact that both he and I had just completed our arrangements to go skiing within days, if not hours. We gave each other a smile but said not a word.

After the ceremonial transfer of ownership, I was invited to go with her in the Prime Minister's car and, as we left, a protestor hurled an egg straight at us. The driver accelerated and the egg landed

harmlessly in the road. The Prime Minister looked as though absolutely nothing had happened, and it was then that I realised that she
was not called the Iron Lady for nothing.

She certainly summed up what she believed in in two sentences in
her book, *Statecraft*, showing all her continuing zeal and cutting edge.
She wrote:

> The demand that power be limited and accountable, the determina-
> tion that force shall not override justice, the conviction that individual
> human beings have an absolute moral worth which government must
> respect – such things are uniquely embedded in the political culture
> of the English-speaking people... They are our enduring legacy to
> the world.

She was very much at home in the House of Commons. She was
a standard-bearer for parliamentary democracy, and that is something of which her own family can be very proud, as can we as
parliamentarians.

Sir Peter Emery
Conservative MP 1959–2001

Sir Peter Emery was first elected as the MP for Reading in 1959 and served there until 1966. He was Member for Honiton from 1967 until 1997 and later East Devon from 1997–2001. He died in 2004.

There are, of course, many stories. One of the least known was when she was appointed by Edward Heath to be the frontbench spokesman on Power, taking over from Sir John Eden and being the first woman to be given this appointment. At the time I was Vice-Chairman of the backbench committee on Power, of which she, as the frontbench spokesman, was Chairman.

I went to brief her in her flat one morning soon after her appointment. We discussed all matters that were dealt with by the ministry, including iron, steel, gas, electricity, nuclear power and the coal industry. Towards lunchtime Margaret had to leave for a luncheon appointment, and I said that the only outstanding matter was the oil industry. I was then a director of Philips Petroleum UK and I said that I could fill her in on this whenever it suited her.

She turned to me and said, with a twinkle in her eye, 'Peter, you don't have to bother. I sleep with the oil industry every night.' Of course Denis was then a Director of Burmah Oil.

Lord Armstrong
Secretary of the Cabinet 1979–87

Robert Armstrong joined the civil service in 1950, serving in numerous senior posi-
tions within the Treasury, Home Office and Cabinet Office, eventually rising to be
Head of the Home Civil Service in 1981. He sits as a crossbencher in the House
of Lords.

I was summoned one morning in July 1979 to a meeting with the
Prime Minister at No. 10, which I hoped – but did not know – would
result in an appointment as Secretary to the Cabinet. I was taken
upstairs to her room and shown in at the door of the study. As I went
through the door, she looked up at me and said, 'Robert, you're looking very tired.' It was not the most promising opening to an interview
in which I was hoping to be offered one of the most onerous jobs in
the public service, so I stammered out something about having been
up rather late the previous night. Then she said, 'Robert, I have asked
you to come in order that I can tell you that I want to appoint you as
Cabinet Secretary to succeed John Hunt in October.' Of course, I
was delighted and accepted the offer. I went downstairs and told the
Private Secretary that the Prime Minister had offered me the job and
that I had accepted it. But I said, 'It was a little bit odd that she started
by saying, "Robert, you look very tired."'

The Private Secretary said, 'Oh, don't worry about that, she's saying
that to everybody this morning.'

She was nothing if not feminine and many of her colleagues, and
many of those who were her civil servants, will recognise that. My
recollection goes back to the first visit that we had from President
Mitterrand of France to Downing Street, in 1981. We were all dreading it because he had no English, or claimed not to, so that everything
had to be interpreted – and, of course, he was French.

Lady Thatcher had greatly disliked his predecessor and Mitterrand
was said to be a socialist, but the meetings went rather well. Despite
the interpretation, they went smoothly and there were good speeches
by both parties at a dinner. When the President finally came to leave

the next afternoon, I went with the Prime Minister to see him off at the front door of No. 10. As we walked back, I said to the Prime Minister in what I suppose was a tone of some surprise, 'That visit went rather well, didn't it, Prime Minister?'

She said, 'Yes, I suppose it did.' Then there was a pause and she said, 'Of course, he likes women, you know.'

Looking back, I recognised that the President had been – how shall I put it? – flattering her femininity throughout the meeting, and that she had recognised that and enjoyed every minute of it.

One afternoon in May 1982, during the war in the Falkland Isles, the telephone rang on my desk. It was the National Security Adviser in Washington: would I please set up the 'hotline', as the President wanted to speak to the Prime Minister? I told the Prime Minister's Private Secretary that the President would be calling to speak to the Prime Minister, activated the 'hotline' and went through to No. 10 for the call.

The conversation began with the usual exchange of pleasantries about health and weather, customary even in such high-level conver-sations, and then the President asked how things were going in the South Atlantic. This was something that the Prime Minister had at her fingertips, and she spoke well and fluently for about a quarter of an hour. Then the President began to speak. After two or three sentences he asked another question. The Prime Minister took the opportunity of dealing with a few points which she had not been able to cover in her first exposition and responded, once again speaking well and fluently for another fifteen minutes. She then thanked the President for his call, expressed her gratitude to him and to the United States government for their help and support, promised to keep him posted on future developments, said goodbye and replaced the receiver.

Not long afterwards I met the National Security Adviser, and I said that we had been a little mystified by the President's call and did not quite know what it was all about. He laughed, and said: 'We shan't try that again.' 'What do you mean?' I said. He said: 'Well, we had a message to convey which we thought that the Brits would find unhelpful, so we figured that it had better be conveyed by the President to the Prime Minister. The trouble was, the President couldn't get a word in edgeways.'

Many years later I happened to meet another American official who had been one of those who were in the Oval Office when this exchange took place. He told me that, during the Prime Minister's second exposition, the President had taken the receiver away from his ear and held it out in front of him so that they could all listen, saying as he did so: 'Isn't she marvellous?'

I think – though she never said as much – that the Prime Minister had a shrewd suspicion that the President was calling in order to convey some unpalatable message, and was not averse to the thought of making it difficult for him to do so.

More than once during the time that I was with her, she told me that her role as Prime Minister was to be the guardian of the strategy. She had a clear vision of what that strategy should be and of the policies required to carry it out. She displayed great courage and determination in pursuing this strategy and in introducing and sustaining the policies which it required, and she could exercise great firmness and all the strength of her personality in making sure of the active support of her colleagues and her civil servants in putting the policies into effect.

She respected the civil service as an institution and valued the traditional virtues of integrity and impartiality. She liked and respected many, but not all, of the individual civil servants with whom she had to deal, and she went out of her way to be considerate and kind to those who worked in her office. But I think that she thought that civil servants in general were too set in their ways and had become too accustomed to the management of decline.

In discussing appointments with her, she never once asked, 'Is he one of us?' She wanted to know whether someone was a doer as well as a thinker, and whether he or she had what it took not just to advise cleverly on policy but to manage a department or division effectively.

She was a glutton for work and took an infinity of trouble to master the detail of every subject that she was called on to consider, often to the discomfiture of those with whom she was going to discuss it.

That was all made easier for her and more challenging for the rest of us by her capacity to manage on three or four hours of sleep a night, not just for a night or two but seemingly indefinitely. For her, the working day was two or three hours longer than it was for any of the rest of us weaker vessels. There was no catnapping during the day. There were times when it seemed like a very unfair advantage. She kept up the pace throughout my time, although I believe that there were some slight signs of weakening towards the end of her time in office.

Lord Coe
Athlete and Politician

Sebastian Coe's athletics career saw him beat twelve world records, win two Olympic gold medals and receive numerous other awards. He became the Member for Falmouth and Camborne in 1992, serving until 1997. He was raised to the peerage in 2000 and helped London secure the 2012 Olympics.

The enduring image of Margaret Thatcher is of an incredibly strong-minded woman with equally strongly held opinions. It was often written during her premiership that she had little time for those who disagreed with her. My own experience of her, long before I became a Member of Parliament or even entered active politics, was not altogether the same.

It was in 1988, in the run-up to the Seoul Olympics. I was invited to a reception at 10 Downing Street at which there were many distinguished people drawn from all walks of British life, not just athletics. Mrs Thatcher was a consummate professional at such events, moving round the room and chatting to her guests. She came up to me and asked how my preparation for the forthcoming Olympics was going. She knew I was expecting to be defending my title for the second time and I told her I thought it was all going really well (little realising that, in the event, the selectors had other intentions!). Her questioning then moved to how long in advance I would be going out to the region to acclimatise for the games and I realised I was getting into a more detailed conversation than I had anticipated. Perhaps naively, I hadn't expected the Prime Minister to have thought about the preparations athletes make. Most people think you turn up, run and come home. I explained I would be going out to Australia to train, on the same time zone as Seoul, and then fly directly to the Olympic holding-camp a few weeks beforehand.

'Oh, you don't need that length of time,' she said. 'Well, I think you do,' I ventured in response.

And so our conversation continued, both of us convinced of our point of view. Our discussion became quite detailed, with Lady

Thatcher increasingly focused on winning me over to her point of view. The rest of the room was, for a while, denied her attention as she pinned me to these questions. For some minutes, there was no other issue that mattered to her. The best efforts of various private secretaries to guide her on to the next person had no impact as our conversation became more and more animated.

Eventually the Prime Minister looked me in the eye and said, 'Mr Coe, I think you're wrong, and I am a research chemist.' To which I replied, 'Prime Minister, I think you're wrong – and I'm a double Olympic Champion.' For a moment, I thought my training would start sooner than I had planned but instead her natural, slightly stern, expression melted and she laughed. 'Right,' she said, 'I am going to instruct our ambassador in Seoul to give you the complete run of the Embassy. You must have everything you need.'

Admiral Sir John Woodward
Commander-in-chief, Naval Home Command 1987–89

Admiral Sir John Woodward, known as Sandy, has had a long and distinguished career in the Royal Navy which he joined at the age of fourteen. He has served on numerous ships and in numerous positions at the MoD, eventually rising to the rank of Admiral and the position of Commander-in-Chief of Naval Home Command. He led the 1982 Task Force in its mission to recover the Falklands. He is now retired.

In 1985–86, I was just sufficiently senior in the Defence Ministry to stand in for the Chief of the Defence Staff as Professional Military Adviser to the Secretary of State for Defence once or twice at a Cabinet meeting. The day after one such occasion, I was having lunch with one of Mrs Thatcher's civil service secretaries (the row of people who sit at the PM's right to record all that goes on) who said, more or less out of the blue, 'You were very lucky yesterday.'

Being unaware of having had any particular stroke of good fortune recently, I asked him what he was talking about. He replied: 'You interrupted the Chairman.'

'Chairman?' I said, 'Chairman? What Chairman?'

'The Prime Minister – Mrs Thatcher – you interrupted her in mid-flow.'

'Oh, that Chairman – well, what's wrong with that? She was giving her views on a professional military matter – and she was getting it wrong. Someone had to tell her.'

'Nothing's wrong with that as such, only...'

'But surely, if the Prime Minister is about to do something fairly crass as a result of less than full knowledge of the subject, someone has to interrupt, give her the additional facts, and let her make her political decision on the basis of a full and proper professional brief. And anyway, she stopped, let me say what needed to be said to keep her straight on military facts, took it in, and went on to arrive at a sensible course of action. What on earth is wrong with that? Where does the luck come in? Isn't this how business is ordinarily conducted, how it should be conducted?'

'Well, yes and no,' he replied, 'the last junior minister to interrupt her like that was fired.'

'Serve him right,' I said. 'He can only have been giving her "professional military advice" from a profound ignorance of the subject, or political advice which, after eight years as Prime Minister, she had already heard two or three times before. Hardly a valuable interruption, indeed a complete waste of her time, most likely. He should have known better.'

My conclusion from this rather odd conversation was that we still had an excellent chief executive – provided only that she retained a few advisers who were prepared to say 'No, Prime Minister' from time to time. Luck didn't enter it.

I have to admit that the conversation is slightly embellished, mainly to make better sense. It is intended to bring out the point that in 1986 at least, she was still a good, if rather intimidating listener to sensible advice. I suspect that the cause of her later downfall was as much to do with running out of such advisers, as anything else.

Lord Freeman
Conservative MP 1983–97

Roger Freeman was elected for Kettering in 1983, a seat he held until 1997. He served as a Defence and then a Health minister in the Thatcher government. In 1995 he joined the Cabinet as Secretary of State for Transport. In 1997 he was raised to the peerage.

Baroness Thatcher was elected an honorary member of the Carlton Club, of which I am now Chairman, in 1975, at a time when women were not members of the club. I am quite certain that her quiet determination and conversations with many ultimately led to the club opening its doors to women members. She did not argue the case, she just quietly and consistently encouraged it, and I think that all members of the club are in her debt. In 1990, some colleagues will remember that our club was bombed by the IRA, and we lost one Member of Parliament and several other members. She came almost immediately to the club and spoke to those who were injured and to the families of those who were killed. That was very much appreciated.

In 1986, which seems a long time ago, I was summoned to Downing Street to become a junior minister. I said to the Prime Minister, 'Thank you very much. This is a great day. My wife has just had a baby daughter.'

She said, 'What's the hospital? What's the telephone number?' Fortunately, I could remember it. She dialled the hospital and the receptionist answered. The Prime Minister said, 'This is the Prime Minister speaking.'

I could hear the lady at the other end say, 'Pull the other leg.' The Prime Minister said, 'I don't think I will, my dear. Just put me through.' That really was appreciated by my wife, who talks about it constantly.

She was a great lady.

Sir Teddy Taylor
Conservative MP 1964–2005

Sir Teddy Taylor was the Conservative MP for Glasgow Cathcart from 1964 to 1979 and for Rochford and Southend East from 1980 to 2005.

One of my exciting times in Parliament was when Mrs Thatcher invited me to join her shadow Cabinet in the post as spokesman on Trade and Industry and then as the spokesman on Scotland.

I have always had the feeling that one of the main reasons why I was appointed at all was because of my position on devolution in Scotland and, happily, the party turned from its previous commitment to devolution under Mrs Thatcher's leadership. It has always been argued that devolution was the only way to undermine the growth of the Scottish National Party who believed in full independence for Scotland, and both Mrs Thatcher and I thought that far from undermining the nationalists, devolution would simply provide them with an opportunity to grow. Happily, by taking the Nationalists head on without the devolution commitment we were able to virtually wipe them out in the 1979 election. The only personal problem, of course, was that by wiping out the SNP vote I lost my own seat in Cathcart in Glasgow and returned to Parliament a few months later as MP for Southend East in a by-election. I think I will never forget the fact that although Mrs Thatcher won the election and was on her way to Downing Street, she nevertheless found the time to phone me the morning after the election to offer her sympathy.

The discussions we had in the shadow Cabinet when I was a member were truly exciting because instead of endeavouring to make political propaganda we seemed to spend most of our time considering detailed and fundamental issues which were to be the basis of the Thatcher administration. Among the most important issues we had to consider were the curbing of trade union abuses, the reduction of levels of taxation and the promotion of privatisation. Papers were constantly brought before the shadow Cabinet and Mrs Thatcher always appeared to like having someone putting forward a contrary view which was subject to real discussion. If she won the argument she always expected everyone in the shadow Cabinet to accept the decision and to go along with her, but if she lost the argument Willie Whitelaw had a habit of stepping in to suggest that the matter should be referred to a subcommittee and that was the end of the issue.

I will always remember Jim Prior who was one of those who was constantly putting forward strong arguments against some of the fundamental changes in policy, but was always among the most loyal and most cooperative members of the shadow Cabinet in giving full support for decisions once they were reached. I enjoyed taking part in all these discussions and expressing my opinions.

Mrs Thatcher ran the shadow Cabinet like a teacher in a school and because of my strong views on the EU I was constantly endeavouring to persuade the shadow Cabinet to adopt a more aggressive policy on the issue. I can well remember an occasion when she reached across the shadow Cabinet table, smacked my hand and with a smile on her face said: 'Do not mention the EU again today Teddy', and there was laughter throughout the gathering.

I think the most impressive aspect of the shadow Cabinet discussions for me was that under her leadership we looked with care and seriousness at problems which she felt had been neglected in Britain for far too long, and because these policies were implemented during her administration Britain was able to overcome many of the problems which other European nations still suffer from. I certainly think she was the greatest of all the politicians I have seen in Parliament in my long service here and she certainly did a great job for the country as a whole.

Lord Palumbo
Former Chairman of the Arts Council

Lord Palumbo is a property developer and an art collector. He was raised to the peerage in 1991.

On one occasion, my wife asked Margaret what she thought of Tony Blair. 'My dear,' she said, 'I do not think of him.' That was all.

Margaret's support for Desert Storm, the first war in Iraq, was clear. We have heard that it was to some extent due to her that there was the backbone to go to war. I asked her some years later what she would have done if the second Iraq War had come on her watch. She said, 'It is not sufficiently or fully realised that I was a scientist before I became a politician. As a scientist what we need are facts, evidence and proof. If we have the facts, and we have the evidence and we have the proof, we can check and recheck, and check as many times as is necessary before coming to a considered view. The answer to your question is that we had very few facts. We had no evidence and we certainly had no proof, so I would not have committed one single member of the armed services to a war from which they may not have returned. What I would have done was to give George Bush the sort of assistance that Ronnie Reagan gave me in the Falklands; that is to say, logistical support and intelligence support, but nothing more. And I would have told Bush so to his face.' She was very definite about that.

When she offered me, some years before, the chairmanship of the Arts Council, she said to me, 'Mr Palumbo, I want you to understand one thing very clearly, and you must not forget it. The government has no money. You are being asked to supervise the distribution of a great deal of money, and you must spend it wisely and carefully because it is taxpayers' money, not government money.' That is advice that I shall obviously never forget, no more than I shall forget a wonderfully kind and utterly magnificent lady.

Lord Burns
Chief Economic Adviser to HM Treasury 1980–91

Terence Burns is an economist. After serving as Chief Economic Adviser to the Treasury he served as its Permanent Secretary from 1991 to 1998. He was raised to the peerage in 1998.

I owe Baroness Thatcher a huge debt of gratitude. Towards the end of 1979, on the advice of the noble and learned Lord, Lord Howe, I was appointed as Chief Economic Adviser to the Treasury, a position that I held throughout the rest of Mrs Thatcher's time as Prime Minister. During that ten-year period, I had the privilege of attending many meetings with her. I had enormous opportunities to watch the particular style of debate and the method that she used when challenged, something that I had never seen before.

Apart from late-night speech-writing sessions which I occasionally got involved in, most of my experiences were of accompanying the Chancellors of the day. By their very nature, we were dealing with the major issues of economic policy and, even more so by their nature, they were usually very controversial. We normally had these sessions because there were some difficult issues to sort out. They were very tense and very often there were tricky issues to resolve. At times one did not expect to reach resolution. On more than one occasion when I left she said to me, 'I just want you to look as you go out at what it says on that door', to remind me that it said First Lord of the Treasury. She was trying to indicate that, in the final analysis, it was going to be her word.

Of course, those people who did not work with Mrs Thatcher assume that by her very nature she began and ended with an entrenched position and refused to listen. That is not at all how the process took place. Part of her enormous talent was her ability to question, challenge and press you on issues as a way of trying to find whether the views that she held herself could stand that stress-testing. I always felt that she was trying to test her own ideas and your ideas to see how they stood up to this process of questioning.

I have heard it suggested that somehow the recent financial crisis has its origins in her approach to economic policy. Nothing could be further from the truth. Those who worked with Mrs Thatcher know that she disliked financial excess whether in the private or the public sector. In the early 1980s, when we were struggling with rapid growth of the money supply, she frequently asked why there could not be some limits to the leverage ratios of banks, even in a deregulated system. She was only very reluctantly put off this approach, which has now become much more fashionable after the events of recent years.

A surprised journalist said to me that after the events of recent years he had been looking at some of the things that Mrs Thatcher had said about the single currency and had been astonished to discover that most of the things that had occurred in the past few years were part of the debate that took place then and why she came to the view that the UK should not be part of the single currency.

Along with many others, I regard myself as enormously fortunate to have played a small part in those momentous years. There was a real greatness about Mrs Thatcher and I feel very privileged to have watched that.

Václav Klaus

President of the Czech Republic 2003–13

Václav Klaus is one of the foremost politicians of post-communist Eastern Europe. He served as Prime Minister of the Czech Republic from 1992 to 1997 and became President in 2003. He has written numerous books on economic policy and has been the recipient of numerous awards for the cause of freedom.

Although Margaret Thatcher and I have met personally many times in the last decade, I would rather speak briefly of her opinions and attitudes than of personal issues. My view is the view of a politician from Central Europe and from a former communist country. That is probably what makes it somewhat specific.

There were certainly sufficient domestic reasons, motives and arguments, but we may say, with only a slight exaggeration, that the revolution in Central and Eastern Europe which brought about the end of communism was initiated in 1979 by the victory of the Conservative Party in the general election placing Margaret Thatcher at the head of the British government. She attacked the ever-expanding state – which represented the dominant tendency throughout the twentieth century. This was a century of socialism with all sorts of adjectives and with a highly varying degree of the humiliation and degradation of the individual – and her fight against socialism was the first example of success. She showed that it was possible to reverse this tendency and return to a liberal political, economic and social system.

Without wishing to be ideological, I cannot but recall that unlike many – more or less – conciliatory Western politicians, Margaret Thatcher understood the dangers of the communist doctrine and it was by her uncompromising attitudes that she contributed immensely to the end of communism.

She did not regard politics as a 'technology of power', but as an instrument for enforcing certain ideas and moral principles. This was the source of her uncompromising stance for which she earned the nickname the Iron Lady. This had nothing in common with her personal characteristics in the way I got to know her. She was not the type of politician who makes compromises. Likewise, her allies either shared her ideas and moral principles or, if they did not, they could not be her allies.

She did not regard freedom as a way to greater efficiency and prosperity. It was a moral principle and the highest value. Therefore, a free society was not just an effective political slogan but a deeply rooted vision, which she continually endeavoured to carry out throughout her life. Those who accused her of being stubborn, persistent or obstinate were people who never really came to understand the real meaning of a 'free society'.

She entered politics at a time when the faith in a 'modern welfare state' and in a 'mixed economy' prevailed. Laissez-faire was considered a relic, belonging to the nineteenth century. Margaret Thatcher opposed these opinions, which were, at the end of the 1970s and the beginning of the 1980s, unique. Fortunately, she found an ally in this 'campaign' for the restoration of old virtues on the other side of the Atlantic in Ronald Reagan.

Neither could she come to terms with the process of the unification of Europe. She always saw Europe as a community of free and sovereign states connected (or united) by free trade. However, the idea of creating some sort of a 'super state' or a federation of Europe began to prevail on the European continent. The bureaucratisation of European structures, the growing of the 'Eurocracy' and the abandonment of the principles of free trade on a global scale discouraged her and she entered the group of the so-called Eurosceptics, to which I am honoured to belong as well.

Her attitudes in politics and her conduct in everyday life prove that she is one of the extraordinary figures of the last quarter of the twentieth century. I have met many giants of world politics but none have made such an impression on me as this exceptional woman.

Lord Bellwin
Conservative Peer

Irwin Bellow became a councillor for Leeds in 1969 serving as the leader of Leeds City Council from 1975 until 1979 when he was raised to the peerage. He was Parliamentary Under Secretary of State at the Department of Environment from 1979 to 1983 and the Minister of State for Local Government from 1983 until 1984. Lord Bellwin died in 2001.

I first met Margaret Thatcher through my involvement in local government. This was in the late 1960s when I was Chairman of Housing on Leeds City Council. Together with Keith Joseph, she was co-chairing a small party policy committee, looking into future housing possibilities.

I continued to meet her over the next few years, as a national/local government leader and being the then Conservative leader of the council in Leeds. We had set up an informal liaison group which met with her three to four times a year.

The Ted Heath years did not produce good local/national government relationships. Heath was very remote and did not really want to listen to what his party leaders throughout the country were saying.

As a contrast to this, Maggie, albeit not over-enthusiastic about local government, was always thirsty for knowledge. Contrary to what is often said of her, in my experience she always listened, thoroughly questioned, and if convinced (not easy to do), she would take on board contrary views. She liked decisiveness and respected knowledge and practical experience, particularly if based on success.

She was invariably encouraging and while she expected loyalty, always gave it herself where she felt it was merited. She was, at all times, a serious, single-minded and focused person, quite formidable really. I always found her to be kind and considerate and certainly caring. She was never one for small talk. Even when greeting visitors at the top of the stairs in Downing Street, she would quickly go straight to the point of the meeting in question.

She first spoke to me about the possibility of my joining her future government a year or so before the event. She asked me if I would like to do this and go to the House of Lords when, not if, but when we won the next general election.

It was never mentioned again for a year or so, but when forming the government over that first weekend in May 1979, she telephoned to ask if I remembered our conversation. This consistency of thinking was absolutely typical of her.

As an amusing aside, when the call came, my late mother-in-law, a dear lady then in her eighties, first answered the telephone. The operator, having confirmed the number, asked her to hold on to take a call from the Prime Minister. 'The Prime Minister,' said my mother-in-law. 'Just a moment, I'll put my earrings on.' When I later told Maggie of this she said, 'How charming.'

Looking back, an abiding impression is the remarkable hours Mrs Thatcher worked. She was always sprightly and immaculately turned out. Occasionally, whatever the lateness of the hour, she used to come into the Lords and sit on the steps to the throne, thereby giving support while listening to the debate. However tired she may have been, she never looked or acted it.

Unlike Tony Blair, she had a great respect for the House and its traditions. She always worked particularly hard in preparing for speaking in the Commons. Her in-depth briefing and preparation was thorough in the extreme. It was undoubtedly a major factor in the excellent performance she invariably gave at the dispatch box.

One amusing incident I recall, albeit after I had left the government, is when she stayed with us at our home in Leeds. She had a 6 a.m. start in the City the following morning and therefore had to stay overnight. It was quite an experience in many ways. I arranged for my grandson, Danny, to stay with us overnight – when would he otherwise get the chance to meet a Prime Minister? I suggested to him beforehand what questions she might put to him and I got almost all right – he was well prepared and did well – he was fourteen at the time.

Although I had not seen her for some time prior to that overnight stay, on sitting down, her very first remarks were to ask what I had specifically meant by something I had said in the House of Lords a week or two beforehand – she had taken the trouble to read the Hansard.

A magic moment was when we noted guards surrounding the house, part of the street blocked off, a bodyguard and secretary in the house and going to bed, my wife asked me if she should put the burglar alarm on!

Lunch on Sunday at Chequers was a memorable experience. It is a somewhat unusual place, not all that easy to find. We circled round looking for the entrance, eventually to be met at the door by the lady herself, on the steps, waiting to meet and greet visitors in her inimitable, dominantly cheerful way.

The morning was spent around the fire with the family, it being wintertime – all most congenial, pleasant, yet businesslike. When we walked into the dining room, the prepared table layout was completely rearranged and everyone reseated by her so that she could be close and most easily converse with whoever she felt could most contribute to such topics as she wished to discuss.

My decision to leave government was something of a wrench. Had I lived in London I would certainly have wanted to continue. She was not happy that I wished to go, but once I pointed out that it was 'not fair to the family' she was most understanding and wrote a typically gracious and kind letter which was published in *The Times*.

I could tell many stories of situations, amusing and otherwise, but always it comes down to my memories of her being a true leader in every sense of the word. Her courage and determination are now legendary – in my experience they have never been more deserved. Critics and opponents may choose to forget the appalling shambles Margaret Thatcher inherited from Labour in 1979. History will remind them.

Lord Ridley
Cabinet Minister 1983–90

Nicholas Ridley was among Margaret Thatcher's staunchest supporters and most trusted colleagues. He joined the Cabinet in 1983 as Secretary of State for Transport and went on to become Secretary of State for the Environment and finally for Trade and Industry. He was raised to the peerage in 1992 and died in 1993. This passage is taken from his book My Style of Government.

Margaret Thatcher was always immaculately turned out herself. She dressed smartly, was well-groomed and expected other people to be so as well. During the 1987 election Nigel Lawson appeared on television with his hair in need of a trim; he got a complaint from next door. She wanted to set an example of high standards in all things, and for her example to be followed by others. She wanted 10 Downing Street to become renowned as a place of quality entertaining. She arranged for it to be redecorated in the mid-1980s with style and much gold leaf. It was transformed into a very grand and elegant house for entertaining the great and the good. It was adorned with good pictures from the national collections – one room contained a particularly lovely group of Turners. She entertained a lot. She saw to it that the food and wine, the flowers and the service, were of the highest quality. Quality was the keynote – not extravagance. Whenever the programme of a visiting foreign dignitary allowed, she would give a dinner for him. These dinner parties were glittering occasions. Important and interesting people were asked; she also liked to have plenty of pretty and well-dressed women among the guests. She expected people to rise to the occasion, and they did. Her speech after the dinner was always a model of fluency, erudition and courtesy. She was a master of the impromptu speech. Some of her speeches when the Eastern European leaders came to London were particularly moving. It seemed to cause her no nervousness or bother when she had to make a speech after dinner. This was not the case with some of her principal guests. I remember being fortunate enough to sit next to President Havel of Czechoslovakia when he dined there. Margaret Thatcher was on his left, and she talked to him for most of the meal. When my turn came, he hastily picked up his speech notes to make last-minute improvements. My attempts to engage him in conversation were dashed by Margaret Thatcher saying to me across him, 'Can't you see, Nick, he's trying to finish his speech.'

In addition to official dinners, she gave frequent receptions – for party workers, or a visiting overseas delegation, or for scientists, artists, musicians or entrepreneurs. She also held lunch and dinner parties at Chequers at weekends, particularly when an overseas visitor was staying there. I remember one particular lunch, given for Lech Wałęsa, the Polish leader of Solidarity. He was very conscious of Poland's debt to her and of all her help and encouragement. But that didn't stop him calling for a lot more in his very effective after-luncheon speech. There was a strange affinity between the fiery Polish shipyard trade unionist and the high-principled British Tory Prime Minister – two people as different as they could be. It was because they both believed in freedom and in democracy with an equal passion that they were in alliance; not so much friendship, as a common cause to fight.

Sometimes groups of colleagues would be invited to lunch. It was after some such lunch that she resolved, after a long conversation with Nigel Lawson, Patrick Jenkin and myself, that another attempt must be made to replace the domestic rates. This was the day that she decided to start the studies which eventually led to the community charge.

She held a Boxing Day lunch every year to which family, friends and loyal supporters, both inside and outside politics, were bidden. It became a little too famous, and the press would find out who was there and who was not, trying to speculate as to who was 'in' and who was 'out'. It was difficult for her to keep any part of her life private. She always used to ask to this and other parties those acquaintances who had been widowed, or had been ill, or had suffered some misfortune, as well as her friends.

She was neither an egalitarian nor a puritan. From the way she entertained, it could hardly be said that she believed in a 'classless society'. She believed in equal opportunity for anyone to qualify to receive an invitation to one of her dinners; but once achieved, this was a distinction in a class of its own.

She liked to drink a little, although never too much. She preferred whisky and rarely did justice to the excellent wines that adorned the No. 10 dinner table. Government hospitality over the years had procured for No. 10 wines from the finest vineyards of France, and her predecessors cannot have done much damage to the stocks. The wine was always both excellent and adequate in quantity. She was entirely tolerant of those who had had one too many, unless they were proposing to drive themselves home. She often asked people before they had a drink whether or not they were driving and was very strict about this. One evening she unexpectedly visited the whips' office in the Commons late at night. One of the whips in the Lords happened to be there. He was considerably inebriated but thought he would go undetected if he stayed put where he was standing and hung onto the table firmly. 'Why don't you sit down,' she said. 'You look far too drunk to stand up.'

Lord Marlesford

Conservative Peer

Mark Schreiber was raised to the peerage in 1991.

M argaret Thatcher could always see the real point. For three and a half years, I was in Whitehall as an adviser and worked a certain amount with a think tank. I remember well that, on one occasion, the presentation made at Chequers by the think tank was to show where the government was going, even if it did not want to go there. I remember that Robin Butler was demonstrating the way in which inflation would reach unthinkable double digits. There was a silence, broken by Margaret Thatcher thumping on her blotter at the Cabinet table in Chequers, saying, 'If that chart is true, we have lost the next election.' Then Tony Barber, who was the Chancellor at the time, waded in to say that it was not true – but of course it was.

Baroness Dean once said what a pity it was that Margaret Thatcher had not tried to talk more to the union leaders, that no one could have tried harder to talk to the union leaders than Ted Heath. Indeed, we had something called tripartite government, which was government, industry and unions. A fat lot of good that did.

After the 1974 election, I used, as a *fonctionnaire*, to attend meetings of the shadow Cabinet. They were very difficult meetings because Mr Heath did not accept that he had made mistakes and that things had to change. He and Sir Keith Joseph used to spar. I remember, on one occasion, Ted Heath saying to Keith Joseph, 'I suppose that you'd let British Leyland go to the wall.' Keith Joseph said, 'Of course I would, if it could not put its house in order.' Ted replied, 'In that case, you would have blood on the streets.' It was all awkward and difficult. As the shadow Cabinet left the room, I was following behind, when Margaret Thatcher came up to me and said, 'Mark, you know, Keith has nearly had enough, and the day he goes, I go.' It was basically from that moment that she realised the need to make a challenge that had never previously been made.

Oliver Letwin
Conservative MP 1997–

Oliver Letwin became the MP for West Dorset in 1997. He was a Special Adviser to Sir Keith Joseph from 1982 and then to the Prime Minister's Policy Unit from 1983 to 1986. He is now a member of David Cameron's Cabinet.

'The Prime Minister will see you now' – terrifying words for a young man, especially one about to be subjected to a job interview by the Iron Lady. And there she was, the victor of the Falklands, sitting in a wing-chair in her study. The 'interview' lasted a few seconds: 'I gather you are joining us.' It was welcome news to my ears – and, as I subsequently discovered, typical of her approach to the mechanics of administration: clear, decisive, no precious time wasted.

Once on the staff, you were a member of the family – and there was pretty much the same plain-speaking as in a family. When coming to discuss a speech I had drafted on science, it was not immediately encouraging to be greeted in the drawing room at Chequers by the PM standing by the fireplace and saying to the Chief Scientific Adviser in that inimitable but much imitated voice, 'Yes, that speech was as much of a dead loss as this one.'

You had to know what you were talking about, and you had to stand your ground. We quickly discovered that when she was interrogating and criticising and opining, seemingly without taking the slightest account of what you were saying, she was in fact at her most attentive – ceaselessly testing, often enough to destruction, the weak points in the argument, the facts that contradicted the assertions, the claims that could not be substantiated. And when, in a certain domain, you had established that you knew, and that you could defend a position, her trust was almost frightening. The memoranda – always to be short and clear – came back, with signal points doubly and triply underlined. In Cabinet committees, a note passed to her would be read out, 'I have a note...' as if the truth had been delivered, not always to the pleasure of her colleagues.

In the end, as in any family, the strongest bonds were those of affection. We loved her – perhaps we were a little bit in love with her, not least because of the tremendous compliment she continuously paid of knowing and knowing that she knew – great as she was, and small as we were – who and what we were. In disaster, there would be flowers sent. In error, there would be support and acceptance. The worst case I can recall arose from the local government expenditure round. I had a little computer and felt terribly proud to have installed a little programme of my own invention to determine the fiscal effects of certain decisions that fell to be made. Alas, in committee, the conversation took an unexpected turn, and it was only the next morning that I discovered my programme failed to work when a negative replaced a positive. Down to the study, to admit the error. Not a single word of reproach from the lady: she was, despite all the appearances to the contrary, wholly able to absorb the idea that her staff were imperfect human beings.

They were turbulent times. It was something of a shock to be sent home one weekend, when the miners were out and the dockers had just come out, to read the histories of the General Strike. But they were also times of seemingly boundless possibility. The impossible was being done – the rolling back of the socialist state – and she was hungry for more ideas. They might be devoured with delight or spat out in disgust: but the appetite for more was always there. It was as if we were living on the edge of a hurricane. We swept forward, blown and buffeted, but hugely exhilarated.

And at the eye of the hurricane, a still calm. She never rushed, never seemed to be aware of time. One Friday night, an urgent minute arrived from one of the members of the Cabinet: should we do something or not – yes or no by midnight? The Private Secretary and I rushed out a memorandum on the pros and cons and hastened to her flat. Up as always, and working on her boxes, she calmly read the minute and the memo. Then the fatal enquiry: *why* the need for a decision by midnight, or indeed before Monday? In our haste to answer the minister's question, we had failed to question the question. For all her energy, she hastened slowly enough to see the point we had missed.

When the day came to announce my departure, she was to be found in her room at the House of Commons. The response was theatrical. On hearing the news, she sat down, as if to steady herself. One knew, of course, that it was for effect – but how touching that she bothered to put on the effect. A politician to her fingertips, yes – but the Iron Lady had charm.

John Redwood
Conservative MP 1987–

After a successful career as an academic and then in banking, John Redwood became the head of Margaret Thatcher's Policy Unit in 1983 and remained there until 1985. In 1987 he became the MP for Wokingham, rising rapidly until he joined John Major's Cabinet as Secretary of State for Wales in 1993. He resigned in 1995 to fight for the leadership of the Conservative Party, a position he fought again for in 1997.

I always remember my first encounter with Margaret Thatcher. As Leader of the Opposition she had heard that I had set out a number of proposals to privatise Britain's unprofitable, unhelpful, unfriendly, lumbering nationalised industries. I was added to the guest list for one of her lunches in the shadow Cabinet room at the House of Commons. The main intellectual dish of the day was devolution. Margaret was about to go to the House to raise just this issue. I watched as a range of constitutional experts told her their thoughts, only to see her more than a match for them, well briefed, deadly in her questions. Now I realise she was fired up and a little nervous before appearing in the House. Then it was quite a spectacle to see such a powerful senior politician in full flight, clearly the mistress of her brief, able to deal with professors and advisers with forceful points and searching questions.

I steeled myself for the challenge. I knew my turn was to come soon. After what seemed like an age discussing devolution where I kept well out of the fray, she turned to me to hear my thoughts on privatisation. I had soon grasped from watching and listening to the previous conversation that you had to be quick and make your best points while you still had the chance. Once you allowed your flow to be interrupted and the questions to begin you were going to be thrust on the defensive. I marshalled my best points. I was sure the position I had adopted was proof against the most forceful of counter-attacks. The questions soon came thick and fast and I held my ground. I was beginning to enjoy it, realising that if you could withstand the barrage you might even shift her position. As the nerves went and the determination increased, Margaret Thatcher decided she had had enough as it was not the subject of the day. With a crushing, 'That's all very well, Mr Redwood, but they'll never let me do that,' I realised my time was up and we were on to the next question.

That first encounter fascinated me. While I could see what many saw, that here was a strong-minded lady who was powerful in argument and gave no quarter, it also struck me very forcefully that here was someone really interested in the issues who was learning by the clash of different opinions. She was, to adapt a phrase she made famous about someone else, 'someone I could do business with'.

I went away realising that if privatisation was to turn from the dream of a few of us to the reality of the many, we needed to create a climate of opinion in which Margaret Thatcher's political judgement sensed it was possible or safe to do it. Here was a canny, cautious, even defensive politician who could often judge the mood of the nation well and who was only going to lead them up to a point. Like all great leaders she knew that on many occasions she had to follow rather than lead. In a democracy the leader has to accept that there are limits to how far he or she can take the people, and there is an absolute prohibition on leading them in certain directions at all.

This first encounter had prepared me well for many meetings, arguments, debates, discussions and exchanges which I had with Margaret Thatcher when I became her chief policy adviser after the 1983 general election. It was satisfying to put to her a memorandum saying that in her second period as Prime Minister she now had the political strength and the financial and economic necessity to get on and privatise large chunks of the public industrial and service sector. It was a pleasure to find that now a lot of the caution and the worry had abated. Now the issue was not 'will the public buy it?' but 'how can we do it technically?' By 1983 Margaret Thatcher rightly sensed that the main problem was no longer public opinion, which was ready for some drastic changes to get Britain on the move again, but opinion in the City, which was extremely cautious.

When I went round the City trawling opinion from my No. 10 base it was a disappointment to discover that many in the City strongly held the view that to sell something worth several billion pounds on the stock market was a technical impossibility. They believed that equity issues could not be larger than a few hundred million pounds and were strongly against selling shares in British Telecom. They preferred the

Twenty-six-year-old Margaret Roberts, Conservative candidate for Dartford, canvassing in her constituency, October 1951.

Margaret Thatcher MP enters the House of Commons after being elected Member for Finchley and Friern Barnet, October 1959.

MT, aged thirty-four, with her twin children Carol and Mark, aged six, at their home in Farnborough, Kent, November 1959.

MT, then Secretary of State for Education and Science, with Britain's newly elected Prime Minister, Edward Heath, and Quintin Hogg, the Lord Chancellor, June 1970.

MT wells up during a BBC interview with Michael Cockerell on the day she won the Conservative leadership contest, February 1975.

Margaret and Denis with Mark and Carol at their Chelsea home on the day of their silver wedding anniversary, December 1976.

MT with a sixteen-year-old William Hague after he received a standing ovation from delegates at the Conservative Party Conference in Blackpool, October 1977.

MT holds her namesake Maggie, a Charolais calf, during her electioneering tour of East Anglia, April 1979. Denis was heard to mutter, 'If we're not careful, we'll have a dead cow on our hands.'

With three members of the Women's Royal Voluntary Service, holding their medals, May 1978.

Celebrating the annual Finchley carnival, MT meets the 'Queen' and her attendants, July 1979.

At a Finchley day centre, MT meets centenarian Mr Brighty, April 1978.

MT chats with schoolchildren in Woodside Park, September 1981.

ABOVE England footballers Kevin Keegan and Emlyn Hughes (right) kissing MT when they attended a reception given by her at Downing Street. Left to right: Ron Greenwood (manager), Kenny Sansom, Trevor Brooking, Kevin Keegan, Margaret Thatcher, Emlyn Hughes, Mick Mills, Phil Neal and Viv Anderson, June 1980.

RIGHT Margaret and Denis take their holiday host's King Charles Spaniel for a walk along the beach at Constantine Bay, Cornwall, August 1986.

BELOW MT takes part in a phone-in on the BBC's *Saturday Superstore* with presenter John Craven. She later judged music videos on the programme's 'pop panel', January 1987.

MT in the kitchen of her flat at No. 10, January 1987.

idea of bonds to finance it in a different way. I proposed to Margaret Thatcher that we could overcome these difficulties with a new structure, selling shares direct to the public by mail order and newspaper advertisements, and selling to overseas interests at the same time as selling some of them through the conventional brokers and banks in the City. She saw the point and became excited by the possibilities and gave me the backing I needed at the Treasury and in the City.

The whole privatisation story illustrated Margaret Thatcher at her best. At first her caution was demonstrated by tough argument. She believed in testing people out, almost to destruction, to see if they could stand their ground. She knew that she would have to stand her ground in a very public way and wanted to make sure that those advising her really did believe in the idea and had thought it through.

It showed her brutal honesty in judging the public mood and judging what the obstacles were at the time. Finally, it showed that she was indeed prepared to change her mind as others helped her make the case and overcome the obstacles.

Throughout the years that I worked for Margaret Thatcher in one capacity or another, the thing that never ceased to amaze me, apart from her remarkable energy, was her constant striving for the truth and her constant willingness to change her mind. It could take months to get her to make a decision on a big issue. She would be argumentatively indecisive for long periods. It was because she knew that, with her style of politics, once she had committed herself to something and went public she had to fight it through all the way. She combined caution with radicalism in a quite remarkable way which enabled her to stay at the top of British politics for so long. It also meant that when people come to write the history of Britain in the twentieth century, with the benefit of some perspective, they will see that, unlike many other Prime Ministers, she did have a general vision, a sense of direction, and she did find the measures and the men to help her carry it through in many important respects.

Privatisation may well go down as her greatest success. From modest beginnings it took off after the sale of BT. It spread around the world. The most unlikely people became converts, from the Labour governments of New Zealand and Australia, through the former communist states of Eastern Europe, to Fidel Castro's Cuba. It even eventually permeated the UK Labour Party.

Margaret Thatcher came to see the connection between privatisation, wider ownership and every man a shareholder. She came to enthuse over it, as she had over her very successful campaigns to sell council houses to their tenants. It was a pleasure to take her such an idea, it was exhilarating to argue it through with her and exciting to see it come to fruition.

Sir Tony Baldry
Conservative MP 1983–

Sir Tony Baldry has held the seat of Banbury since 1983. He was made an Energy minister by Margaret Thatcher in January 1990 and he served in various ministerial capacities under John Major.

I first met Margaret Thatcher when she was Secretary of State for Education and I was a student at Sussex University who was active in student politics. From that, I became Margaret Thatcher's personal aide and research assistant in the October 1974 general election. The Conservative Party was in opposition and Margaret was a member of the shadow Cabinet as shadow Housing and Planning minister. In those days, Members of Parliament did not have numbers of research assistants – they had just a single House of Commons secretary – so the core campaign team in Finchley was small: Mrs Thatcher's secretary, Alison Ward, now Lady Wakeham, her agent and me. What struck me first about working for Margaret Thatcher was her prodigious work ethic, her indefatigable determination to analyse and understand any brief that she was given and the considerable attention she paid to the last detail. I think that that was helped by the combination of her training both as a research chemist and, for a while, an extremely able junior at the tax Bar.

Working for Margaret and producing research briefings for her, I knew that I had to be ready and able to deal with any of the supplementary questions that she might ask – or, at the very least, know who could provide those detailed answers. The simple fact was that at any meeting – I suspect that this was the case throughout her time as leader of the party and as Prime Minister – Margaret was always the best-prepared person in the room, because invariably she had taken the time and effort to ensure that she was the best briefed.

When writing speeches for Margaret in the October 1974 general election, we used two books for primary source material. The first was F. A. Hayek's *The Constitution of Liberty* and the other was a book written and published in the 1930s called *A Time for Greatness*. To my shame, I cannot now remember the author's name, but I well recall that Margaret's reflection of these two books was along these lines: if the state takes all in taxation and spends all, we all become slaves of the state.

Margaret Thatcher was also incredibly kind, particularly to those who worked for her. Of course, she revelled in the Iron Lady sobriquet given to her by the Russians and others – it was a badge of respect for her steadfastness and determination – but there was also a much softer and more caring side to her. Perhaps I can give one example with which I think every Member could empathise. One of my intake, Patrick Nicholls, was a very effective junior minister, but had had to resign from office following a road traffic offence. Not surprisingly, he was cross with himself and very frustrated, and thought he had let people down.

One evening, Patrick had a telephone call from his whip, telling him to be in the division lobby at five to ten, shortly before the ten o'clock vote. Patrick asked why and was told simply to be there. Patrick arrived, as instructed, at five to ten, and shortly afterwards Margaret Thatcher walked in, put her arm through his and said, 'How are things going, Patrick? How are you?' As the division bell rang and as the lobby filled with parliamentary colleagues, the Prime Minister slowly walked through the lobby, arm in arm with Patrick, chatting to him all the way – a kind and clear gesture of support for someone who had been a hard-working junior minister and who continued to be an extremely hard-working and loyal backbencher.

Margaret also had a great sense of humour. In the 1983 general election, another of our intake, Jeremy Hanley, won Richmond with a majority of just seventy-four votes. The day after the general election, Margaret telephoned Jeremy to congratulate him on winning Richmond. The Conservative vote in the constituency had been about 21,000. The conversation went like this. Jeremy: 'Thank you very much, Prime Minister, for getting me the seventy-four votes that I needed.' Prime Minister: 'Jeremy, I got you the 21,000 votes – you just got the seventy-four.' Indeed, I often think there were two Margaret Thatchers: the real Margaret Thatcher for those who knew and worked with her and the caricature Margaret Thatcher of some press commentators, satirists and political opponents.

During the winter of 1974–75, I gave some help to Airey Neave in the Conservative leadership campaign. When Margaret became leader of the Conservative Party, I joined her private office for a while as the personal link between her and the Britain in Europe campaign that was going on as a consequence of the EU referendum. I therefore had a good opportunity to see how Margaret worked, in the early part of her leadership, with parliamentary colleagues and advisers. Yes, Margaret Thatcher was certainly a person of robust views. She liked a good discussion – robust argument, even – but she was always willing to listen and heed the views of others. There were, I suspect, countless occasions when having heard the arguments – having heard the advice of Willie Whitelaw, or, on more personal matters, heeded the good counsel of Denis – Margaret would accept other people's contributions and advice, perhaps saying something like, 'All right, we'll do it your way, but you had better get it right.'

I was elected in 1983 when Margaret secured a majority of 144 in the Commons. I do not think any of us who were elected in June 1983 were in any doubt that we owed our election to Margaret Thatcher and the affection in which she was held by huge numbers of voters. This, for me, is best recalled in a single sound bite in Banbury market. One of the television stations had come to do some vox pop on the election in Banbury. They went up to a chap who ran the fruit and veg stall. 'What do you think about the general election?' they asked. 'I don't know much about politics,' said the guy, 'but this I do know: No. 10 – Maggie's den.'

Sir Malcolm Rifkind
Cabinet Minister 1986–97

Sir Malcolm Rifkind served as MP for Edinburgh Pentlands from 1974 to 1997 and is now MP for Kensington. He joined Margaret Thatcher's Cabinet in 1986 as Secretary of State for Scotland. He was a Cabinet minister throughout John Major's administration, latterly as Foreign Secretary.

Those who were privileged to serve in Margaret Thatcher's Cabinet will always be grateful for the experience. She had her own distinctive style of Cabinet government.

For her, a Cabinet discussion was a series of bilateral exchanges rather than a collective analysis of the issues of the day. Whereas John Major would keep his own views to himself until his Cabinet colleagues had expressed theirs, Mrs Thatcher would open the discussion by indicating the conclusion that she wished and expected.

On one occasion she sat down at a Cabinet committee and began by saying, 'I haven't much time, today. Only enough time to explode and have my way.' As each minister expressed his view she would often engage him in battle before moving on to the next.

While this could be an alarming experience for a new member of the Cabinet it was neither as distressing nor as difficult for the Cabinet as a whole as this introduction might suggest. For all her bossiness and aversion to compromise, Margaret Thatcher was a constitutionalist and a believer in Cabinet government to her fingertips.

Unlike an American President who is quite entitled to ignore his Cabinet – none of whom, except the Vice-President, having been elected by the nation – a British Prime Minister is *primus inter pares* and often Mrs Thatcher found herself in the minority. This she accepted with varying degrees of enthusiasm but she never challenged the right of her colleagues to decline to accept her wishes. Indeed, when she went into battle she relished an adversary who was prepared to disagree with her as long as he knew what he was talking about. It was John Major's willingness as a mere junior whip to tell her in front of his colleagues that she was wrong and misguided that first brought him to her attention and led to his ultimate coronation as her successor to the Tory crown.

As long as she was Prime Minister her natural gut instincts were tempered by the need to carry her colleagues and ensure acceptable government. After her retirement that was less of a constraint. One recalls Gladstone's comment on Sir Robert Peel: 'Former Prime Ministers are like great rafts floating untethered in a harbour.'

I was privileged, along with Ken Clarke, to serve in Margaret Thatcher's government for the full eleven years of her term of office and to be in her Cabinet for almost half that time. It was never dull. Each day we saw political leadership and statesmanship of the highest order and a Prime Minister with remarkable personal qualities. It was sometimes said that she did not have a sense of humour, and it was true that there was very little wit in many of her speeches, but I recall on one occasion that she was asked, 'Mrs Thatcher, do you believe in consensus?' To our surprise, we heard her saying, 'Yes, I do believe in consensus; there should be a consensus behind my convictions.' I thought at the time that this was an extraordinary example of wit, but as the years have gone by I have realised that she was actually being deadly serious.

It was also said that Margaret Thatcher could be very intolerant of those who did not agree with her. That was also a parody of the truth. She was intolerant of people who were woolly and who argued that things could not be done because they would be unpopular or that it was too difficult, but when she met someone able to argue from a point of fact and whom she respected, she not only listened but could change her mind. I was moved to the Foreign Office at the time of the Falklands and she recalled Sir Anthony Parsons, our ambassador at the Security Council, to ask him how it was going at the United Nations. He had never met her before; he was a rather grand diplomat. When he started trying to report to her, she, not uncharacteristically, kept interrupting him and he was not used to this. After the fourth interruption, he stopped and said, 'Prime Minister, if you didn't interrupt me so often, you might find that you didn't need to.' She not only kept quiet but six months later appointed him her foreign policy adviser.

Having spent a lot of my time in the Foreign Office, I am conscious of the fact that diplomats in the Foreign Office were not her favourite. I went to see her when I was Defence Secretary some years later, after she had retired, and she said to me, 'You know, Ministry of Defence, your problem is you've got no allies. The Foreign Office aren't wet – they're drenched.' When it came to the Foreign Office and to diplomats, she sometimes had a remarkable capacity to distance herself from the government of which she was Prime Minister.

On one glorious occasion in which I was personally involved, we had a difficult negotiation getting a package of sanctions against South Africa. They did not include economic sanctions, but she was very unhappy that one of the proposals at the European Community Council was that we should withdraw our defence attachés. The Ministry of Defence did not mind but it took an awful long time for Geoffrey Howe to persuade her to go along with this, and she was basically unconvinced but did go along with it. Some weeks later, we had a visit from the President of Mozambique and I was asked to sit in on the meeting at Downing Street. The President rebuked her for not doing enough against apartheid in South Africa. I will never forget her response. She bridled and said, 'Mr President, that is simply not the case. We are refusing to sell arms to South Africa. We have initiated the Gleneagles agreement whereby we don't have any sporting contact with South Africa. We're using all diplomatic means to try and bring down apartheid.' 'We, we, we', she said – and then suddenly she stopped, pointed at me and said, 'They've decided to withdraw our defence attachés,' adding, 'I don't know what good that will do.' The President of Mozambique was rather bemused by what seemed to be happening.

Although she may have had mixed feelings about the Foreign Office, she actually owed it a great debt of gratitude, because one of her greatest triumphs – her relationship with Mr Gorbachev and what flowed from that – was a result of the diplomats in the Foreign Office spotting at a very early stage that the youngest new member of the politburo, Mikhail Gorbachev, was a man to try to cultivate, and she had the wisdom to accept their advice. We should not underestimate what followed from that, which was her persuading Ronald Reagan to accept her view that Gorbachev was a man with whom we could do business. Reagan would not have accepted that advice from most people but, coming from the Iron Lady, he said, 'Well, if she believes that, then I can proceed on that basis.' The result was not only a remarkable set of initiatives but the end of the Cold War and the liberation of Eastern Europe without a shot being fired – a remarkable epitaph.

One of the big issues that is relevant to the debates we have today is whether, in the relationship with the United States, British Prime Ministers always have to agree with the President or otherwise we risk that relationship. All I can say is that Margaret Thatcher had no doubt that the answer was, 'No, you don't have to.' On several occasions she had deep disagreements with Ronald Reagan, one of her closest friends. For example, when British companies had contracts to help to build a Soviet oil pipeline in the early 1980s, the Americans threatened sanctions against those British companies and Margaret Thatcher bitterly criticised them. I was sent off to Washington as a junior minister to have meetings with Mr Kenneth Dam, the American deputy Secretary of State. We reached a compromise. The only thing we could not agree on was whether the compromise would be known as the Rifkind-Dam agreement or the Dam-Rifkind agreement.

Margaret Thatcher had openly and publicly disagreed with Reagan on the Reykjavik summit, when she felt that he was surrendering too many nuclear weapons without getting enough in return, but most important of all, she bitterly resented the invasion of Grenada. Grenada had been invaded by the United States, which had forgotten, unfortunately, that Her Majesty was the Head of State of Grenada and had not even informed the British government of what it was about to do. Margaret Thatcher not only criticised it but she went on the BBC World Service attacking the United States and saying that it could not behave like that. Some days later, Reagan recorded in his memoirs that he was sitting in the Oval Office with some of his aides and he was told that the British Prime Minister was on the phone and would he take a call. Yes, he said, of course he would. She started berating him in a rather strident way down the telephone. It went on for only about a minute, but some of us who have been on the receiving end know how long that can feel. When she was in full flight, Reagan put his hand over the receiver so that she could not hear, turned to his aides and said, 'Gee, isn't she marvellous?' Far from resenting it, they appreciated that sometimes they got it wrong and even their closest allies were entitled to point it out.

Lord Flight
Conservative MP 1997–2005

Howard Flight was the MP for Arundel and South Downs from 1997 to 2005. He was raised to the peerage in 2011.

During the great years of Margaret Thatcher's premiership I was actually doing one of the things she advocated and set British citizens free to do, being an entrepreneur and building Guiness Flight as a successful fund management business. As a result, I cannot claim to know the great lady well, but have admired and supported her from afar for twenty years.

The first time I met Lady Thatcher socially was at a reception at No. 10 in the 1980s, where I was the guest of an MP friend. His wife commented on introducing us to Sir Denis and Maggie that Denis looked just like my father. While remarkably true, Maggie was not amused!

In 1988 I wrote a book about currencies with the rather pretentious title *All You Need to Know About Exchange Rates*. I sent a copy to Lady Thatcher but received no response – I think my diagnosis for the purposes of the book were too financially clinical.

Just prior to the 1997 general election I was pleased to be invited by Maggie to a reception for those known to be of sound views on Europe and the euro. I recollect Denis interrupting while Maggie was holding court on the ghastliness of the EU, to the effect 'We should get the hell out.' Maggie continued without drawing breath. At the same occasion, Nick Gibb took photos of us all with Lady Thatcher, but with a pair of curtains in the background – I felt Maggie did not feel it appropriate for her to be contrasted against a pair of curtains!

At a more recent and equally enjoyable reception given by Lady Thatcher, I was talking with her when in particular it struck me what a very attractive and vital woman she still is.

Tom Utley
Writer

———

Tom Utley is a regular columnist for the Daily Mail.

M argaret Thatcher arrived more than an hour before anybody else
for my father T. E. Utley's funeral in 1988. She took her place in
a pew at the front of the church and sat silently there alone, waiting for
the other mourners to arrive and the service to begin.

My mother and the rest of us were surprised and terribly touched
that the Prime Minister had decided to come. She had just arrived
back in London from a summit meeting in Toronto and she was off to
another one in Paris straight after the funeral. It was true that she had
known my father fairly well and he had helped her with some of her
speeches. But he was never a prominent public figure and his friendship with the Prime Minister was not so close as to put her under any
sort of obligation to attend his funeral. She had already done more
than her duty by my mother by writing her a long and moving letter in
her own hand from Toronto on the night of my father's death.

It was my father's vicar who told me that the Prime Minister had
already been there for more than an hour. I asked him why on earth
she had come so early and I will never forget his reply. 'She told me,'
he said, 'that she didn't want to upstage the widow.' Lady Thatcher
took no formal part in the service – my brother and I did the readings
– and she left with no sort of fuss or fanfare when it was over: just a
word with my mother, a handshake for the vicar, a nod to me and my
siblings, and she was gone.

James Baker III
Chief of Staff to President Reagan

James Baker served as Chief of Staff and Treasury Secretary in the Reagan administration. He was George H. W. Bush's Secretary of State.

From their first meeting in 1978, President Reagan recognised Margaret Thatcher as a philosophical soulmate. Both passionately believed the doctrines of democratic liberalism. Both instinctively understood the ruinous consequences of communism, socialism and excessive government regulation. And both spoke with such plain eloquence about these things that they won the trust of their electorates and, with it, the power to transform their nations and – in time – the world.

When Prime Minister Thatcher took office, the clock had run down on Britain's post-war experiment in socialism. Inflation reached 25 per cent, state industries lost millions each week and the top marginal tax rate was 83 per cent. In the US, inflation, unemployment and interest rates soared, casting the economy into stagflation. Declinism was in the air. Experts said we should stop thinking about growth and start thinking about the limits of growth.

But Prime Minister Thatcher and President Reagan shared an optimistic dream of what she later called 'boundless opportunity built on enterprise, individual effort and personal generosity'. Beginning in 1979, she attacked the 'British disease' with determination. But when Reagan took his oath nineteen months later, her privatisation campaign, tax cuts and other programmes had not yet borne fruit. At first, Reagan's tax cuts (from 70 per cent to 50 per cent, later to 28 per cent), deregulation, free trade and sound money also failed to break the grip of recession. But both leaders stood firm. 'The lady's not for turning,' she famously declared. 'People are prepared to put up with sacrifices if they know those sacrifices are the foundations of future prosperity.'

In November 1982, the US economy started growing again. Britain regained its proper place among the most vibrant world economies.

And elsewhere, the demonstration effect of the Thatcher–Reagan revolution ignited what one commentator called 'a startling burst of innovation, economic growth and political freedom' that has meant opportunity, hope and better lives for billions of men, women and children worldwide.

Thatcher and Reagan, armed with deep faith in personal freedom, also had the courage to speak truth to the Soviet Union. It was an 'evil empire', Reagan told Parliament in 1982, to Thatcher's happy applause at hearing her own long-held ideas echoed by an American President. (And by the way, it was the Soviets who in the 1970s first called her the Iron Lady and they didn't mean it as a compliment.) Both leaders also clearly understood what most others did not: that communism would eventually fail, that it was, as Reagan said, 'destined for the ash heap of history'.

Yet they were also realists. The nuclear-armed Soviet Union was still dangerous. When others would not, Thatcher allowed new and better US missiles to be stationed on British soil and supported the American President's rejection of unverifiable treaties. But she also recognised – earlier than we – that the West could do business with Gorbachev. Together, they engaged the Soviets in talks that began the process of East–West reconciliation.

In 1989, the Berlin Wall fell, validating the doctrines of peace through strength and cautious engagement. It then fell to the first President Bush to assure that the Soviet Union died with a whimper, not with a bang. He avoided triumphalism, assured Soviet leaders that the West had no military designs and won their cooperation in the Gulf War and Madrid peace conference. And in this, he had no better ally and friend than Great Britain. The special relationship gave Thatcher license to disagree on German reunification, the role of the United Nations in the Gulf War and other points. But she never ceased to be our trusted adviser and ally, nor we hers.

Domestically and internationally, Thatcher and her American presidential allies simply won the battle of ideas. Today, democracy and free markets are widely honoured (though sometimes grudgingly) and outright collectivism rarely defended. Even old political foes and other critics comfortably inhabit the structures that Thatcher and her Yankee friends created. Ideas that once seemed radical are now commonplace.

Napoleon called Britain a nation of shopkeepers. It fell to a British shopkeeper's daughter to demonstrate that what was intended as an insult was, in fact, the clue to Britain's greatness. The same personal, economic and political freedom that produces a nation of shopkeepers also produces general happiness and prosperity for the shopkeepers' nation. The job of government, Margaret Thatcher well understood, is simply to preserve the security and freedom of all its people, so they can run their own shops and their own lives.

Lord Butler

Principal Private Secretary to Margaret Thatcher 1982–85

Robin Butler served in numerous positions in the civil service from 1961 onwards but is best remembered as the Principal Private Secretary to Margaret Thatcher from 1982 until 1985, and as Cabinet Secretary and Head of the Home Civil Service from 1988 to 1998. He sits as a crossbencher in the House of Lords.

My dominant recollection of working with Margaret Thatcher was the certainty of her instinctive reactions. When the IRA bomb exploded in the Grand Hotel Brighton at ten to three in the morning on the last day of the Conservative Party Conference in 1984, I was with her in the sitting room of her suite at the hotel. She had just finished her conference speech and I had given her a paper on which a decision was needed by start of business next morning. Denis had gone to bed next door.

When the bomb went off, I thought it was a car bomb outside. I said to her, 'We should move away from the windows.' As we went across the room we could hear the noise of collapsing masonry through the bedroom door.

Without hesitation she said, 'I must see if Denis is all right.' She opened the bedroom door, whereupon the noise of structural collapse became louder, and she disappeared into the darkness. I paused in the sitting room, wondering what I should say to the tribunal of inquiry if she was killed by the collapsing building. To my relief she and Denis emerged almost immediately, Denis pulling on some clothes over his pyjamas.

We then moved into the corridor. Miraculously the lights had stayed on. (Thereafter Margaret Thatcher carried a torch in her handbag in case the same thing happened again – she always learned from experience.) Some others joined us and we began to debate what we should do next. I suggested returning to London – only one hour away.

Margaret Thatcher said, 'I'm not leaving the area.' The decision was then taken out of our hands by the arrival of a fireman who – after one false start – led us down the main staircase and out of the back of the hotel, not without Margaret Thatcher breaking off to ask whether all the staff in the foyer were accounted for.

We were taken to the training accommodation at Lewes Police Station where the Thatchers were allocated bedrooms. At that stage I did not know that the bomb had been in the upper part of the building or that anyone was missing. I lay on the bench in the day room at 5 a.m. At 5.45 the telephone rang. It was John Gummer, then Chairman of the party. He said, 'It's worse than we thought. The Tebbits, the Wakehams and others are trapped in the collapsed building.'

I decided not to wake Margaret Thatcher but turned on the television to watch the news, including Norman Tebbit being brought out. Margaret Thatcher appeared just after eight; she had seen the news on a television in her room. 'We must make sure the conference re-starts on time,' she said. I was appalled. I said, 'Surely you can't go on with the conference when your colleagues and friends are being dug out of the rubble.' 'It is what they would want,' she said. 'We can't allow terrorism to defeat democracy.' But just before the speech she was sitting in the green room, saying, 'I am not sure I can go through with this.' Gordon Reece said, 'Of course you can go through with it.' I am absolutely certain that she was always going to go through with it. Many times I saw her say beforehand that she was not sure she could do something and then go out and give a bravura performance.

Another quality is that she never seemed to waste energy by looking back and worrying about whether she had done the right thing. What was done was done. The only thing worth using energy on was what to do next. I remember travelling back with her from a lunchtime engagement in the City during a bad moment in the coal miners' strike, when the dockers were for a short time also on strike and the prospects of importing the energy supplies needed were threatened. On this journey back we suffered another blow, learning that the government had lost its case in the High Court over the banning of the GCHQ unions. Margaret Thatcher was faced with making a statement in Parliament in front of a jubilant opposition. She was immediately clear about what she would do. 'I will make clear that we will appeal the GCHQ case to the House of Lords and, if we lose, we shall accept the judgment of the court. We cannot fight for the rule of law in one area if we don't accept it in another. Now back to the miners' strike.' The government won its appeal in the House of Lords.

The legends about Margaret Thatcher's physical toughness and stamina are justified. In December 1984 she went to Beijing to sign the Hong Kong agreement and then went on to Hong Kong to reassure opinion there. Believing that Ronald Reagan was in the Western White House in California, the Foreign Office suggested that she should visit him on the way home following his re-election as President. Even if this information had been correct, the geography would have been dubious since it is a shorter distance from London to California than from Hong Kong. In fact, Ronald Reagan was in Washington and the visit involved a 24-hour flight from Hong Kong on the VC10 but only a twelve-hour time change. While the staff decided that we would get what sleep we could, Margaret Thatcher announced that she would stay awake and study the Anti-Ballistic Missile Treaty and Cap Weinberger's speeches in preparation for her talks with Ronald Reagan on the Strategic Defense Initiative.

She did this to such good effect that, faced with the President and the US defence establishment at Camp David, she persuaded them to accept the four principles which preserved the principle of nuclear deterrence. We returned home in time for Christmas Eve having flown right round the world. The full trip had lasted five-and-a-half days or 130 hours, of which fifty-five hours had been spent in the air. I had occasion to telephone her on Christmas Day and asked whether she felt tired. 'Certainly not,' she said. 'Why ever should I?'

On another occasion she had a dental appointment in the morning. On her return, I asked her whether she had had any trouble. 'I'm afraid the dentist said that I had to have my impacted wisdom teeth out,' she said. Later that day, at the end of the usual round of meetings and engagements, I asked when she would like an appointment made with her dentist for the removal of the wisdom teeth. 'He did it this morning,' she said.

What was the secret of Margaret Thatcher's energy? Apart from the certainty of her instincts and her physical stamina, she seemed to have an inexhaustible supply of adrenalin. No occasion was too trivial for her not to take seriously, whether it was a school prize-giving or a confidence debate in the Commons. All were the subject of intense and detailed preparation.

When I was Principal Private Secretary, in briefing her for Prime Minister's Questions, I did not brief her on the facts – other people did that – but regarded my job as being to calm her down, usually by reassuring her that her case was good in answer to a question and, just occasionally, if she was sleepy after lunch, to work her up a bit and say, 'Prime Minister, I think you have to worry about this question, this is quite difficult.' It was about getting the horse to the starting gate with exactly the right amount of perspiration on the flanks, and then she would perform superbly in the House of Commons.

Lord Powell and his wife were splendid to Lady Thatcher in her latter days. Indeed, I think that on the Sunday evening, he was the last person, outside her family, to visit her. About a month ago, he said that he had been with her on a Sunday afternoon. I asked him what he talked to her about because, of course, in her latter months, she found conversation difficult. He said, 'We didn't talk. We turned on the television and we watched *Songs of Praise* and we sung the hymns together.'

When judicial review was gaining force and I was head of the civil service, I suggested to Margaret Thatcher that we might arrange a seminar between senior civil servants and some of the judges so that the judges would know more about the way in which decisions were taken in government. 'Absolutely not,' she said. 'I am not going to have any appearance of the executive appearing to interfere with the independence of the judges. We must keep them strictly separate.' That is an aspect of her principles and her administration that I do not think has been much mentioned.

I was her Principal Private Secretary between 1982 and 1985. Inside No. 10, having the privilege of seeing her in that intimate setting, we of course saw a very different person from the one that the public saw outside. The public saw the bravura performances and the confidence. She has been charged with being overconfident, even arrogant, but you saw a very different picture before the great public appearances inside No. 10, somebody whose motivation and force was not built on overconfidence but was in fact built on lack of self-confidence. I say that because I heard her say it herself publicly, after she left office. She said it was something that the media never really realised about her. I believe that that was the driving force behind her perfectionism in her appearance, in her dress, in her speeches and in her grip on her briefing. All those things had to be perfect before she would appear in public.

I offer an anecdote which relates to a time after she had ceased to be Prime Minister and after I had ceased to be Cabinet Secretary. She very kindly came to my college at Oxford to talk. In the course of her remarks to the students, she said that one of the things that she worried about in modern life, and the life facing their generation, was the number of children born illegitimate. When it came round to questions, one of the students said to her, 'Lady Thatcher, don't you think it is a little unfair to use the word "illegitimate" of a child throughout its life when it has had no influence over the circumstances of its own birth?' Her eyes flashed and she said, 'Well, what would you call them? I can think of another word but I think it would be even more unkind.' I thought, 'Goodness, what's going to happen?' but the moment passed. She came to dinner and chapel, and in the lighter part of the evening we were having a drink in the Master's Lodgings before she and Denis went back to London. We were talking about other things completely when she suddenly said, 'You know, Robin, that young man who asked me this afternoon about the word "illegitimate" had a point didn't he?' That was quite characteristic. I will wager that she never used the word illegitimate again. She was always prepared to learn, even from a student. She hit back immediately but then she thought about it and took the point.

I never had any doubt while I was working with her as Private Secretary and Cabinet Secretary that I was a witness to greatness as well as to great events. Those are memories that I will treasure all my life.

On the evening of the day when Margaret Thatcher left Downing Street, I invited her and Denis to a farewell party in my office with some of the civil servants I knew she regarded most highly. I said, 'When we are very old the thing which our grandchildren and great-grandchildren will think most interesting about us is that we worked with Margaret Thatcher.' I believe that still and I am glad that I said it to her at that moment.

Alan Clark

Conservative MP 1974–92 and 1997–99

Alan Clark was the MP for Plymouth Sutton from 1974 until 1992. He returned to Parliament in 1997 as the MP for Kensington and Chelsea. He served under Margaret Thatcher as Minister for Trade and then Minister of State at the MoD but he is best known for his notoriously indiscreet diaries. This extract is taken from his bestselling Diaries. *Alan Clark died in 1999.*

Monday 19 November 1990

The whole house is in ferment. Little groups, conclaves everywhere. Only in the dining room does some convention seem to have grown up (I presume because no one trusts their dining companions) that we don't talk 'shop'.

'Made your Christmas plans yet?' All that balls. God, the dining room is boring these days, even worse than Pratt's. Big, slow, buffers 'measuring their words' oh-so-firmly; or creepy little narks talking straight out of Conservative News.

But in the corridors it is all furtive whispering and glancing over shoulders. The institutional confidence (seen at its most obvious in those who have served a prison term, and which I first noticed in my early days on Warren Street), that special grimacing style of speech out of the corner of the mouth, eyes focusing in another direction, is now it seems the only way of communicating.

Most people are interested – not so much in the result, as in knowing what the result will be in advance, in order to make their own 'dispositions'. To ingratiate oneself with the new regime – a new regime, I should say, because the outcome is by no means certain – even as little as a week before it is installed, looks better than joining the stampede afterwards. The issue which can be discussed semi-respectably is who is most likely to deliver victory at the general election? But it is packaging, conceals a great basket of bitterness, thwarted personal ambition and vindictive glee. Talk of country, or loyalty, is dismissed as 'histrionics'.

And there is a strange feeling abroad. Even if the lady wins –

and here I am writing 'even if', pull yourself together Clark, say 'even after she's won' – there will be no escaping the fact that at least 150 of her parliamentary colleagues will have rejected her leadership. That's a big chunk. Some people, particularly those who pose as party elders, like Tony Grant, are intimating that it might be 'better' if, faced with so blatant a show of no confidence, she decided to 'heal' the party by announcing her intention to stand down at a given date (i.e. become a lame duck which the Labour Party could taunt and torment on every occasion, and a busted flush internationally).

And as the savour of a Heseltine victory starts to pervade the crannies and cupboards and committee rooms, so more and more people are 'coming out'. 'Oh, I don't think he'd be so bad, really...' 'He's got such a wide appeal.' 'My people just love him, I must say...' 'I know what you mean, but he'd be so good at dealing with...' (fill in particular problem as appropriate).

Most conspicuous in canvassing are Hampson (loonily), Mates (gruffly) and Bill Powell (persuasively). Michael himself is quite shameless in offering all and sundry what they have always wanted. For example, he would probably have got Paul's support anyway, but 'sealed' it with an assurance that Paul would be Speaker in the next House; Soames fell straight away for the 'your talents are long overdue for recognition' line, as did little Nelson and Rhodes James ('you've been treated abominably').

Michael stands in the centre of the Members' Lobby, virtually challenging people to wish him good luck. He gives snap 'updates' to journalists and greets supplicants who are brought along for a short audience by his team. The heavier targets he sees in his room. The Cabinet play their cards close to the chest, although Mellor, apparently, speaks to Michael twice a day on the telephone. Some, like Kenneth Clarke, want her out so badly that they don't need even to blink. And I would guess that there is a fair coterie of Ministers of State and parly secs like Sainsbury and Trippier who feel uneasy with the lady and like the idea of a change.

At the top of the ministerial staircase I ran into Garel Jones. He was bubbling with suppressed excitement. I don't think he actually wants 'Hezzy' as he (spastically) calls him, to win. It would be disruptive of the Blue Chip long-term plan. But he's high on the whole thing.

Tristan said, 'Of course every member of the Cabinet will vote for the Prime Minister in the first round.' Like hell they will.

I said to him, hoping he'd deny it, 'One cannot actually exclude the possibility that Heseltine will score more votes than her on the first ballot.'

'No, I'm afraid one can't.'

'Can one, even, be completely sure that he will not get both the largest total and the necessary margin to win without a second ballot?'

'No, I'm afraid one can't.'

This was really chilling. Apocalypse. Because time is horrendously tight if we have to organise an alternative candidate.

Four working days and a weekend. But if Michael scoops it in one gulp then that is the end of everything.

Maddeningly, I had to return to the department. Meetings and an official lunch. Scandinavians.

'I assume that there is no likelihood of Mrs Thatcher being defeated for the position of Prime Minister?'

'Oh no. None whatever. It's just one of these quaint traditions we have in the Conservative Party.'

But the encounter made me realise the enormity of what we're doing changing the Prime Minister – but without any electoral authority so to do. I thought I'd have a talk to Peter, although he doesn't encourage it, and I cancelled my early afternoon engagements and went back over to the House.

I listened outside the door. Silence. I knocked softly, then tried the handle. He was asleep, snoring lightly, in the leather armchair, with his feet resting on the desk.

Drake playing bowls before the Armada and all that, but I didn't like it. This was ten minutes past three in the afternoon of the most critical day of the whole election. I spoke sharply to him. 'Peter.'

He was bleary.

'I'm sorry to butt in, but I'm really getting a bit worried about the way things are going.'

'Quite all right, old boy, relax.'

'I'm just hearing bad reactions around the place from people where I wouldn't expect it.'

'Look, do you think I'd be like this if I wasn't entirely confident? What's the arithmetic look like?'

'Tight-ish, but OK.'

'Well, what?'

'I've got Michael on 115. It could be 124, at the worst.'

'Look, Peter, I don't think people are being straight with you.'

'I have my ways of checking.'

'Paul?'

'I know about Paul.'

'The Wintertons?'

'The Wintertons, funnily enough, I've got down as 'Don't Know's.'

'What the fuck do you mean, 'Don't Know'? This isn't a fucking street canvas. It's a two-horse race, and each vote affects the relative score by two, unless it's an abstention.'

'Actually, I think there could be quite a few abstentions.'

'Don't you think we should be out there twisting arms?'

'No point. In fact it could be counter-productive. I've got a theory about this. I think some people may abstain on the first ballot in order to give Margaret a fright, then rally to her on the second.' (Balls, I thought, but didn't say.)

'What about the '92? They're completely rotten. They've got a meeting at six. Are you going?'

'No point. But I think you should.'

In deep gloom I walked back down Speaker's corridor. It can't really be as bad as this can it? I mean there is absolutely no oomph in her campaign whatsoever. Peter is useless, far worse than I thought. When he was pairing whip he was unpopular, but at least he was crisp. Now he's sozzled. There isn't a single person working for her who cuts any ice at all. I know it's better to be feared than loved. But these people aren't either. And she's in Paris. '*Où est la masse de manoeuvre? – Aucune.*'

I went into the Members' tearoom. The long table was crowded with Margaret supporters, all nonentities except for Tebbit who was cheering people up. Much shouting and laughter. Blustering reassurance. Norman was saying how unthinkable it was to consider dismissing a Prime Minister during a critical international conference. 'Like Potsdam in 1945,' I said. No one paid any attention. If they heard they didn't or affected not to understand the allusion.

The crowd thinned out a little and when he got up Norman said that he wanted a word. We went into the Aye lobby and sat at that round table in the centre with all the stationery on it.

'Well...?'

'It's filthy,' I said.

'It could be close. Very close.'

I agreed, 'Fucking close.'

'If it's like that do you think she should stand in the second ballot?' I simply don't know the answer to this. Governing would be very difficult with half the party against her. She might have to make concessions to the left. I asked Norman if he thought she would have to bring Heseltine into the Cabinet.

'She'd certainly be under a lot of pressure to do so.'

'Renton.'

'Yeah.'

I said that the key tactic was to get Chris Patten to stand and draw off the left vote. At least the hard left vote, Charlie Morrison, Bob Hicks, all the wankers. Norman said, 'And Ken Clarke.' I told him no, if you have too many candidates people just get in a muddle and Heseltine walks through them, just as she did in 1975. Norman said that a lot of people now regarded Michael as a right-wing candidate anyway.

'Well, we know different.'

'Too true.'

Norman said, 'If it's open season, I'm damn well going to put my name in. The right must have a candidate they can vote for.'

'You'd lose.'

'It's likely I would, but at least we'd know our strength. That could be useful in a changed situation.'

'Look, Norman, we want to put additional names in to reduce his total, not ours. I don't think Heseltine has that big a personal vote. It's just an anti-Margaret coalition.'

I could see he was thoughtful. But he didn't want to prolong the conversation, which we were conducting in tones just above a whisper, though still arousing the curious attention of passers-by.

Raising his voice Norman said, 'Well, this time tomorrow everything will be settled,' and gave one of his graveyard cackles.

The '92 meeting was in one of those low-ceilinged rooms on the upper committee room corridor. The mood was tetchy and apprehensive. There was a kind of fiction running from several (Jill Knight, for example, shockingly), just as Norman had foreseen, that 'Michael' – as defectors call him (supporters of the Prime Minister always refer to him as 'Heseltine'; and this is quite a useful subliminal indicator of how the Speaker is going to vote when he or she is being deliberately or defensively opaque) – was 'really' on the right.

The trouble with this club, to which I was elected almost as soon as I arrived here, but with which I have never really felt comfortable, is that it personifies in extreme form two characteristics found in the majority of MPs: stupidity and egomania. It is only the shrewd and subtle guidance of George Gardiner that has prevented them becoming a laughing stock in recent years. But such integrity as they might originally have possessed has been eroded by the inclusion of many from marginal seats. None are quite as awful as Elizabeth Peacock, who spoke squatly and fatly against Margaret – why bother, she won't be here in the next Parliament anyway – but most are concerned solely with saving their own skins. I spoke loyally, and should have been movingly, of our debt to the PM. But there was a hint of what's-she-ever-done-for-us from the audience and with some justification, so few ministerial appointments having come out of the '92. I tried to make their flesh creep with what Michael would do, got only a subdued ritual cheer when I said Margaret is undefeated, and never will be defeated either in the country or in this House of Commons. I'm not particularly popular with that lot. They think I'm 'snooty'. Perhaps my boredom threshold shows. But in the ballot tomorrow I'd say they will divide no better than 60/40.

After dinner I had a word with Norman Lamont. He'd just come back from somewhere-or-other. 'I don't like the smell,' he kept saying. 'There's a bad smell to the whole place.' He's right, of course. It's the smell of decay. It's affecting everything, the badge messengers, the police, the drivers. Something nasty is going to happen.

I write this very late and I am very tired. Perhaps I'm just needlessly depressed. I'd ring the lady if I could, but she's at a banquet. She's not even coming back for the ballot. Lovely and haughty.

Ronald Reagan
President of the USA 1981-89

After his career as a film actor and as Governor of California, Ronald Reagan became President of the USA in 1981 and held the office for two terms until 1989. His great friendship with Margaret Thatcher and their shared political priorities cemented relations between Britain and the USA throughout the 1980s. This extract is taken from his memoirs An American Life. *Ronald Reagan died in 2004.*

On a trip to England in 1978 I bumped into Jason Dart, one of the Californians who'd been in my Kitchen Cabinet, and he said he wanted me to meet a friend of his who had recently been elected the first woman to head the British Conservative Party.

I'd been planning on spending only a few minutes with Margaret Thatcher but we ended up talking for almost two hours. I liked her immediately. She was warm, feminine, gracious and intelligent and it was evident from our first words that we were soulmates when it came to reducing government and expanding economic freedom. At a reception that evening, an Englishman who had heard about our meeting asked me: 'What do you think of our Mrs Thatcher?'

I said I'd been deeply impressed. 'I think she'll make a magnificent Prime Minister.'

He looked at me out of the corners of his eyes with a kind of mocking disdain that seemed to suggest the idea was unthinkable: 'My dear fellow, a woman Prime Minister?'

'England once had a queen named Victoria who did rather well,' I said.

'By jove,' he said. 'I'd quite forgotten about that.'

Throughout the eight years of my presidency, no alliance we had was stronger than the one between the United States and the United Kingdom. Not only did Margaret Thatcher and I become personal friends and share a similar philosophy about government, the alliance was strengthened by the long special relationship between our countries. The depth of this special relationship made it impossible for us to remain neutral during Britain's war with Argentina over the Falkland Islands, although it was a conflict in which I had to walk a fine line. After the landing on South Georgia Island, Margaret Thatcher called me and said that Britain would never submit to a takeover of one of its crown colonies. She asked me to telephone Leopoldo Galtieri, President of the military junta that ruled Argentina, to urge him not to proceed with the invasion and to say that Britain would use whatever force was necessary to keep her colony. I spoke to Galtieri but couldn't budge him.

The junta misjudged not only Margaret Thatcher's will but the strength of our ties to England. We assured Margaret Thatcher that we were fully behind Britain. Margaret Thatcher, I think, had no choice but to stand up to the generals who cynically squandered the lives of young Argentinians solely to protect the life of a corrupt and iron-fisted totalitarian government. She did so, I believe, not because, as was speculated in Britain, her government might fall if she did not, but because she believed absolutely in the moral rightness of what she was doing and in her nation's obligation to guarantee the handful of people living in the Falklands the right of self-determination.

Sir Ronald Millar
Margaret Thatcher's Speech-Writer

Sir Ronald Millar was an accomplished playwright and film-script author. He began writing speeches for Prime Minister Edward Heath in the early 1970s. He was then invited to continue as speech-writer firstly to Margaret Thatcher and then John Major. He was the author of a phrase that has entered our language – 'the lady's not for turning'. Sir Ronald died in 1998 and this extract is taken from his autobiography A View from the Wings.

Margaret Thatcher was elected leader on 11 February 1975 but stubborn loyalty to her predecessor was still with me when, six days later, I was summoned to meet her in the House of Commons. At this first meeting her attitude to me was guarded as was mine to her. I had the feeling she was thinking: what sort of writer is this who worked for Ted? Not one of us, that's for sure. I was thinking: she must have something special or they wouldn't have made a woman party leader, but I wasn't clear what it was and in any case not at all sure that I wanted to be further involved politically.

I had heard that she was intent on change and fine, I thought, change is not only inevitable, it's desirable, but let's not wipe out yesterday like a wet sponge cleaning a blackboard. No one had said she intended this but the word was that she was a force to be reckoned with, a woman with all the determination of a man and therefore, in all probability, up to no good. However, seeing her in daylight for the first time, and suppressing one of those cliché assessments that were to dog her throughout her political life, there was a kind of senior girl-scout freshness about her that was rather appealing, as though she had stepped straight out of *The Sound of Music*, though I doubt if 'soft woollen mittens and whiskers on kittens' were ever her favourite things.

She offered me a chair and a coffee and said she had inherited a five-minute party political broadcast that was to have been given by Mr Heath and she understood that I helped with these broadcasts, was that right? 'Helped' was an understatement, but I nodded. Well now, would I consider doing this one for her? I explained that my play was opening in a few days' time and I was completely taken up with final rehearsals. She said she understood but that the broadcast only required a five-minute text. Couldn't I find time to squeeze it in?

I pointed out that a five-minute text took rather more than five minutes to write and in any case I'd no idea what she wanted to say. 'Just set out my stall in general terms. There won't be any time for more than that. My politics aren't quite the same as Mr Heath's, you know.' Yes, I did know that. I also knew that as well as strong views she had a sense of mission and people with missions could be difficult to work with.

'Well?'

Assuming I could find the time, exactly when did she want it?

Could I manage a draft by tomorrow morning, say about eleven? This really was rather tiresome. Reluctantly I said I would see what I could do.

'Thank you. Till tomorrow, then.'

A polite smile, which I returned. There had been no instant meeting of minds, rather on my part, a feeling of irritation at being diverted from something more important to me, if not to the charismatic new leader of the Conservative Party. I too could be stubborn on occasion. I really shouldn't have agreed so easily. I hurried away from the Palace of Westminster and sat at the back of the stalls in the Haymarket, my eyes on the stage and the actors and my mind concentrated nine-tenths on the play. During the lunch break I scribbled a few thoughts in my Rymans notebook but couldn't think of an ending. If stuck, 'go for a quote' is a cliché but it's not a bad fall-back position. I managed to remember some lines from a speech attributed to Abraham Lincoln, his most memorable after Gettysburg, which I had learned once for an audition.

Next morning at eleven I returned to the new leader's office. 'May I have it?' she held out her hand. On a sudden impulse I said, 'May I read it to you?' She seemed surprised but indicated a chair some way from her across the room. Then she sat down and half covered her eyes with her left hand. Was the light troubling her or did she fear the worst? 'It helps me concentrate,' she said. 'Go ahead. I'm listening.'

When I had done there was a total silence. I thought, well, that went down like a sack of potatoes. I'm off the hook. Glory hallelujah! But then she took her hand from her eyes and reached into one of these large holdalls in which nowadays women carry everything but the microwave. From this receptacle she produced a handbag. Out of the handbag came a wallet and from the wallet a piece of yellowing newsprint. All this was done very slowly and methodically without a word being uttered. Finally she got up and came across the room to me and handed me the piece of newsprint. 'It goes wherever I go,' she said. It was the Lincoln quotation.

There are moments in life when something goes 'click' in what one assumes to be the brain and you find yourself without warning on the same wavelength with a total stranger. This appeared to be just such a moment. I started to explain that I'd turned to Lincoln because I hadn't really had time for a peroration; my mind had been up there on stage with the actors. She said: 'If that's what you can do when you're not really trying, what will it be like when you are?' And this time the smile was more than polite. It was a dazzler.

Lord Howe
Cabinet Minister 1979–90

Geoffrey Howe was Margaret Thatcher's first Chancellor of the Exchequer and held the post from 1979 to 1983. He went on to become Foreign Secretary from 1983 to 1989 and Deputy Prime Minister from 1989 to 1990. His resignation in 1990 over European policy and his savage speech in the House of Commons were key factors in Margaret Thatcher's eventual downfall. These reminiscences are drawn from Lord Howe's memoirs, Conflict of Loyalty.

Arthur Seldon sought my view of Margaret Thatcher as a possible target for the Institute of Economic Affairs. My response was cautiously encouraging: 'I am not at all sure about Margaret. Many of her economic prejudices are certainly sound. But she is inclined to be rather too dogmatic for my liking on sensitive issues like education and might actually retard the cause by over-simplification. We should certainly be able to hope for something better from her – but I suspect that she will need to be exposed to the humanising side of your character as much as to the pure welfare-market-monger. There is much scope for her to be influenced between triumph and disaster.'

February 1975
Two days after her election as leader of the party, Margaret Thatcher came to address the regular Thursday meeting of the 1922 Committee. The room was packed. Unusually, shadow Cabinet members were present as well. The new leader, escorted by the Chairman, Edward du Cann, entered the committee room through the door opening onto the platform. She was flanked only by the all-male officers of the committee. Suddenly she looked very beautiful – and very frail, as the half-dozen knights of the shires towered over her. It was a moving, almost feudal, occasion. Tears came to my eyes. The Conservative Party had elected its first woman leader. And this overwhelmingly male gathering dedicated themselves enthusiastically to the service of this remarkable woman. By her almost reckless courage she had

won their support, if not yet their hearts. A new bond of loyalty had
been forged.

June 1979: Tokyo

The real star of the summit was Margaret Thatcher, making her first
appearance on the world stage as Prime Minister. In those days it
was still the custom for each head of government to make a separate closing statement to the final press conference – a fearful recipe
for competitive tedium. As the newest member, Margaret was the
last head to perform. The 'press corps' assembled at the new Otani
Hotel contained a startlingly large clutch of Japanese women – some
journalists, no doubt, but many more diplomatic and political wives,
secretaries and the like, all fired with curiosity by this female phenomenon. Margaret did not disappoint them. Speaking without a note
(but far from extempore) she sparkled alongside the soberly scripted
statesmen who had gone before. For the first time I realised just how
powerful an international champion Britain now had.

Spring 1982

One colleague had concluded that: 'The way in which Margaret oper-
ates, the way her time is consumed, the lack of a methodical mode of
working and of orderly discussion and communication on key issues
with other colleagues, mean that our chance of implementing a carefully worked out strategy is very low indeed...' There never was any
real improvement in Margaret's working methods of the kind that he
would have liked. Yet the important agenda items were being tackled,
albeit in a less systematic way than he or I might have wished. This
was happening, above all, as a result of Margaret's input, authority
and, sometimes, judgement. The difference from our more analytical
approach was that her influence was deployed much more opportunis-
tically and instinctively than we should have planned. But throughout
Whitehall and Westminster her instinct, her thinking, her authority,
was almost always present, making itself felt pervasively, tenaciously
and effectively. It came gradually to feel, as the months went by, as
though the Prime Minister was present, unseen and unspeaking, at
almost every meeting. The questions were always being asked, even if
unspoken: how will this play at No. 10? What's the best way of getting
the Prime Minister on side for that? And so on.

May 1983: Williamsburg Summit
Ronald Reagan was a splendidly natural host, with a straightforward and engaging tenacity on points that mattered. There was a sponta-neity about his mutually supportive attitude towards Margaret. She likewise blossomed with admiring, almost affectionate, directness towards him. It was for both of them a personally satisfying and politi-cally supportive relationship.

September 1983: Foreign Policy Seminar at Chequers
I explained to Margaret that her own unique relationship with President Reagan, and her standing in Europe and elsewhere, could give Britain a voice in the Alliance which it badly needed at a time when the Soviet campaign against our deployment of intermediate range nuclear forces was obviously entering its peak period. 'One notable success,' said one official, 'had been to convince the PM that there was very little scope for destabilising the Soviet Union or Eastern Europe.' This important advance in understanding was probably to prove crucial to the successful outcome of Margaret's first encounter, still more than twelve months ahead, with Mikhail Gorbachev. The force with which Margaret later expounded this and argued the case for dialogue with Moscow was no less crucial in turning President Reagan away from the 'evil empire' rhetoric and encouraging him towards a similar relationship with Gorbachev. I sometimes think this may be seen by historians as her greatest achievement in foreign affairs.

March 1985: Funeral of General Secretary Chernenko
The style of Margaret's second meeting with Mikhail Gorbachev, late-evening at the Kremlin, was to the point and friendly. Scheduled for only fifteen minutes, we were there for almost an hour. Margaret enthused over Gorbachev's recent London visit ('one of the most successful ever'). 'We must,' replied Gorbachev, 'continue to meet and talk to one another.' 'People in Britain,' concluded Margaret, 'took great pleasure in Gorbachev's appointment and would be pleased to see Gromyko in London.' Gorbachev chuckled. 'Mr Gromyko,' he said, 'is waiting for the London fog to clear.' Certainly the two leaders were attracted to each other, relished each other's company. But neither Margaret nor Mikhail ever completely lowered their guard.

February 1984

It was her unflattering perception of union loyalty that caused Len Murray and his colleagues such distress. For them the charge of disloyalty to the crown, which Margaret implied was a consequence of union membership, was equivalent to a charge of treason. It was that insult, as they saw it, which made them angry. But this was a case where Margaret was at the end driven by her 'all or nothing' absolutist instinct. She could not find room in her thinking for acceptance of the parallel legitimacy of someone else's loyalty. It was probably the clearest example I had seen so far of one of Margaret's most tragic failings: an inability to appreciate, still less accommodate, somebody else's patriotism. A great patriot herself, with an enormous instinctive loyalty, she found it hard to respect or sympathise with the sense of loyalty of others, or even with the idea of a wider or different loyalty for herself. Even Welshness, I sometimes felt, she regarded as somehow beyond some unspoken pale – still more Irishness. A citizen, she seemed to feel, could never safely be allowed to carry more than one card in his or her pocket, and at GCHQ that could only be Her Majesty's card.

October 1985: Commonwealth Heads of Governments, Nassau

Before the world's television cameras, Margaret set out to present not the successful achievement of a concerted Commonwealth policy for change in South Africa but only the triumphant insignificance of the concessions *she* had had to make to achieve it. With forefinger and thumb only a few millimetres apart and contemptuously presented to the cameras, Margaret proclaimed that she had moved only 'a tiny little bit'. With four little words she had at one and the same time humiliated three dozen other heads of government, devalued the policy on which they had just agreed – and demeaned herself. She had certainly ensured that things would be a good deal less easy at any future such meeting. Even I could scarcely believe my eyes.

March 1987: Russia

It was marvellous to behold the impact which Margaret herself had on ordinary Russians whose path she happened to cross. The three Soviet television journalists, who interviewed her for the long, uncensored interview which they broadcast, had never encountered anything like the whirlwind that swept them aside. The nationwide television audience loved it. This was indeed reflected in the reaction of Russians in the streets of Moscow and, even more, of Georgians in the streets of Tbilisi. When Margaret decided, as she did on more than one occasion, to make an unconventional exit from her Zil limousine to greet passing pedestrians, she was instantly overwhelmed by enthusiastic recognition and acclaim. 'Her driving personality,' said the *Mail on Sunday*, 'puts her head and shoulders above anyone else on the world stage.'

September 1988

I was driven finally to conclude that for Margaret the Bruges speech represented, subconsciously at least, her escape from the collective responsibility of her days in the Heath Cabinet – when European policy had arrived, as it were, with the rations. Margaret had waited almost fifteen years to display her own distaste for the policies which she had accepted as a member of that government. I began to see her – and I do so even more clearly now – as a natural member of the gallant but misguided backbench group of Enoch Powells, Robin Turtons and Derek Walker-Smiths, who had fought so long and hard against the European Communities Bill in 1971. Yet her deeds from day to day generally continued to belie that analysis. For she went on acting, for the moment at least, as though she was indeed the Prime Minister of a Member State of the European Community. And we had to continue conducting business on that basis. It was, I imagined, a little like being married to a clergyman who had suddenly proclaimed his disbelief in God. I can see now that this was probably the moment at which there began to crystallise the conflict of loyalty, with which I was to 'struggle for perhaps too long'.

Conclusion

And so came the years of triumph that ended in tragedy. Margaret Thatcher's eleven years as Prime Minister still stand as a period of remarkable achievement, albeit marred by decisive errors in her final term in office. She was beyond argument a great Prime Minister. Her tragedy is that she may be remembered less for the brilliance of her many achievements than for the recklessness with which she later sought to impose her own increasingly uncompromising views. For Margaret Thatcher in her final years, there was no distinction to be drawn between person, government, party and nation. They merged in her mind as one seamless whole. Her interests were axiomatically those of Britain. Any criticism of her was an unpatriotic act. The insistence on the undivided sovereignty of her own opinion dressed up as the nation's sovereignty was her own undoing.

Lord Crickhowell
Secretary of State for Wales 1979–87

*Nicholas Edwards served in Margaret Thatcher's Cabinet as Secretary of State
for Wales from 1979 until 1987 when he was raised to the peerage. He became
Chairman of the National Rivers Authority in 1989, a position he held until 1996.
The following piece is a shortened version of an essay about Margaret Thatcher
and the work of the Cabinet in his book,* Westminster, Wales and Water.

Meeting in the Prime Minister's room in the House of Commons,
we were discussing education policy. Keith Joseph, who she liked
and admired and to whom she owed an immense debt of gratitude,
but who she sometimes treated badly, was interrupted with increasing
frequency as he attempted to present his case. At first these astringent
interjections came every few sentences and then with the staccato bark
of an automatic weapon they ripped every sentence into increasingly
minute fragments. Most of us examined our papers in silence with
increasing irritation and embarrassment; but Nigel Lawson, deciding
that enough was enough, suddenly leant across the table and snapped,
'Shut up, Prime Minister, just occasionally let someone get a word in
edgeways.' There was a stunned silence: we all looked up waiting to
see what would happen. For the first and last time I saw Margaret
Thatcher blush and then for twenty minutes she was silent, and during
this extraordinary lull Keith presented his paper and we went on to
have one of the most constructive discussions that I ever remember in
a Cabinet committee chaired by the Prime Minister. I don't remember
any other occasion when a Cabinet colleague was quite so blunt but
it is nonetheless a myth that we were all always supine and subservient. The techniques for standing up to the Prime Minister's extremely
combative conduct of business varied but they were more effective
than has been generally acknowledged. In reality she seldom behaved
quite so badly as on that occasion with Keith Joseph and there is much
to be said for the technique of testing the strength of a case by vigorous argument, though there were a few members of the Cabinet who
found it unendurable.

Margaret Thatcher loved an argument and respected those who stood up to her when they had command of their subject. She invited contributions from around the table, sometimes from those of us who would have preferred at that particular moment to stay silent. The system of testing a case to destruction had the great advantage that it frequently exposed a flaw and prevented a disaster; the drawback was that it sometimes destroyed perfectly good policy and prevented it being pressed further. As time went on, the runners in the race also found that the challenge had been made more severe by the simple manoeuvre of packing the committees with hostile critics. After the industry committee had produced a series of decisions and recommendations with which the Prime Minister disagreed, she regained control by assuming the chair herself. Committees that were not considered sufficiently robust found that the membership was changed, or decisions were taken by ad hoc groups of ministers, frequently without the circulation of papers or adequate interdepartmental consultation. There was nothing very new in this but the Prime Minister carried the process further than most of her predecessors. Despite these manoeuvres there were frequent occasions when the Prime Minister did not get her way and when she accepted, sometimes with visible irritation, the majority decision.

She always came to the table impeccably well briefed. The Treasury commentary would be to hand; she would have underlined key passages in the papers before her with a yellow marking pen; her extraordinary memory provided a further challenge. On occasions she positively overwhelmed the opposition. This was always relatively easy if the unfortunate minister's colleagues simply did not believe that this was a policy for which they were prepared to fight and risk injury or worse. For most ministers the injury they feared most was the loss of some treasured policy of their own: if your own paper was next on the agenda, you would not prejudice its progress by stirring up advance hostility. Having said that, it is also true that in the great majority of cases when the minister sought approval for a policy he considered important and was prepared to fight, he would get his way, although sometimes it did not feel like it at the time.

An account that concentrates on arguments round the Cabinet table inevitably gives a partial and distorted picture of the Prime Minister's character and conduct. The aggressive and dominating characteristics which she used to such effect in Cabinet discussions were frequently matched by acts of great personal kindness. She always seemed to know a great deal about her colleagues and their troubles, and a Member of Parliament would be surprised to be stopped in a corridor with an inquiry about a recent sickness or a family problem. It was because of actions of that kind that she was so much loved by her staff at Chequers and No. 10, and by all those who worked closely with her.

She paid numerous visits to Wales and for nearly eight years gave me all the support I could have wished, even though my instruments were government agencies and regional policies that she did not much favour. As in so many other cases, she was more pragmatic and flexible in achieving her objectives than many of her critics have understood or acknowledged. She seemed most at home with the people of Wales in the period before tight security restricted her movements and cut her off from contact with ordinary people. On the last Christmas in opposition before she became Prime Minister, we arrived in Wrexham late one evening when the streets were packed with shoppers. She went from stall to stall in the market buying groceries and talking to stall-holders and customers and then we emerged into the main street just at the moment that a huge float bearing Father Christmas appeared round the corner. The crowd surged forward and in a moment of inspiration, and perhaps because there was almost nowhere else to go, we pulled her up onto the float beside Father Christmas and there through the packed crowd they travelled together to a surging, warm, enthusiastic welcome that was unique in all my experience of politi-cal life. During the last election campaign in which I took part in the summer of 1987, things were very different – every move was carefully scheduled. Security was tight, contact with crowds was minimal. I took her down to Cardiff Bay and, as we drove away, a small but noisy group booed and one man raised his fingers in an obscene gesture. The Prime Minister visibly froze, obviously offended, and turned to me saying, 'Oh what dreadful people, we are really wasting our time – what is the point of all your efforts if they appreciate them so little.' One felt that she was not at her best and this was alien territory, far from the England that she knew and understood. In a way it was the Scottish story all over again. Her efforts to help were not rewarded; the support that she gave for her Secretaries of State was not appreci-ated; there was a barrier that somehow she was not able to surmount.

My formal responsibilities as Secretary of State finally came to an end on election day and that weekend, as I sat in my Welsh home with Ann, I was surprised to receive a telephone call from No. 10.

'The Prime Minister would like to speak to you.' There were a few words said about the way that the election had gone, sadness at seats that had been lost, and then she said, 'I have decided to appoint a very senior member of my Cabinet as Secretary of State for Wales.' 'Oh, yes, Prime Minister,' I said, 'And who is that?'

'Oh, I can't tell you,' she replied, 'Because I have not yet told him.'

'In that case I cannot really comment,' I responded.

By this time Ann was in a fever of excitement, all agog to know who it was to be – we had been speculating long and hard. 'Well I will tell you if you promise not to tell anyone,' she said.

'Of course,' I replied.

'I have decided to ask Peter Walker to take on the job,' she told me.

'Peter Walker,' I repeated clearly, at least in part for Ann's benefit, 'I am sure he will do it excellently, what a brilliant idea.'

After she had rung off, I wondered why she had telephoned. It cannot be that if my reaction had been hostile she would have changed her mind. In any event I was rather touched and I appreciated the fact that she had taken the trouble to tell me, particularly as Peter Walker was apparently still totally ignorant of his fate.

'Will he accept it?' said Ann doubtfully. 'Oh, yes, I am sure he will,' I said. 'After all, he knows the difference between being in and out, and in the circumstances he will have an almost free hand to do anything he likes.'

Baroness Trumpington
Conservative Peer

Raised to the peerage in 1980, Jean Trumpington served as a junior minister from 1985 until 1992. Initially a Parliamentary Under Secretary of State at the Department of Health and Social Security, she took up the same position at the Ministry of Agriculture, becoming the Minister of State for that department in 1989.

I owe Margaret Thatcher everything since she made me a life peer in her first honours list as Prime Minister. That was a huge surprise and I shall never cease to be grateful to her.

Having said that I am and always shall be terrified of her.

I well remember the first occasion I attended a full Cabinet meeting in the place of John MacGregor. I was a brand new MAFF [Ministry of Agriculture, Forestry and Fisheries] minister and I had been instructed to press for a particular professor to be appointed for a job. My only briefing was given at the last moment and consisted of the bare words that the Department for Education agreed with this appointment.

When it appeared that my great moment had arrived all I could do was to repeat the above words, several times, with less and less conviction.

Feeling a total prat and surrounded by the great and the good I subsided in much sweat.

As the Prime Minister left the Cabinet room she patted me affectionately on the shoulder and said 'Don't worry dear, we will see your professor gets the job.'

The reason I think I am so frightened of her is because I never feel I can say the sort of thing I would say to my women friends, but always feel I have to ask her something meaningful about the state of the world. I am sure it's my fault, and I have never been afraid of sticking to my guns when I felt deeply over any issue. She never held that against me.

I was so lucky to have worked for her and with her, and fought with her. The fighting was part of the process. She liked to have something to fight against. It gave her ideas and helped her make up her mind later. I remember a poor man who sat between us at a dinner. I said, 'The *Daily Mirror* is quite right about the mentally handicapped.' She said, 'The *Daily Mirror* is never right.' That started us off. I think the poor man thought we were going to hit each other, and probably him, in the middle of the dinner. That was the way it was.

It was either death to the end or eternal friendship – and I know which I would choose. I send my very warmest sympathy to her family and say what a great loss it is to me personally and to all her friends and admirers, wherever they are.

She was a beautiful woman. It took a French President to appreciate that, even if his remark had a twist – but that is typically French.

Frank Field
Labour MP 1979–

Frank Field was Minister for Welfare Reform in Tony Blair's first administration. He is the author of several books, including Neighbours From Hell – The Politics of Behaviour, *and has held the seat of Birkenhead since 1979.*

David Sheppard was a left-wing Bishop of Liverpool, who was much admired and also loved. In one volume of his autobiography, he recalls his meetings with Mrs Thatcher – or, rather, the lead-up to those meetings. He recalls the state he would be in – the feeling of illness as the dreaded hour approached. On one occasion, I asked her, a year before she would appoint a new Archbishop, whether she would appoint David Sheppard if his name was one of the two on the list that came to her from the royal commission. Her reply was immediate: 'Yes, of course.' I was slightly staggered by that response, so I asked why. She said, 'He always tells me to my face what he thinks and we always have a good argument.' It therefore seems proper that in the tributes we pay to this extraordinary person we should follow her example and not be frightened of argument or even of division – we mock her if we are frightened of that.

Mrs Thatcher was not uncritical of her own record. On one occasion I asked her, 'Mrs T., what was your greatest disappointment in government?' Again, as though she had thought long and hard beforehand about it, she said, 'I cut taxes and I thought we would get a giving society, and we haven't.' She thought we would, by low taxation, see that extraordinary culture in America whereby people make fortunes and want, perhaps publicly, to declare what they are doing with them. That had not taken root here.

She was also brilliant on detail, and that was part of her power in Whitehall. I once had to see her to discuss a defence order for Cammell Laird. Indeed, my relationship with her began after the second meeting I had as MP for Birkenhead, when the shop stewards said, 'Cut out all this old stuff. We want a cross-party group and we want you to lead it. We want all the parties in the Wirral lobbying for orders.' That was the beginning of my friendship with her.

Our discussion took place the day she returned from a meeting with President Bush to decide on the first Gulf War. She had every reason to cancel it, but the meeting took place in her study. I had never seen her in such a state. She was marching around the study saying, 'You've no idea what a struggle it is putting backbone into him.' I said, 'Prime Minister, come and sit next to me because I have some things I would like to discuss with you.' She kept talking about putting backbone into the American President in order to fight this great war. Finally, she took pity on me and asked, 'What do you want?' I made the plea for the defence order and she said, 'Fine. Anything else?' When I said no, she immediately got up and continued, 'You've no idea the victory I've had today over this.' I was really rather excited to be this very small footnote in history.

Of course, courtesy dictated that whichever of the Wirral MPs had lobbied her would tell the others, but in my excitement I forgot to do so. About thirty-six hours later I saw David Hunt walking down the corridor and I remembered, so I began apologising. He said, 'There's no need to apologise, Frank. The relevant Secretaries of State have received a prime-ministerial minute and it has been copied to their permanent secretaries.' There was a Prime Minister who was making history, for right or wrong – for right, I think – and who was extraordinarily wound up by the events that she had managed to bring about, and she had no staff with her, but before she went to bed that night she wrote that minute to implement what she had agreed. She was wonderful to lobby, because I knew within seconds whether she would do something or whether she thought it was a barmy idea, in which case there was no point discussing it further.

Let me make one last point. Towards the end of her time as Prime Minister, Mrs Thatcher was captured by a court on the government benches whose members made it difficult not only for many government backbenchers but particularly for someone such as me to see her. I wrote to the court and said that if they continued to block my chance of talking to her and lobbying her, I would kidnap her and tell her what they were doing – and would also lobby her. I got a note back late in the debate saying that the Prime Minister would see me at ten o'clock. This is a good lesson for the Prime Minister and the Leader of the Opposition. She had a hugely impressive voting record. In my experience, she was one of the last out of the lobby and she was there for people to talk to – rather than going in, out and away to do what was thought to be more important business.

As she passed by, I said to her, 'Prime Minister, should I follow you?' She said, 'People do.' As there was no mirror in front of her, I have never worked out whether she was smiling. I hope she was. Following her is a challenge to us. Do we see her record as though it had been brought down from Mount Sinai on tablets of stone or would she have recognised, as I have hinted in the few conversations I have had on this specific point, that there is now a new agenda and that whatever principles one has must be applied to it?

What mattered were ideas and whether one could defend one's corner. I mourn her passing.

Baroness Fookes
Deputy Speaker of the House of Commons 1992–97

Janet Fookes served as the Member for Merton and Morden from 1970 until 1974 and for Plymouth Drake from 1974 until 1997. She became a Dame of the British Empire in 1989 and was raised to the peerage as Baroness Fookes of Plymouth in 1997.

More years ago than I now care to remember, I was confiding my own political ambitions to my boyfriend of the time, a dental surgeon. He rather poured cold water on the idea saying that his father, who was a leading Conservative agent, had seen a very able young woman turned down by the selection committee in his constituency and both father and son thought that women were never going to get very far in politics. The able young woman concerned was none other than Margaret Thatcher. I was therefore delighted when she finally obtained her seat in Finchley and soon after her election came down to speak in my own constituency. Although I heard her speak many times thereafter, this first one will always remain in my mind as typical of her single-minded energy in pressing a point home. The theme on this occasion was that 'politics is the art of the possible'.

Lord Lamont
Chancellor of the Exchequer 1990–93

The MP for Kingston-upon-Thames from 1972 until 1997, Norman Lamont served as a junior minister in the Department of Energy, the Department of Trade and Industry, the Ministry of Defence and the Treasury between 1979 and 1989. In 1989 he became Chief Secretary to the Treasury in Margaret Thatcher's Cabinet and in 1990 he became Chancellor of the Exchequer, a position he held until 1993. He was raised to the peerage as Lord Lamont of Lerwick in 1997.

Margaret Thatcher was one of the greatest ever peacetime Prime Ministers. I was very happy to be in her government for all eleven years. But Margaret Thatcher was generally thought to be a somewhat fearsome colleague and demanding Prime Minister. However, she liked people to stand up to her and whatever her manner she respected those who put a good case against her. It was important also not to take everything she said literally.

She could sometimes be very unpredictable in meetings. I remember one occasion when she had been on a plane coming back from the United States. She sat next to the head of MGM – 'More Gutsy Movies' – a man called Lew Wasserman, who was the chief executive. Somehow on that journey he persuaded her that her crowning glory as Prime Minister would be the state financing of film studios in Rainham Marshes in Essex. I was Chief Secretary to the Treasury at the time and this was revealed to me. I expressed some bewilderment and astonishment at this proposal and said to her, 'But I thought we believed in controlling expenditure.' I received a glare. I said, 'I thought we believed in low taxes. I thought we didn't believe in subsidies to inefficient industries.' I got more and more desperate and said, 'Prime Minister, there's no unemployment in Essex. We would have to build the roads in order to get to Rainham Marshes.' I remember her glowering at me very fiercely and in desperation I said, 'You do know, Prime Minister, that we'll have all the environmentalists against us because there's a very rare bird' – I knew about these things – 'called the Brent goose that breeds there.' She looked at me and said,

'You are utterly hopeless. All you ever say is "No, no, no". You do not have a constructive idea in your head. If you had been in my government since 1979, I would have achieved nothing.' I said, 'Well, Prime Minister, you're always right about everything but there's one thing you're wrong about. I've been in your government since 1979!'

I went back to the department and said, 'The Prime Minister's made a very strange decision but we must get on with it.' A few hours later, a call came through saying that she did not wish to pursue the matter. I saw her the next day, beaming. She congratulated me on something but there was no reference whatever to that matter.

It was often the case that if one put objections to her they might be overruled at the time but nonetheless they were absorbed. Contrary to what critics said she both listened and was flexible.

One thing that Margaret always did when there were factory closures in a constituency was to agree to see the local MP. I know that she had innumerable meetings with Labour MPs representing some constituencies because there were frequent closures. Some very improbable and unlikely friendships were struck up between Margaret and people who opposed her and her policies on the floor of the House.

Another characteristic of Margaret Thatcher was that she was always extremely thoughtful about all those who worked for her. She really did mind about them and their families. I was once told by the manager of Smythson, the stationers in Bond Street, that their largest buyer of notelets was Mrs Thatcher. Certainly she was very adept at sending little handwritten notes commiserating with people or congratulating them on this or that. I have several such notes from her. I am quite sure that Mrs Thatcher has carried out many private acts of kindness that are unknown to the wider world because she simply has not told anyone about them and only the individuals know.

She was extremely loyal to people. I always remember when one of her PPSs, Fergus Montgomery, was accused of shoplifting. It was all over the *Evening Standard*. What was the first thing she did? She took him into the tearoom and went around the House of Commons with him, showing that she thoroughly supported him. Of course, the charges were all subsequently dropped.

Mrs Thatcher had a very strong sense of the need to honour one's obligations. One year my Conservative Association in Kingston decided to ask the Prime Minister's husband, Denis, to speak at a function which was being held in the Banqueting Suite at Twickenham Rugby Ground. On the Saturday afternoon I was sitting at home reading a newspaper in an armchair when the telephone rang and a voice said, 'The Prime Minister for you.' Mrs Thatcher then came on the line and said 'Denis has strained his back and can't be with you tonight at Kingston.'

I replied 'Well, Prime Minister thank you very much for ringing, it is very good of you to tell me and I know everybody will understand.'

The PM went on, 'No no, you don't understand what I'm saying. I'm coming instead.'

I replied, 'Prime Minister that is extremely kind of you but it isn't really necessary because everybody will understand that Denis is not at all well.' I was rather worried as I didn't think it was a grand enough occasion for a Prime Minister. Some people would be annoyed they didn't know she was coming. I was also concerned about the short time available to lay on the necessary security and all the other complications that would follow from an unexpected visit by the PM. But Margaret was insistent. 'We always keep our promises, and I am coming,' she said. She did. She stood in for Denis at the dinner and of course the evening was a huge success.

I remember once helping her to host a party in Downing Street. I do not remember quite what it was for but after it was all over she invited the waiters who had been pouring the wine to sit down with her on the sofas and chairs. She poured them all a glass of wine and carried on chatting to them, discussing the party.

It was sometimes said that she was compassionate and concerned about drivers, secretaries and doorkeepers but not at all about ministers. That is not true, although on one occasion I protested to Keith Joseph about how she had handled a particular colleague during a meeting. He looked at me in utter astonishment and said, 'Oh really? You know her method. She deals in destructive dialogue.' Then he said, 'She gives me the lash. They send a stretcher for me.'

I remember hearing of a meeting at which Ferdy Mount in the Policy Unit was present, an important Cabinet subcommittee. He had a terrible cold and kept coughing. Margaret said to him, 'You've got to do something about that cough. What you need is this.' She named a particular medicine. He said, 'No, no, no, no.' She said, 'Just a minute', and disappeared out of that important meeting, went upstairs for about ten minutes and came back with a whole packet of capsules which she then insisted that he took there and then. Of course, colleagues were thoroughly annoyed that that very important meeting had been disrupted, but she was so informal in that way.

Dealing with Margaret Thatcher was always unpredictable. She used to say, 'Thatcher's law is that the unexpected always happens,' and she made sure that that was the case. She was a wonderful person – someone whose name will, as I said, always be synonymous with courage. She was a person who always did things for the right reasons. It was a huge privilege to have known her and an even greater privilege to have been in her government.

Olga Polizzi
Designer

Olga Polizzi is a well-known designer. She redecorated Downing Street in 1988 at the request of Lady Thatcher and is a main board director of Rocco Forte Hotels.

In 1988, just after her third election victory, Mrs Thatcher asked me to help her redecorate some of the public rooms in Downing Street.

At the time I was Design Director for Forte plc, the hotel company founded by my father, Lord Forte, a great admirer of Britain's first woman Prime Minister. It was Alistair McAlpine, the treasurer of the Conservative Party and a great friend of hers, who suggested I could do the job. I had met her before at various dinners that the McAlpines gave and at conferences in the early 1980s. I was young, and very much in awe of her.

As the testimonies from left, right and centre in Parliament last Wednesday showed, few people were not impressed by her vision and passion. Getting to know her, I was equally struck by her politeness and kindness.

The day before I had my first appointment with her at No. 10, I stayed up most of the night with a colleague, sorting materials and schemes for the rooms. Frugal as ever, she had given us a very small budget for the work.

The next day we nervously presented the schemes to her. She did not like any of them. In one of the large drawing rooms, she envisaged flowered curtains, which we thought would clash horribly with a beautiful multicoloured Ziegler rug already there. I gently tried telling her so. My colleague was less gentle and told the PM that such curtains would be inappropriate.

'Don't you think so, dear? All right.'

We settled on plain silk curtains but then had a disagreement on the treatment of the windows. I suggested that the very tall eighteenth-century windows needed pelmets and quite an elaborate curtain design. She was dead against pelmets, but when I insisted that they would be the correct style, she acquiesced but said, 'Perhaps we could put a strip of brown paper on the top of the pelmets. Then two or three times a year, we could remove the paper and the dust that has gathered on top.'

And so we did.

She wanted bright colours and bright lights – too bright, I thought, though now that I am getting older and have poorer sight, I understand why. She chose a cheerful yellow for the staircase lined with the photographs of all the former Prime Ministers. That colour is still there. She wanted English paintings for the house, but the government art collection was almost spitefully difficult about providing fine works. I still wonder why, as Downing Street should be a showcase for British art.

Working with her made me realise how adored she was by all the staff, from doormen to secretaries to cleaners. When two men delivered a sofa, after first bouncing up and down to make sure it was comfortable, she offered to make them a cup of tea herself. The idea that she was cold and unfeeling has always struck me as ludicrous. There is the famous picture of her leaving Downing Street for the last time in tears. But what the picture did not show was the throng of Downing Street staff almost all weeping as they said goodbye to her. No wonder she was moved to tears.

I was always prejudiced in her favour because my father adored her and she respected him because he had come from Italy to Britain with nothing and built up a substantial business. And they shared a huge love of Britain. 'There's no other country in the world better to live in,' my father used to say.

He had been a great supporter of Hugh Gaitskell but, like many others, he was horrified by what had happened to Britain under Labour in the 1970s. After Mrs T. began her reforms, he described her as 'an angel sent by God to save Britain in its hour of need'.

She was clearly comfortable with men, and did not always find it easy to talk to women, but I didn't mind; I always thought that the fact a woman had risen to the top in the patriarchal 1970s Britain was a huge encouragement to other women to strive for the top. Far more irritating was how self-important men continued to condescend to her.

She could go from discussing an international crisis on the telephone with President Reagan to comforting a secretary whose mother had died with equal understanding and commitment. At Christmas at Chequers, her beloved jewel in the English countryside, she always let the staff go off after lunch, and she and her guests served a cold-cuts dinner themselves. One Christmas, someone gave her a large pot of caviar that all her guests tucked into. But when its price was mentioned, she quickly put on the lid and said to Romilly McAlpine, 'We had better put it back in the fridge, dear.'

After her fall from power, she came to dinner at my house just before Christmas; she was on very good form, considering. She took a fancy to the rather pretty crackers on the table and when Denis was about to pull one, she called across the table, 'Stop Denis, we are taking it home!' Denis pulled it anyway but other guests gave her theirs – she left carrying half a dozen crackers for her own Christmas table.

I consider myself lucky for having known a woman that I both liked and admired as much as I did Margaret Thatcher. As David Cameron said, she rescued our country. Of course that involved painful decisions, but don't let anyone ever say she did not care.

She was a true Christian, moral and kind. Her ambition was always to be PM in order to change Britain for the better, but she was aware how difficult it was. Britain's problems then were huge – as they are again today. Margaret Thatcher cared more than any other politician I have ever known about the everyday lives of people and their difficulties.

As she famously put it, she was determined that the state should be the servant of the people, not its master. Britain has changed in almost every way for the better as a consequence of her governance.

Andrew Mitchell
Conservative MP 1987–97 and 2001–

Andrew Mitchell served as PPS to William Waldegrave and John Wakeham in the Thatcher administration. Under John Major's government he held the position of Government Whip, Vice-Chairman of the Conservative Party and Parliamentary Under Secretary of State at the Department of Social Security. He was Secretary of State for International Development in David Cameron's administration from 2010 to 2012.

I was first introduced to Margaret Thatcher by a much-loved family friend, Ian Gow MP. It was just before the 1987 general election when my father, David Mitchell MP, a staunch supporter of Mrs Thatcher from the early days, and I were both standing for Parliament.

Conservative MPs and candidates had assembled at the QEII Centre, the other side of Parliament Square, for a pep talk by the Prime Minister as the campaign that would see her third historic victory got underway. I remember she told us, 'We shall remain cool, calm and elected.'

'This,' said Ian Gow, 'is David's boy and he is standing in Gedling. They will be the only father and son team for many years to serve together in the House of Commons.' I stuttered a few words when she asked why I was not following my father into the family wine business! I remember she said how important family businesses are to the lifeblood of the economy. She wished me well and said she looked forward to seeing me on the government benches after the election.

Once elected I would see her occasionally, usually bustling down the long corridors of the Commons. As she approached, always surrounded by a retinue, I would stand stiffly to attention receiving a smile as she passed. She would often come into the tearoom in those days (she did so much less as time passed which was, perhaps, a mistake) and a colleague would fetch her a cup of tea while those of us at the table at which she had alighted would sit in terror as she enquired about our views on the latest money supply figures or a just published report which she naturally presumed we had spent the previous night reading. She was always careful to find a suitable resting place for her handbag – which seemed to be a bottomless repository for important information of every possible kind.

The one occasion which I will never forget occurred on the night of 21 December 1988. Patrick McLoughlin and I (we both had significant constituency mining interests) had become immensely concerned about the government's treatment of the Union of Democratic Mineworkers (UDM). These brave men had continued working during the mining strike which had taken place during the previous Parliament – often at great personal risk and with considerable bravery – while the militant NUM (National Union of Mineworkers) had been striking with the clear intention of destroying the elected government. The UDM had literally kept the lights on by courageously crossing picket lines and continuing to work.

The mining industry was inevitably slimming down and Patrick and I were concerned that the UDM should be supported and wherever possible their pits kept open. I had raised this issue with Mark Lennox-Boyd, her PPS, and very much to my surprise the Prime Minister had not only agreed to meet us but had summoned us both to dine with her in the House of Commons Members' dining room.

As dinner started Patrick and I managed to get a few sentences out before she spoke. She did not draw breath for quite a while! Our food remained uneaten. She quizzed us on what was happening in the Nottinghamshire and Derbyshire coalfields. Patrick's knowledge as a former miner impressed her. As a regular visitor to the Gedling pit (where Dennis Skinner's brother, whom I met several times underground, worked) I reported on what my mining constituents were saying.

Just at the moment where we had got her attention and some hard-won support, her agitated PPS appeared at the table. Reports were coming in of a bomb exploding in an aeroplane over Lockerbie. Mrs Thatcher immediately asked a series of questions, set up emergency meetings and said she would go to Scotland at dawn the next morning. I remember being particularly struck by her saying 'this awful tragedy has taken place in Hector's seat [Hector Munro was the local MP]. Find him now and brief him and make sure he comes with me on the plane tomorrow morning.'

For months after, on the rare occasions when I was standing

anywhere near her in the voting lobbies, she would ask me about the UDM and the mining families who lived in my then constituency of Gedling. Her personal interest and concern are sharply at odds with the hard-hearted portrayal of her in much of the media.

Lord Hill
Conservative Peer

Jonathan Hill is Leader of the House of Lords. In the 1980s he worked in the Conservative Research Department and as a Special Adviser to Ken Clarke. He was Political Secretary to John Major and was raised to the peerage in 2010.

It is true that great leaders are not always easy people. I think that it is fair to say that patience was not a virtue that Mrs Thatcher had in abundance, and that she did not always instantly get the point. The great Ronnie Millar, who helped with her speeches for many years, told me the lovely story of an occasion when he was trying to reassure a rather nervous Margaret Thatcher with some soothing words just before she was due to speak at her first party conference as Prime Minister. 'Piece of cake, Prime Minister.' 'No, not now, thank you, dear.' Those who knew her best all testify to the warm side of her character: the countless personal kindnesses, the loyalty and the small, thoughtful acts.

For someone who so defined a decade, it was perhaps not such a surprise that a new decade ushered in change and that after eleven-and-a-half years the longest-serving twentieth-century Prime Minister resigned and, a little over eighteen months later, joined your Lordships' House. It was perhaps typical of Mrs T. – now Lady T. – that she began with a maiden speech on Europe, on Maastricht, in fact. Perhaps it was typical also that she began by reminding her new home of one or two home truths. She began:

'Mine is a somewhat delicate position. I calculate that I was responsible as Prime Minister for proposing the elevation to this House of 214 of its present members. That must surely be considerably more than most of my predecessors – and my father did not know Lloyd George!'

Sadly, that was to be one of few speeches to which we would be treated in the subsequent decades. The light that had burned so brightly began to dim as she suffered the loss of Denis and ill health. However, although we may not have been blessed with her words, her presence was keenly felt and was sustained by her many friends in the House of Lords.

Perhaps Margaret Thatcher's greatest strength as Prime Minister was her refusal to accept Britain's decline. In taking that stance, the obstacles she faced were monumental, but her belief in the ability of the British people to better themselves, and of our country to better itself, was paramount. She was a once-in-a-lifetime Prime Minister and one of the most remarkable leaders this country has seen.

Conor Burns
Conservative MP 2010–

Conor Burns fought Eastleigh in 2001 and 2005 and was elected to Parliament in May 2010 in the seat of Bournemouth West. He was a close personal friend of Lady Thatcher.

I heard the news that Margaret Thatcher had died as I landed at Heathrow and turned on my mobile phone to find ninety-seven new text messages. It was the news that we had been dreading for some years. Yet she had come through so many health scares, we always sort of thought she would still be there. In the memorable lines of Charles Wolfe:

> If I had thought thou couldst have died,
> I might not weep for thee;
> But I forgot, when by thy side,
> That thou couldst mortal be.

As I watched the television coverage about this remarkable lady, I felt a deep sense of personal loss. Some of us have lost a dear friend, who in my case was not only a friend but a mentor and protectress – someone I loved and cared for very deeply. Margaret Thatcher, Prime Minister, is immortal. Lady T. was a very human human being. She was my childhood hero and the inspiration for my entering politics. I cared for her very much.

I first met Margaret properly when, in 1997, I drove Denis to a golf day in Dorset where he was the guest speaker. Returning to London earlier than planned, DT insisted that I come in 'and meet The Boss'. Lady Thatcher was perched on an armchair, shoes on the floor, with her legs tucked under her. A large tumbler of whisky was on the go and she was reading the *Wall Street Journal* and making notes.

As we entered the living room, she insisted on making DT and me drinks, and almost had to be restrained from going downstairs to make us an omelette. She returned instead with crisps and nuts. That evening we engaged in a fantasy Cabinet reshuffle. Lady T. enjoyed it greatly, as she always did any political conversation.

Over the years, she was enormously supportive of my efforts to get elected to Parliament. I remember that in 2001 she came to support me in Eastleigh. We took her to a health club in a visit covered live on Sky News. The chief executive of the entire group had come to welcome her. She announced to him, 'These places are a complete waste of time – up and down stairs keeps me fit!'

In 2002, I had what must have been the unique privilege of welcoming Ted Heath and Margaret Thatcher to Eastleigh in the same month. When Ted was coming, I warned the people in my association, 'For goodness' sake, don't put out the Thatcher-Tebbit fliers!' Well, they did. Ted reached for one of them, looked at it and said to me, 'What on earth are you doing with those two?' I said, 'Well, they agreed to come.' He then said what I suppose for him was a grudging compliment, 'I suppose that is something of a coup.'

In November 2002, despite her office announcing that she would never 'ever' speak in public again, she came to speak for me at a dinner in Eastleigh alongside Norman Tebbit. It was on that occasion that she gave a clue as to her contentment with the security of her record. Asked by a guest at the pre-dinner reception what her greatest achievement was, she replied robustly: 'Tony Blair and New Labour – we forced our opponents to change.'

It was at that same event that I was to see DT's capacity to remain unaffected by alcohol. The Thatchers had arrived very early – in no small part due to Lady T.'s obsession with not being late. As she went to the room to work on her speech, DT was offered a drink. Having protested that it was too early, he then managed four pints of Hampshire ale before dinner. It was also then that I realised why she had stopped speaking. She became increasingly nervous and uptight, and even – incongruously – announced that the 500-plus guests were there to eat, not to hear her. DT calmed her down and all was well. But it was hard to see.

Margaret came down to Eastleigh again in 2005; alas, it was not to be and Chris Huhne won.

In January 2010, in the run-up to the general election, Lady Thatcher came to what turned out to be the last dinner she ever had outside her home or the Ritz. She came to do an event for me and another candidate which we had given the rather novel title 'Women, for men to win'. Ann Widdecombe was the guest speaker and Margaret was the guest of honour.

As the years went on, I would see more and more of her. I would often accompany her to receptions and dinners, or take over from her devoted Private Secretary and escort her, holding on to my arm, to make sure she always knew who she was meeting and to help with tricky questions. The small, tight group both loved and protected her in equal measure. Yet my private visits were the most rewarding and precious. They were, for me, a small way of repaying her kindness to me when in her prime.

In recent years, I spent almost every Sunday evening with Lady Thatcher. We had great conversations on those Sundays. They ranged very much depending on how she was on a particular day. If we were in good form, we would go through the papers. I remember last November showing her a poll in the *Sunday Telegraph* that showed the Conservatives were 9 per cent behind the Labour Party. She asked when the next election was, so I said that there was a little over two years to go. She said, 'That's not far enough behind at this stage!' I texted that information to the Prime Minister from the living room of Chester Square; I do not know whether it cheered up his Sunday evening at Chequers, but I am sure it reduced my prospects of promotion. We couldn't read much into his reply of, simply, 'Thank you. DC'.

It was always a joy to visit her. Even on my informal Sunday evening calls she was always immaculately turned out, the only concession to informality being her smart black leather slippers. Her living room was a subtle combination of the comfortable and the formal. The room was dominated by a large portrait of Lady Thatcher from the early 1990s and below it, in pride of place at the centre of the mantelpiece, was the silver bowl inscribed to her on the tenth anniversary of her becoming Prime Minister by the 1992 Committee. Each side of this were framed photographs of her grandchildren, Michael and Amanda, and one of her devoted DT.

Sometimes, in recent years, I would point out a particular painting – maybe of Chequers or Downing Street – or a photograph to spark conversation. Yet she remained utterly lacking in introspection or interest in raking over past events. One evening last autumn, I said to her, 'You must look around the room, Margaret, and think, "Not bad. Not bad at all.'" Her reply surprised me. 'Yes,' she said, 'but as my father always said, it's not what you've done that counts. It's what you do next.'

On one occasion, I took a taxi to Chester Square to see Lady Thatcher on a particularly wet and awful evening. The taxi driver said, 'Which end of the square do you want, guv?' I said, 'The house with the policeman outside.' 'Maggie Thatcher's, guv?' 'That's right.' 'What you doin' there, then?' 'I'm going to have a drink with her – she's a friend of mine.' 'What d'you do then?' 'I'm a Tory MP.' As we pulled up, I went to pay the driver, but he refused to take the fare. I apologise in advance to the Prime Minister for repeating this story, but the driver said, 'Your fare tonight, guv, is you go in there and you tell 'er from me that we ain't had a good'un since!' I imparted that message to Margaret, who looked at me and said, 'Well, he's quite right.' I was then on the receiving end of a lecture about how he probably had a wife and child to support, how I should have paid him and how it was monstrous that I had not.

My encounters with her were often a mix of high-end politics and domesticity. During the same visit, we could range from her complimenting the Christmas pudding I had made for her, to discussing the inevitability of the demise of the euro. It was never routine.

One of the things we used to talk about was her time in office and some of her remarkable achievements. Quite recently, towards the end of last year, I remember saying to her, 'You must have made mistakes.' She said, 'I suppose I must have done.' I said, 'Can you think of any specific examples?' She replied, 'Well, they usually happened when I didn't get my own way.'

Much has been made in the media about the controversial nature of Margaret Thatcher as a politician and of her premiership. We should not shy away from that and nor should we on the Conservative benches be afraid to talk about that. That would be to betray who she was: she was a robust, principled, confrontational character. Yes, she divided; yes, she pursued her policies with vigour and persistence. She believed, as she said to me, that politics at its purest is philosophy in action. She believed in the battle of ideas – something that we would welcome returning to domestic politics today.

In some ways, the protests are the greatest compliment that could be paid to Margaret Thatcher. Even in death, the left have to argue against her. She would take great pride in these protests. She would not get angry about them; she would regard them as utterly and completely absurd. All I would say to those engaged in those protests is that they should look at how gracious she always was in what she said whenever her political foes departed the scene – most recently in the statement she issued about Michael Foot.

Her enduring legacy is not just in what she achieved and the fact that the Labour Party has not reversed much of it. Her true legacy lies here on these benches and in those who are coming up behind us. After the 2010 general election, I had the honour of organising a small number of receptions to introduce her to new colleagues. She drew great solace and comfort from the number of those colleagues who told her that they were in Parliament because of her inspiration and because of what she believed and did. Only two years ago, Tony Abbott, as the aspirant Prime Minister of Australia, asked to come to see her and told her that his philosophy was informed by watching what she had done when he was at university. While she was divisive to some degree, controversial certainly, she was an inspiration to many people way beyond these shores.

I visited the Reagan Library in California in the year of President Reagan's centenary, and was presented with a copy of the newly published *Ronald Reagan – The Notes*. This gem of a book contains some of Reagan's favourite one-liners, stories and anecdotes, all easily digestible in small paragraphs. I knew immediately that it would be a perfect addition to the other books Lady T. kept at her side. I asked Fred Ryan, the wonderful former Chief of Staff who will represent the Reagan family [at Mrs Thatcher's funeral], if I could have a copy for Lady T. A beautifully wrapped book was given to me to take back.

On my next visit, I poured Lady T. and myself a couple of G&Ts – what DT called 'proper ones' – and gave her the present. The look of delight as she opened it and saw Ronnie Reagan's face on the front was one of undiluted pleasure. That delight increased when she saw a handwritten inscription from Nancy Reagan to 'Dearest Margaret'. That book remained beside her for many months to come.

Lady T. remained, to the end of her life, interested in ideas. She thought her principles could be applied to the new challenges of today. She was especially proud to remain an inspiration to young people. She had an intrinsic disregard for the trappings of power or office. She found statues uninteresting, although accepted that they would happen.

The legacy she would most have wanted would have been a living one – teaching her beliefs to a new generation. That's why, in the closing years of her life, we talked often about creating a modern Swinton College – the party's old training centre – to promote her philosophy. Lady T. said at President Reagan's funeral, 'But we have one beacon to guide us that Ronald Reagan never had. We have his example.'

Now we have her example, also. The beacon burns twice as bright today. As Lady T. burnished the torch of freedom in life, so we must carry it on after her death.

Lord McNally
Liberal Democrat Peer

Tom McNally was Political Secretary to Prime Minister James Callaghan and MP for Stockport South from 1979 to 1983. He was a founder member of the SDP in 1981 and is now Leader of the Liberal Democrats in the House of Lords, and a Justice Minister.

Due to some serendipity, for about five years at the State Opening of Parliament I found myself sitting on the bench opposite next to Mrs Thatcher and spending time with her as we awaited the Queen's arrival. The one thing I want to share with the House took place in the year her husband died, when she had already had a number of minor strokes and did not speak a great deal. She suddenly turned to me and said, 'My husband died earlier this year.' I said, 'Yes, Baroness Thatcher, I know.' She paused again and then said, 'I miss him very much.' That tremendous partnership between Baroness Thatcher and her husband, which was so much a factor in her own political life, is remembered today.

I was present for two exchanges that took place between Enoch Powell and Mrs Thatcher. To appreciate fully the quotations that I am about to give, one will have to imagine that slightly nasal, Black Country twang in which Mr Powell spoke, but which I shall not try to imitate. The first is Enoch Powell addressing Mrs Thatcher after the Falkland Islands had been invaded. Speaking on 3 April in the House of Commons, he said:

The Prime Minister, shortly after she came into office, received a soubriquet as the Iron Lady. It arose in the context of remarks which she made about defence against the Soviet Union and its allies; but there was no reason to suppose that the Rt Hon. Lady did not welcome and, indeed, take pride in that description. In the next week or two this House, the nation and the Rt Hon. Lady herself will learn of what metal she is made.

My second quotation is from some ten weeks later – 17 June 1982 – after the British victory in the Falklands War. Enoch Powell said:

> Is the Rt Hon. Lady aware that the report has now been received from the public analyst on a certain substance recently subjected to analysis and that I have obtained a copy of the report? It shows that the substance under test consisted of ferrous matter of the highest quality, that it is of exceptional tensile strength, is highly resistant to wear and tear and to stress, and may be used with advantage for all national purposes.

That was the only time in my experience that Enoch Powell made a joke.

Lord Baker
Cabinet Minister 1985–92

A junior minister in the Conservative government of 1970–74 and in the early years of the Thatcher administration, Kenneth Baker joined the Cabinet in 1985 as Secretary of State for the Environment. He went on to become Secretary of State for Education and Science, Chancellor of the Duchy of Lancaster and ended his ministerial career in 1992 as Home Secretary. He was raised to the peerage in 1997.

In popular memory Prime Ministers are remembered for a characteristic feature. For Disraeli it was the monocle and the small wisp of a beard; for Gladstone, the great shock of white hair; for Chamberlain, the umbrella; for Churchill, the cigar; for Harold Wilson, the Gannex mac; but for Maggie, it would have to be the handbag: she was never without it and it became a formidable weapon. When she joined the Lords there was a cartoon which depicted the peers cringing away from an empty front bench on which was deposited just one handbag.

I have attended meetings where Maggie would 'handbag' a colleague. But in all fairness that colleague usually deserved it. She liked a good argument and she always respected people who would argue strongly and stand up for their corner, as long as they knew their facts and had researched their argument. Woe betide the minister who was casual or careless – those are the ones who would get the full blaze of her contempt.

But Maggie had another use for the handbag. It contained not only all the things that women carry in their handbags, but also little scraps of paper. At a Cabinet meeting she would have a brief prepared by the Cabinet Office under the guidance of the Cabinet Secretary. This, you could be assured, was well-read, underlined and marked even to the last page. Then she would have a second brief prepared by her political advisers from the Number 10 Policy Unit and this, too, would be carefully marked. That brief came to her in a separate box which the civil servants did not see. These were to arm her for the debate which would take place on the issue under discussion.

The minister leading the discussion would have no idea what was in either brief but you knew from an early stage what her view was. Her style was not to go around the table like John Major collecting the voices and then coming down upon the side which had the majority. Maggie knew what she wanted but on several occasions she did not get her way.

When Maggie was really up against it and the argument was running against her, she would then pick up her handbag, put it on the Cabinet table and, opening it carefully and slowly, she would take out a piece of well crumpled and thumbed paper. This was the brief that came from no one knows whom – a friend, or someone who had rung her up who had a particular view about the matter in hand. It was unpredictable, sometimes illuminating, at others weird, sometimes an interesting new light, at others a worthless piece of gossip. Whenever she drew out a piece of paper like this the Cabinet Secretary would pale and the minister would raise his eyes to the ceiling knowing full well that he was about to be grounded.

When I was Education Secretary, I did discover one of Maggie's private briefers – her hairdresser. He had a child in one of the inner London comprehensive schools and when he was doing the Prime Minister's hair she would hear about his child's poor experiences. The Prime Minister would then tell me and her colleagues that something more had to be done.

Discussions at Cabinet are never predictable. Many are the ministers who have cursed the contents of that wretched blue handbag.

The following passage is an extract from Kenneth Baker's memoirs The Turbulent Years.

Early on the morning of 22 November 1990 I was telephoned by Andrew Turnbull from No. 10 and told that the Prime Minister had decided to resign. A great leader of our country, a very great Prime Minister, had been struck down by a collective loss of nerve among her colleagues. It was the end of an era and of a very great Prime Minister.

When I arrived at No. 10 I found my fellow Cabinet colleagues waiting outside the Cabinet room in a funereal and uneasy silence, not at all keen to catch each other's eye. The Prime Minister came down the stairs a little after nine o'clock and with head lowered went alone into the Cabinet room. After a few minutes we were sent in to take our places. Margaret looked very red-eyed and under considerable strain. She began by saying that before the formal business of the Cabinet she wanted to make her position known. She started to read from the paper in front of her, but when she reached the part which said, 'having consulted widely among colleagues', she broke clown and could not continue. The words choked in her throat and she wiped away tears from her eyes. She started again falteringly and said, 'I am so sorry.' Cecil Parkinson, sitting next but one to her, suggested that the Lord Chancellor should read the statement. Margaret blew her nose, shook her head and continued, 'I have concluded that the unity of the party and the prospects of victory in the general election' – here she paused again and choked on the words, but went on – 'will be better served if I stood down to enable Cabinet colleagues to enter the ballot for the leadership. I should like to thank all those in Cabinet and outside who have given me such dedicated support.'

David Waddington was dabbing his eyes at this stage, and others were close to tears. Some, while remaining expressionless, must have been relieved. But nobody around that Cabinet table had ever thought they would witness such a scene. Margaret went on, 'It is vital that we stand together. The unity of the party is crucial and that's why I am giving up. I couldn't bear all the things I have stood for over the past eleven years being rejected. The Cabinet must unite to stop Michael Heseltine.'

Slowly Margaret recovered her composure. It had been a moving scene. Never before had she broken down in front of her colleagues. But at the end she was a real person of flesh and blood, not the cold, unfeeling automaton she was so often portrayed as. Then the Lord Chancellor, James Mackay, read the passage which Robin Butler, the Cabinet Secretary, had prepared for him, recording the Cabinet's tribute to Margaret's leadership of the country.

'As Party Chairman,' I said, 'you have and will always continue to have the love and loyalty of the party. You have a special place in the heart of the party. You have led us to victory three times and you would have done so again. Speaking as one of the longest-serving Cabinet ministers,' I added, 'those who have served you recognise that they have been in touch with greatness.' Then Douglas Hurd said he wanted to place on record the superb way in which Margaret had

carried herself at the Paris conference over the last three days, especially with the pressures of the leadership election upon her.

We then turned to other matters, the business of the House and
so on. When it came to foreign affairs, Margaret gave a spirited, very
detailed and long report on her talks with Gorbachev and Bush. She
was clearly getting back into her stride. But towards the end of the
meeting I could see she was close to tears again.

We were all asked to stay on for coffee, which we then had sitting
around the Cabinet table. We talked about the future. Margaret was
very keen and insistent that it should be a member of the Cabinet who
was elected to succeed her. 'I think the Cabinet will have to do everything it can to ensure this. You will have to work very hard,' she said.

During this meeting I passed a note to Douglas Hurd asking whether
he had come to any agreement with John [Major] about the candi-
dacy. I had assumed that some time over the last twenty-four hours
they must have talked together about this and come to an arrangement. Douglas sent back a note saying they were going to issue a joint
statement declaring that they had worked very closely together and
would continue to do so but, in all the circumstances, the best way of
uniting the party would be for both to go forward in the next ballot. It
would be a friendly contest. Douglas drafted this statement then and
there, and passed it to me. It was perfect, a masterly composition. One
of Douglas's great gifts is his capacity to draft elegant statements at the
drop of a pen. Norman Lamont, who had been promoting John's cause
for some time – he had actually canvassed Cecil Parkinson twenty-four
hours earlier – could now openly become John's campaign manager.
It was clear to me that despite the disavowals of the two protagonists
a good deal of preparatory work had already been done by the two
camps to marshal their campaign teams.

Cecil was quite scathing about the whole situation. He said both
campaigns would be negative if the contestants were going to be
friendly. 'If they are going to be friendly, why bother to turn up and
vote for them?'

As the meeting broke up I told Cecil and Douglas that as Chairman
of the party I would make a statement to the cameras outside No. 10
on behalf of the Cabinet. I jotted something down outside the Cabinet
room, and then went out to the massed cameras opposite the front
door of No. 10 and said, 'This is a typically brave and selfless decision

by the Prime Minister. Once again Margaret Thatcher has put her country and the party's interests before personal considerations. This will allow the party to elect a new leader to unite the party and build upon her immense successes. If I could add just a personal note, I am very saddened that our greatest peacetime Prime Minister has left government. She is an outstanding leader, not only of our country but also of the world – I do not believe we will see her like again.'

I was deeply moved by the events which I had just witnessed. I was very close to tears myself in the Cabinet room. I had started by being cool about Margaret Thatcher, but over the years I had come to admire her. She has traits of character which can make her not particularly endearing. As Prime Minister she was personally dominant, supremely self-confident, infuriatingly stubborn and held a strange mixture of broad views and narrow prejudices. But Margaret also had a strength of character that made her a natural leader. She was a patriot, always putting the interests of Britain first. She also realised that Britain had to be saved from economic and institutional collapse. No Prime Minister I have known since the war would have seen through that tough Budget of 1981 which deepened the recession we were then going through but proved to be the foundation of the prosperity of the middle and late 1980s. No Prime Minister I have known would have had the courage to launch a sea and land offensive 8,000 miles away to secure the independence of a small group of colonial islands. No Prime Minister since the war would have withstood a miners' strike for over a year. And no Prime Minister since the war would have reduced the power of organised labour in the way that Margaret did.

Sir Gerald Kaufman
Labour MP 1970–

Sir Gerald Kaufman has served in Parliament for more than forty years. In the 1980s he was a member of Labour's shadow Cabinet, covering first Environment, then Home Affairs and finally Foreign Affairs.

For many, of course, Margaret Thatcher was synonymous with 'milk-snatcher' and it would be idle to pretend that to us in the Labour Party, and to millions of our supporters, many of her policies were other than anathema. But Margaret was much more complex than that, both as a politician and as a person, and her international significance was emphasised quite recently when, almost twenty-four years after she had stopped being Prime Minister, an actress in Hollywood could win the 'best actress' Oscar for portraying her almost as well as she used to portray herself.

I served in the shadow Cabinet for ten years when Margaret Thatcher was Prime Minister. I saw her in action, and I often opposed her in action. After she left office – or rather, was ousted from office by some of her colleagues – I had contact with her from time to time.

It was my job to oppose her right-to-buy legislation, whose impact on the availability of social housing persists to this day, which is quite a charge sheet, not to mention the blunders that finished her off: the poll tax and 'no, no, no' to Europe. But after all, she was a Tory Prime Minister and was not elected to implement policies that I or my constituents favoured. Unlike Winston Churchill, Harold Macmillan or Ted Heath, she broke the post-war consensus; that was her objective and that was her achievement.

In personal relationships, and in some policy areas, Margaret Thatcher could be more than civilised – indeed, punctilious and cordial. I was a junior housing minister when she was shadow Environment Secretary, and I recall an occasion when one of her frontbench spokesmen violated the kind of across-the-floor frontbench deal on which the functioning of this House depends. It was Margaret who sought me out to apologise and to say that she knew nothing about it, and would have stopped it had she known.

After she became Prime Minister, she baulked at railway privatisation. It was imposed by John Major, and its messy consequences we suffer to this day. Although she won her second and third elections with enormous majorities, she was always accessible. She announced that any Member of Parliament with employment problems in his or her constituency could come and see her at No. 10, and I availed myself of that offer when a computer multilayer board factory in my constituency was at hazard. We met in the Prime Minister's study in 10 Downing Street and I explained the problem. 'But how are we to save it?' she asked. I suggested that it could be taken over by the National Enterprise Board, which had been created by Labour. Kenneth Baker, the junior minister responsible for this policy area, was present, so she turned to him and asked plaintively, 'Kenneth, what did I do with the National Enterprise Board?' I am sorry to say that the factory is now a blood transfusion centre but, still, she meant well.

Margaret Thatcher was brave. In the parliamentary week following the Brighton bombing, in which terrorists tried to kill her and her entire Cabinet – and British democracy, by seeking to do so – she came here; she was present, bright and perky in the House of Commons for the government statement, to which I responded. She was also absolutely right on a considerable number of foreign policy issues. Against timorous nerve-trembling on both sides of the House and attempted international interference, she was utterly determined that the people of the Falkland Islands, who wanted to be British and who still want to be British today, should not be the victims of a fascist dictator. How some Labour Members of Parliament could actually want to water down a response to an aggressive fascist dictator, I could not understand then and I still do not understand today.

When Saddam Hussein seized Kuwait, she was actively part of the preparations to oust him by force. I was shadow Foreign Secretary at this time and had to seek to carry with me our backbenchers, some of whom were spineless. In the debate, I therefore told the House that Labour policy was based not on supporting the United Kingdom government, but on implementing United Nations Security Council resolutions. She knew what I was up to, and she dug the Foreign Secretary in the ribs with her elbow and smiled a wry smile. She was also much more far-sighted than most United Kingdom Prime Ministers about rightward trends in Israel and in the Middle East. When, as shadow Foreign Secretary, I visited Morocco, I was told by the United Kingdom ambassador there that she had given him a direct instruction to approach the leaders of the then substantial Moroccan Jewish community and urge them to exhort the sizeable number of Moroccan Jewish immigrants in Israel to vote Labour – Shimon Peres – in a forthcoming election.

Until her final debacle, she generally found ways of getting her own way. There had been a Lionel Bart musical called *Maggie May* and the saying went, 'Others may not, but Maggie may', and that was very much her watchword. I saw her from time to time after she had left office. On one occasion I attended a social event and when I came in she bustled over to me. I had recently had published in a newspaper an article about protecting children from pornography on TV and videos. She told me how much she admired the article and said, 'I carry it with me everywhere in my handbag.' To be part of the contents of Margaret's handbag – what greater apotheosis could one possibly hope for?

Lord Jopling
Conservative Peer

Michael Jopling served as Conservative MP for Westmorland (later Westmorland and Lonsdale) from 1964 to 1997. He was Margaret Thatcher's Chief Whip from 1979 to 1983, before his appointment as Secretary of State for Agriculture, Fisheries and Food from 1983 to 1987. He was raised to the peerage in 1997.

Much has been said about Margaret Thatcher. Indeed, much of it has been said several times, but let me add two or three of my memories. I remember Margaret Thatcher above all as a particularly kind woman. I give one example. At the first Christmas for which she was Prime Minister, in 1979, she said to me, 'Do you know of any of our people in the House of Commons who are going to be alone – through death, divorce or whatever – over this Christmas period? If you do, I would like to ask them to Chequers to come and stay over Christmas.' That, I thought at the time, was one of the most generous things from somebody with all the pressures on them of being Prime Minister.

There are some who say that she was a very bad listener. I would argue strongly with that. Maybe she was not a very good listener when some of her colleagues were embarking on what I call waffle. However, often I was at a meeting of ministers when a Secretary of State had to come and propose a new policy. She would begin the discussion in her typically strident way, saying, 'Well, Secretary of State, I am not very attracted to what you want to do, but let us hear it, if you must.' He would then explain what he wanted to do. Others would come in. Having listened, she would say, 'Well, Secretary of State, if that is what you want to do, you'd better go on and do it. But if it all goes pear-shaped, don't come back to me to bail you out.'

Of course, Margaret Thatcher loved, probably above all, an informed political debate. I have a memory of a very small lunch in Downing Street, when Pierre Trudeau come over from Canada to complain because we were not expediting as much as he would have liked the legislation to release British control over the Canadian constitution. At lunch, we quickly got that out of the way. Then Margaret Thatcher and Pierre Trudeau, who clearly disliked each other, embarked on a gloves-off confrontation of political philosophies. Francis Pym and I were the only outsiders present. It was a memorable experience to be a fly on the wall and listen to those two going hammer and tongs together.

Alexander Haig
Supreme Allied Commander in Europe 1974–79

General Alexander M. Haig Jr served in the Korean and Vietnam wars. He was White House Chief of Staff for President Richard Nixon, Supreme Allied Commander in Europe and President Ronald Reagan's first Secretary of State. He died in 2010.

Margaret Thatcher is a giant among contemporary world leaders. She is a woman of conviction, courage and principle.

I first met her in the mid-seventies while I was serving as the Supreme Allied Commander in Europe (SACEUR). I recall being urged by one of Great Britain's leading Conservative political leaders to meet with an upstart Conservative lady who believed she could be the next Prime Minister of Great Britain. He urged me to meet her in Brussels and brief her on the European security situation, adding that her intellectual well was somewhat dry on such things. Because of the position of the caller, I agreed, and after spending approximately one hour with this attractive, bright and enthusiastic political hopeful, left with the impression that my contact's assessment had been an accurate one as it applied to European security issues.

I saw Margaret Thatcher six or eight months later at a point when she had become the nominee of the Conservative Party. In the brief intervening period between our two meetings, she had acquired a level of military knowledge that was both remarkable in scope and the match for a professional with years of European security background. During the remainder of my time as SACEUR I met frequently with the then Prime Minister, and remained in awe of her military and geopolitical acumen.

Some years later, as America's 59th Secretary of State, I came to know Margaret Thatcher in an environment where the vital interests of both of our respective nations were at stake on several important occasions. Perhaps the most difficult of those occurred at the end of my service in the Reagan Cabinet during the Falklands War. In my first book entitled *Caveat: Realism, Reagan, and Foreign Policy* I described this remarkable woman in the following brief paragraph:

> In the Falklands, the West was given a great victory by Great Britain. I do not mean the defeat of Argentinian soldiers by British soldiers. Every man who fell on either side represented a loss to the free world. British arms prevailed, but principle triumphed. The will of the West was tested and found to be equal to the task. The rule of law was upheld. The freedom of a faraway people was preserved. For this, the free world may thank the men of the British Task Force and Mrs Thatcher, who was by far the strongest, the shrewdest and the most clear-sighted player in the game. In times of acute national crisis, a leader will always hear advice that clashes with his inner convictions. Easier courses than the right course will be thrust upon him. It is the leader who, knowing where the true interest of the nation lies, resists such counsel and perseveres in his principles, who deserves the name of statesman. Margaret Thatcher belongs in that company.

Lord Steel

Leader of the Liberal Party 1976–88

David Steel was leader of the Liberal Party for almost all of Margaret Thatcher's period as Prime Minister. He led the party into an Alliance and later a merger with the SDP, and became a founding father of the Liberal Democrat Party. Sir David Steel was the first Presiding Officer of the Scottish Parliament.

I have two contradictory memories of Margaret Thatcher. The first is the public one: her strident uncompromising battling at House of Commons Question Time, especially her memorable (but rather flattering) put-downs of me: 'Let me tell this young man...'

The second is a private one. On one of the many occasions when she felt obliged to invite me as leader of the Liberal Party to dinner at No. 10 for a distinguished foreign guest (we always parade our multi-party democracy on such occasions) my wife was struck down with flu and could not travel from Scotland. She greeted me, 'So sorry to hear Judy is ill. I didn't want you to be alone so I've arranged for Carol to join us and partner you into dinner.' A genuinely thoughtful and kind touch.

Mark Menzies
Conservative MP 2010–

Mark Menzies was elected to Parliament in 2010 in the seat of Fylde, having stood in Glasgow Govan in 2001 and Selby in 2005.

My mother was widowed at an early age and forced to raise me on her own. She was a Labour voter. She worked in a factory and she was a trade union member. She often had to get up at five o'clock in the morning to catch the bus, determined that she could give me the best possible chance in life. A good education and stability were important to my mum. Balancing working shifts and doing her own child care was always a huge challenge. One of Margaret Thatcher's key policies provided my mother with a huge lifeline. I refer, of course, to the assisted places scheme, for this policy had a huge benefit in my life. People from my background in Scotland did not go to private school, nor did they go to university, and the scheme gave me and others that opportunity. It not only allowed private boarding school education to become affordable to someone like my mum but succeeded in broadening my horizons at an early age.

While private education is not necessarily the best option for everyone – indeed, Lady Thatcher herself showed what can be achieved through the grammar school system – I know how fortunate I was to receive a place on the scheme. It certainly gave me confidence and a jump-start in life that would never have been possible without Lady Thatcher's hard work and belief in the power of education. I almost certainly would not be in Parliament today without that push. As I say, my story is not unique. Some 800,000 children were ultimately supported by the assisted places scheme between 1981 and its abolition in 1997, with an average of £10,000 in total spent on their schooling – just a few thousand pounds per year.

I was privileged to meet Lady Thatcher on a number of occasions, but none sticks out in my memory as much as the first time I met her, when I was a teenager. I was nervous, and she was prime ministerial, but she took time to talk to me, and she made me feel like the only person in the room. One thing I never did was to say thank you for the assisted places scheme, so may I correct that mistake now? I say thank you, Margaret Thatcher, for the assisted places scheme and for giving children such as me an opportunity that we would never otherwise have had.

Andrew Roberts
Historian

Andrew Roberts is one of Britain's most pre-eminent historians and has written extensively about Winston Churchill and the Second World War.

Sir Winston Churchill, about to enter a public meeting, once paused and turned to a fellow Conservative MP as he took a large cigar out of his breast pocket. 'Never forget your trademark,' he said, as he lit it and put it in his mouth.

After Churchill himself, no Tory premier had quite so many trademarks as did Margaret Thatcher. There was the handbag, the 'Iron Lady' jutting jaw, the shoulder pads, the big hair, the basilisk stare, above all that unmistakable, highly trained voice that could run through every quaver and crotchet, from the cooing-dove softness of her 1979 St Francis of Assisi quotation on the steps of No. 10 to the stridency of her 'no, no, no' to the single European currency in October 1990. Yet the woman behind the trademarks was a very different person from the one who used them all so deftly during her eleven and a half years in Downing Street.

At a dinner given by Lord Cranborne in his house in Chelsea in the mid-nineties, Boris Johnson and I were by turns incredulous and mystified by the praise that Margaret – it was what she asked me to call her in life, and I see no reason to revert to formality after her death – heaped upon John Maynard Keynes. 'Wasn't he the Bloomsburyite inventor of inflation, the author of socialist economics?' we asked.

'What else could Britain have done in 1945?' she replied, before going on to lavish praise on his architecture for global economics as set out at Bretton Woods. Boris and I looked at each other, wondering if we were being subtly teased in some way, but she then went on to praise Keynes's anti-unemployment policies of the 1930s and it was clear she meant every word.

The idea that she was politically utterly inflexible was one that she never minded if other people promoted – she was a diligent curator of her own myth – but it never really corresponded to reality. Here was a premier who backed away wounded from the threat of confrontation with the National Union of Mineworkers in 1980 and 1981, knowing that Britain's coal reserves were not sufficiently high to risk a second Tory defeat at the hands of Arthur Scargill in a decade.

Here, too, was a right-wing Conservative who effectively turned over Rhodesia to Robert Mugabe at Lancaster House in 1979, and a convinced Unionist who gave the Dublin government a say in the government of Ulster in 1985. (One of the few errors she admitted in public came in a *Daily Telegraph* article soon after Enoch Powell's death in 1998 in which she confessed the Anglo-Irish Agreement to have been a mistake.) Above all, it was her ministry that signed the Single European Act and joined the European exchange rate mechanism. A robotic right-wing ideologue would have done none of those things; she was always a far more complex political operator than she liked to acknowledge.

For all that she was regarded in left-wing demonology as the skin-flint cutter of public services, she was personally very generous. When in 2005 I was chosen by Margaret to take her place as a trustee of the Margaret Thatcher Archive Trust, I discovered just how munificent she had been to the Churchill Archives Centre in Cambridge. Offered an eight-figure sum for her private papers by an American university, money that could have gone straight into her and her children's pockets, she instead nobly agreed to deposit the papers at Cambridge, where British scholars could consult them with ease. (Of course, Oxford would probably have got them had it not behaved so spitefully in refusing her an honorary degree in 1985.)

Far from the unthinking, even bloodthirsty, warmonger portrayed by the left, Margaret Thatcher was profoundly saddened by the deaths of British servicemen during the Falklands War. She wrote personally to the families of every one of the 255 soldiers, sailors and airmen who gave their lives in that conflict, and was able to recall the names of scores of them for years afterwards.

When in the 1983 general election Neil Kinnock replied to a heckler who had shouted that Mrs Thatcher had 'showed guts' during the Falklands conflict, with the words: 'It's a pity that others had to leave theirs on the ground at Goose Green to prove it,' she was understandably disgusted.

'Disgusted' and 'appalled' were also the words she used to me when I asked her about her reaction to John Major's affair with Edwina Currie.

For all that she despised John Major, Margaret's reputation for holding grudges was another myth. As Geoffrey Howe, whose 1990 resignation perhaps did more than anything else to destabilise her premiership, afterwards acknowledged: 'We see each other from time to time in the Lords and quite often sit alongside one another. We are perfectly civil and courteous.'

Even Sir Edward Heath, who, when she fell in 1990, apparently cried 'Rejoice! Rejoice!', was subsequently invited to a large gala Tory dinner. In 2005 she was spotted chatting happily to Tam Dalyell, who during the Falklands War had accused her of killing 368 Argentine sailors on the *General Belgrano* in order to prolong the war.

There were many other surprises about her likes and dislikes; at a dinner in Gstaad one year, I managed to draw her out on the various Labour leaders who had opposed her and, while she entertained a very high regard for Harold Wilson, both as a politician and a man, she regarded James Callaghan as a sneaky, essentially untrustworthy politician – the precise mirror image of the popular view of the two men. She rated Michael Foot highly as a politician – primarily because of his oratorical skills – but simply could never understand why he had worn a donkey jacket to the Cenotaph on Remembrance Day.

Her views on history were very often not the conventional ones that one might have expected from her. Like many politicians, she was interested in British political history and enjoyed discussing what she might have done in certain historical situations. Sitting next to her at a dinner in the House of Commons, I posited how she would have reacted if she had been in Asquith's Cabinet in November 1916, when Lord Lansdowne had proposed making peace with the Kaiser's Germany before any more people were killed on the Western Front.

I expected the standard Tory response that such a suggestion was appeasement, tantamount to treason, impossible to consider when our boys were fighting in the trenches, and so on. Far from it; Lady Thatcher said that such a peace at that stage of the Great War would have saved Russia from revolution, the British Army from the tragedy of Passchendaele and probably saved Germany from the Nazis. 'The only problem that I can see with such an agreement,' she said, reverting to expected type, 'is, could you trust the Germans to implement it fully?'

Her attitude towards the interwar Conservative appeasers such as Chamberlain was similarly understanding of the pressures on them, and not at all the knee-jerk ultra-Churchillian stance her reputation might have implied. There was, in short, a reflective, considered side to Margaret Thatcher that was utterly belied by her trademarks. Of course when she did act instinctively – such as when she veiled the 'ethnic' tailfin on the BA model plane with her handkerchief, or when she reached out to touch Ronald Reagan's flag-draped coffin – the result could be as dramatic as it was delightful.

In all the years that I knew her, I never once came across the central failing of which many of her political enemies accused her – of refusing to listen to other points of view. Peter Walker, who served in all three of her Cabinets, was 'the wettest of her wets' yet he agrees: 'It's a myth that she wasn't a good listener. She always gave access to anybody who wanted to speak to her. I admired her – there's no hostility.' Because she enjoyed the intellectual stimulus of argument, she could sometimes be perverse, but that is not the same as not listening.

Margaret loved the attention that continued to be lavished upon her after her fall in November 1990, taking it for granted that she would be the centre of attention in any room. In that sense she was not unlike most politicians. The difference was that she would be able to return the favour, even if only for a moment, making each person upon whom she turned her attention the sole recipient of it, a technique that many in public life fail to master. The result was that when she thanked everyone down to the cloakroom attendant at the end of an evening, each of them would feel they had had their moment with Maggie.

I well remember her explaining, in a restaurant in the Swiss Alps one night, about how to bomb a railway from the air – you zig-zag across it apparently, rather than trying to strafe along it – and as she did so I realised that she was quite aware that everyone on the nearby tables was listening too, and that she was rather playing to the gallery as a result.

We were staying in Switzerland with a mutual friend, Lady Colyton, the widow of one of Churchill's ministers, and one night she invited along for dinner Yehudi Menuhin, Princess Marie-Astrid of Luxembourg and her husband, the Archduke Christian of Austria. The conversation got around to what Europe would have been like if Archduke Franz Ferdinand had not been assassinated in Sarajevo in 1914, which led on to the present state of European integration. This time Margaret certainly did not play the counter-intuitive game; indeed, Lord Menuhin, a very committed Europhile, left the dinner early, so outraged was he by her violent strictures against the European Union.

'Why don't you come out in public and say you favour withdrawal?' I asked her after he'd left. 'No one's ever asked me the question,' she answered, somewhat disingenuously. Far from being the outspoken back-seat driver she was accused of being, Margaret never came out publicly for Britain's withdrawal from the European Union, for all her passionate belief that it was the right course to take. This was because she knew the schismatic effect it would have on an already profoundly bifurcated Tory Party under John Major.

When left-wingers accused Margaret of being a Grantham shop-keeper's daughter with petit bourgeois instincts and a Poujadist mentality, they often meant subtly to impute anti-Semitism to her political make-up. In fact, there was not so much as a scintilla of it in her. Her family took in a Jewish refugee from Nazi Germany in the 1930s and she appointed more Jews to the Cabinet than any previous premier, enjoying the intellectual stimulus they provided.

The only racial grouping that was ever traduced in my hearing was the Welsh – and that was by Denis, because Geoffrey Howe and Tristan Garel-Jones were Welsh, and Michael Heseltine was brought up in Wales. 'As you'll recall, my maiden name was the same as Andrew's surname, Denis,' she said in mock admonishment, 'so I hope you won't go too far down this particular road.'

Recollections of the events of November 1990 were painful to her, of course, so I didn't tend to bring them up, but she would occasionally return to them, using the startling phrase she had employed on a BBC documentary in October 1993, when she had called her betrayal by the party 'treachery with a smile on its face'.

There was a modesty to Margaret which is rarely acknowledged. When I asked her what she felt about a rather ordinary painting of her fetching £440,000 at the Winter Ball in 2005, she answered that she assumed it was some kind of tax-efficient way to donate money to the Tory Party rather than any reflection on her political legacy. At a dinner in a private house within the precinct of St James's Palace, she meekly retired from the table with the other women as the cigars and port arrived, telling us that she wanted to talk about clothes upstairs. When we joined them shortly afterwards she was in fact playing animatedly with the host's Jack Russell, another image few people would have of her.

Just as men-about-town such as Cecil Parkinson and Alan Clark were indulged by Margaret in a way that the strait-laced schoolmarm of popular mythology never would have, so fairly heavy drinking was never considered a capital offence either. In the drawing room of the Taipei Hilton's presidential suite one evening, a well-known historian and I were enjoying a drink with her and Denis and her Chief of Staff Julian Seymour when, on trying to stand up, the historian keeled over and fell face down in the small gap between Margaret's knees and the vast, sharp-edged, marble-topped table. An inch to either side would have meant his landing either in Margaret's lap or braining himself on the table. 'Jet lag can be a terrible thing,' was all she said, a twinkle in her eye. Since the historian and I had been in Taiwan for several days, and she had flown in only that morning, it was not to be taken at face value. There was a lack of condemnation about minor human failings that was immensely attractive about her, and quite unlike her popular image.

Similarly the standard line that she had absolutely no sense of humour has been wildly exaggerated. It is true that she did not tell anecdotes, and had no real interest in set-piece gags, but there were several occasions on which she could jolly along a dinner party using humour. At one formal Adam Smith Institute dinner, after no fewer than five male economists had given speeches before her, she began, 'The cocks might crow, but it's the hen that lays the eggs.'

The Labour MP Frank Field, who wrote in 2005 about their friendship, said that, 'Two traits became apparent to me: her humour and her resolve.' The resolve everyone knows about, but the humour was there too. A sense of humour involves both telling jokes and getting them. It is true that she rarely told unscripted gags – many women of her age and background don't – but she was fine at laughing at other people's.

It is, however, true that she had absolutely no small talk. Her idea of a greeting was: 'Hello Andrew, what do you think about what the UN is doing in Srebrenica?' This could be unnerving when one was mentally preparing some anodyne remark about the weather, but it did save time. Saying goodbye she could be equally unnervingly direct: 'Never forget, Europe brings us problems, but America the solutions!' she once called downstairs, pretty much apropos of nothing, as Norman Lamont and I left one of her Christmas parties at her offices in Chester Square.

In anyone else such a farewell might be considered a mild eccentricity, but in Margaret it was always depicted by her opponents as monomania – or even dementia. (Her regal stance at the top of the stairs could be unnerving: at one of Margaret's Christmas parties in Belgrave Square, Lady Annabel Goldsmith whispered to me as we walked in: 'For God's sake remind me not to curtsey; that's what I did last time!')

There can be no doubt that Denis's death in June 2003 took a dreadful toll. At the end of the reception after the funeral in the Guards Chapel, I asked her who had chosen the beautiful hymns and readings. 'I chose them with my ministers,' she replied. When told by her devoted Private Secretary that it was time to go, she said, 'I will as soon as I find Denis,' looking about for him. 'He's around here somewhere.'

The pathos of the moment was heavy, but the extraordinary thing was how Margaret rebounded from that very sad period, her capacities very soon strengthening and rebuilding. Within a couple of months she was taking on semi-public engagements, working hard and moving her offices into the House of Lords. At a dinner party at her home in Chester Square only a few months after the funeral she was on fine form, extolling the quality of the sermons at her adored Royal Hospital Chelsea, where she worshipped regularly and where she could be certain of no happy-clappy liberal clerics wagging fingers at her.

Yet instead of being allowed the untroubled twilight years she so deserved, Margaret was then faced with the possible imprisonment of her son Mark in South Africa on charges of having helped finance an attempted coup d'état in Equatorial Guinea. Having pre-lunch drinks with Margaret at Mark's house in Cape Town on Christmas Day 2004, it soon became apparent to me how much of a toll his legal quagmire had taken on her, and despite her sweetly trying to make conversation with my 5-year-old daughter – thankfully not about the UN's role in Srebrenica – the strain on her of Mark's tribulations clearly showed. The plea bargain that ended that episode came as a huge relief to her, although she was saddened that it resulted in Mark not being allowed to visit.

The only time I spoke to her about her own death was at Chester Square, when the conversation got round to Charles Moore's forthcoming biography of her. It was slated only to be published after her death, and like an idiot I blurted out the question: 'Is it to be a cradle to the, er, er...' not quite wanting to finish the morbid sentence I'd stupidly started. 'I think the word you're looking for is "grave", Andrew,' she replied good-naturedly. 'And the answer is yes.'

Edward Pearce
Author and Journalist

A former columnist for The Scotsman *and former Commons sketchwriter for the* Daily Telegraph, *Edward Pearce has published twelve books including* Machiavelli's Children, The Lost Leaders *and a biography of Denis Healey.*

Personally, unlike most contributors to this book, I am not a fan of the lady – too rigid, too narrow, too full of animus, a sort of Protestant ethic gone rogue. Oddly, she was so much better with what we inadequately call 'ordinary people' than with coadjutors. There is a nice story about custard. At a Cabinet dinner, a very inexperienced and frightened young waitress spilt a great dish of custard all over Geoffrey Howe. Instead of berating her, or going all steely silent, Margaret threw her arms round the girl and said 'My dear, you mustn't cry. Anyone could have an accident,' and to Geoffrey Howe who was ineffectively sponging away at his suit, 'Geoffrey! Stop making such a fuss.'

It could be of course that the victim being Geoffrey, between whom and herself there was something of a sympathy deficit, charitable feeling came very easily. But it shows her very nicest side and wasn't the only example.

When her chauffeur died, she didn't send a card, she went to the funeral in person. Contrast, under the present Tory regime, the death of Giles Shaw earlier this year [2000]. He was a Minister of State, a former serious candidate for the Speaker's Chair and very widely liked. The only sitting MP at his funeral in Yorkshire was Tam Dalyell!

I saw most of Margaret Thatcher in opposition and really rather liked her. Pity about the politics. Actually, I mean that seriously. She did behave well enough and pretty nicely away from politics. The excesses came with the party struggle. After all, Neil Kinnock isn't a communist, but Maggie thought he was and said so in the Commons. 'He is a Marxist, a crypto-communist.' It was an unbelievable remark, but instructive. The good nature and manners of ordinary life would regularly be swept away in the political context, but so was all sense, sophistication and judgement.

The same is true of that outburst on TV, instantly recalled and apologised for – 'drooling and drivelling about the poor'. It is one thing to be hard-headed, but that spoke a partisan rage beyond party, directed rather at a class. Would she ever have embarked on the poll tax which fell so heavily on the claimant, canned beer-drinking, football-watching, undeserving part of mankind if the 'drooling and drivelling' outlook hadn't been an underground stream in her nature? Like I said, a Protestant ethic gone rogue.

Class was central with her and I'm not alone in noticing. At a seminar at Durham about five years ago I set out before lunch the notion of Margaret Thatcher, class warrior. Alan Clark, her great fan, breezed in on time for what he would have called 'pudding', and afterwards launched himself onto the thesis, 'It's all absolute crap of course to talk about liberal market theory. What Margaret is on about is the class war.'

I don't mind the fierceness. Where Blair cringes, she bops and when she does, sometimes you find yourself at the other end of the telescope approving!

I was at a dinner for her in 1985 where Charles Moore was attacking the new Anglo-Irish Agreement, 'Robert Armstrong's revenge' as some of us called it. 'What about the Protestants?' he asked in the odd Orange way of so many English Catholics. She leant into the table and in her best, taut, intense, Puff the Magic Dragon way, said 'Yes, Charles and what about the Catholics?' She had heard John Hume's great speech not long before she was actually listening to people like Armstrong. Consequently all the fierceness which she would misuse in hating the Germans and despising the unemployed was turned towards getting a decent equity for the minority. It was wonderful.

'Am I no a bonny fighter?' asks Alan Breck. Yes, indeed, but too much so in Margaret Thatcher's case. For she started fighting her own side. When a leader of a party creates factionalism as she did in her last two years – and during the term of her successor when she called in backbenchers to bully them into voting against the Tory whip – it is simply ruinous. For a head of government to summon a seminar to collectively analyse the character faults of a notably friendly neighbour, Germany, was to do something against reason. And in politics, whatever the joys of raging conviction, reason has its uses.

She was 'the little girl with a curl, right in the middle of her forehead'. And you know how that ends.

Daniel Hannan

Conservative MEP 1999–

Daniel Hannan was first elected as a Member of the European Parliament for South East England in 1999. He is a former speech-writer to Michael Howard and William Hague and is President of the Young Britons Foundation.

It's oddly fitting that the last thing Margaret Thatcher watched on television, the evening before she died, was *Songs of Praise*. She appeared on TV far more often than she watched it, but that weekly compilation of hymns was something she always enjoyed.

The reason I know is that I once stupidly attempted to make polite conversation with her on the subject. Around the turn of the millennium, the great woman came to lunch with a group of *Telegraph* writers. Determined not to ask a sententious question about public policy, I instead blurted out: 'Is there anything worth watching on television at the moment, Lady Thatcher?'

She fixed her fierce blue eyes on me, trying to remember who I was. (On a previous occasion, I had managed to thump her on the elbow while making an expansive point, and she had been wary in my presence ever since.) Then she softened. 'We enjoy the Sunday evening programmes, dear, especially those stirring Methodist hymns. But we find that *even they* are becoming a little wishy-washy these days.'

It is often said that Margaret Thatcher had no small talk, but this is another way of saying that she took even the paltriest things very seriously. Applied to television, her earnestness was bathetic. Applied to the rescue of a great country, it was absolutely necessary.

Just as Churchill, a rotten peacetime politician, brought the qualities that were needed to a war, so Margaret Thatcher's achievement cannot be divorced from the context of her times. During the 1970s, it felt as if Britain was finished. It is already hard to recall the sheer awfulness of that era: the strikes, the power-cuts, the three-day week, the prices and incomes policies, the double-digit inflation. As a 1978 headline in the *Wall Street Journal* put it: 'So long, Great Britain, it was nice knowing you.'

To turn such a situation around required the single-mindedness that became Margaret Thatcher's defining characteristic, and was the central theme of the Meryl Streep film.

'At least you knew where you stood with her,' people say, and it's true. But inflexibility, on its own, is no virtue. Such virtue as it has comes from its deployment in a good cause. What made Margaret Thatcher a great leader was not stubbornness, but being right. Her single-mindedness, like Churchill's, was placed at the service of a correct analysis of what needed to be done. He knew that there was no point in trying to compromise with Nazism; she that there was no point in trying to compromise with socialism.

Had she been wrong, but equally stiff-necked, she might have been a second Heath. The grocer, if anything, was even more obstinate than the grocer's daughter. He was certainly pricklier, more autocratic and more convinced of his indispensability. But he got the big calls wrong, accepting the Attlee consensus, seeking to treat with the trade unions and forcing Britain into its unhappy relationship with what is now the European Union.

That's the point about Lady T.: not that she was single-minded, but that she was right. Right, for what it's worth, about Wesley's hymns and the milk-and-water quality of religious broadcasting; and right, too, about what it means to live as independent citizens in an independent country.

Peter Riddell
Political Journalist

Peter Riddell is director of the Institute for Government. In the 1980s he was a political journalist for the Financial Times *and* The Times. *From 1991 to 2011 he was chief political commentator for* The Times.

Margaret Thatcher did not have much time for working political journalists, like those of us who ran political teams in the press gallery. She regarded us as a mixture of the ill-informed, the ill-intentioned and the ill-directed. Journalism was not a proper job. She would never use a term like 'reptiles' about us as her beloved husband Denis did. But there was a similar feeling of detachment and contempt.

Her preferred media contacts were with proprietors and ideologically sympathetic editors and columnists – those who were 'one of us'. This was in marked contrast to some of her predecessors like Harold Wilson, and all her successors who – at least during their rise to the top and in their early years as Prime Minister – cultivated friendly relations with political editors and correspondents, using first names at press conferences.

For Mrs Thatcher, it was always Mr Riddell, never Peter. And, in many ways, quite right too. I have never called a serving Prime Minister by their first name, however well I knew them beforehand, and however friendly our relations afterwards. Mrs Thatcher – and I will call her that throughout this contribution since that or Mrs T. was what she was known to us all at the time – created a mystique out of distance. There was always a little danger about her, apprehension of a damning put-down or memorable eruption. She was clearly different, someone who was willing to challenge the drift and defeatism of that unhappiest of political decades, the 1970s. It took some time for many of us to realise that she was changing the political landscape – the 1981 Budget and Cabinet reshuffle, followed by the Falklands.

Bernard Ingham was her faithful emissary to us, with his bluff Yorkshire bark and occasional bite. He was his mistress's voice – intuitively understanding her instincts and moods – even, if often, he anticipated rather than directly reported her views. Bernard was always the loyal retainer, below stairs, not a confidant. He was an interpreter and not himself a player – unlike, say, Alastair Campbell during the Blair years. Bernard was there to handle the media on her behalf, so that she would not have to do so.

Revealingly, my most striking memories of her are mainly away from Westminster, at party conferences, during elections and during her overseas visits. Mrs Thatcher was never a natural orator. Her success came from the power of her personality, the force of the conviction politician, the sabre rather than the rapier. Hence her most memorable speeches were all about the circumstances – the Iron Lady being tested during the Falklands conflict or in the aftermath of the Brighton bomb in October 1984. On both those occasions, it was less the soon-to-be-forgotten words that impressed than the expression of the personal will of the leader.

Only once did I see the mask fall – in January 1986 after the great Westland debate in the Commons. After weeks of infighting, disclosures and the resignation of two Cabinet ministers, her hold on power appeared to be under threat. The case against her, and her advisers in 10 Downing Street, was strong. That morning, as she left for the Commons, she said it might be her last day as Prime Minister. In the event, Neil Kinnock made a mess of his attack on her, she delivered a competent reply and Michael Heseltine, her great challenger, drew a line under the affair in what Michael Foot called his re-ratting speech. Despite everything, the Tory Party did not want all the upheaval of changing their leader. When the dramas of the afternoon had been played out, I bumped into her with Archie Hamilton, her faithful Parliamentary Private Secretary, in one of the small corridors by the terrace. I made some no doubt inane remark and she replied, for once, incoherently, looking utterly drained and exhausted. The curtain had fallen, the exam was over, the final lap had been run and the victor had nothing left.

If Mrs Thatcher seldom saw political journalists at Westminster, she was very accessible during election campaigns. That was when the party leaders still held daily news conferences, then in and around Smith Square. She treated these events as seminars, as her daily chance to educate backward political journalists. Each Political Editor was given his – and it was still largely his rather than her – chance to ask a daily question. Even if the question was addressed to some other minister, she invariably intervened. While the broadcasters sat at the front, to catch the cameras, some of us preferred to sit towards the back, in order to hear the comments of Denis Thatcher who stood there and offered an audible running commentary – 'bloody silly question', 'a lefite' etc. It was the world of *Private Eye*'s 'Dear Bill' letters made flesh.

Otherwise, my most vivid memories were on overseas trips when she was invariably at her most formidable – dealing with Presidents Reagan and Gorbachev. On the final day of her successful pre-election trip to the Soviet Union in spring 1987, in Tbilisi, the capital of Georgia, she looked, with her fur hat, almost like a Russian empress. As an elderly woman kissed her hand opposite the seminary (now a museum) where Stalin had trained and had been expelled, I remarked to Bernard Ingham that nobody in London would believe the scene. 'It's your bloody job to tell them.' As, indeed, it was. On the crowded and noisy VC10 flying back over the Black Sea and up the Danube, she famously said she would go 'on and on'. Ingham muttered, 'Now, I'll never be able to retire.' Hubris is always followed by nemesis and three and half years later, he, and she, did.

Sir Stephen Sherbourne
Political Secretary to Margaret Thatcher

Stephen Sherbourne was Margaret Thatcher's Political Secretary throughout her second term of office. He took on the same role for Michael Howard between 2003 and 2005.

One of Margaret Thatcher's great strengths as Prime Minister was that she never allowed herself to be taken captive by the establishment. Often, in the flat at No. 10, with just Denis and a few of us, after we'd been working late, and while we were eating the lasagne or shepherd's pie which (yet again) had come out of the freezer, she (and Denis) would litter the conversation with complaints about the government: 'too left-wing', 'spineless ministers', 'need to get off their backsides' etc. Had the transcripts of these conversations been read without knowing who'd been saying it, you would have thought it was some middle-class, middle-aged couple living in Surrey, but certainly not the person heading up the government.

One specific example of her ability to be detached from, and critical of, her own government came in a letter she once wrote. Every evening, Mrs Thatcher would have to sign dozens of letters (which she 'topped' and 'tailed') which had been put in her red box by her private office who were always meticulous in ensuring that the letters they drafted were totally in line with government policy. On one occasion, the Prime Minister topped and tailed a one-and-a-half page letter, which had been drafted and typed as usual by her office. But, on this occasion, she didn't stop once she'd signed 'Yours sincerely, Margaret Thatcher'. She continued to write in her own hand, for a further page and a half, the following: 'That is the official reply. My own views are as follows...' There then followed a policy quite at odds with official government policy. But to the great credit of her private office, it was sent out exactly like that.

Chris Moncrieff
Political Journalist

Chris Moncrieff was Political Editor of the Press Association from 1980 to 1994.

Nothing could be further from the truth than to portray Margaret Thatcher as a woman with a flailing handbag, constantly barking orders. It is true that she regularly had European grandees cowering before her – and she once said of her own ministers that she did not mind what they did, so long as they did what she said.

But her kindness to all whom she dealt with has been widely chronicled, especially her affinity with children.

But let me start at the beginning. My first meeting with Mrs Thatcher involved a degree of deception – on my part.

Edward Heath had just won the general election of that year. He marked the occasion by inviting members of the parliamentary lobby, and their spouses, to a reception at 10 Downing Street. At the time, my wife was heavily pregnant with our fourth child, so it was not really practical that she should go.

Instead, I invited (with my wife's and her husband's permission) the wife of the local publican, who had to pretend to be my wife.

Once inside, the pair of us stood drinking in a corner, when Margaret Thatcher, then Education Secretary, came over and asked us – it being that time of year – where the pair of us were going for our summer holidays.

And in virtually one and the same breath, my 'wife' replied 'Sardinia' and I said 'Walton-on-the-Naze'.

It was the first – and only time – I saw her rock back on her heels.

And on one occasion, a spectacular parade was planning to welcome her to Beijing and scores of tiny children, clad in the flimsiest costumes, gathered in the famous Tiananmen Square to take part.

It was a bitter day and the children were shivering with cold. This infuriated Mrs Thatcher who immediately button-holed a senior Chinese army officer and told him in no uncertain terms that unless some warm clothing were found for these children, she would leave immediately.

The officer knew he had met more than his match – and dutifully ushered the children into the warmth. Mrs Thatcher had taken on the might of the Chinese army – and emerged triumphant.

On another occasion she attended, as guest of honour, the Christmas party for children held by the press gallery in the Commons.

She spent some of the evening badgering the children to eat up their sausages and baked beans – with varying degrees of success. A year later, one of the parliamentary reporters asked his small daughter if she would like to go to the press gallery party again that year. There was a short pause and the little girl replied: 'Only if that nice dinner lady is there this time…'

Her husband Denis accompanied her on most of her foreign trips, although he openly said he did not much enjoy going anywhere east of Suez. Sometimes he would wander down to the 'steerage', the press end of the Royal Air Force VC10 on which she invariably travelled.

There, he would join us in what were sometimes pretty raucous and rowdy drinking sessions, consuming, as was his wont, considerable quantities of gin.

On one such occasion, we heard the dreaded footfall of the Prime Minister moving towards our end of the plane. She took one look at Denis and said: 'I thought there was going to be no gin on this trip, Denis.'

He momentarily looked taken aback, but recovered himself quickly to say: 'It's only tonic, dear.' Whereupon, he slurped back the remains of the gin in his glass and slunk back with her to the VIP area.

She was, as everybody knows, a stickler for British things. Once, she raged about the provision of French Perrier water at a press conference. 'What's wrong with British water?' she inquired.

And at another press conference she discovered – horrors – that a reporter's suit had been made in an Eastern European country. She decided to ask all the other journalists present for the provenance of their attire.

I cowered in the background, hoping she would not notice me, but she did. 'And your suit,' she asked, 'where was that made?'

With great trepidation, I examined my inner breast pocket. To my great relief, it said 'Burtons'. She looked at me, looked at my suit and after a brief pause said witheringly: 'I thought they had started to make snappy clothes there…'

And neither before nor since have I ever seen a politician engage in the childish game of 'stare me out' with an animal. But Thatcher, in the Falkland Islands, found herself engaged in a staring challenge with a passing penguin.

The two of them, unblinking, gazed at each other's eyes for fully two minutes before the penguin, realising it had met its match, surrendered and tottered away, vanquished. Another Thatcher triumph.

Mrs Thatcher may not have read the papers – she relied on her Press Secretary Sir Bernard Ingham to give her a digest every morn-ing – but she was nevertheless Fleet Street savvy.

On the Saturday after the 1987 general election, I had to go into No. 10 to pick up copies of the exchanges of letters between the Prime Minister and ministers who, for one reason or another, were not included in the new Cabinet.

As I waited in the lobby, Denis, expressing huge relief that the campaign (he hated electioneering) was over, entered carrying a copy of the *Financial Times* under his arm. A few minutes later, Mrs Thatcher arrived. They were going off to Chequers for the remainder of the weekend. She was carrying a copy of the fashion magazine, *Harpers & Queen*. Someone whispered to her that there were still TV cameras outside. Mrs Thatcher did not wish to be seen in public with anything so 'trivial' as a fashion magazine so she snatched the copy of the *Financial Times* from under her husband's arm, wrapped it around the magazine, thus hiding it, and turned to me, saying: 'You didn't see that. You didn't see anything, did you?'

Whereupon the pair of them marched out into the sunshine.

Sir John Major
Prime Minister 1990–97

Sir John Major served as a junior whip, social security minister, Chief Secretary to the Treasury, Foreign Secretary and Chancellor of the Exchequer under Margaret Thatcher. He was Prime Minister from 1990 to 1997.

My role as Treasury Whip led me into a serious row with the Prime Minister. Each summer, by tradition, the whips' office entertained her to dinner, and in June 1985 we met at No. 10. Margaret Thatcher was never noted for her small talk with colleagues and the first two courses passed with only desultory exchanges. It was evident that she wished to turn to some serious political discussion and John Wakeham said, 'The Treasury is at the heart of policy. I'll ask the Treasury Whip to begin.'

I regarded it as my role to tell the Prime Minister what the back-benchers were saying, and I did so. 'They don't like some of our policies,' I told her. Margaret did not like the message at all and began to chew up the messenger – I thought her behaviour was utterly unreasonable and repeated the message. She became more shrill in her criticisms. 'I'm astonished at what you're saying,' she snapped. I made it clear again that I was merely reporting the views of many Members, but she continued to attack me, became increasingly annoyed and I said: 'That's what colleagues are saying whether you like it or not – it's my job to tell you, and that's what I'm doing.' Her tirade continued. By now I was past caring about tact, shaking with anger, and nearly walked out. I repeated the message once more but made no impression at all and, as she raged on, the whips around me became very uncomfortable. I was almost beside myself with fury, and made no attempt to hide it. Even as I spoke, I thought I might be wrecking my career, but I was too angry to backtrack – which, in any event, would have been craven. I may not be promoted, I thought, but I'm not going to be humiliated.

Carol Mather intervened to support me. Margaret turned on him with an angry word. Bob Boscawen hastened to support Carol. He was met with a glare. I had no intention of backing down and pitched in again. The meeting was dangerously close to collapsing in mutual recrimination. Jean Trumpington, one of the Lords' whips, attempted to lower the temperature and had her head bitten off for her pains. It was an extraordinary performance by the Prime Minister, and I have never forgotten it. As we rose from the table for post-dinner drinks her husband Denis came up to me. 'She'll have enjoyed that,' he remarked, and drifted off happily, clutching a gin and tonic. John Cope sidled up and suggested I might make my peace with Margaret. 'I think,' I told him, 'that it's up to her. You'd better tell her that.'

The next day, to my astonishment, this extraordinary woman did just that. Since phrases like 'wets' and 'dries', 'one of them' or 'one of us', were already part of the Thatcher folklore, I assumed that after our argument I would be cast into outer darkness at the first opportunity. My career, I was sure, would be on hold if not on stop. But I was wrong.

In the late afternoon I was sitting as the whip on duty on the Treasury bench in the Commons. Margaret swept in from behind the Speaker's Chair and sat beside me. She could not have been more charming. She mentioned some ideas I had previously put to her, so inconsequential I cannot now remember them, and said she wished to discuss them. Another whip was summoned to the bench, and an ad hoc discussion commenced in the whips' office, with the Prime Minister and me seated in armchairs. Without the fracas of the previous night being mentioned, peace was declared.

A few weeks later, in the autumn reshuffle, I was promoted to my first ministerial post in a department. Not for the first or the last time, Margaret Thatcher had surprised me.

Neil Hamilton
Writer and Broadcaster

Neil Hamilton served as Conservative MP for Tatton from 1983 until the 1997 general election. He was a member of the No Turning Back Group of MPs. He is a writer and broadcaster.

Contrary to popular mythology, Margaret is not at all stuffy or narrow-minded and has a good sense of humour. She likes raising a chuckle by acting up to her caricature handbagging image – a joke all the more amusing to observe when played on someone who thinks she is being serious.

But I have to admit that getting her to see the point of someone else's jokes is sometimes no laughing matter – as I occasionally discovered to my cost. After *The Spectator* awarded me the title 'Parliamentary Wit of the Year' in 1988 she engaged me as a resident jokesmith to add some souffle lightness to the bread-and-butter pudding of a prime ministerial speech.

It was no easy task. For example, in October 1989 I was at Chequers helping with her speech for the debate on the Queen's Speech. This annual debate concerns the government's programme for the year ahead but technically arises on a motion to present a loyal address to the monarch, thanking her for 'her gracious speech'. The government chooses two of its own backbenchers for the honour of proposing and seconding the motion – the first, usually an amiable old buffer long past his sell-by-date, and the second, usually some oily young man on the make. They are followed immediately by the Prime Minister, who has to shower compliments upon them before getting on with the serious business.

The seconder in 1989 was an amiable young buffer, Jeremy Hanley, then Tory MP for Richmond and Barnes. A chartered accountant by training, he was also a member of MENSA, the club for the very brainy. But his roots were more theatrical – his mother being star of stage and screen, Dinah Sheridan; his father, the well-known comedian, Jimmy Hanley. Jeremy was an excellent and amusing raconteur in his own right and could be relied on to rise to the occasion.

What could Margaret say about him? I suggested a mild witticism, combining a reference to his intelligence and amiability: 'He is very clever and amusing but he never allows his brains to go to his head.' The joke seemed pretty obvious to me, but not alas to Margaret, who exploded: 'I can't say that! If his brains aren't in his head, where will people think they are?' We grappled with the abstruse metaphysics of the humour for some time but, try as I might, I could not get her to see the punchline – she was convinced everyone would think she was suggesting his brains were in his backside!

In 1990 I was a government whip during Michael Heseltine's leadership challenge. I wanted to help her and was amazed when Chief Whip Tim Renton forbade whips getting involved.

Although we all owed our jobs to her, he said we had to be neutral: 'In the long-term interest of the party.'

I was not convinced; she was irreplaceable and had to be saved. Renton also happened to be a patrician 'wet' and former aide to Geoffrey Howe, whose resignation speech had precipitated Heseltine's challenge so I naturally ignored his advice and fed all my intelligence into her campaign. Sadly, this had no effect because her campaign managers were grossly incompetent and she spent vital days in Paris at a world summit instead of rallying support in the Commons.

When she did return I and other members of the No Turning Back Group told her what we thought of her campaign. I proposed she ask for a statement of support from all the Cabinet. I knew many ministers would secretly vote for Heseltine and hoped to push them into a corner. I advised her to ask each of them individually rather than en masse, thinking most would be too gutless to tell her to her face.

Unfortunately, I had miscalculated.

Her fatal absence from Westminster had caused backbench support to leech away so only a handful of Cabinet members promised to back her unequivocally. The rest said that although they would back her if she decided to fight on, she could not win and she should withdraw.

The No Turning Back Group had a routine dinner planned for that evening but there was only one topic. By this stage, there was dispute even in our ranks as to whether she could win. Peter Lilley, then a Treasury junior minister under John Major, announced he thought she should resign rather than be defeated. I angrily denounced this as 'establishment treason' and suspected a Treasury plot to shoehorn

Major into the leadership. At about 9.30 p.m., we got a message from No. 10 that she was thinking of resigning. At this, Michael Portillo and Michael Forsyth rushed over to bolster her resolve.

I stayed behind to continue our arguments. An hour or so later, hearing no further news, Michael Brown and I also went to No. 10. We were ushered into the Cabinet room where the atmosphere was like a morgue. Margaret sat with a small group of ministers, sunk in gloom. It was the saddest sight of my life.

Here was this giant of a woman, sitting there, with the stuffing knocked out of her. She had won three general elections, won the Falklands War, seen off Arthur Scargill and restored prosperity and pride in being British. She and Ronald Reagan had just destroyed the Soviet Union. She was the greatest peacetime Prime Minister of the century. How could we even be thinking of ditching her? I was aghast. Apart from Portillo and Forsyth the others present (including John Gummer and Attorney-General Nick Lyell) were all defeatists.

I said it was ridiculous to give up now; she had a solid majority on the first ballot of MPs and had failed to get the required 15 per cent majority over Heseltine by only four votes. If she could do so well after a disastrous campaign while she was abroad, there was everything to play for in the second ballot. Wearily, she said it was too late. After eleven years as PM she could not canvass MPs.

I refused to accept this and tried to cajole her. Was she not a warrior queen like Boudicca? Better to die heroically in battle than leave the field. I tried everything. Each time the dismal Jimmies shook their heads and advised it was hopeless.

They began to slink away.

At 2 a.m., I was the only one left. She said she would go to bed and consider things but I knew the game was up. Like some battleship holed below the waterline, she was sinking and passing into history. I was distraught and went home to tell Christine. The first news bulletins in the morning broke the story.

Several days later, I sat next to her as she gave her last Commons speech in a no confidence debate opened by Neil Kinnock. Despite this being a valedictory speech, it was a barnstormer.

She wiped the floor with him and the Tory MPs cheered. I looked around at my colleagues and wrote in the whips' book: 'PM cheered to the rafters by 150 hypocrites [who had voted against her].'

I was one of a small group who lunched with Margaret in the Members' dining room on her last day in the Commons in 1992 and continued to see her regularly. My saddest memory of these twilight years was the reception following Denis's memorial service at the Guards Chapel. I spoke to her for about ten minutes and then she said she had better go see where Denis was. Then, after a pause, she said: 'Oh, I can't do that anymore, can I?' I gave her a big hug and shed a tear.

Philip Davies
Conservative MP 2005–

Philip Davies stood in Colne Valley in the 2001 election but was later successfully elected in 2005 as the Member for Shipley.

Margaret Thatcher was my political inspiration. I only wish that I had been in Parliament when she was Prime Minister.

My earliest political memory was of the Falklands War of 1982. I was ten years old and remember coming home from school to see what was going on over in the Falklands. It was during that crisis that I built up my admiration for Margaret Thatcher. I was born in Doncaster and my father was involved with the local Conservative Party – there are not many Conservatives in Doncaster – and as soon as I was old enough to deliver leaflets and knock on doors, my father had me out delivering leaflets and knocking on doors. I loved elections – we never used to win any, but I still loved them.

People have often said to me that it must have been incredibly difficult going around mining communities in the mid-to-late-1980s supporting Margaret Thatcher and a Conservative government. It was not difficult at all. I believed in Margaret Thatcher to my core and when we believed in somebody in the way I believed in Margaret Thatcher it was not difficult to go knocking on doors to support the great things she did for this country. It was not Margaret Thatcher who ruined those mining communities; it was Arthur Scargill who ruined them – and let no one forget that.

Margaret Thatcher was a conviction politician. She believed that politics was all about trying to persuade people of what she believed in rather than just telling people what she thought they wanted to hear. That is the kind of politics that I believe in. She did not need focus groups or opinion polls to tell her what to believe. She was instinctively in tune with the British public.

I remember from working at Asda that the best retailers were the ones who instinctively knew what the customers wanted without having to go to a focus group to ask. The worst chief executives of retailers were the ones who always had to be told what the focus groups were telling them and what the opinion polls were telling them. For me, it is exactly the same with political leaders. The best political leaders such as Margaret Thatcher instinctively know what the public want and where they are – they do not need opinion polls – and the worst political leaders are those who have to rely on those polls because they know no better themselves.

Margaret Thatcher won three general elections on the trot, and the best way to sum up her achievement is to recognise that more people voted Conservative in her third general election than they had done the first time she won in 1979. That is a remarkable achievement showing how she built support over those eight years. Tony Blair, on the other hand, won three general elections but lost 4 million voters between the last and the first election. That goes to show the difference in calibre between those two politicians who might otherwise be closely compared.

Margaret Thatcher was voted out by her own party. I have utter contempt for those in our party – people who were not fit to lick her boots – who ousted her in 1990. That did an awful lot of damage – but not just to the country; it did long-term damage to the Conservative Party as well.

Anyone wanting to sum up Mrs Thatcher should look at her final performance from the dispatch box as Prime Minister. It was one of the finest performances that has ever been seen in Parliament. I think it was Michael Carttiss who said from the Conservative benches that she could wipe the floor with the lot of them, and that was absolutely true – she could. During that debate, I wonder how many Conservative Members wondered, 'Oh, Lord, what have we done?' They got rid of the greatest Prime Minister this country has ever seen. There will never be another like her.

Lord Dobbs
Novelist and Broadcaster

A former Chief of Staff and Deputy Chairman of the Conservative Party, Michael Dobbs is most famous as the author of the House of Cards *trilogy of political novels.*

They sow the seeds of their own destruction, even the greatest. And so it was with Margaret.

The date was 4 June 1987, exactly one week before the election triumph that returned her to Downing Street for a record third time. Her victory was unprecedented, and it was to be her last.

I was Chief of Staff of the Conservative Party and on that fateful day was sitting in my claustrophobic room in Conservative Central Office. When I had been appointed to the position I had been told by Norman Tebbit, the Chairman of the party, what to expect. 'There comes a point in every war when the generals require that someone be taken out into a courtyard, put up against a wall and shot. Your job is to find the body. Or to be the body.' I had thought he was joking.

A Gallup poll the night before had shown an alarming reduction in the size of the Tory lead. On the basis of the poll we were headed for trouble, but every other piece of information suggested we were going to win, and win big.

It was a rogue poll.

It didn't, however, stop the panic. Margaret was holding a morning summit in the room next door to mine with Norman, David Young, Willie Whitelaw and Stephen Sherbourne. Suddenly John Wakeham burst into my room and asked for the press advertising that was proposed for the following day. I was not responsible for the advertising but it had been left in my room for security. I handed the layouts to John, but he shook his head. 'I'm not going back into that room without you.'

So I took the layouts and walked into the room. If John had been kind he would have offered me a blindfold. It was time to be stood up against the wall.

The next few minutes of what became known as 'Wobbly Thursday' remain distinct in my mind, but I won't report the gory and distasteful details here, except to say that although the confrontation that took place was ostensibly about advertising, it had far more to do with power, access and intrigue. For the Court of Queen Margaret had turned into a Byzantine maze of crossed wires and conniving acolytes. Margaret was at the height of her powers, and it seemed that everyone wanted their own individual piece of it.

And that is the point of this story. She was at the height of her powers. She could rant and rage to the point of incoherence (and did during those minutes); I felt as though the handbag had been buried deep in the back of my skull. Willie Whitelaw rolled his oyster eyes at me in sympathy, but only Norman Tebbit tried to stand up to her, to restrain her, to direct her onto safer ground. It was to no purpose. In more than a decade of working for her I had seen her in pain, in tears, in triumph, but never had I seen her in such a condition.

She was the leader, one of the greatest leaders of the century, and about to score another historic victory. Except she seemed to doubt that herself.

As we left the meeting we were all shaking. I walked next to Willie Whitelaw, that wise and often underrated old bird, who said something that was to change my life. 'That is a woman who will never fight another election,' he muttered.

It seemed a preposterous suggestion. She bestrode the world. Yet three weeks later, as I sat beside a swimming pool in Gozo, the thought was still bothering me. I worked it over. They never know when to go, the great leaders. They all have to be pushed, shoved, hacked from office. Lloyd George. Churchill. And Thatcher, too. I realised that Willie was right.

She had lost the sensitivity and patience that had guided her so successfully through the difficult years when she had rebuilt a party in tatters and set it upon a course that transformed the country. It wasn't so much a matter of principle or policy but of personal style that, in the end, forced away from her even many of her closest allies. She became a political Chernobyl from whom so many were to distance themselves.

That realisation transformed my life. I sat down beside the swimming pool and began work on a novel about the destruction of a Prime Minister. It was called *House of Cards*.

Like so many of the ancient gods, she could not be brought down by mere mortals. She could only be brought down by herself. Oh, but while it was good, wasn't she magnificent!

Lord Hattersley

Labour Peer

*Roy Hattersley was Labour MP for Birmingham Sparkbrook from 1964 to 1997
and served as Deputy Leader of the Labour Party between 1983 and 1992. He was
raised to the peerage in 1997.*

In 1973, when I was shadow Education Secretary and Margaret
Thatcher was the real thing, the Tory government published a
White Paper called 'A Framework for Expansion'. It announced great
increases in spending on schools and universities and confirmed the
new generosity with a statistical appendix that I couldn't understand.
So, in preparation for the House of Commons debate, I consulted
Maurice Peston – not then a peer, merely a professor of economics. He
said the figures were phoney.

Impatient at my inability to understand his explanation, Peston
drafted me a paragraph that he suggested I read to the House
of Commons. I stuttered it out with as much conviction as I could
muster. There was an immediate explosion of incredulous contempt.
The notion that Thatcher had got her figures wrong was regarded
as ridiculous by everyone – including the education correspondents
of the major newspapers. Stuart Maclure, Editor of the TES and
doyenne of education journalists, told me that he proposed to discover
the extent of my error by consulting the only real expert on the subject
– Professor Maurice Peston.

The result of the Peston adjudication was a unanimous outcry
among education correspondents that the government had got it
wrong. Nobody said that I had got it right. I wrote to Thatcher
demanding an apology. She didn't reply. I challenged her to a debate.
She didn't respond. One day, I met her in the lobby of the House of
Commons and said: 'Sooner or later, you'll have to admit that you
were wrong.' She looked me in the eye and said: 'Never! Never! Never!'

When, ten years later, I became Deputy Leader of the Labour Party,
I occasionally stood in for Neil Kinnock at Prime Minister's Questions.
Another peer (C. C. P. Williams of Oxford and Essex) suggested that

I should approach her in the manner of a spin bowler. My first question should, metaphorically, be a slow, long hop, which she hit for six. The second should be cunningly disguised so that, when she attempted a second boundary, she was bowled. More often than not, she scored off both my deliveries. But occasionally, it worked.

Once I persuaded her to denounce me for suggesting that the poll tax assessment was inaccurate and was then able to tell her that one of her ministers had admitted it that morning. Her reply was that I was 'trying to cause trouble'. Simon Hoggart wrote that it was the nicest thing anyone had ever said about me.

Her last speech in the House of Commons – on the day she gave up the premiership – was not half as good as people make out. It was the way in which she opened the debate on the Westland affair that left the most lasting impression on me. Knowing she was in trouble, Thatcher simply reminded her backbenchers that she was the champion of the ideology that they supported. That was, of course, her strength, and her contribution to British history. She changed the ideological climate. After Thatcher, nearly everyone hated public expenditure and loved the free market.

Lord Wakeham
Chief Whip 1983–87

John Wakeham was Conservative MP for Maldon, later South Colchester and Maldon, from 1974 to 1992. He joined the whips' office in 1979 and was appointed Chief Whip in 1983. In 1987 he became Leader of the House of Commons and was appointed Energy Secretary in 1989. He was elevated to the peerage in 1992 and became Leader of the House of Lords, a position he relinquished in 1994.

I entered the House of Commons in 1974 – one year before Mrs Thatcher became leader of the Conservative Party. I left it for the House of Lords barely eighteen months after she left No. 10. My time as an MP was therefore dominated by this giant figure – one of the greatest Prime Ministers this country has ever seen, and probably will ever see.

Tributes elsewhere in this timely volume testify eloquently to the dramatic changes she wrought in British politics – permanently transforming an economy in decline into the powerhouse we have today, and turning us into a nation of owners with stakes for the first time in our businesses, our major industries and, for many, many more, in our own property. Few dispute that success, and the permanent legacy, even among Margaret's detractors.

I do not want to add to this catalogue – but rather to add my own personal memories of the saddest point of Margaret's premiership, her resignation in November 1990.

Those of us who were closest to her knew that a challenge to her leadership from Michael Heseltine was almost inevitable from the moment Geoffrey Howe made his famous speech in the House of Commons. It seemed then a question not of if, but of when.

I had little part in her campaign during the first ballot, because it fell during the climax of the electricity privatisation for which I was responsible. One thing I knew was that the result could never be certain: far too many of my colleagues in the Parliamentary Conservative Party would be telling Margaret's campaign managers what they wanted to hear, not how they were really intending to vote.

The result when it came was a great body blow – so near yet so far, with the outcome of a second ballot far from certain.

It was at that point that Margaret asked me to run her campaign for the second ballot. Before we could make any plans, I knew there was one central issue we had to confront. In a parliamentary system such as ours, no Prime Minister can long remain in office if he or she does not have the support of the Cabinet – and, in this case, that support was regrettably far from clear.

I knew, therefore, that Margaret had to see all the members of the Cabinet to ascertain where they stood. If they were all behind her, there was a very good chance of victory in the second ballot; if they weren't, then that victory was far from clear.

On the afternoon of Wednesday 21 November, Margaret gave an accomplished performance in the House of Commons during a statement on the Paris summit. After that, she agreed rather reluctantly to see her Cabinet colleagues one by one in her office overlooking Parliament Square. She asked each of them their views.

Many Cabinet colleagues said they would stick by her to the end. Some reaffirmed the view expressed by Cranley Onslow, the Chairman of the 1922 Committee, that she should permit the contest to be widened to allow in figures like John Major and Douglas Hurd. At least three warned her that they were prepared to resign if she stayed on. A large number added that they thought, whatever their own decisions, support in Parliament was crumbling away – and that standing again may risk handing victory to Michael Heseltine.

To those who told her they could not see her winning the second ballot, or who themselves refused to support her, she mused that politics was a funny old world. She had won a record three elections; she maintained the overwhelming support of the Conservative Party in the country; she had never lost a motion of confidence in the House of Commons; and the first leadership ballot had shown she still commanded the support of a substantial majority of Conservative MPs – although not quite enough to win through the antiquated and eccentric electoral system that then existed.

Two quite amusing incidents occurred during this round. The first was when Peter Brooke went in to see her and give his support. He was dressed in white tie and tails on his way to a City dinner and he remarked to me that there was a time in his days at Oxford

when white tie and tails was the only appropriate dress in which to
make important decisions.

The second came when the late Alan Clark also rushed in without an appointment and said 'Prime Minister, you must fight on – of
course you will lose but what a glorious defeat!'

That round of meetings finished at about 8.30 p.m. and Margaret
told me she was going back to No. 10 to think things over. She was
clearly very depressed – and had to face hours of work on her speech
for a confidence motion, moved by Neil Kinnock, the next day.

To try and prevent the formation of cabals among Cabinet ministers
and others, it was made clear to colleagues that Margaret was going to
sleep on things. The Cabinet meeting was brought forward to 9 a.m. to
allow decisions to be reached before the formal business began.

By morning – and after consultation with the most important person
in her life, Denis – she had decided that it was impossible to carry on
and she said so to the Cabinet. It was, understandably, an emotional
moment, but composure was soon regained and the meeting ended
quite quickly.

The rest, as they say – including her bravura final appearance at the
dispatch box – is history.

I look back many times at that awful week and ponder whether
anything different could have been done. Each time, I come up with
the same conclusion – that, against the background of the first ballot,
we did everything we possibly could.

The manner of Margaret's departure has, I hope, faded from
memory. After all, she deserves to be remembered for all that she
achieved for the British people in eleven magnificent years – not for
the way it all ended. Those achievements live on, and always will,
because she changed Britain for ever.

Sir Robin Day
Political Journalist

Sir Robin Day, who died in August 2000, was among the most distinguished and best-loved political journalists of our time. He started working as a political correspondent for the BBC in 1954, quickly establishing his reputation as a hard-hitting interviewer. He is best known as the presenter of Question Time, *which he chaired from 1979 until 1989.*

Of Thatcherism there will be many conflicting definitions. Here, in fairness, recorded for history, is her own exposition – the authorised version, as it were, or the gospel according to Margaret. She gave it in answer to this question from me on television, three days before polling day in June 1987:

Q: But you have stamped your image on the Tory Party like no other leader has before. We now hear of 'Thatcherism'. What is it that 'Thatcherism' means?

A: Sir Robin, it is not a name that I created in the sense of calling it an 'ism'. Let me tell you what it stands for. It stands for sound finance and government running the affairs of the nation in a sound financial way. It stands for honest money, not inflation; it stands for living within your means, it stands for incentives, because we know full well that the growth and economic strength of a nation comes from the efforts of its people, and its people need incentives to work as hard as they possibly can. All of that has produced economic growth. It stands for something else. It stands for the wider and wider spread of ownership of property, of houses, of shares, of savings. It stands for being strong in defence; a reliable ally and trusted friend. People have called those things 'Thatcherism'. They are in fact fundamental common sense and having faith in the enterprise and abilities of the people. It is my task to try and release those. They were always there. They've always been there in the British people, but they couldn't flourish under socialism; now they've been released. That's all that 'Thatcherism' is.

She may have learned this off by heart. If so, she had learned it well.

She spoke it with a fierce and fluent vigour, with that rare political gift of making simple and familiar words sound new and compelling.

Margaret Thatcher was a political phenomenon. Not only was she the first woman to be Prime Minister of the United Kingdom. Not only did she lead the Tory Party for over fourteen years. What was also phenomenal about her was that she, a bourgeois Conservative, proved to be a radical Prime Minister. In adopting Thatcherism, she buried socialism, or at least she buried 'Clause Four' socialism. She was driven by conviction and instinct, rather than by intellect or reason. She was admired for her 'conviction' politics by that left-wing opponent of consensus, Tony Benn. And she is much admired by Tony Blair, who is apt, unless my ears deceive me, to echo these words of Margaret Thatcher:

'I decide with others the way we are going, then I bend every single effort to getting that through, overcoming all obstacles. It is not arrogant in my view. It is determination and resolve.'

From the poor Tory performances in the 1989 Euro-elections it looked as if the Thatcherite ascendancy was coming to an end. What with rising inflation and industrial stoppages, an American TV reporter quipped: 'The Iron Lady is showing signs of metal fatigue.'

There was the acrimonious resignation of her Chancellor, Nigel Lawson. And after the messy Cabinet reshuffle, in which she booted the long-suffering Sir Geoffrey Howe out of the Foreign Office, the Thatcherocracy ended sooner than expected.

In her 1988 Bruges speech, she signalled her determination to prevent the EC from becoming a super-state: 'We have not successfully rolled back the frontiers of the state in Britain,' she declared, 'only to see them reimposed at a European level.' This appalled the pro-European establishment.

Did she set out to whip up Euroscepticism? Or was she responding realistically to a cooling of Euro-enthusiasm among the British people? Who can say? But there are no prizes for guessing how she will urge us to vote in the euro referendum.

Until the end came, Mrs Thatcher dominated her Cabinet like no other recent Prime Minister. There was no obvious successor to her. She achieved all this – and here was a strange feature of the Thatcher phenomenon – without being a great parliamentarian, without being a brilliant orator, without having a gift for words or memorable phrases, and without displaying a notable sense of humour. Probably more than any Prime Minister in my lifetime, she was anathema to many intellectuals, such as the petty-minded Oxonians who shamefully voted to refuse her an honorary degree.

But her style of leadership, however domineering or strident, did not prevent her from winning another huge majority (102) in 1987. She thus became the first British Prime Minister to have been elected to three consecutive terms of office since Lord Liverpool over 160 years ago.

At that 1987 election, strong claims could be made for Margaret Thatcher's leadership. Had she not rolled back the state, curbed the trade unions, defeated Scargill, Galtieri and Ken Livingstone, and defied terrorism? Had not her Chancellors, Howe and Lawson, reduced the top rate of income tax from a monstrous 83 per cent to 40 per cent? The pound was strong. Inflation had stayed in the 4–5 per cent range. The economy was growing.

But the second Thatcher government had seen some rough weather. There was no shortage of ammunition for critics of Thatcherism. There was the violence during the prolonged miners' strike and in the printers' dispute at Wapping. There was the Westland helicopter affair, when normal Cabinet government disintegrated. Michael Heseltine stalked out of the Cabinet and Thatcher came perilously near to falling from power. As she herself said to someone in Downing Street as she left for the Westland debate: 'I may not be Prime Minister by six o'clock this evening.' Thus for about three hours on the afternoon of Monday 28 January 1986 did Sir Geoffrey Howe seriously think that he might become Prime Minister that day.

Labour, with its media skills, including a brilliant film boosting its new leader, Neil Kinnock, was widely held by the chattering classes to have won the 1987 campaign. Bur Labour lost the election.

So that election was a triumph for what had come to be called Thatcherism. Few people, if any (certainly not I), then thought that this three-times victor, this invincible vote-getter, this woman so admired around the world, would soon be forced out of office. Yet only three years later, in 1990, that is what happened to Margaret Thatcher. For the first time ever in peacetime a British Prime Minister in good health, commanding a majority in the Commons, was kicked out of office.

This was not only the end of an epoch, but the extraordinary end of an extraordinary epoch. Whether you were glad or sad to see her go, she was the only Prime Minister whose name has been given to an 'ism'. No one ever talked about Disraeli-ism, Macmillanism, Heathism or even Churchillism. As Margaret Thatcher herself tearfully remarked at her very last Cabinet meeting, 'It's a funny old world.'

My favourite memory of her will always be that 1987 election interview. She was on top form, in full flow, almost unstoppable. In content and style, this was vintage Thatcher. My attempts to interject were frequently cut short. At one point I was driven to suggest that we were 'not having a party political broadcast, but an interview which must depend on me asking some questions occasionally'. The Prime Minister replied, 'Yes indeed, *Mr* Day', and went on exactly as before. According to Richard Last, the admirable TV critic of the *Daily Telegraph*, 'Sir Robin was crushed with the effortlessness of a beautifully coiffured steamroller flattening a blancmange.'

I do not remember her as 'Maggie', or ever hearing anyone ever call her 'Maggie'. To me she was 'Prime Minister' or 'Mrs Thatcher'. If I spoke of her, it would be as 'Mrs Thatcher' or 'Margaret'. But never Maggie.

Cheryl Gillan

Conservative MP 1992–

Cheryl Gillan became the MP for Chesham and Amersham in 1992 after serving as Chairman of the Bow Group. She was Secretary of State for Wales from 2010 to 2012.

'So when are you going to try and become a Member of Parliament? We need more women in politics.'

These words were spoken to me at a formal dinner, just before the general election of 1979 and readers might be surprised to hear, given some of the widely circulated mythologies about the lady involved, that those words were addressed to me by Margaret Thatcher.

At the dinner I sat next to Mrs Thatcher, who was then Leader of the Opposition. We chatted about how hard everyone was working to win the election and how she was about to become the first woman Prime Minister. She also shared reminiscences of what it was like to be a Cabinet minister. When Mrs Thatcher asked whether I was interested in politics, I replied that I had always had a strong involvement. This is why I joined the Bow Group, which gave me a way to fulfil that interest in politics. Mrs Thatcher then asked her question, which set me off on a quest to become an MP and ultimately led to my election to the House of Commons on 1992.

Despite what many people have said about Margaret Thatcher, she really did encourage women to participate in politics – as I can testify.

Terry Major-Ball
John Major's Brother

Best known as the brother of John Major, Terry Major-Ball held numerous jobs including, famously, garden gnome maker. He wrote his life story in Major Major, *from which this memory of Mrs Thatcher is extracted. He died in 2007.*

I am often asked what I think of Mrs Thatcher, and I have to say I have always admired her, even when her policies led to Philips making redundancies and me losing my job in 1989. I have met the lady only twice, once at No. 10 and once in the Chancellor's office in the House. She was very polite to me, only correcting me when I referred to the 'poll tax'. She told me 'community charge' was the correct term but appeared not to take any offence.

The question I hate being asked is why Lady Thatcher has been saying less than helpful things recently. For many years I was one of her most enthusiastic supporters and I remained one even towards the end of her time, when with many others I began to think she was losing her touch and was disregarding the people who voted for her. Many of the people I worked with were beginning to say that she had to go, that we needed someone more in tune with our way of thinking. After John was made Chancellor the stick I had to take about her increased. I became an obvious target for remarks by many people in the office where I worked who were fed up with her ways.

Whenever they said she must go, I stuck to my ground, saying: 'Look at all the great things she has done.' When they said she was arrogant and didn't care about ordinary people I had a stock reply. 'Oh yes, she does,' I would say with some authority, 'John tells me so.' I would relate little tales I had been told to demonstrate the other, less cold side to her nature – like the time a young lady serving dinner at Chequers tripped and deposited meat and gravy all over a minister and she went to comfort the girl, not the minister. I continued to support her, even after I was certain a change was needed, because I felt that if an expert like John was prepared to support her, I should too. I just hoped she would stop looking for fights and get on with the job.

After my firm closed and I found myself redundant, people would ask me: 'How can you support Thatcher when you're out of a job and can't get another?' 'Look abroad,' I would say – it was always the same answer. 'We're better off than a lot of countries. Things will come round in time. We've had all this before and come out stronger.' I was saying this right up to the time of the leadership challenge, despite my private thoughts. Why? Because I knew John was prepared to vote for her right up to the wire. How? Because of our conversations. As far as I'm aware, John only agreed to stand himself after he knew there was no hope for her. I have to admit I was hurt and mystified whenever I read of the criticism Margaret was reported to be making of John, the man we are told by the media whom she had chosen and supported as her successor and who had been so loyal to her.

I was especially hurt when I remembered how she complained about the treatment she received from her predecessor. Apparently she thinks her case is different because she never lost an election, whereas Ted Heath did. I find this reasoning odd. It is strange too that she has saved former colleagues whom she chose for the Cabinet herself. What happened to her judgement then? Recently I heard her say on television that it was better to have them in the Cabinet than on the benches making trouble. Why did I have a feeling of déjà-vu?

Now that her memoirs have been published and she has had her say, perhaps her sadness at leaving office is passing and peace can reign. I hope those historians who were planning to say, as a footnote to her achievements, that she didn't know how to retire from office gracefully will return their pens to their stands unused. I and many others can remember her great deeds while forgetting her miscalculations.

I'll even be prepared to say sorry for using the vulgar expression 'poll tax' to her face on that occasion when we met. She is a great and remarkable lady.

Patrick Minford
Economist

The Professor of Economics at Cardiff Business School, Patrick Minford is among the most respected economists of recent times. He has published numerous books and papers and his work was highly influential upon the development of Thatcherite economic policy.

For me Margaret Thatcher was the epitome of thorough hard work on policy. A big issue would be centre stage – monetary policy and inflation, unemployment and benefits, for example – and the basics and the prejudices aired, the hard work would begin.

The civil servants would of course produce their briefs and reports, and that would be the start for a general canvassing of views around those with the same aims as her. But the critics' views too must be synthesised and dealt with convincingly – how long would the monetary policy take to bring down inflation? Would cutting unemployment benefits have enough effect?

The whole process would often come to a grand climax in a Chequers seminar, as it did in the case of these two topics – where she presided, heckled or intervened with more dramatic emphasis, reducing strong men to quailing silence. But the objective was to test the preferred policies to destruction (sometimes too literally, as the burden of proof was on the effectiveness of change – political capital would be used up and there must be the probability of noticeable results).

I remember on one occasion someone (one of her wets, or one of her closest advisers? I forget; it could easily have been either) said something limp and silly; this provoked one of those fearsome diatribes (a 'handbagging') which became legendary. Then later on I was the object of her ire – I fought back, which got me into even deeper water. But the fact was that she didn't care what feelings were trampled on in the process of getting to the nub of good policy – only those (men typically) with too much personal pomp and worth would not understand that vital objective; and she had no patience for people who couldn't take it in such a cause.

To those unfamiliar with the usual brutal seminar methods of reaching truth this was all pretty hard; but I noticed that among those close to her the survivors were a tough intellectual breed. When the country had become so used to failure in policy after policy, it was indeed vital that pretty stringent tests were applied to the new ones; they could not be allowed to fail.

The Chequers seminars were rounded off by her chivvying everyone to eat properly; one got the impression that if she had only had the time she would have cooked it too. One minute the hectoring platonic dialogue, the next the attentive host bringing round the soup. The point was this: we men had settled for second, third and fourth best for her country and a small woman was going to see us and such pathetic compromise with mediocrity off, once and for all. It was startling, wonderful stuff; and how badly we needed it and how much hard work and bruised *amour-propre* it took.

Baroness Nicholson
Liberal Democrat Peer

Emma Nicholson was the MP for Torridge and West Devon from 1987 to 1997. In 1995 she famously defected from the Conservative Party to the Liberal Democrats. She was raised to the peerage as Baroness Nicholson of Winterbourne in 1997.

I believe that unlike the most successful Tory Prime Minister of the twentieth and nineteenth centuries, Mrs Thatcher lost her way on the road to a new, liberal, radical synthesis. She lost her way, I believe, because the Brighton bomb effectively locked her away in a Nixonian bunker, staffed by overzealous, ideological activists and cut off from the voters she needed to see and hear and touch. The IRA won a more profound victory than was immediately apparent from her survival. Her isolation led her to harden policies which destroyed the post-war political consensus that she inherited and helped develop a climate of acquisitive greed.

Four winters will be sufficient to watch her trajectory: 1976, 1982, 1984 and the five days from Thursday to Tuesday in November 1990 when it all came falling down.

In 1976, after an extended struggle, I was selected for the role of sacrificial lamb in Blyth, Northumberland, to fight the second strongest Labour constituency in the country: the scene of my own father's triumph in 1931 as a reforming Conservative. Facing sure and certain defeat I called on the new party leader for advice in her office in the Palace of Westminster.

This first meeting with Mrs Thatcher revealed to me a pacing tigress, full of warmth and reformist resolve, overflowing with a fighting spirit and a zeal for conquering socialism by going directly to the people. Eyes flashing bright blue, golden hair, radiating a feminine energy unknown outside the home to the Tory male establishment, she got right down to business: 'Go door to door, Emma, let them know you, as a person.' I moved north every weekend and lived at a £3-a-night bed and breakfast on the High Street while my principal opponent, the Labour MP, stayed in the nearest five-star hotel way outside the constituency issuing press releases headed 'Blyth Working Men's Club'. I went, alone, door to door, dressed in my best to honour the electorate in wind and snow through the council estates promoting her vision of freedom from socialist control, and I polled the best Tory score in half a century.

1982 marked the bleak winter in a different hemisphere which had a major impact on her career, threatening to plunge her political trajectory perpendicularly downwards. I refer to the Austral winter of 1982 when General Galtieri's invasion of the Falkland Islands came just when her political rating stood historically low, restored only by the professionalism of the British armed forces in a particularly 'close-run thing', which cost a thousand lives, and many more wounded. From pacing tigress she turned to Viking mode, conquering, scorning the vanquished enemy even in death and victory. She spurned aside the Archbishop of Canterbury's prayers for the fallen and their families.

By winter 1984 I was Tory Vice-Chairman with special responsibility for women with regular private access to the Prime Minister. But something was changing in her: she was moving more and more swiftly away from her Methodist Liberal roots to the consensus of the nouveau riche grandees of the Monday Club and the seriously rich of her North London constituency. Cabinet and junior ministers, nearly all male, worshipped, genuflected and deprived her of the perspectives, the arguments that kept her democratically alert. Ever the scientist, Thatcher was gradually losing her intellectual challengers. She lost the opportunity to talk around all facets of an issue and was starved of real debate inside her own party. Eventually she would resist my reasoned arguments on poll tax relief for non-working married women, telling me that the nature of marriage was that women should be financially dependent upon men. I saw then that the modern world had grown away from her as her supplicants kept her in ignorance.

The Brighton bomb was the turning point. Crouched behind military security and Special Branch police, forbidden on real pain of death to act as a normal politician and work the street, she fell slowly into the warm, cuddly routine of being the House Goddess to the blindly ambitions of her immediate official circle. Bit by bit the new party donors became the glitzy circus from whom she only received supportive views and approval. She stopped reading comment about herself in the newspapers, finding it too hurtful.

Thursday to Tuesday: November 1990

It was intensely clear to me that Mrs Thatcher had lost her hold over her strongest political allies in the Cabinet. She was trapped in a room with enemies, with bright-eyed young men such as those who passed through junior minister posts in education and could see that the scientist PM wanted to destroy the levelling influence of learning in our country. She was, indeed foolishly, pulling up the ladder, as Reagan had done in Sacramento and the White House, strangling the access of new talent to the top. And these young Tories could see it happen: they became the inner core of the mutiny, waiting only for the courage of a Heseltine or a Howe to trigger the overthrow.

I tried three times, finally in public statement, to tell Mrs Thatcher that I was going to vote against her. Neither she nor her circle were able to grasp my message. They lived in a cocoon of mutual admiration and the passing out of considerable public wealth.

When they finally appreciated my determined stand, although it was too late, they instantly treated her with such disloyalty that I was appalled: all they could think about was when to find a new post, a better job, not to see her out with the dignity she deserved.

The day before the vote, I convinced two fellow Tories: one would vote with me, against her, and the other would abstain. We made the determining two-vote margin by which she lost. She left behind a party unreformed, slavishly following transatlantic models, out of touch with a Britain packed with diversity whose talents were struggling to break out of the government controls that she, a partial Liberal, had mercilessly imposed.

Lord Lawson
Chancellor of the Exchequer 1983–88

Nigel Lawson was elected to Parliament in 1974 and joined the Thatcher govern-
ment in 1979 as Financial Secretary to the Treasury. He was made Energy
Secretary in 1981 and promoted to Chancellor after the 1983 election. He retired
from the House of Commons in 1992 and was elevated to the peerage in the
same year.

It is twenty years now since I wrote my memoirs. I concluded, then,
in these terms:

'It was a great adventure on which we embarked in 1979; an
adventure to rescue Britain from economic and political decline of a
kind that is now barely remembered, but which stank to high heaven
at the time; the adventure of charting a radically new way forward
and – despite universal doubt and cynicism – seeing it through. It
could not have been done without Margaret Thatcher, who will go
down in history as one of the greatest Prime Ministers this country
has known.'

Much has happened over the past twenty years. In the UK, New
Labour has come and gone, and we now have a new Conservative-led
government trying to grapple with some of the same problems that
confronted us then. And my judgement of Margaret has, if anything,
been reinforced by the passage of time.

She was also the only Prime Minister of modern times to have given
their name to a particular constellation of policies, values and beliefs.
What 'Thatcherism' meant was a mixture of the rule of law, sound
money, free markets, financial discipline, firm control of public spending, lower tax rates, patriotism or nationalism (the distinction is largely
in the eye of the beholder), Victorian values (of the Samuel Smiles
self-help variety), privatisation and a dash of populism. She saw these
as much as moral as economic (or political) imperatives. And (at least
most of the time) they imparted a clear sense of direction, which the
country understood, even if it did not always like it.

An essential part of her (and her government's) success – what

Andrew Marr (no Tory) has called 'the most extraordinary and nation-changing premiership of modern British history' – was a willingness to extend the bounds of the politically possible.

There was, for example, widespread acceptance at the time that inflation was a major economic and social evil, that all attempts – by governments of both parties – to contain it by incomes policies had not only failed but brought significant political and economic disadvantages of other kinds, and that the problem was getting worse, as inflationary expectations became embedded. But it was equally widely assumed that the alternative approach of a fierce monetary squeeze would bring levels of transitional unemployment that made it politically impossible. In the event, transitional unemployment rose rather more than we had expected, and lasted slightly longer. But it did not make the policy, which was pursued to a successful conclusion, politically impossible.

Again, there was general agreement that nationalisation of a large and important sector of the economy had failed, having brought neither business efficiency nor industrial peace (as its original architects had hoped, by ending conflict between workers and their capitalist bosses), and that this was a significant part of the explanation for Britain's poor economic performance. But the obvious remedy of recognising this and embarking on a policy of denationalisation – or privatisation as it came to be known – was assumed to be politically impossible: a rupture of the post-war settlement which the people did not desire and the trade unions would not permit. And, of course, it had never been done – neither in the UK nor anywhere else. Yet we did it.

It was widely accepted, too, that the trade unions had become an over-mighty subject, more interested in exercising political power than in raising the living standards of their members, and had made the country almost ungovernable. But following the unsuccessful attempts of both the Heath Conservative and Wilson Labour governments to deal with this problem, it was equally widely seen as politically impossible to achieve.

Again, the 'savage cuts' on which we embarked to deal with an unsustainable budget deficit and a bloated and unaffordable public sector were widely considered to be politically impossible and a recipe for intolerable civil strife and unrest. Yet we persisted, albeit rather more gradually than we had originally intended, and the public finances were, in my time, brought into surplus.

There is a lesson to be learned from this. Governments in a democracy have always to be conscious that there is a limit to what is politically possible. But they tend to assume that limit to be more constrained than it is – provided (and the proviso is important) they decide first what it is necessary to do and then how to explain to the people why they are doing it, rather than deciding first (after consulting focus groups) what the people are prepared to accept. That lesson is not the least part of the heritage of Margaret Thatcher.

Margaret Thatcher was a womanly woman and always considered it important to use her woman's skills to the utmost. Before sitting down she always had a little movement – and I've never seen another woman do it – of hitching up her skirt, so she wasn't sitting on it. Her bum was sitting on the chair – well, her knickers, of course – so when she got up her skirt was uncreased. She always thought things out. She was a great details person.

Margaret felt closer to the woman who goes out to work than the one who stays at home. I don't think she had a great deal of sympathy for the housewife. She felt she was part of a sisterhood of so-called working wives. Women have many great qualities and Margaret had a lot, but there is one male quality that is usually important in politics and that she lacked – clubbability.

Mitterrand described her as having the mouth of Marilyn Monroe and eyes of Caligula. Whether he meant it or whether he was trying to charm her in order to undermine her resistance to whatever it was he wished to do, I don't know. I think she could turn it on if she wanted to, but sexiness wasn't the most obvious thing about her. She was also extremely headmistressy.

She never bullied me. The only one she really bullied was Geoffrey Howe. Listening was never her strongest attribute, but she was infinitely better in the first half of her premiership. It was a gradual process. The real deterioration set in at Christmas 1987, when Willie Whitelaw had to resign on health grounds. That made a huge difference. Until then, his presence at her side concentrated her mind.

There had never been a Cabinet with so many Jewish men – me, Michael Howard, Leon Brittan. I wondered why, and the conclusion I came to is not that she had a thing for Jews, but that she was one of those rare politicians without the faintest whiff of anti-Semitism.

Margaret's mind operated on at least two levels. There was the saloon-bar populist, but there was also the sophisticated, calculating politician. She switched from one mode to the other. She wasn't an intellectual in the sense that Keith Joseph was. She was more like a clever lawyer, quick at picking up a brief and mastering all the detail. She liked the company of intellectuals, enjoyed the debate, but she thought of herself more as a woman of action.

Margaret's political philosophy was shaped greatly by her family background, particularly her father. She was very close to him, but not her mother, who didn't go out to work.

She had a Protestant work ethic and felt that everybody should have the opportunity to make their own way by their own efforts, and that no one should stand in the way of people bettering themselves. So when groups appeared to have ancient privileges of one kind or another, she would go for them – such as the restrictive practices of the legal profession. She wasn't a class warrior.

One wouldn't say Margaret was totally humourless, but her sense of humour was not highly developed. She did once make me laugh. I showed her a new commemorative coin and said approvingly at the head on the coin: 'Ooh, she looks just like Rita Hayworth!'

Bob Hawke

Prime Minister of Australia 1983–91

The trade unionist and Labour politician Bob Hawke is among the most influential figures in Australian politics. He became Prime Minister of Australia in 1983, remaining in that position until 1991. This passage is taken from his book The Hawke Memoirs.

On Saturday afternoon at Lyford Cay the forty-nine Commonwealth heads met without officials. The meeting followed a plenary on that morning where heated argument had erupted over Margaret Thatcher's lone opposition to sanctions. Debate was at times bitter and the atmosphere spilt over into the afternoon. Margaret was implacable as she fought back against attacks by a number of the speakers. She had a terribly rough time, and although I repudiated her stance, I sympathised with her for the enormous physical and emotional strain she was under.

The afternoon session delegated to a committee of seven (Prime Minister Lynden Pindling of the Bahamas, Margaret Thatcher, Rajiv Gandhi, Brian Mulroney and myself, with Presidents Robert Mugabe of Zimbabwe and Kenneth Kaunda of Zambia) the Herculean task of trying to reach some common ground on the sanctions issue. The seven of us met that evening, with Robert and Kenneth preferring, literally, to sit on the sidelines. We were to witness a vintage Thatcher performance, Margaret at her best and worst.

Margaret Thatcher was the hardest working head of government I ever met. Her application was prodigious and she was always extraordinarily well briefed for every meeting. Whatever the subject, she could press her sometimes jarring and belligerent viewpoints with great authority, and for that I deeply respected her. But while she had first-class application, she did not always display a first-class mind. In argument she often seemed to be playing catch-up. She sought to buy time while exchanging views so that she could more easily absorb contrary positions and give herself room to marshal her thoughts and responses.

In my experience she had two techniques for stalling debate. First she was an inveterate interrupter. I never dealt with a leader who interrupted other speakers so often. It was a cause for irritation among many of those with whom she dealt. Her other technique for slowing the pace of discussion was what I called her delay-by-parenthesis approach. If a leader was unwise enough to attach a parenthetical observation to the main thrust of his argument, Margaret was away. She would grab hold of the parenthesis like a terrier with a bone, tearing into it and worrying it to a degree that often made her interlocutor and the rest of us wild with impatience.

A bizarre example of this technique surfaced in the Lyford Cay committee meeting. We were discussing the Eminent Persons Group and the stage-by-stage concept of sanctions. Brian Mulroney was developing his main argument in support of Rajiv's and my attempt to persuade Margaret to come in behind the idea. Brian was unwise enough to refer to an aside she had made during the afternoon's discussions: 'Margaret, when you said that, I thought that the fat was really in the fire.'

At that her eyes blazed and she pulled herself erect in the chair. 'What do you mean the fat was really in the fire? Just what do you mean? What fat? What fire?' she asked imperiously. 'Brian, I was brought up to mean what I say, and to say what I mean. What do you mean, the fat was really in the fire?'

'My God!' I thought. I couldn't refrain from jumping in: 'Margaret! for Christ's sake! Forget the bloody fat and the bloody fire, it's got nothing to do with anything. Just listen to what Brian's saying, will you.' Margaret looked at me in some astonishment but, to her great credit, she copped it. Then I turned to my friend Mulroney and said: 'Brian, get on with it, and leave the fat out of the fire.'

Margaret could also, I thought, be a little less than straightforward at times. There was one occasion when she seemed to me to almost deliberately misunderstand a proposition. One of the proposed sanctions included the proposition that governments would agree not to enter into contracts with majority-owned South African companies. In our private discussion Margaret said she couldn't agree to that because in South Africa there were so many companies with whom Britain had to deal. 'Margaret, we're not talking about in South Africa, we're talking about in our countries. The Australian government won't have a contract with a majority-owned South African company, you there in the United Kingdom shouldn't deal with such a majority-owned company,' I explained to her. 'Oh, I see,' she replied.

But the very next day she did not see and in our discussion she went off on the same thing again. I thought she was being a little slippery. I do not intend these comments to disguise the fact that I have a certain admiration for Margaret Thatcher. There is so much of her philosophical approach to domestic and international politics that I cannot share, but she is a formidable and remarkable person – applied, committed, dogged, dogmatic, determined and certainly courageous.

Baroness Williams
Liberal Democrat Peer

Shirley Williams was a leading member of the Labour Cabinet of the late 1970s. She was a founder of the SDP in 1981 and went on to lead the Liberal Democrats in the House of Lords.

M rs Thatcher and I followed one another at Somerville College, Oxford. She became the first woman President, I think, of the Oxford University Conservative Association, and I came, nearly five years later, to be the first woman leader of the Oxford University Labour Club. Somerville was the cradle for Prime Ministers, including Mrs Gandhi, and it very much embodied and understood Mrs Thatcher, who, above all, had the most incredible single-mindedness, determination, dedication and self-discipline. I do not think in my entire political life that I have ever met anybody who combined those four qualities in the way that she did. From the very beginning, she knew what she wanted to be and what she wanted to do, and managed to overcome virtually every obstacle one can think of.

It was not easy to put yourself forward as leader of the party or, later, as a Prime Minister in those days. Our society was still a deeply masculine one, where any woman who stood up opened herself to patronage, to the assumption that she was of a second level of intellect and to all the rest that went with that. It is important to say – hopefully with respect but with some memory of what things were really like – that, for example, the then Prime Minister, Mr Heath, was clearly not too happy to have that particular woman in his Cabinet and rather cleverly seated her five seats away from him, so that she could not be seen if she got up and tried to speak. We remember that she had an extraordinary capacity to overcome – and even not notice in some ways – the objections that were raised to her as a woman. The assumption when Airey Neave took over her campaign for the leadership was that she would be most unlikely, on those grounds, ever to succeed.

In that context it is perhaps worth telling an anecdote. According to Sir Denis Thatcher, at one stage he was sitting at home in Flood Street while Mrs Thatcher was ironing his shirts, which she was very keen on doing, and getting breakfast. She said, in a sort of rather casual way, 'Denis, I am thinking of running for the leadership'. To which he responded, 'Leadership of what, Margaret?' That somehow sums up the wonderful balanced detachment and humour of Sir Denis. I cannot underline too strongly the extent to which I think Mrs Thatcher began to lose her life when he passed away. He was absolutely central and key to her whole personality and her ability to become what she was.

When she and I were in opposite positions – we were both Secretaries of State for Education, and sometimes opponents – she did not try to pretend that there was no difference between us. She loved it. She relished argument. She relished confrontation.

Christine Hamilton
Writer, Broadcaster and Battleaxe

The wife of former Conservative MP Neil Hamilton, Christine Hamilton first came to public attention for her vigorous defence of her husband during the 1997 general election. She capitalised on her image by writing the Bumper Book of British Battleaxes *for Robson Books and now works as a presenter on radio and television.*

During the 1992 general election Margaret came to speak at a rally for Neil in Knutsford, arriving at our home for supper beforehand. It had been an exciting day. That afternoon she had done a walkabout in Stockport for Tony Favell and had been attacked – fortunately only with a bunch of daffodils. Margaret, of course, carried on with supreme sangfroid but her minders were understandably alarmed by the breach of security.

On arrival with us, all memory of daffodils had been expunged and she beetled in through the front door, reluctantly stepping on the pristine red carpet we had rolled out for the occasion, demanding to know 'What are the trade figures? What are the trade figures?'

She marched into the drawing room where Neil steered her to an armchair. Adjacent to this we had carefully placed the cardboard cut-out figure of Margaret which I had bought in Carnaby Street back in the mid-70s which normally sat in our hall to frighten off burglars (very successfully). It was exhilarating to have the real three-dimensional Margaret sitting next to her two-dimensional replica but she affected not to notice, perhaps thinking there was nothing unusual about this and that every home should have one!

Into the dining room for supper and, among a multitude of goodies normally classed in our household as 'forbidden or controlled substances' was a magnificent rich, dark chocolate torte which I had lovingly made. I knew that, although chocolate was one of Margaret's favourite foods, she had given it up for Lent. I assumed, therefore, that she would refuse the proffered delicacy and accept the fruit salad alternative. Not a bit of it! She took a particularly large wedge and rapidly demolished it with gusto. When I gingerly expressed my surprise, she replied in a magisterial tone of mock stern rebuke: 'I have given up chocolate BARS – this is quite different!'

The torte had the desired effect – at the rally, she gave a breathtakingly spectacular tour de force, speaking for over an hour without a single note.

Kenneth Clarke
Cabinet Minister 1985–97 and 2010–

Kenneth Clarke was first elected to Parliament in 1970. He joined the Heath government as a government whip in 1972 and was a Cabinet minister at Industry, Health and Education under Margaret Thatcher. Under John Major he was Home Secretary and Chancellor and in David Cameron's Cabinet he has served as Lord Chancellor and Minister without Portfolio.

I was a government whip in the early 1970s, and Margaret was Secretary of State for Education. She was a tough and striking character, and I got on perfectly all right with her, but I became aware that Ted Heath was thinking of sacking her. Margaret had become involved in a silly row, where the Labour Party and the newspapers decided that taking milk from schoolchildren was a dreadful, Victorian thing to do. It plainly existed for the benefit of the farming industry – it was a way of dumping milk on schools, and no longer had anything to do with the avoidance of rickets – but she became an object of criticism. We were all aghast that Ted was thinking of sacking the only woman in the Cabinet. He was persuaded not to, but no doubt he occasionally looked back and regretted that he did not have the foresight to get rid of the person who proved to be his most formidable rival.

When we went into opposition in 1974, there was huge pressure to get rid of Ted. Many people wanted Keith Joseph, on the party's right, to stand. Keith was a brilliant but indecisive character; he went through agonies, and then made a somewhat ill-judged speech (on sexual promiscuity and social deprivation) which, in the stupid daily atmosphere of politics, was instantly assumed to have cost him his chance. Margaret had been close politically to Keith, so there was a rush to get her to stand. The result was that Margaret was the only opponent Heath had on the first ballot, and she came ahead for the simple reason that she wasn't him. She gathered an enormous protest vote that had no ideological content, which made her unbeatable in the second ballot. So Margaret became one of the most unexpected leaders of the party that we had ever had.

As opposition leader, she had a rocky ride, because she had not fully matured as a politician. She was a bit typecast; people used to make rude remarks about her twinset and pearls – she epitomised a right-wing, *Daily Mail*-reading, suburban housewife. She was subject to a great deal of muttering: the other members of her shadow Cabinet had all been shocked by her becoming leader; a lot of the grandees deeply resented that she was leading the party and they were not.

She was a difficult woman to get to know, and I'm not sure I ever did. I combined my job with being a barrister, and one day, coming back from court in the West Midlands, I fell asleep on the train. I woke up to find, opposite me, Margaret and Ian Gow, who had got on at some station and were teasing me. But she offered me a lift in her car from the station. She took me back to her room in the House of Commons and offered me a cup of tea. She was wandering around, finding dirty teacups, washing them in the sink, throwing a tea-towel at me and getting me to dry them – she was remarkably feminine, and normal.

We were all believers in free-market economics; we all thought the trade unions were a dreadful, over-powerful vested interest. We all thought we should stop bailing out lame-duck industries and pouring the taxpayer's money into over-manned, overpaid and inefficient nationalised industries. But once we came to government in 1979, if it hadn't been for Margaret, I'm not sure many of us would have had the courage of our convictions. She gave us all the courage to do what we all believed ought to be done. Over time, we pushed the boat out further and further, and became more and more unpopular with the public – but she made us put our tin hats on and get on with it. To our astonishment, we survived as a government.

The poll tax was her undoing. I always said it was great fun working in her government so long as you could stand the hassle. But unfortunately, as always happens if people stay in office for too long, she got carried away with her own infallibility. The poll tax was the worst example of that. She got some sycophantic young men around her, whom I will not name because they are friends of mine, and she wouldn't discuss it with her more senior colleagues, who disagreed with her. We'd had many policies that were unpopular, but many of us knew in our bones that the critics were right on this: it was an uncollectable tax. She'd always flown by the seat of her pants, by her gut instinct – but that time her gut instinct was wrong.

As soon as any Prime Minister starts thinking of his (or her) role in history, it's the beginning of disaster. But I don't think she did that much: she probably took the woman of destiny bit for granted. Although she did once come out in Cabinet with a bizarre statement: 'Why do I have to do everything in this government?' To which I think I wasn't the only person sitting round the table thinking: 'The trouble is, Margaret, that you believe that you do have to. And you shouldn't. And you can't.'

At the end, when she was talked into seeing the Cabinet one by one, she saw me first because somebody had told her that I was the most vehement (in believing) that she couldn't go on. She tried to jolly me out of it, so I explained forcefully, as is my way, that in my opinion she'd lost and ought to stand down. She accused me of being defeatist; I said that she had been defeated.

I didn't see her much (after that). She never came to terms with losing the leadership. She became embittered and persuaded herself that it had all been treachery and some kind of plot, which was paranoid nonsense.

Whenever I ask myself the mystifying question of why the Conservatives, the natural governing party for centuries, dissolved into civil war and swung so violently to the nationalist right, I think that in some mysterious way it goes back to the trauma of Margaret's defeat. I think there was a section of the right wing of the party that never came to terms with it; that believed the stuff about plots, and regarded John Major's government, in some peculiar way, as a betrayal of Margaret's legacy – when it followed Thatcherite policies pretty consistently. What we tried to be in Major's government was Thatcherite with a human face. But we were destroyed from within by people who considered themselves the most loyal followers of Margaret. It was left to Tony Blair to take over Thatcherism with a human face.

She was one of our great recent Prime Ministers. She'd be outdone by Churchill, and possibly, although he was a much more flawed character, by Lloyd George. But anybody writing the history of the twentieth century in Britain will regard Thatcher as one of the dominant political personalities, and her era as one of the decisive phases in our history. Which is why it was such a privilege to serve in her government; as you may have gathered, I found it rather enjoyable.

Lord Deedes
Journalist

W. F. Deedes was a veteran Daily Telegraph *journalist and columnist. Sir Denis Thatcher was one of his best friends. He was a Cabinet minister in Harold Macmillan's government. He died in 2007.*

On the night of 19 May 1982 Margaret Thatcher gave a dinner at 10 Downing Street for the Duke and Duchess of Kent and Prime Minister Muldoon of New Zealand, who was paying us a friendly visit. It was the eve of the contentious Falklands War. On our arrival just before 8 p.m., both Mrs Thatcher and her then Foreign Secretary Francis Pym were, unsurprisingly, missing.

'Talk to Muldoon,' Denis Thatcher ordered me, 'and keep talking.' Dinner was late, awaiting our hostess. I sat between Mrs Thatcher and the renowned singer, Kiri Te Kanawa, an easy companion because we shared an interest in golf. The Prime Minister engaged Muldoon, who was sitting on her right.

As the main course arrived, a long message was brought to Mrs Thatcher. She read it, pencilled some notes and returned it. 'Awkward,' she said to me. 'United Nations will be on the telephone at 9.45 p.m. It will interfere with the speeches.' She sent a message suggesting that the UN call at 10.30.

The only sign of her abstraction was that her wristwatch had stopped. She had forgotten to wind it. Then, putting the UN on one side, she resumed talking to Mr Muldoon about figures they liked and disliked on the international scene. Muldoon had just returned from Dublin, where he visited Ireland's Prime Minister, Charles Haughey. His government had declined to support sanctions against the Argentine. It was not Haughey's wish, she explained to Muldoon, but his people 'had insisted on it'. From Mrs Thatcher's face I judged Charles Haughey stood in low esteem.

With the coffee, a message then arrived at our table from the UN in New York. They would call at 10.30 p.m. Margaret Thatcher rose and delivered a polished speech of welcome to the Prime Minister and her royal guests. The Foreign Office had given her the date of our first import of lamb from New Zealand, we learned subsequently. It went down well in the company assembled at No. 10.

In the distant past, I reflected, I have occasionally sent flowers to my hostess in return for dinner. Presenting a destroyer was original, probably unique. Duty fulfilled as hostess, Margaret Thatcher retired with her Foreign Secretary and chiefs of staff to deal with the UN.

I admired the steely self-control of her performance that evening, the more because I knew that along with it there lurked an altogether softer side to her nature. We saw it a couple of years later, after the IRA had attempted to murder her at Brighton by blasting her hotel during the party conference of 1984.

One Sunday soon afterwards, a beautiful autumn day, Margaret Thatcher emerged from church in tears. 'It went through my mind,' she said by way of explanation, 'that this was a day I was not meant to see.'

Mikhail Gorbachev
President of the Soviet Union 1985–91

Mikhail Gorbachev was the last President of the Soviet Union. He presided over a period of intense change in his country and is credited with the introduction of the modernising policies of perestroika and glasnost. He famously attempted to foster peace between the superpowers and received the Nobel Peace Prize in 1990. This extract is taken from his memoirs.

At my first meeting with Mrs Thatcher in late 1984, we had established what proved to be a good and lasting relationship. We both appreciated the contact and got on very well. This first meeting might be the reason why the Soviet–British dialogue made such a good start on my taking the helm of the Soviet Union in 1985 – although British policy towards us during the first years of perestroika was not exactly what you would call friendly. Great Britain was the first Western country to support the American Strategic Defense Initiative and to participate officially in its development. Margaret Thatcher viewed the Reykjavik meeting as a failure and fully supported Ronald Reagan's position, blaming the Soviet Union for the lack of an agreement. The British government made a big show of expelling a group of Soviet officials, accusing them all of being agents of the KGB.

But at the same time the British spoke out in favour of a 'constructive long-term dialogue' with the Soviet Union. It is revealing that Margaret Thatcher took the initiative in visiting the Soviet Union after my election as General Secretary. She was a frequent guest in Washington, and it seemed as if she intended to represent Western European interests in the dialogue between the superpowers.

Mrs Thatcher came to Moscow in late March 1987. Our talks took place in the Kremlin, in the presence only of our personal assistants and interpreters. Stressing the significance of her visit, I remarked that the last high-level visit to the Soviet Union by a British Prime Minister had taken place more than twelve years earlier. She corrected me immediately, saying that the last British Conservative Prime Minister had visited the Soviet Union more than twenty years before.

Before getting down to business, I expressed my astonishment at a speech she had made in Torquay only a week before leaving for Moscow, delivered in the spirit of Reagan's anti-communist crusade. I said that we even had the impression that she might cancel her visit.

Mrs Thatcher had maintained that the Soviet Union aspired to 'establish communism and domination worldwide' and that 'Moscow's hand' could be seen in virtually every conflict in the world. Obviously I could not leave it at that and replied that much of her speech in Torquay as well as most of the accusations she had made were Conservative stereotypes going back to the 1940s and 1950s. But Mrs Thatcher stood her ground: 'You are supplying weapons to the Third World countries,' she rejoined, 'while the West supplies the food and aid in addition to helping establish democratic institutions.' The discussion became very heated.

Looking back I must admit (and it seems to me that I have already done so) that our policy towards developing countries had been highly ideological and that, to a certain extent, Mrs Thatcher had been right in her criticisms. However, it was well known that the West had always been the prime supplier of weapons to the Third World and thus supported authoritarian and even totalitarian regimes, working on the principle that 'that dictator is a son of a bitch, but he is our son of a bitch'.

Our discussion had reached a point where I considered it necessary to say: 'We have frankly expressed our respective views on the world in which we live. But we have not succeeded in bringing our standpoints any closer. It seems to me that our disagreements have not become less after this conversation.'

My partner struck a more conciliatory note. Suddenly changing the course of our conversation, she said: 'We follow your activity with great interest and we fully appreciate your attempts to improve the life of your people. I acknowledge your right to have your own system and security, just as we have the right to ours, and we suggest taking this as a basis for our debate. In spite of all the differences between our systems,' she added, 'we can still exchange some useful experiences. We are deeply impressed by the vigorous policy of reform you are trying to implement. We have a common problem here – how to manage change.'

We went on to discuss our main topic: arms control. At the time Soviet–American talks on strategic arms were being held in Geneva. I went on the offensive, asking Mrs Thatcher directly: 'Is the West ready for real disarmament or have you been forced into negotiations under pressure from public opinion in your countries? I would appreciate it if you could clarify your position.'

Mrs Thatcher advanced the familiar argument that nuclear weapons represented the best guarantee for peace and that there could be no other guarantee in present conditions. 'We believe in nuclear deterrence,' she continued, 'and we do not consider the elimination of nuclear weapons practicable.'

In reply I delivered quite a long harangue, the gist of which was that the West did not want a solution, but was only interested in complicating the issue. I concluded: 'Today, we are closer than ever before to making a first step towards genuine disarmament. But the moment we were given this opportunity, you hit the panic button. Is the Tory policy exclusively aimed at hindering disarmament and the reduction of the level of confrontation in the world? It is amazing that Great Britain should feel comfortable in such a position.'

Mrs Thatcher seemed somewhat taken aback by my tirade. 'That's what I call a speech!' she exclaimed. 'I don't even know where to start.' And she assured me that the West did not in any way intend to make life difficult for us or complicate reform in the Soviet Union by rejecting disarmament.

Again and again, Margaret Thatcher repeated her main argument: nuclear weapons are the only means to ensure the security of Great Britain in the event of a conventional war in Europe. For this reason, Britain did not intend to commit itself to limiting in any way its nuclear arsenal. In short, our conversation was going round in circles. In an attempt to ease the tension, Margaret Thatcher told me about a 'funny occurrence', as she put it, which happened during a meeting with Hua Guofeng. The meeting was scheduled to last one hour. The Chinese leader spoke for forty-five minutes, and when Mrs Thatcher asked one single question, he continued his monologue for another twenty minutes. Seeing this, Lord Carrington (the British Foreign Secretary) handed the Prime Minister a written note: 'Madam, you tend to speak too much.'

Mrs Thatcher came to Moscow in June 1990. I had returned from my trip to the United States and Canada on 5 June, a few days before her arrival. She seemed greatly impressed by the results of the visit and complimented me on the 'extraordinarily successful meeting' with George Bush. Indeed the talks with the American President had dispelled a number of mutual concerns, including issues we had often discussed with Margaret Thatcher.

During our first conversation, she remarked that she believed it was essential to emphasise the positive aspects in our relations and to point out our convergent views on a number of issues at our joint press conference. 'Journalists tend to highlight negative aspects,' she said, 'and we must therefore concentrate on the positive achievements. It seems to me that many people, including many of the press, have not yet fully grasped how far we have come and how much the summit meetings contributed to this.'

'In 1986 my idea of a nuclear-free world was perceived as wishful thinking,' I reminded Mrs Thatcher. 'Today we are about to conclude an agreement with the Americans on a 50 per cent cut in strategic nuclear arms, and we have agreed on the elimination of our chemical weapons stockpiles. We have made much headway in only three years! Or, to take another example, the idea of a political settlement of regional conflicts was seen as another utopia. Today, the process has begun. And I must say that you personally have greatly contributed to this.'

My last meeting with Margaret Thatcher in her capacity as Prime Minister took place in Paris on 20 November, on the occasion of the European conference. We concentrated on the situation in the Gulf. I had discussed the issue with Mr Bush on the eve of our meeting, and Margaret Thatcher 'OK'd' our exchange of ideas. However, she admitted that she did not believe that a political settlement was possible and thought the use of force was inevitable. Hence she proposed that the next UN Security Council resolution (we had discussed it with George Bush) should be formulated in more severe terms, complaining that the Americans seemed to be 'somewhat over-cautious'. Needless to say, we also talked about the situation in the Soviet Union. The British Prime Minister did not hide her concern – she was an experienced politician and she perceived the dangers. We bid farewell at the entrance to my residence. 'God bless you!' she said in a soft voice.

The elections to the leadership of the British Conservative Party took place in Mrs Thatcher's absence. She failed to obtain the necessary majority on first ballot. She had told me that she had enemies – in eleven and a half years at the helm, this is virtually unavoidable. Yet she seemed to have no intention of capitulating. In Paris, when she was informed of the result of the election, she declared to the waiting press that she was 'going to show them' back home. Upon her return to London, however, she announced that she would resign. It was a noble act. Nonetheless, I regretted it.

Margaret Thatcher did much to support our perestroika. Needless to say she had her own views on the reforms, perceiving them as winning the Soviet Union over to Western positions, as a Soviet version of 'Thatcherism'. Nonetheless, she genuinely wanted to help us and to mobilise the efforts of the Western countries in support of our policies. During the August 1991 coup, she spoke out in defence of the Soviet President and his family.

One must give her credit for her services to her country. Mrs Thatcher took over at a time when the United Kingdom was lagging behind the other Western nations, and she succeeded in radically changing both the domestic and international situation of Great Britain. However Mrs Thatcher's tough methods and her inherent authoritarianism soured even her closest supporters, not to speak of the opposition, and eventually led to conflict situations. I had the impression that, in order to work with her, you had to accept her style and character unconditionally. Her authoritarianism and her penchant for forceful methods were manifest in British foreign policy. In crisis situations, she spoke out in favour of military sanctions. Even after her resignation as Prime Minister, we would occasionally receive information that 'Mrs Thatcher is suggesting air raids'. She was particularly tough in her approach to the Gulf crisis.

Margaret Thatcher was not an easy partner for us, and her fierce anti-communism would often hinder her from taking a more realistic view on various issues. Still, one must admit that in a number of cases, she was able to substantiate her charges with facts, which eventually led us to review and criticise some of our own approaches. All in all, she was a strong advocate of Western interests and values indeed.

Margaret Thatcher had much of what I would call the 'Old English Spirit', at least as we Russians usually imagine it, which shows in her commitment to traditions and 'tried and tested' values. During our official meetings she was always very considerate and courteous. We eventually came to know each other better and she showed genuine warmth towards me and Raisa Maksimovna – despite the differences in our views and our political arguments.

Malcolm Fraser

Australian Prime Minister 1975–83

Malcolm Fraser was elected to the Australian Parliament in 1955 at the age of twenty-five. He was elected leader of the Liberal Party in March 1975 and became Prime Minister in November of the same year.

You could get Maggie within reach of reasonable results if you could get her to turn her intellect to a question. She had a good mind, but if you engaged the emotions rather than the intellect, you just got this awful jingoism, and then she could be so very stubborn. If ever she thought her prestige or Britain's prestige was at stake, well, then you couldn't move her.

Once ministers settle in, they become attached to all sorts of programmes of their area, and they don't want to put a hot knife through them, so it gets harder to cut. I gave Maggie Thatcher that advice when she was elected. I told her to take an axe to things early, because it was harder later, but she didn't really do it either.

Mark Prisk

Conservative MP 2001–

Mark Prisk is a surveyor and a former National Vice-Chairman of the Federation of Conservative Students. He was elected as MP for Hertford and Stortford in 2001, and is Minister for Housing in David Cameron's government.

Over the last thirty-odd years I've had many encounters with Lady Thatcher. She was originally one of the main reasons I came into politics, because she showed that an individual can make a real difference. Ideologically she inevitably helped shape my views, though I've not always agreed with her. Yet it is perhaps my first meeting with her which helped me form my view of the woman behind the -ism.

I first met the then Mrs Thatcher in Truro City Hall, in the run-up to the 1979 general election. I had recently become Chairman of Cornwall Young Conservatives and was determined to meet our party's leader. The hall was packed, yet somehow when she entered at the back everyone sensed it and turned. Not great in stature she bustled into the hall and strode towards the platform, her support team trailing behind. She spoke with energy and clarity, and as she did so she dominated the audience. Yet it wasn't her speech which I remember most. There were two other incidents that showed a hint of her true personality.

During her speech a photographer, perched on a high stand, fell quite heavily. She stopped speaking and made sure that he was OK. Most politicians ignore such things, but she seemed genuinely concerned – when she might perhaps have been annoyed at the interruption.

Then after speaking, as she was leaving I collared her and asked what a Conservative government would do for young people. She turned and simply said, 'Do for you? Shouldn't we let you get on with it for yourself?' Momentarily I was taken aback. Had I blown it with the leader? Yet it wasn't intended as a rebuke, just an honest response, which saw through the question to the assumption beneath. It reflected that unsentimental part of her character, which was often caricatured as uncaring. All she was expressing was the same notion

President Kennedy has previously been lauded for: 'Ask not what your country can do for you, ask what you can do for your country.'

I have often found these two incidents instructive. A woman genuinely concerned for others' welfare, but able to distinguish between care and sentimentality. In this age of hand-wringing emoting, it's a quality much missed.

Javier Pérez de Cuéllar
Secretary-General of the United Nations 1982–92

Javier Pérez de Cuéllar was Secretary-General of the United Nations for a two-term period of office from the 1982 to 1992.

Dealing with a woman at the height of power in a great European nation was something which immediately brought to my mind the great Elizabeth I, and was somewhat of a challenge for a newly appointed Secretary-General of the United Nations.

My first acquaintance with the Prime Minister was on the occasion of the serious problem which arose in April 1982, following the Argentinian occupation of the Falkland Islands. Immediately I assumed that the Prime Minister would be concerned by the fact that the Secretary-General of the United Nations was South American; I therefore made it a point of honour, as was my duty according to the Charter and my own conviction, to show total independence and impartiality.

From the beginning the Secretary of State, Alexander Haig, offered his good offices to both parties and kept me continually informed of the progress made. However, as is customary in the UN Secretariat, I decided to set up a small preventive working group comprising my immediate collaborators to put forward ideas to the parties involved, if necessary. When the endeavours of the United States proved fruitless, the British and Argentinean representatives agreed to continue within the framework of the United Nations. During this time it was clear that on the British side the Prime Minister was personally in charge of the British endeavours and we maintained indirect contact throughout. Although we were no more successful than the state department, the rigorously technical manner in which the Secretary-General contributed towards finding a peaceful solution to the difference of opinions was proof of the organisation's complete impartiality, and I believed it was recognised as such by the British side.

I have to mention that when a military confrontation became unavoidable I received an unexpected telephone call from Mrs

Thatcher, during which she asked me to do all I could to keep 'my boys' from being killed. I was moved to hear the voice of a mother. I must add that through various interviews with the Prime Minister I was able to appreciate her extraordinary intellectual capacity, her profound knowledge of the long-standing and arduous international problems affecting the international community, such as those of the Near and Middle East, and although we did not always agree, I admired the clarity of her position, at times inflexible, and her willingness to listen to the arguments of her interlocutors. She was indisputably a great stateswoman. Finally, let me say that I treasure the very kind letter she sent to me on giving up her office as Prime Minister, which I was so honoured and proud to receive.

Tony Benn
Labour MP 1950–83, 1984–2001

Tony Benn served as a Labour MP for fifty years before leaving Parliament to 'spend more time on politics'. He was a Cabinet minister at the Departments of Industry and Energy in the Wilson and Callaghan governments.

Margaret Thatcher was a very powerful, right-wing force in society. She followed her beliefs and had clear objectives. Her policy was to reverse the trends in modern politics that were made possible by the trade unions being legalised. She decided to eradicate the power of the unions, undermine local government and privatise assets – and therefore the three policies of the Labour movement.

It was a major attack on democracy and at first it carried some public support, but then it became unstuck and, in the end, it was rejected. But ideas always come back and the modern Tory Party is influenced by her ideas.

Although I thought she was wrong, she said what she meant and meant what she said. It was not about style with her; it was substance – I don't think she listened to spin-doctors, she just had a clear idea and followed it through.

I remember her at the funeral of MP Eric Heffer. I was asked to make a speech and as I was waiting, there was someone behind me coughing. It was Mrs Thatcher, and at the end I thanked her for coming and she burst into tears. She had come out of respect for someone whose opinions she disagreed with.

Eric Forth

Conservative MP 1983–2006

Eric Forth served as a junior minister in Margaret Thatcher's and John Major's governments in various positions, ending his government career as Minister of State at the Department of Education and Employment. He was the MP for Mid Worcestershire from 1983 until 1997, when he became the MP for Bromley and Chislehurst. He died in 2006.

The organisation of which I was Chairman – Conservative War Forward, dedicated to perpetuating the principles and policies of 'Thatcherism' – organised a dinner in 1999 to celebrate the twentieth anniversary of Margaret's first great general election victory.

Throughout the evening, tribute after tribute was made to Margaret and to Thatcherism. At the close, another one seemed unnecessary, so instead I was able to pay tribute to Sir Denis – 'without whom Thatcherism could never have happened'.

I think it pleased both Margaret and Denis!

I am proud to be a member of No Turning Back, a group of Conservative Members of Parliament set up in 1984 to support Margaret Thatcher in her determination to challenge the bastions of socialism, public ownership and trade union power in Britain in the late 1970s.

Margaret attended one of our dinners in, I think, early 1986. During a rare lull in the conversation, Margaret asked if I had anything to say. To my colleagues' horror, I opined that there were too few sound 'Thatcherites' in her government, not least among NTB members present!

There was a stunned silence – and Margaret quickly moved on to another subject without comment.

By the end of 1986, at least three of the members present were in the Thatcher government – and by 1990, nearly half the group!

Harvey Thomas
International Public Relations Consultant

Harvey Thomas was the Director of Press and Communications at Conservative Central Office from 1985 until 1987. He continued to serve as Director of Presentation to the Conservative Party until 1991.

I suppose I am one of the original people accused of being a spin-doctor. It amazes me now how little 'spin' we needed to do with Mrs T. compared with today's requirement for constant spin on every-thing and everybody in politics, in an apparent desperate attempt to make it look as though they know where they are going.

Agree with her or not, Maggie knew where she was going and for the most part, the media was so busy keeping up that 'news manage-ment' was pretty straightforward.

But that never really included too much on the personal side. Behind the unavoidable 'public personae', Denis and Margaret Thatcher were, and are, pleasantly private people. So, perhaps the memories that are most appropriate for me are those that illustrate her personal touch – and her concern for, and loyalty to, friends.

The phrase that I recall hearing more than others, was, 'Because it's right.' People would suggest political direction or action and Mrs T. would say time and again, 'No, we've got to do it this way, because it's *right!*'

In many ways, her thinking was quite simplistic – even though she has considerable capacity to master detail as well. But, 'because it's right', has always been the driving motive in her private as well as her public life.

In 1985 I had gone to New York to prepare for her speech to the United Nations 40th Anniversary Celebration.

She had been out of the country for more than two weeks – I believe at the Commonwealth Heads of Government meeting in the Bahamas. While she had been away, a number of critical comments about me had appeared in the *Times* Diary, the Peterborough Column in the *Telegraph*, and one or two other political gossip columns. Nothing in the mainstream news passed on to the Prime Minister in the Bahamas – but enough to be personally hurtful.

When the Prime Minister arrived at the hotel in New York, she came full steam into the suite, and the first thing she said was, 'I hear there have been some nasty comments in the papers, Harvey – don't worry about it. I know where they are coming from and I'll make sure they stop.' I would never have brought it up – and I have no idea who did – but she certainly made my day!

And in private, she has a dry sense of humour. Four of us were sitting with her having a sandwich lunch in the Finchley constituency office during the 1987 election. It had been a frantic morning and we had afternoon and evening visits ahead of us.

After two weeks of campaigning, we were all struggling to keep going and as we shovelled the sandwiches down, I said, 'Boy, I am ready for a siesta now.'

The other three nodded and agreed and I looked at Mrs Thatcher at the other end of the table and said, not very hopefully, 'Well that makes it almost unanimous.'

'It's certainly not unanimous,' she said, 'it's a majority of one against!'

I'm not sure that Maggie ever really understood that it was simplicity and integrity that gained her so much support, especially inside the Conservative Party.

The media consistently speculated on whether we deliberately kept applause going at the big rallies in the eighties. And if so, how we did it! We did, and it wasn't hard. I would zoom the cameras projecting her picture onto the giant screens into a tight close-up shot of her face.

I first used this approach with Billy Graham fifteen years earlier. When the audience sees a speaker's face occupying a whole 20-ft screen, the eyes are about two feet wide – and they give away all the speaker's emotional feelings.

Integrity shines through and, perhaps surprising to some, Mrs T.'s eyes at the end of a speech always had the message, 'Wow, you're all being a bit overgenerous with the applause – but thank you!'

It was as though those words were printed across the screen – and as long as we kept the cameras close-up, the applause would continue – once in a while helped by a 6-inch tear appearing out of the corner of an eye!

For her, she was simply 'telling it like it is' and for all of us who saw our role as 'a ministry of helps', that just made it easy for people to get the 'Maggie Message'.

Shimon Peres
President of Israel 2007–

Shimon Peres has served twice as Prime Minister of Israel and twice as Foreign Minister. He is a recipient of the Nobel Peace Prize.

While commonly alluded to as the Iron Lady, throughout our acquaintance – and I may even venture to say our friendship – and well before she was made Baroness in recognition of her outstanding accomplishment and achievements, to me, Margaret Thatcher was simply the lady.

My encounters with Margaret Thatcher were many and each and every one of them was a learning experience that I treasured. Talk by the nature of things centred on a huge tapestry of global issues – terrorism, globalisation and the economy, the collapse of the former Soviet Union, the Falkland Islands, statesmanship and the domestic and international political arena and, of course, the Middle East conflict, and these are just random samples of our discussions. No matter the topic, our exchanges were always intense, never less than stimulating, at all times enlightening. I invariably felt humbled by the razor-blade sharpness of her mind, her acute perception of things and the clarity of her thoughts.

It is these very qualities, combined with an unflagging tenacity of purpose, fearlessness in the face of fierce opposition and indomitable faith in her way, which became an infinite source of inspiration to us, her admirers. It is her strength and compassion, free spirit and capacity to champion vital causes, together with her remarkable determination and commitment to her undertakings, that led me to compare her to another formidable leader with whom I had the privilege of closely working: Golda Meir. While Golda was never dubbed the Iron Lady, she was often referred to as 'the only man in the government'! Because Golda, like Margaret, pierced the glass roof of the government and soared to the very peak of political power, not by a twist of fate, but on the wings of her uniqueness.

The analogy is not random, for both became popular icons not only in the restricted circumference of their own countries, but were the object of admiration among their peers on a global scale, for they were both forged from uncommon fabric, propelled by an undaunted spirit and motivated by an unswerving resolve to build a better tomorrow for their respective people. Albeit in different parts of the world, they both played a major role in turning the direction of events at their most crucial crossroads and indeed, left an indelible mark on history. In their own distinctive manner, and with banners raised high, they fought their battles courageously and uncompromisingly, twentieth-century revolutionaries and the epitome of women of valour.

In a world of change, Margaret Thatcher has helped it change. In a world of globalisation, she was a catalyst in helping it globalise. She made a clean sweep of many old embedded notions and injected new energy into a stagnating situation. Supported by a measure of luck and armed with the strength of her convictions, Margaret Thatcher viewed her missions pragmatically and judiciously used the tools at her disposal to turn her vision into reality. History and the world owe much to Margaret Thatcher. So do I.

Sir Rex Hunt

Governor of the Falkland Islands 1980–85

After an eventful colonial and diplomatic career, Sir Rex Hunt became the Governor of the Falkland Islands. He was present at the invasion in 1982, removed by the Argentinians and returned after liberation. This extract is taken from his book My Falkland Days. *He died in 2012.*

The last of the service chiefs to visit us in 1982 had been the Chief of Air Staff, Air Chief Marshal Sir Keith Williamson. He stayed in Government House and, on the first morning, asked to see me alone in my office. There he disclosed that the Prime Minister intended to visit the Islands from 8 to 12 January and handed me a letter from Sir Robert Armstrong, then Secretary of the Cabinet and head of the civil service. Written in his own hand, with paragraphs and lines thoughtfully lettered and numbered to ease reply, Sir Robert stressed that security must be maintained and that the only person with whom I should discuss the programme was the Military Commissioner, Major-General David Thorne. If news of the visit leaked out, it would be cancelled. He sketched a possible outline for a four-day visit, finishing with a postscript: 'The PM does not like much spare time on visits like this.' David and I mapped out a provisional programme and I sent it back in a handwritten letter to Sir Robert. He wrote again with a few further comments and told me to reply only if we disagreed. That was that. It was the easiest VIP programme I had ever arranged. Normally, and particularly where the military were concerned, such visits entailed weeks of preparation and discussion, with voluminous programmes and numerous printed revisions. For the Prime Minister, three handwritten letters sufficed.

It was not, of course, quite as simple as that for David, who was responsible for the Prime Minister's protection. On a strict need-to-know basis, he and his staff prepared a contingency plan 'for the visit of a VIP to the Falkland Islands'. No names or dates were mentioned, but it was planned for a Saturday arrival and Wednesday departure. The giveaway was that one of the party was shown as 'VIP's wife/husband'.

ABOVE On 4 May 1979, Margaret Thatcher is elected Britain's first woman Prime Minister.

BELOW MT and husband Denis attend the funeral of friend and political adviser Airey Neave, in April 1979. Neave was killed in an IRA car-bomb attack outside the House of Commons.

ABOVE MT with (l–r) Lord Home, Liberal leader David Steel and opposition leader Mr Michael Foot at the Cenotaph in London for the Remembrance Sunday Service, November 1981.

BELOW President Ronald Reagan and MT smile as they cavort around Camp David, December 1984.

MT is joined by Queen Elizabeth II and five former PMs at No. 10 as she hosts a dinner celebrating the 250th anniversary of the residence becoming the London home of Prime Ministers, 1985.

MT and French President François Mitterrand sign the Channel Tunnel agreement, February 1986.

MT in a
British tank
during a visit
to British forces
in Germany,
September 1986.

'Someone I can
do business with.'
MT with Soviet
leader Mikhail
Gorbachev
in 1987.

The bullet-proof
election battle
bus of 1987.

MT wins a third term as Prime Minister after the Conservatives beat Labour by 376 seats to 229, June 1987.

MT, as she was rarely seen in public, in spectacles, July 1987.

LEFT Celebrating
British National
Day in Australia,
August 1988.

BELOW MT outside
10 Downing Street
with her son
Mark, daughter-
in-law Diane, and
two-month-old
grandson Michael,
May 1989.

ABOVE Pakistani Prime Minister Benazir Bhutto and MT in the rose garden at Chequers, July 1989.

LEFT Prime Minister Margaret Thatcher, watched by husband Denis, makes her final speech outside No. 10, before leaving for Buckingham Palace to offer her resignation to the Queen, November 1990.

As no announcement about the visit could be made beforehand, the journalists who would normally have accompanied the Prime Minister were to follow twenty-four hours later. There was a BBC television team in the Islands, led by Nicholas Witchell, but it had been there since before Christmas and was due to leave on 5 January, three days before the Prime Minister's arrival. That morning, I received a call from Bernard Ingham, the Prime Minister's Press Secretary, telling me to keep the team on the Islands but not to disclose the reason. I rang Nicholas at the Upland Goose, where he and his colleagues were happily packing, and asked him to come to my office. There I explained that something was likely to happen over the next week that he might wish he had stayed for and my advice was for him to post-pone his departure. He said that must mean that we were expecting someone we wanted to see or someone we did not want to see; either way, he would stay (at the time, there were rumours that an Argentine intended to bring some next-of-kin to the Islands to pay homage to their dead). I think he guessed that the Prime Minister was coming but, to his credit, he kept it to himself.

I told Mavis, of course, about our forthcoming guests, but we had to pretend to the staff that they were preparing for a party of journal-ists who could not be accommodated at the Upland Goose. In the village atmosphere of the Falklands, the slightest hint of an impending visit by the Prime Minister would have been flashed round the Islands by 'diddle-dee radio' within minutes and Don, for all his excellent virtues, would have been one of the first on the air. I hoped that he would forgive me for denting his reputation as a reliable newsmon-ger. I warned Patrick Watts and other local journalists to be at the airport by 4.30 p.m. on Saturday 8 January, but did not tell them who was coming.

As soon as Mrs Thatcher stepped off the Hercules, Patrick telephoned the FIBS studio, which interrupted its normal programme to announce her arrival. In the twenty minutes that it took Don to drive along the four miles of potholed airport road, the Stanley townsfolk flocked out of their houses and gathered along the route to welcome the Prime Minister. At her request, Don stopped at various points and she and Mr Thatcher got out and shook hands with scores of people. She said to one group, 'You were all marvellous,' to which Mike Bleaney, who was standing with young Daniel on his shoulders, replied, 'You didn't do too badly yourself, ma'am!' As we passed near Harold Bennett's house, he came to the taxi window and handed Mrs Thatcher a single rose. His eyes were moist and he was too choked to speak. He turned away but the Prime Minister told Don to stop, jumped out of the taxi and hurried after him. I followed and introduced him. He still could not speak and I could see that Mrs Thatcher, too, was deeply moved as she thanked him for the rose. All along the route, the crowds had gathered. It seemed that the whole of Stanley had come out to greet her. For a normally undemonstrative community, it was a remarkable display of affection – spontaneous, sincere and from the heart.

The Prime Minister's party consisted of the Chief of Naval Staff, Admiral Sir John Fieldhouse, who had been the commander of the Task Force operations from April to June 1982, based at Northwood; her Principal Private Secretary, Robin Butler, who was later to take Sir Robert Armstrong's place as Secretary of the Cabinet and Head of the Home Civil Service; a Private Secretary, John Coles, who was seconded from the Diplomatic Service; Press Secretary Bernard Ingham and a duty clerk, Alan Logan. There was no security officer or personal detective. I showed Mr and Mrs Thatcher to their room and pointed out the Argentine bullet holes in the ceiling. The Prime Minister elected to sleep in the bed beneath them. As she tidied up, Mr Thatcher came down to the small drawing room and stood warming himself in front of the peat fire. Our first engagement was a briefing at HQ BFFI and I was surprised to see that he made no move to get ready. 'Oh, I can't come,' he said, 'I've not been security cleared.'

I ran through the programme with him and the secretaries who had now joined us, and pointed to one or two items that might be omitted if they thought that we had given the Prime Minister too much to do. I got a few rueful smiles in response and an assurance that she would fulfil every bit of the programme, and probably more. At the briefing, it was interesting to see the close rapport between the Prime Minister and Sir John Fieldhouse and the detailed grasp that she had of military matters. Afterwards, we had a small dinner party at Government House with a few of the leading Islanders. There were only seventeen in all, but even this was a bit of a crowd for the small drawing room. Nevertheless, that was where we stayed because the Prime Minister decided that she preferred it (as we did) to the main drawing room. After the other guests had gone, she naturally gravitated to Mavis's chair beside the peat fire, kicked off her shoes and relaxed with a whisky and soda – a practice she was to follow each evening.

Sunday started with a visit to Stanley airport to see the RAF units and to visit the engineering works at the nearby quarry. The Royal Engineers were producing thousands of tons of crushed stone to build roads from the airport to the Coastel sites along the Canache. The first Coastel had arrived from Sweden in December on the *Ferncarrier*, a semi-submersible heavy-lift vessel, and we had hoped to have it in position in time for the Prime Minister to open, but the wind and tides had to be exactly right and the correct combination did not occur until the evening of her departure.

In the latter part of the morning, the Prime Minister attended a joint meeting of executive and legislative councils, followed by lunch at Government House with councillors. They each expressed their thanks and undying gratitude to Mrs Thatcher for sending the Task Force and reiterated their loyalty to the Queen. Looking to the future, they emphasised that Islanders had no wish to resume negotiations with the Argentines for as long as the Argentines equated negotia- tions with the transfer of sovereignty. They were grateful to Britain for providing the necessary security and for responding generously to Lord Shackleton's recommendations: they recognised that it was now up to Islanders to make the most of the opportunities thus created. Councillor Tony Blake urged the breakup of more of the larger farms and Councillor Tim Blake pressed for the development of the Islands' deep-sea fisheries by using the 150-mile protection zone in which to license fishing. Tim also explained the work of the select committee, of which he was Chairman, on revising the constitution and the electoral procedure for the Islands and expressed the hope that proposals would be forwarded to HMG by July.

After lunch, the Prime Minister visited the Rookery Bay minefield and the Camber, where the Gurkha engineers, RAF Search and Rescue and several Royal Navy units were based, and then flew back across the harbour to see the Port Squadron of the Royal Corps of Transport, finishing a busy afternoon with a visit to the Field Post Office and the bakery. The latter was, literally, a museum piece. Used in the First World War, it had been taken out of an army museum and transported to the Falklands, where it performed magnificently until the troops moved to the Canache, after which it was returned to the museum. Parked under canvas between two FIC warehouses, it was a popular place to visit not only because of the appetising smell of freshly baked bread but also because it was the warmest place in town.

Before evensong in the cathedral, the Prime Minister laid a wreath at the cross of sacrifice for those Falkland Islanders who had lost their lives in the two World Wars. She had brought a number of wreaths from England, all beautifully made with flowers rarely seen in the Falklands. David was host for dinner that night in Britannia House.

Monday was, if anything, busier than Sunday. We visited four settlements in East Falkland and two in the West. At each place the Prime Minister gave speeches to the Islanders and to the troops and spoke to a large number of them individually. In order that she might meet as many Islanders as possible, David had kindly arranged for helicopters to bring them in from outlying settlements, so there was a large crowd (by Falklands' standards) wherever we went. Local journalists and the BBC team were joined by others from Britain who had flown in on the Sunday. Microphones and cameras were thrust in front of the Prime Minister at every opportunity and she sustained the barrage with unfailing good humour and patience. We travelled in a Sea King, with a Chinook for the press and the infantry escort. Mrs Thatcher was welcomed with tremendous warmth wherever we landed, but none more so than at Goose Green, where the men, women and children who had been incarcerated in the community hall gave her three resounding cheers and gathered round to shake her hand and offer their personal thanks.

Brook Hardcastle and Eric Goss took us to the grave of Lieutenant Nick Taylor RN, where Mrs Thatcher laid one of her wreaths and Eric assured her that the people of the settlement would tend the grave with loving care for evermore. We then visited 'Y' Company of the 1st Battalion, the Royal Hampshire Regiment, accompanied by the battalion commander, Lieutenant-Colonel Hastings Neville. Sited near the remains of the old schoolhouse between Goose Green and Darwin, theirs was the first camp to be provided with portacabins and was well on the way to completion. The Prime Minister was concerned about the welfare of the garrison and hoped that David's objective of having most of them out of tented accommodation by the onset of winter would be achieved.

From Goose Green we flew to Port San Carlos, where Alan Miller and his small band were sharing the settlement with the RAF Chinook detachment, the Harrier forward operating base and a platoon of the Royal Hampshires, and thence to San Carlos to lay a wreath at Blue Beach cemetery. Pat and Isabel Short provided lunch for the Prime Minister's party: after so many VIP visits they were becoming expert hosts. Indeed, I never ceased to admire Isabel for the seeming ease with which she adapted to the changed circumstances. Before the war, she had been extremely shy and retiring, but now she chatted easily to all and sundry, from the Prime Minister down. This I noted was a heartening characteristic of Islanders in general: they rose to the occasion, whether at home, like Isabel, or the UN, like John Cheek, or in London, like Lewis Clifton.

San Carlos Water was still protected by Rapiers, the crews of which lived in dugouts reminiscent of the trenches in the First World War, but their morale could not have been higher, as the Prime Minister discovered. At Kelly's Garden, across the bay from San Carlos, the Royal Engineers were busily constructing a camp, which was intended to house the Chinook detachment and the headquarters of the ground air defence battery. Like most of the camps under construction, the biggest enemy was mud. We wore wellingtons as we splashed from hut to helicopter.

The Prime Minister refused to wear wellingtons for our next port of call, which was Port Howard cemetery. In fact, she was quite indignant when I suggested on the aircraft that she should put them on. 'I am not wearing wellingtons to Captain Hamilton's grave,' she said firmly, and promptly donned her best shoes. A Gurkha guard of honour presented arms as she walked through the mud to lay a wreath on Captain Hamilton's grave. I followed in my wellies, wondering whether a male Prime Minister would have been so sensitive.

After chatting to the people in the settlement, we flew from Port Howard to Fox Bay East, where Islanders from Fox Bay West, Port Stephens and Chartres had assembled. It was also the base for 'A' Company, the Royal Hampshires, whose camp was taking shape a little way up-river, at Doctor's Creek. Returning to the triangle after so many take-offs and landings, and so long in a noisy helicopter, I think that we were all feeling tired; within half-an-hour, however, we were changed and heading for a public reception at the Town Hall. On the short journey from Government House, I warned the Prime

Minister that we had a surprise in store. Councillors had decided to confer upon her the freedom of the Falkland Islands, a unique honour in that only the freedom of Stanley had been awarded before (and that only to the Royal Marines and the West Yorkshire Regiment, which had been based there in the Second World War). Harold Rowlands, as the most senior kelper in the FIG, had been chosen to present the scroll; I would introduce him and we would both speak for no more than two minutes. She would be expected to say a few words in reply, but not to make a long speech.

The Town Hall was packed. There must have been 600 or more there, in a room normally considered crowded with 200 (indeed, the Director of Public Works was concerned that the floor might not take the weight). The atmosphere was electric and the Prime Minister perked up as soon as she entered: she was engulfed in a sea of grateful well-wishers and it took the best part of an hour to guide her through the crowd to the stage at the other end of the hall. I introduced Harold and stuck to my allotted two minutes. Harold was equally brief: describing the occasion as the greatest moment in his life, he said that he was echoing the sentiments of all Falkland Islanders in expressing his pleasure at being able to thank Mrs Thatcher in person for their liberation and pledged Islanders to build a better future to ensure that the war had been worthwhile and that British lives had not been lost in vain. He read out the formal proclamation, presented the scroll and then brought the house down by kissing the Prime Minister. Clearly elated, Mrs Thatcher made what many of the audience told me afterwards was the best speech they had ever heard. It lasted for twenty minutes, without notes or briefing (none of us had prepared any material for her), and struck exactly the right chord. She received the most enthusiastic reception ever witnessed in the Falkland Islands. The biggest cheer came when she said: 'Today again the Union Jack flies over Port Stanley, and may it ever fly there.' This had of course particular significance for me, for it was here in the Town Hall that General Garcia had told me that the Argentines would stay 'forever'. It was an intensely moving experience for us all, including the Prime Minister's party. Bernard Ingham came up afterwards and smothered me in a huge bear-hug. Dinner that evening was a lively affair, with all the day's fatigue banished. Indeed, though well past midnight, Mr Thatcher had difficulty in persuading the Prime Minister to go to bed.

Tuesday was largely a nautical day but, before flying to HMS *Antrim*, the Prime Minister visited the junior and senior schools, the hospital, the post office, the power station, PWD, the Brewster houses and the FIGAS hangar, where the Beaver was being reassembled. At sea, she went from HMS *Antrim* to the RFA *Fort Grange*, the *Stena Inspector* and HMS *Charybdis*, returning in the evening to give interviews to the Penguin News and the local radio. David was host at a tri-service dinner that night, which lasted until after midnight. Relaxing in front of the peat fire before going to bed, the Prime Minister suddenly said, 'I haven't seen a penguin, I must see a penguin before we leave.' As she was due to depart at 8 a.m. that morning, there was not much time to arrange a visit to a penguin colony. Then she added, 'And I should like to walk over Tumbledown.' I groaned inwardly. 'It will mean getting up at five Prime Minister,' I said. 'That's fine,' she replied. After she and Mr Thatcher had retired, David organised a helicopter and I got hold of Ian Strange. We agreed that we should be able to fit in both Tumbledown and Seal Point before breakfast.

It was a miserable morning, blowing and raining. Undeterred, the Prime Minister jumped into the Sea King and we landed in the wet on Tumbledown. Mr Thatcher urged her to put a scarf over her head, but she would have none of it. Although the dangerous ordnance had been removed, there was still plenty of evidence of the battle, hangars and foxholes festooned with bits of webbing, tattered clothes and the inevitable tubes of toothpaste. Surveying the difficult terrain in the wind and the rain, the Prime Minister marvelled that the Scots Guards had been able to storm the Argentine positions. From Tumbledown, we flew down to Seal Point, on the tip of Port Harriet, and the jackass penguins obliged the Prime Minister by coming out of their burrows and eyeing her curiously. Thanks to the helicopter, we were back at Government House and having breakfast by 7.15 a.m.

Everything had gone without a hitch up till now; we had even managed to keep the Prime Minister's departure a secret. To convince the press that she would not be leaving until the following day, one of the crew of her Hercules had been told to stay up late drinking with the journalists (who were sharing the Upland Goose with them). He played his part so well that, when the rest of the crew climbed out of their bedroom windows at 4.30 a.m., he failed to surface and had to be quietly spirited away by his colleagues. Most of the press had accepted an invitation to be flown on a wildlife tour for the day and were on their way to a penguin colony when we escorted the Prime Minister to the airport. We bade our farewells and the Hercules door closed at precisely 8 a.m. As it was raining hard, David and I sought shelter in the helicopter and sat waiting for the Hercules to take off. We were congratulating ourselves that everything had gone well when the intercom crackled and our pilot reported that the Hercules was taxiing back. Apparently all four engines had lost power as the pilot opened the throttles. There was no danger because he had scarcely started his take-off run; but it was worrying. David and I dashed out of the helicopter and across the apron to be at the foot of the steps again as the Prime Minister and her party disembarked. We waited in the Station Commander's portacabin while the RAF decided what to do. The Prime Minister was naturally perturbed about losing precious time; her programme was as full as ever, with a big reception at Ascension on her way home (she had passed through unknown on the way down) and she wanted to be back in London for Question Time in the House of Commons the following afternoon. The choice lay between checking the faulty engines, which might have taken several hours, transferring the special caravan, which had been fitted into the Prime Minister's aircraft, into the press Hercules, or taking the press Hercules as it stood. As switching the caravan would also have taken several hours, the Prime Minister elected to go in the press Hercules, without trimmings. After almost an hour's delay, we said farewell a second time and breathed sighs of relief as the heavily laden Hercules lumbered off the runway and disappeared into the overcast skies. We had thoroughly enjoyed the visit, but another day at that pace would have been hard to bear. 'Early night, tonight, David,' I said, as we flew back to the triangle, with which he heartily concurred.

Before she left, Mrs Thatcher said that she had been deeply touched by the warmth and kindness of the welcome she had received every-where she went and from everyone she had met. She knew that what was being expressed to her was the loyalty of the Falkland Islanders to Britain and their gratitude for the professionalism and gallantry of the Task Force in freeing them from the domination of a military invader. But that was only part of the story. What in truth the Islanders were expressing was their gratitude to Mrs Thatcher for sending the Task Force and never wavering in her determination to liberate the Islands.

They believed that, had she not been the Prime Minister at the time, the Task Force would never have sailed and they would have been under Argentine domination 'forever'.

In coming 8,000 miles to meet the Islanders, the Prime Minister boosted morale as nothing else could. The citizens of shabby, shell-shocked Stanley needed a tonic and the Prime Minister's visit was the perfect medicine. It was fitting that she should come in the month that marked the 150th anniversary of continuous British settlement, the date by which the Argentines had determined that they would achieve sovereignty over the Islands. Her clear, unequivocal commitment to the Islanders both reassured them and instilled confidence in the future. Whatever other politicians or the Foreign Office might do or say, Islanders knew that they had a staunch champion at the helm in London.

Lord Gilbert
Labour MP 1970–97

John Gilbert was a minister throughout the Wilson and Callaghan governments of the 1970s and after being raised to the peerage in 1997 served under Tony Blair as Minister for Defence Procurement.

I am going to talk about something a little unfashionable about the late Baroness – her luck. She was a very lucky Prime Minister and a very lucky politician. There is nothing wrong with that. I am sure that I will be corrected by historians, but I am told that whenever a name was put to Napoleon Bonaparte for promotion to general, his first question was, 'Is he lucky?' It is a very good question indeed. Baroness Thatcher was very lucky. To say that is in no way to diminish her achievements and accomplishments.

But look what happened at the beginning. It was only because not a single man was prepared to stand against Mr Heath, whether on the grounds of reticence, gentlemanliness, loyalty or timidity, that she was the only one. That was luck. She could not have arranged that in advance, so what brilliant luck. I remember when it happened. I was in the same committee as the noble Lord, Lord MacGregor, when the news came through. I remember rejoicing with my noble friend Lord Barnett, who was leading for the government. He was Chief Secretary and I was Financial Secretary to the Treasury on that occasion. We rejoiced and said, 'That's marvellous. The Tories will never win a seat north of Watford from now on.' It just shows how wrong and stupid one can be.

Then we get to the 1979 election. Who could have lost the 1979 election against a government where the dead were going unburied, the garbage was piling up in the street and the country was in a state of utter shambles? She could not have lost. Anybody leading the Tory Party would have won the 1979 general election. We created Margaret Thatcher, in that sense.

As for the next two general elections of 1983 and 1987, I have to be rather careful. I know that it is said that you make your own luck in this world. I do not know whether Margaret Thatcher had a big part in the choice by the Labour Party as to who was to lead them into the 1983 and 1987 general elections, but she could hardly have done a better job, in my view. If I say any more, I will probably get the whip removed from me, so I must be very careful.

She really did not have it that difficult in those two general elections. As for some of the other people whom she was up against – Arthur Scargill, I ask you. Would you not love to have Arthur Scargill as your opponent in any debate going, a man who is frightened to go to his own members to get them to vote for a strike that he called? I cannot find parliamentary language to use to describe Arthur Scargill. Mrs Thatcher did not create Arthur Scargill; the National Union of Mineworkers, or certain branches of it, did, although not in my part of the world, I am glad to say, not in the West or East Midlands.

After Arthur Scargill, she was up against a bunch of fascists from a tinpot banana republic in South America. It was a gift. I am told that it was a very close-run thing: that we might not have won in the Falklands. I do not share that view, although I know that that is an unorthodox view. I know that certain things happened down there that should not have happened and that there was a certain amount of military bungling, which was our fault – not Mrs Thatcher's fault. As far as world opinion was concerned, to be up against a bunch of tinpot fascists was absolutely brilliant. She was lucky. She did not decide that the Argentines were going to invade the Falklands. She did not decide what a bunch of so-and-so's they were to have running their country. That was all her good luck. Good luck to her, but do not let us forget that she had an enormous amount of luck right through her career from beginning to end.

That is in no way intended to diminish her achievements, because the important thing in this world is that if you get your luck, you use it and take advantage of it, and she did, ferociously, without any quarter given. I admire her greatly for that.

I was once present at a conversation between Mrs Thatcher and Ted Heath. I was the only other person present: beat that. She had only recently become leader of the Conservative Party. It was an extraordinary event that brought that to pass.

I had gone to a memorial service for Hubert Humphrey. It was held on a day when the Cabinet was meeting. The Cabinet was going to come, but had not showed up because the meeting had overrun. The first three rows on the left-hand side of the aisle were left empty, and I parked myself in the middle of the fourth row. I had not been sitting there long before a figure came up and sat down next to me on my left. It was Margaret Thatcher. She was looking sparkling and effervescent. Needless to say, do I regret it? No, I do not – I tried flirting with her. I thought I was doing rather well, actually. Of course, I would, would I not? I complimented her on how her dress suited her, the colour of her eyes and all that sort of thing. We were getting on famously.

The rest of the pew was empty until, all of a sudden, a shadow appeared at the other end of the pew, escorted by the ushers, and was sat down next to me on the other side. It was Ted Heath. There then ensued a conversation between Margaret Thatcher, me and Ted Heath, which was a very unusual conversation in that nobody said a thing to anybody from start to finish. Considering the personalities involved, I think that is probably unique.

We have lived in the shadow of greatness. We shall never see her like again.

Carol Thatcher
Journalist
***

Carol Thatcher is a freelance journalist, author and daughter of Margaret Thatcher.

For a workaholic, No. 10 was the perfect home: a staircase of just seventeen steps led from the private flat to the Prime Minister's study on the first floor. It had to be the shortest commute in London.

The flat quickly dispelled the popular image of grand living. It was converted out of attic rooms during Neville Chamberlain's time. When it was portrayed in a Bond film, we all looked enviously because it was much more glamorous than the real thing.

I recall domestic arrangements being very do-it-yourself. Often, guests who came up to the flat for an early-evening gin and tonic would find one or other of my parents coordinating glasses, with one of us racing down the stairs to the catering kitchen to fill up the ice bucket from the machine there because no one had thought to refill the ice trays in our own freezer. My father wasn't keen on ice in drinks, though. 'Dilutes it,' he used to claim.

My mother regarded food simply as fuel and had no claims to being a foodie. The late playwright Ronnie Millar, who used to come in for speech-writing sessions often on a Sunday evening, used to raise his eyebrows and mutter: 'Lasagne again.'

My mother had total tunnel vision when it came to work. As kids, my brother and I were watching a pop music show on TV while she was doing constituency paperwork in the same room. I asked if she wanted me to turn the volume down. 'No,' she replied. She hadn't realised it was on.

When I was at boarding school she was meticulous about turning up to school functions but always had a file of paperwork to sign or read when there was a lull in proceedings.

I think she was the most practical, efficient and organised person I have known. I once read that she was described as 'fanatically tidy' while I was 'fanatically messy'. I couldn't argue.

On the evening of Friday 2 April 1982, my father was downing a gin and mixer in the drawing room of the flat at No. 10, when a message was delivered by a member of the Prime Minister's staff. Argentina had invaded the Falklands. Now, Denis prided himself on his geography, but this caught him out. 'I remember looking at *The Times Atlas of the World* to find out where the bloody hell they were – and I wasn't the only one.' Denis was already in fighting mood. 'As an ex-soldier I thought: how the hell are we going to get a force 8,000 miles away? I looked at the distances and it was a logistical nightmare – but I had no doubt that we had to do something.'

An emergency session of the House of Commons was called and the Prime Minister's own survival was in doubt. I had never seen my mother on her feet in the House of Commons as Prime Minister and it occurred to me that, if things were as bad as they appeared, this might be my last opportunity. I slung on some clothes, went to Westminster and joined the queue for the public gallery.

My mother later described the mood of the House as 'the most difficult I ever had to face'. She began solemnly, but then her voice took on a harder edge. 'It is the government's objective to see that the Islands are freed from occupation and returned to British administration at the earliest possible moment.'

There were several interjections, including one by Edward Rowlands, Labour MP for Merthyr Tydfil, who blanched at the PM's reference to Southern Thule, which was occupied in 1976 when a Labour government was in power. He said it consisted of 'a piece of rock in the most southerly part of the Dependencies which is completely uninhabited and which smells of large accumulations of penguin and other bird droppings'.

As I left the public gallery, my mind was filled with farcical images of bird shit and scrap-metal dealers. It made the cries of shame seem rather over the top.

Back at No. 10, I gently opened the door of the sitting room, not quite knowing what to expect. I genuinely feared that my parents might be moving out of No. 10 within days. A few months earlier, my mother had gone round the flat with little sticky dots marking anything that was ours as opposed to Her Majesty's Government's. The idea was that, if we had to move in a hurry, the removal men would find their job easier.

'Hello,' I said cautiously. She was sitting on a gold-coloured velvet sofa. There was no sign of doubt; this was Britain's first female Prime Minister auditioning for the part of war leader. 'Are you OK?'

'Fine,' she said, stuffing her hands into the pockets of her dress. 'We're down but not for long. I've just been downstairs and told Peter [Carrington] and John [Nott] that we're going to fight back.'

By the following morning, her resolve had hardened even further. Having been to the local church near Chequers, she marched purpose-fully across the Great Hall and announced: 'I'm going back to London. I know we can win. I know we can get them back if only I had six strong men and true. And I don't know if I've got them.'

During the first few days of the crisis, my father saw very little of Margaret. She didn't need reassurance – at least, not from her husband, who shared her views entirely. If it had been down to Denis, he would have dispensed with the diplomatic foreplay and evicted the 'Argies' at the first opportunity. 'From the word go, I said: "Get them off!" I never had any doubts that we were going to win but it was such an enormous operation.'

I was working for the *Daily Telegraph* at the time and would drop into No. 10 occasionally to pick up mail and hopefully see my mother. She was rarely home, but one weekend I found her sitting on the floor in the drawing room surrounded by peace plans – one brought back by Francis Pym, the new Foreign Secretary, another from Al Haig; there was even a proposal from Chile. They all had a conciliatory tone, suggesting things like 'interim administrations' and 'mutual withdrawals'. The Prime Minister wasn't prepared to 'bargain away the freedom' of the Falklanders and insisted: 'I'm not agreeing with anything until they get off.'

And get off they did. On a Monday night two months later, I was driving down Ebury Street when I heard my mother's voice on the car radio. 'There are reports of white flags flying over Port Stanley,' she said, and I took my hands off the wheel and cheered. Slamming on the brakes and parking, I listened to the rest of the speech, feeling absolutely elated.

My main emotion was relief for my mother. Although I had seen very little of her, images of her leaving No. 10 dressed in black, on her way to give bad news to the House, showed the strain she was under.

Denis wasn't in the gallery for that statement. Instead, he waited in the Prime Minister's room and they went back to Downing Street together, saying goodnight to the policemen on the door of No. 10. 'We went inside, and as we walked past the famous bulldog-pose portrait of Winston Churchill by Salisbury, hanging in the anteroom to the Cabinet room, I swear the great man bowed and said, "Well done, girl."'

Baroness Seccombe

Chairman of Conservative Women's National Committee 1981–84

Baroness Seccombe was raised to the peerage in 1991 after many years of loyal service to the Conservative Party, having served in numerous positions including Chairman of the Conservative Women's National Committee and Vice-Chairman with special responsibility for women.

In 1982 I was Chairman of the Conservative Women's National Conference. It had been the custom for the leader of our party to be the speaker at the last session. On assuming office as Prime Minister Margaret Thatcher continued the practice, much to the pleasure of our members.

On this occasion the country was embroiled in the battle to regain the Falkland Islands following the Argentinean invasion. It was a particularly sensitive time as earlier in the day there had been loss of life and two British ships had been sunk. There was enormous concern as news of the action was being released continually. This led to a barrage of media assembled to hear the British Prime Minister give an up-to-the-minute account of the situation.

I accompanied Baroness Young, then party Vice-Chairman with responsibility for women, to greet Margaret outside the conference hall. It was immediately clear that she was deeply moved by the happenings 8,000 miles away. She talked of the families of our servicemen and the sadness of those bereaved. At the same time she knew that in the hall it was not only the conference representatives who were going to hang on every word. It was the national and international media who were waiting to beam her words round the world.

As we approached the time for her to enter the hall I was acutely aware of the demands she had to make on herself in preparation for her expected powerful message. When she spoke I marvelled at her remarkable capacity to speak with such brave resolution.

In private she had shown us her sensitivity, compassion, misery and vulnerability but then drawing on an inner strength she was able to speak in such an authoritative and robust way.

On that day I saw the two sides of Margaret Thatcher – the warm, caring sensitive woman and the international statesman. It was a privilege I shall never forget.

Sir Richard Needham
Conservative MP 1979-97

Richard Needham joined the Thatcher government as a junior minister in the Northern Ireland office, where he remained until 1992. Between 1992 and 1995 he was Trade Minister at the DTI. This extract is taken from his memoirs Battling for Peace.

During the seven years that I held a government post under Margaret Thatcher there were only two occasions when I was summoned in attendance. The first was a general meeting of all Parliamentary Private Secretaries in the Downing Street whips' office. Everyone fell over themselves to be ever more sycophantic in an often vain effort to impress on the PM, within the thirty seconds allotted, why they possessed more shining talents than their colleagues. The whips stood around the back of the room making mental notes and smirking. The second happening was an invitation to lunch at No. 10 in early 1988 when I had been two-and-a-half years a minister. There were eight of us including Lord Young, Willie Whitelaw, Ian Stewart, Colin Moynihan and Edwina Currie. The PM started to savage Ian Stewart. 'What are you doing to tighten up spending in the Defence department?' she demanded. His attempts at explanation were cut off in mid-sentence when the guns were turned on Edwina. Edwina was made of stern stuff and fought her corner. The PM then turned on little Colin Moynihan. 'Why do we need a Minister for Sport?' she demanded. 'To deal with drugs,' he replied. This nonplussed her. 'Explain,' she rasped. 'Well as you know Prime Minister, drugs are endemic in sport. When there are governing bodies which need government money or subsidy we can insist on internal rules and procedures that can eliminate drug taking. We are being successful, particularly in sports such as athletics, but the biggest problem is snooker.' 'Snooker?' she asked incredulously. 'That dreadful game where everyone smokes and drinks and which Denis watches late at night in the flat? What drugs do they take?' 'Beta-blockers Prime Minister. They slow down the heartbeat so the player does not jerk as he plays his shot.' 'I've never

heard of them,' she reflected. 'Then none of us round this table would
ever have any need of them, would we Willie?' Willie blinked and as
he pushed his little pillbox under his napkin, boomed out: 'Certainly
not, Prime Minister!'

Andrew Rowe
Conservative MP 1983–2001

Andrew Rowe was the Director of Community Affairs at Conservative Central Office from 1975 until 1979. He became MP for Mid Kent in 1983 and Faversham and Mid Kent in 1997 until 2001. He died in 2008.

As Director of Community Affairs in Conservative Central Office from 1975 to 1979 I was responsible for arranging many of the annual conferences she attended. In those days the party had a Federation of Conservative Students which was in control of over 100 student unions. It also had a lively and effective Young Conservative organisation and a growing trade unionist group.

The Community Affairs department suggested to the Chairman and to Mrs T. that as part of the general election campaign of 1979, we should try to destroy the allegation that the party was anti-trade unions by staging a rally of Conservative trade unionists at the Wembley Conference centre. We had the advantage of having as one of the members of our team Harvey Thomas, who had been trained by the Billy Graham Evangelist Association. We also had in every Tory Party area young members of the Community Affairs team who, under the leadership of John Bowis, had been fostering good relations with the trade unions for several years.

It was a gamble, of course, and the enormity of it was borne in on me in the early morning of the day itself when the news came that two of our planned busloads from the north-west would fail to arrive because of a strike by transport workers. My immediate thought was that this was the TUC's response to our initiative and that instead of the 3,500 people we expected we should have only the office staff and 180 people from Scotland who had arrived by train the night before. Mad schemes of throwing them round the conference centre and pretending that they were a militant-tendency picket came and went in my anxious mind.

All went well, however, and soon the centre was filled with enthusiastic trade unionists. We had taken great pains to ensure that everyone present had a current membership card since we were sure that the press would be checking.

Inside the hall, under the skilled control of Dick Tracey, a lively programme unfolded until at last Maggie herself appeared. At that point into the hall came a long procession of men and women each carrying a placard declaring: 'ASTMS for Maggie', 'TGWLJ for Maggie' and so on. It was impressive and Maggie herself was clearly delighted. She made a rousing speech, was enthusiastically received and went on her way rejoicing.

It was, in many ways, a landmark event. Not only did it secure a prime spot on the six o'clock news, but its verve and glamour made it a precedent for subsequent political campaigns. Maggie herself wrote a very warm letter of appreciation to me for the whole team.

I need not dwell here on the agonies to which it led. Our suggestion of a similar rally called 'Youth for Europe' to help with the European elections met with such a long hiatus before a decision was finally taken, that we were given about three weeks in which to organise 3,000 young people to appear in the National Exhibition Centre. But we managed and a new form of British electioneering was firmly established.

Lord Fowler
Cabinet Minister 1979–90

After a career in journalism, Norman Fowler became the MP for Sutton Coldfield in February 1974. He served in Margaret Thatcher's Cabinet from 1979 as Minister of Transport, subsequently becoming Secretary of State for Social Services and later Secretary of State for Employment. He was Conservative Party Chairman under John Major from 1992 to 1994. He was raised to the peerage in 2001.

In the leadership election of 1975 I voted for Ted Heath, and then followed that by voting for my noble and learned friend Lord Howe. It is fair to say that that was rather an exclusive campaign. We had twenty-five definite promises and pledges and we ended up with nineteen votes, that being entirely par for the course in House of Commons elections. We had some good quality, however, in my noble friend Lord Brittan and my right honourable friend Kenneth Clarke. As we chewed over the result in a small room upstairs, none of us was convinced that the party had made the right choice. It was then, to my total amazement, that Margaret Thatcher put me into her first shadow Cabinet; it is fair to say that that amazement was widely shared. I had never done a frontbench job before. I was put in charge of health and social security against Barbara Castle; I think that is known as a baptism of fire.

However, that proved a point about Lady Thatcher. Margaret was sometimes seen as surrounding herself with known supporters and yes-men. She had the confidence and the self-belief not to do that. You did not have to be 'one of us' to be in her Cabinet. All three of us at the time were doubters, but all three of us became members of her Cabinet, and our very good candidate – who sadly got only nineteen votes – became her excellent Chancellor of the Exchequer, to whom she owed so much.

In 1975 I was also not at all sure whether Margaret Thatcher was electable. That was not because she was a woman. I had never regarded that as making any difference one way or the other in electoral terms. It was because in the mid-1970s she appeared to the public as aloof and most certainly not one of them. Although she had come up the hard way, she gave the impression that she was to the manor born. This was not an accurate picture of the woman but that was how she was seen. In the years after her election she was given media advice which she was wise enough to take, but above all she began to project her real self. A much grittier Margaret Thatcher emerged.

She was personally kind and generous, and much concerned that her ministers should not lose out in any way. I learned about that in a roundabout way. After about eighteen months I was moved from health and social security to transport. It was not the move that I was looking for. 'What? Transport?' I said to Margaret indignantly. She said, 'Norman, I did transport. You can do transport.' That is exactly what happened. It proved to be a lucky move, for when the new government was formed I went into the Cabinet, never having been even a junior minister. Margaret Thatcher had a lengthy apology to make. She said, 'I'm afraid we can pay in full only twenty-two Cabinet ministers and you are the twenty-third, so we will have to pay you at the rate of the Chief Whip.' She said, 'I am really very sorry about that.' I thought it best not to say that I would probably have done it for nothing had she asked, and we moved on.

My opposite number was a communist, M. Fiterman. The great thing was that after all these great events, you need a communiqué. It was a very genial meeting but there was nothing much we could agree on. The one thing we could agree on, at least in principle, was the need for a Channel Tunnel. The communiqué became about the Channel Tunnel. It ceased to be just an aspiration of the Department of Transport and from that moment became a proposal of No. 10 and went onwards.

There were undoubted crises, such as the Falklands. That was the only time I remember Margaret Thatcher going round the whole Cabinet table and asking each minister, one by one, whether they were in favour of sending a task force. Virtually everyone agreed; there was only one exception. However, I am bound to say that I at least agreed with my fingers metaphorically crossed because I joined the army for my national service in 1956, at the time of Suez. That was not our greatest time. It seemed to me that if we could not get our forces efficiently from Cyprus to Egypt, it would be very difficult to get them to the other end of the world in the way that we did. The success of the

Falklands was a tribute to our totally professional armed forces and to the consistency, determination and courage of Margaret Thatcher. My lesson from that was that the MPs who had voted for her as leader in 1975 had been proved absolutely right.

So what was the secret of a leader who had won three elections and survived crises that would have toppled a lesser person? Stamina obviously; courage certainly; but if I were to choose one factor, it would be professionalism. Her attitude to the televising of Parliament is a case in point. She was a strong opponent of televising the House. She thought it would change the character of Westminster and, I suspect, put more power in the hands of the media, including her *bête noire* the BBC. At times I felt that she regarded me – a supporter of television and a former journalist – as personally responsible for this invasion. Yet when the decision was made and a majority, including half the Cabinet, voted for television she settled down to work. Most of the rest of us took the view that there was not much you could do. You would either come over well or not. Margaret Thatcher studied the angles of the cameras, considered how the pictures would be appearing in sitting rooms all over the country, and emerged as the undoubted star of Westminster. Whatever may have been Neil Kinnock's hopes of this new opportunity – and remember that Kinnock made his first national reputation on television – he lost. It was the same professionalism which took Margaret Thatcher from an opposition leader without experience of foreign affairs to one of the world's best-known and most respected statesmen. It was the same professionalism which drove her into the early hours of the morning working on the multitude of red boxes produced by the departments of Whitehall. The same quality took her into the tearoom and the dining room of the House of Commons, rather than taking the night off; and at party conferences she was entirely tireless as she went from one function to another. She did not much like the annual trial of her speech at the Conservative Party Conference. She would sit there all week listening to her best lines being used by other speakers but knowing that the delegates would expect a sparkling performance at the end. With her speech-writers she would be up half the night preparing her text. It was the price that the leader of the party had to pay and she paid it willingly. It was this complete professionalism which set her apart.

Margaret's family provided the indispensable background rock of support, and a clear and uncomplicated instinct about what was right and wrong provided the certainty of direction. She had a strong feeling of what was honourable and what was not. She was intensely loyal to the officials who most closely worked with her. If she ever lost her temper it was because of attacks on advisers like Bernard Ingham or Charles Powell. She regarded an attack on officials who could not answer back as basically cowardly. Critics were trying to get at her through her advisers. To her this was a particularly despicable example of dishonourable conduct.

Her view of ministers was more complex. She was loyal to them in the midst of a dispute and under attack but she also felt that they should be capable of looking after themselves. However close she might be to a minister (for example, Nicholas Ridley), if the minister insisted on digging himself into a hole then ultimately he had to live with the consequences. The interests of the government took precedence over the interests of an individual minister. The same is true in a rather less stark way of the frequent reshuffles. Ministers were moved out of jobs in the interests of keeping the government's face fresh. In the process quite a number were roughly treated. Leon Brittan should not have been moved from the Home Office; Patrick Jenkin should have been moved from the Environment department, not sacked; Peter Rees should not have had to suffer the entirely avoidable fate of reading about his demise in the papers for week upon week before it happened. All the Thatcher governments would have benefited had ministers stayed both longer in jobs and longer as ministers.

Ultimately, however, success as a political leader is not measured by skill in the television studio or how you appear to your colleagues. It is about what you achieve. Political leaders have to win elections, but it is much more important that they win respect for doing the right things rather than an easy reputation for geniality. Margaret Thatcher's achievement was to take over a country which gave every appearance of being down and very nearly out and turn it round. The change was slow and at times painful but the chances are that much of the change is permanent. She took over a country which had been brought to its knees by uncontrolled trade union power and presided over a decade of reform. Any party which seriously tampers with that record does so at its electoral peril. She took over a country where too much industry and too much activity was controlled, not very successfully, by the state.

Virtually no one today believes in widespread renationalisation and a reintroduction of controls. She took over a country where millions of people were excluded from ownership. With the sale of council houses and wider share ownership important steps were taken to extend the traditional Conservative aims of one nation and a property-owning democracy. And she also took over a country where for decades tax rates had been too high but where it had become accepted that that was the inevitable way of things. Tax rates came down and my estimate is that most people in Britain would now like to keep them that way. These were real and substantial reforms which singled Margaret Thatcher out as one of the most successful political leaders this century.

Above all, serving with Margaret Thatcher was always exciting. It was sometimes also great fun. Some say that she stamped all over her ministers. It is true that if you were prepared to be handbagged she would oblige. She did not respect ministers who came in with a proposal that they immediately withdrew when they heard the initial response from the Prime Minister. I learned very early on that she really did enjoy an argument. Sometimes you actually won that argument as well.

She was an activist, she was a radical and she was, above all, a leader.

Margaret King
Fashion Designer

Margaret King was a fashion designer with Aquascutum.

I first met Margaret Thatcher about six days after she had become Prime Minister. She came into Aquascutum to buy a new coat; she already had one but it was quite old – she was very careful with her clothes. She also wanted a dress, but the one she liked was made in Italy and she insisted that she only wore British. She was very attuned to our country. I rushed into Liberty, bought some silk, and we made her a dress in three days, copying the Italian design. On the Monday morning it was perfect. I sent it up to Downing Street and she left for France on her first foreign visit as PM. In the evening, I saw her on television wearing that dress.

I didn't do anything else for her – she had her own dressmaker – until 1987, when she was due to go to Russia to meet President Gorbachev. She needed a coat, but I wanted to do more. As our leader, I felt she should look absolutely devastating.

We made up four coats for each day of her visit. I then phoned up the milliner, Philip Somerville, and asked for this great big fox-fur hat, and also found her a statement brooch.

Margaret Thatcher's arrival was dramatic and the press was glowing. The Americans were mad about her, saying how she truly looked the part of a Prime Minister. Everyone was very excited. The French, for instance, originally disregarded her and thought she looked rather frumpy. After the Russia trip, however, they were all over her; they couldn't stop talking about her. The Italians were the same. That was the turning point for her and her style.

Our relationship grew from there. Women need to have an image. On one of my early visits to Downing Street, I persuaded her to put on smoke-coloured stockings and black shoes, close her eyes, put on a coat and hat, and turn around to look in the mirror. She just knew she looked good. Margaret had wonderful posture, too. A person who holds herself well gets away with a lot.

Our Aquascutum factory started to make all of her clothes, but I also worked on her whole image. The press referred to her 'bagging' everyone, so I persuaded her to stop carrying a handbag and start carrying a clutch. The pussycat bow – I got rid of that, too. Women often try to look feminine by putting a bow around their neck, but it can make the neck appear very short. She was also very conscious of saving money so the same items were worn again and again.

Her mother was a dressmaker, so Margaret knew about cloth and finish. She really cared about clothes; she loved it when people like President Reagan admired how she looked. She was very conscious when she sat down not to show a lot of leg – although she was blessed with lovely pins.

I was conscious about her upper half. When women sit, their shirt starts riding up, so I created these pop-in bibs that were attached to the top of each of Margaret's jackets with press studs. I inserted a little V-cut into each of her suits, and would pop the bib into the suit. It stayed neatly static when she sat or moved around. In the Commons, she would have a plain one, and if she was going out, I'd have one with beads on it to give her a different look.

When she packed for trips abroad, Margaret would take a special book detailing each outfit for each day and occasion. It was all minutely planned; she was very organised. When the trip was anything to do with business, she wore more sober colours. But when she was representing the country abroad, or standing in a photograph with men in black and grey suits, she would wear colour; I particularly remember a deep coral outfit she wore to the Rocky Mountains in 1990. Pink was very good on her. I didn't want to put her in too much Conservative blue. She was careful to preserve her British image, so she would never have gone to India and worn an adapted sari, for instance.

If Margaret trusted you to do something, that was it – she trusted you. I felt very close to her, and working with her was an amazing chapter in my life.

Linda McDougall
Broadcaster and Writer

Linda McDougall is a documentary maker and author. She is married to Labour MP Austin Mitchell.

Now she's gone, everyone of my generation will be reflecting on the part Margaret Thatcher played in our lives. Like writing in a stick of rock, she runs through the memory of everyone over forty. She was even more than that to me. Both at the beginning and near the end of my career as a documentary maker, I got an insider's view of life in the Thatcher family.

On 4 February 1975, Thatcher won the first ballot for the leadership of the Conservative Party. She got 49.1 per cent, not quite enough for instant victory, but enough to make Edward Heath resign immediately. The previous night, Tory backbenchers had crowded round the few TV sets in the House of Commons to watch Granada Television's *World in Action – Why I Want to Be Leader,* by Margaret Thatcher. They were impressed by her natural demeanour and approved of her ability to chat in a relaxed fashion with ordinary people. They were charmed by her, surprised by her, and they voted for her in the secret ballot on the Tuesday.

I was the young, ambitious *World in Action* producer who jumped off the programme's normally left-wing platform and begged to be allowed to make a film about her. With no fuss and no reservations, she agreed to take part. On the first day of filming we arranged to meet at her home in Flood Street, Chelsea. The kitchen door was open and Margaret was standing at the sink with a Brillo Pad and a dessert dish, attacking stuck-on sponge. 'Come in, dear,' she said, wiping her hands on her hostess apron.

Gordon Reece, her political strategist, was waiting in the living room. For the next ten days Thatcher and Reece were cooperative and charming and did everything they could to make the process easier for a film crew of nine to follow her around her small house. We visited schools and shops, businesses and old people's homes. Thatcher was charming and smiled and listened carefully to all her constituents. We came across some gravediggers in a churchyard. Thatcher chatted with them cheerily and listened to their gripes. As she was about to leave, one of the men got down on his knees and offered to wipe the mud from her feet. 'Thank you very much,' she said, lifting her sensible, medium-heeled court shoe and pointing her toes in his direction.

On Sunday morning we were back in Flood Street to film the family with the papers. The Thatcher twins, Carol and Mark, were twenty-one and gave us what turned out to be an accurate foretaste of the way their personalities would develop. Carol was witty and charming and clutching the latest *Private Eye*. She read out unflattering comments about her mother whenever there was a gap in her parents' analysis of what the broadsheets said about Margaret's chances. Mark, who was still suffering from acne, was sullen and tetchy. Denis was generous and expansive. The minute the filming was finished he offered us all a G&T.

Many years later, in the autumn of 2002 a friend took me to meet a woman who had a good idea for a TV series. It turned out to be Carol Thatcher, who wanted to interview the consorts of world leaders. She would start with her father, Denis, and move on to others she had met through her mother. Denis was famous for never having been interviewed, so it was not hard to sell the idea to Channel 4.

Carol was lovely – witty, fun, generous and utterly indiscreet. She talked absolutely freely about her family, their finances and the people who surrounded her mother. Most evenings Carol would be up for a drink after work and it would often stretch to dinner. Carol's worries were all about her mother. She said the doctors thought she had had a series of small strokes. She often seemed confused and had become very repetitive. Carol adored her father but seemed eager to keep her distance from her mother. She said many times that Mark was especially close to her mother. Mark and Carol had a tempestuous relationship. They squabbled and argued when they were together, she said, and kept out of each other's way as much as possible. Mark was then living abroad, and when he arrived in London to visit his parents, Carol seemed to retreat into her shell. I could always tell when Mark went back to America or South Africa. Carol would be back on form again.

The Thatcher house was a narrow central London terrace on five floors with a police station in the basement. There was a silver sculpture in the centre of the dining table, engraved: 'To Margaret from the Cabinet'. A large oil painting of Baroness Thatcher in full evening dress hung over the fireplace, and there was another of Denis on the stairs. On a table in the living room was a plain silver bowl, engraved: 'The lady's not for turning'. The house was a bit like a museum, with little sign of real life. It certainly didn't look like a comfortable home for a couple of OAPs. I began to realise just how isolated the Thatchers had become. She lived on as an icon, but the real woman had been abandoned and forgotten, with few close friends to share her old age. We managed to film a marvellous interview with Denis when Margaret was away for the day, visiting her sister in a nursing home. Denis drank steadily, smoked regularly and told jokes throughout.

After Christmas Denis went into hospital for a check-up. His doctors discovered all was not well and he had an emergency double heart bypass. He recovered well and after a couple of weeks of convalescence he set off to visit Mark in South Africa.

Margaret was distressed when Denis was away. She kept asking Carol where he'd gone and forgetting the answer. I asked Carol if we could do a small interview with her mother, just to reminisce about her husband and their time together. I thought it might cheer her up a bit and Carol agreed.

On the day of the interview Margaret came downstairs from her bedroom carefully gripping the banister. She was wearing high-heeled court shoes and a coat and dress of heavy silk damask in dark green. She held out her hand to me. I led her to the chair we had chosen and explained that she could look at the shot of herself on the monitor next to the camera. She sat down, and before she looked at anything she put her hands to her throat and sighed: 'The neck – it's the first part of a woman to go, the neck.' The lights were soft and the picture was flattering, but I was shocked by the changes in her.

Her skin was as white and flat as unglazed china and her eyes were full of fear. Gone was the flush of power, the translucence that seemed to last decades longer for her than for other women. Over the years I had envied her confidence, enjoyed the challenges she sent out when she engaged with you. That day I could see only fear and uncertainty. She seemed aware that changes were happening to her and felt powerless to stop them. 'Sometimes I forget the words for things,' she whispered and looked carefully for my reaction. 'Don't we all,' I burbled as reassuringly as I could. 'Don't worry. We can cut out any mistakes – stop and start again if you want to.' Carol sat down and the interview began.

All her old fire came back when she reminisced about the Brighton bomb and the Falklands and the support her husband had given her on both occasions. Like Denis she became most passionate when Carol asked her about being kicked out of Downing Street. 'If you're in politics you expect to be knifed in the back. What I will never forgive is that I was away in Paris and there was a vote on whether I should continue as leader. And this was after nearly eleven years, when I had taken Britain from the slough of despond to the heights. It was the most difficult night of my life. I shall never forget that and I shall never forgive.'

Ruud Lubbers
Prime Minister of the Netherlands 1982–94

Ruud Lubbers was elected Prime Minister of the Netherlands in November 1982 and led three successive governments through to August 1994. During his terms he was instrumental in introducing the 'Dutch Model', which led to the successful turnaround of the Dutch economy.

In 1989 I celebrated my fiftieth birthday. My wife put together a marvellous video of world leaders who wished me a happy birthday who included George Bush, Helmut Kohl, Rajiv Gandhi and Margaret Thatcher. Now, many years later, I am delighted to record my own personal tribute to Margaret.

Although we met before she became Prime Minister, when I was leader of the Dutch Christian Democrats, our first meaningful meetings began at the end of 1982. I remember the European Council in Copenhagen where I had to mediate between President Mitterrand, who represented continental Europe and Margaret, the Atlanticist. It worked surprisingly well.

In the autumn of 1983, Margaret visited me in The Hague. She said jokingly that I should not ruin her reputation. This was an allusion to the nickname of Ruud Shock, which the press had given me. We started to work together on the INF deployment in response to the Soviet SS20 missiles. It was still the time of Ronald Reagan and we all worked towards the achievements at Reykjavik.

I admired Margaret for what she did for her own country, but I was really impressed at how she combined a strong anti-Soviet posture with excellent personal relations – even mutual admiration – with Mikhail Gorbachev. In 1989 she invited me to Chequers to discuss the European Monetary System. Margaret was adamant in pointing out the advantages of flexibility. But I dared to tell her that I drive my car in a more relaxed manner when I use seat belts. We were together in Paris when the political curtain fell for her. We had lunch one-to-one and Margaret confided to me that she would resign but not before John Major was sure of replacing her in the driving seat.

Indeed, by then she had done her job in the UK; in the Commonwealth; in Europe – where she and I quarrelled about how to end apartheid, and where we did our bit to end Soviet oppression. Margaret was a wonderful friend and colleague during those years. The chemistry between us surprised many of our colleagues and there was undoubtedly some jealousy. Later we worked together in the Atlantic Initiative and we continued to practise our common values. Gradually – that is life – we spoke to each other less and less but my gratitude to my dearest Margaret remains as strong as ever.

Lord Waddington
Cabinet Minister 1987–92

Raised to the peerage in 1990, David Waddington served in Margaret Thatcher's Cabinet as Chief Whip and then as Home Secretary. In 1990 John Major appointed him Lord Privy Seal. He was Governor of Bermuda from 1992 until 1997.

Margaret Thatcher was a towering figure, but I saw signs of human frailty. I was with her behind the stage in the conference hall in Brighton in 1984. She was waiting to go in front and make her great speech. She was slumped on a sofa and I think it was Gordon Reece sitting on the arm of the sofa. Margaret was saying, 'I don't think that I can go through with this.' He said, 'Of course you can, of course you can. When you get out there, the whole world will be cheering for you.' She said three bishops had just called in to pray for her and had had her on her knees, but when she added crossly 'as if I had nothing better to do' I knew the old spirit was there and she would put on a great show. She did. She went out in front of that audience and gave one of the most marvellous speeches of her whole life.

Moments after arriving at my desk in the Home Office on the morning of 30 July 1990 I received a call from the police telling me that Ian Gow, Margaret's Parliamentary Private Secretary when she first became Prime Minister, had been blown up in his car. Margaret had been very fond of Ian and he of her, and when I got to No. 10 a few minutes later she was telling her staff: 'Give me work. Cancel no engagements. I have got to keep busy.' And she forced herself to carry on with her normal programme.

On the morning of the 22 November 1990 the Prime Minister, visibly distressed, told her Cabinet that after her failure by four votes to be re-elected leader of the party she intended to resign. But that afternoon she was in the House of Commons replying to a censure debate and to all appearances enjoyed herself hugely as she laid about her, demolishing the opposition case. Words seemed to come easily, but she had sat up half the night preparing for that last great occasion.

Margaret Thatcher came out to help me in the Clitheroe by-election in February 1974. It was a very cold day and after an hour or two we repaired to a place to have lunch. I sat the constituency Chairman on her left. He was so intimidated by the occasion that he could not think of anything to say for five minutes. He then burst into song and said, 'Leader of the Opposition. Don't you think it's time we went for PR?' I thought that the Leader of the Opposition would explode. She choked on her prawn cocktail, gave a great gulp and then said, 'Well, of course, if you never want the Tory Party to win another election that is a very good idea.' The constituency Chairman slumped into his seat and never said another word.

Margaret did not suffer fools gladly but she could be immensely kind, somehow very tolerant of ordinary human failings. The other day I read a book written by Carol Thatcher. In that book about her father, Carol said that she asked him one day what was his idea of the perfect afternoon. He said, 'It is sitting in a deck chair on a hot afternoon with a bottle of bubbly by my side reading a good book, and Margaret in a reasonably calm frame of mind.'

But she loved an argument which usually took the form of her trying to test to destruction every proposition advanced by others than herself. On most matters she was convinced she was right, but who can blame her? She usually was. Two hundred and eighty-four economists wrote to *The Times* saying her policies would not work. They did; and Britain is benefiting to this day. Many doubted whether the Falklands could be retaken. She said they had to be and they were. Everyone said the government could not beat the National Union of Mineworkers: Margaret Thatcher knew better. The Treasury told her Britain had to enter the ERM. She felt in her bones it would end in disaster, and it did. She knew that those opposed to her in her government and in her party were risking the end of Britain as an independent nation state. That was something she was not prepared to countenance, and the fact that she was brought down for that principal reason is something of which she can be immensely proud.

Margaret Thatcher had great qualities of leadership which stood the country in good stead in times of peril, and she was a giant on the world stage. In those days it was somewhat difficult to describe her save in adjectives familiar to the reader of *Jane's Fighting Ships* – Indefatigable, Indomitable, Intrepid, Courageous.

Her determination to resist every threat to peace from the Soviet Bloc, her willingness to face any amount of unpopularity at home if that was necessary in order to see her own country properly defended and the West secure, led to the deployment of the cruise missile in Britain. That in turn gave her the moral authority to speak for the West and made the Soviets realise that they had no hope with their own far more limited resources of forever preventing democracy in Eastern Europe, let alone extending their particular brand of tyranny further west. Margaret Thatcher deserves much thanks from the British people and all who love freedom.

It would not be right to finish without a word about her family and Denis in particular. I think it was during the summer of 1988 that I, as government Chief Whip, and Peter Brooke, as Party Chairman, were having supper with the Prime Minister in No. 10 to talk about possible ministerial changes. We had just sat down when Margaret said: 'Poor old Denis upstairs in the flat, eating all on his own. He must be very lonely and fed up.' 'Oh!' I said, glancing at Peter and having a good idea which way the wind was blowing, 'we can't have that. He must come down. We want to see him, don't we, Peter?' 'Do you really?' said the Prime Minister. 'I promise you he won't say a word.' Well, it did not work out quite as the Prime Minister promised, but it brought home to me what a marvellous relationship she had with Denis and how much she depended on him. I think he was her great strength in moments of appalling strain. We also owe *him* a lot.

You have to say that Margaret was not always absolutely calm when you were working with her. She was always challenging, always relishing a good argument. Sometimes, when you had endured the flame and the fire, you came out of it thinking you might have won but you were never quite sure.

Margaret was absolutely free of side and self-importance. Once, I had an argument with her as to whether the BBC licence fee had been discussed in various committee meetings that we had had on the Broadcasting Bill. I said that I was absolutely sure that the licence fee had never been mentioned; she said that she was sure that it had. The minutes were called for; a man came into the room with a great bundle of documents. She seized the documents, threw them on the floor and flung herself on the floor to read them, bidding me to join her. After three or four minutes of fruitless search, someone knocked on the door and came in. Seeing that extraordinary sight, they might have been quite embarrassed. Margaret was not at all embarrassed. She got to her feet full of bad temper, not embarrassment. She flounced out of the room saying that the discussion would soon be resumed and that she would soon prove how pathetic was my memory.

She was a great person, a great person to work with, and I am immensely proud to have had the opportunity of serving under her.

Helmut Kohl

Chancellor of Germany 1982–98

Helmut Kohl was the Chancellor who reunited East and West Germany. He became Leader of the Christian Democratic Union in 1973 and became Chancellor nine years later following the resignation of Helmut Schmidt.

Margaret Thatcher had a fulfilled and remarkable life. She served her country with great passion and dedication over many years in a most prominent position. During her time as Prime Minister she transformed and successfully modernised her country in many areas. It is predominantly thanks to the reforms she undertook in the 1980s that Great Britain is today among the most economically successful countries in Europe. Her name will forever be linked with the modernisation of her country.

Whenever I think back to our many discussions, I do so with respect and gratitude – in spite of different views on several issues. She always presented her arguments openly and clearly and was fierce in defending them in the face of opposition.

Margaret could look back on her life's work with deep satisfaction. She achieved great things for her country.

Richard Stone

Artist

Richard Stone has painted portraits of the Royal Family for nearly three decades.
He was commissioned to paint several portraits of Lady Thatcher.

'I do hope that the light in here is all right for you?' enquired Lady Thatcher, extending a hand to greet me. She listened attentively while I explained how I hoped the sittings would progress. It was clear she wanted to give her best and be a good sitter. With some minor adjustments to the room, a comfortable armchair was positioned to allow the light to fall gently across her face. Coffee was summoned and the first of many enjoyable sittings began.

It was the beginning of a new adventure. Margaret Thatcher had been such an influential Prime Minister, much revered by my family and an inspiration to many of my generation. Her reputation was well known, as was her appearance from countless photographs and caricatures. I started work on the portrait a few days after meeting her for the first time. Not wanting to record just a superficial likeness, I needed to capture something of the strength and determination that a nation has always attributed to her. The trademark blue suit, the ubiquitous handbag not far from her side and the perfect haircut succinctly enshrined the public perception of the country's first lady Prime Minister.

With a ramrod-straight back and hands neatly clasped in her lap, we gradually broke into conversation. There was talk of the Brighton bombing, the Falklands War, her friendship with Ronald Reagan and most surprisingly, traditional home cooking. Memories of the Falklands took an emotional turn. With a catch in her voice, recalling the lists of casualties brought the reality of the conflict, fought far away, back home. Recollections of the SAS invasion strategy were graphically illustrated over the tea table, with the cups and saucers, sugar bowl, milk jug and teapot used as landmarks to describe the scene.

At times, the conversation was vigorous, with robust opinions expressed giving me moments to see the fire still behind the eyes.

Although each sitting would be an hour-and-a-half in length, time would fly as I flung paint on the canvas. Often oblivious to an agitated secretary wanting to draw things to a close, our time together would regularly overrun. On many occasions, when I was tired from the intense concentration, I would be invited to stay on for a drink to relax and continue our conversation. After time, there emerged a softer, more tender aspect to the Iron Lady. She would ask questions and listen carefully to my responses.

It was at moments such as these that I was able to see a more sensitive side that I felt it was necessary to allude to in the portrait. There emerged a different woman, with a kindness, a good humour and indeed a gentleness that was not revealed in the painting. Although the picture was practically finished, I was about ready to start all over again, as I now felt I knew her as she really was.

While I had invited Lady Thatcher to view the work as it evolved, she made it clear that she would prefer to see it only on completion. When the work was finished, she stood quietly contemplating her image. Placing a hand up to her pearl necklace and considering her words carefully, she remarked, 'It is how one would like to be remembered.'

Earl Ferrers
Conservative Peer

Robin Ferrers had the distinction of serving as a minister in every Conservative government from Harold Macmillan through to John Major. His memoirs Whatever Next? *were published in 2011. He died in 2012.*

I had three memorable 'initial' meetings with Margaret Thatcher. The first was in the late 60s or early 70s. Margaret Thatcher was a young backbencher, in her early forties I suppose. One of the doorkeepers in the House of Lords came to see me and said that Mrs Thatcher was in the peers' lobby and would like to see me. I did not know her. Nevertheless, quietly flattered, I went to the peers' lobby and saw this lovely, blonde lady waiting for me. She smiled and said 'I am so looking forward to seeing you on the train tonight – the 11.50.' I looked puzzled. She then realised that she had made a crashing mistake. She had got the wrong man. Her face went deep puce. Endless apologies and regrets. I took my leave – just a little disappointed.

The second time was in a hotel in Portman Square where all the members of the Conservative Party in the Commons and Lords, were meeting to 'elect' a new leader. The new leader had in fact been chosen, but this was the formality required to show that the chosen one had the approval of the party. The room was packed. I was late and I landed up backstage. Someone was speaking on the platform. There, beside me, was a frightened, trembling, elegant lady. It was Margaret Thatcher, waiting to go on to the stage to do her stuff. I would have trembled too. I never saw her tremble again.

The third time was in 1979, just after the general election, and she had invited me to be Minister of State at the Ministry of Agriculture. She had asked all the members of her new government to a welcome drink at No. 10. One of her *bête noires* was quangos. They were intolerable. They had mushroomed and must be cut down. I thought it prudent to enquire, before I went to No. 10, how many quangos there were in the Ministry of Agriculture. About five of us from the House of Lords were all chatting together in a group, when up looms the

Battleship. The conversation was minimalistic and trenchant. 'How many quangos are there in the Ministry of Agriculture?' 'Thirteen, Prime Minister', or whatever the number was, thanking merciful Heaven that I had ascertained the number beforehand. 'Get rid of them,' she replied and moved on.

She was a hugely formidable lady, of whom I always felt frightened, but whom one could not fail to admire and to respect. I was once asked to lunch at No. 10, itself a great honour. There were twelve of us. In the middle of lunch, Mrs Thatcher became involved in a frantic argument with John MacGregor, who was sitting opposite her. I slithered down in my chair. I was sitting next to Mark Lennox-Boyd, Mrs Thatcher's Parliamentary Private Secretary. 'Have you ever had a ding-dong with the Prime Minister?' he asked. 'No I prefer to keep my head below the parapet,' I replied. 'Oh, she respects people who have a good argument with her.' Maybe, I thought, but I don't want to be made mincemeat in front of this lot.

She was very kind and very caring. In August 1979, when we had only been in government for some three months, my daughter, who was in America, became very ill and we had to go to see her. When we arrived in Washington, we were met by one of the Embassy staff who said that the Prime Minister had rung up to enquire how Selina was and wanted to be kept informed of her progress. I was a junior minister and was virtually unknown to the Prime Minister, but she was kind enough and gracious enough, among all her other problems, to care about one of her minister's daughters.

Many years later in 1999 when we were in opposition, I had an amendment down at committee stage for the House of Lords Bill. The Bill referred to 'a' hereditary peer. I suggested that it should be 'an hereditary peer'. It was about ten o'clock at night. There were not many peers in the Chamber, but I put the amendment to the vote. The division bell rang and, as happens on these occasions, the peers appeared out of the woodwork – from everywhere. Lady Thatcher was at a function in the Cholmondeley Room and came scrambling up the stairs to vote. The whips said, 'You can go back. The front bench has decided not to support this amendment.' She was turning round to go and said. 'Whose amendment is it?' 'Robin Ferrers's.' 'Robin Ferrers? I shall certainly support him.' And she turned round and went into the division lobby. That was typical of her – even if we did not win the division!

Mrs Thatcher was a person to whom one could only look up to. She was kind, gracious, determined and statuesque. She could stand her corner with the best of them – like few others. To be 'handbagged' was an insult when the term was first used. In fact, it was a dramatic description of her force of character. She always looked the part and played the part. She was smartly and correctly dressed. Every hair of her head seemed in the right place – always. When one interviewer asked her why she always dressed so smartly, she replied, 'I dress in a way that I think people expect a Prime Minister to dress.' She was so right. You have to look the part as well as be the part. People do not want a Prime Minister to be 'one of us'. They want a Prime Minister to be on a pedestal.

Mrs Thatcher was a forceful and determined lady, intent on pulling the country out of the doldrums. And she did. Eighteen months or so after she had been in office, when the British people went abroad, they could once again hold their heads up high. What an achievement – only one of many.

Sir Christopher Lawson
Director of Marketing, Conservative Central Office 1981–87

Sir Christopher Lawson was a management consultant. After a career in marketing with Mars plc he joined the staff of Conservative Central Office to introduce modern direct marketing techniques into the party's campaigning methods. He died in 2007.

It is not difficult to understand that many people think of one of our greatest Prime Ministers as merely a single-minded, hard politician, for that was due to her total dedication to her task. I have a very different memory of her. I saw many occasions when she was concerned for others at times when it would have been better to have that concern for herself. I think especially of her worry for others after the Brighton bomb.

I also remember that on the day after the 1983 election results and also the day after those of 1987, both a Saturday morning, I received a letter from her thanking me for my help in the campaigns. She must have been up all night writing her 'thank you' letters!

After each of the 1983 and 1987 elections the Prime Minister gave a celebration party at No. 10 for the new Members of Parliament. At each of these her 'staff' were expected to enthuse the new Members and remind them that now was the time to prepare for the next election.

She had the great ability to enthuse others and did so in many ways through her uncanny depth of understanding of the problems of ordinary people.

At Downing Street parties she would circulate freely, guiding, thanking, encouraging, sometimes demanding of those attending these functions. After the guests left she would often kick off her shoes, have her first drink and relax completely. This was a Margaret Thatcher that most never saw!

I remember being at Chequers in early 1990 when I warned the PM that she was in danger from within the party and that she was likely to be challenged. She walked me around the garden and said that she was not worried. She was undoubtedly misled by her staff, who had told her that she had no problems. History proved differently!

Margaret Thatcher to me showed the world that Britain could and would cure itself of being the laughing stock of the Western world. In this she succeeded and the country owes her a great debt.

Those of us who can remember the 1970s will never forget the changes that developed during 'The Thatcher Years', when once again one became proud to be called 'British'.

Viscount Tonypandy
Speaker of the House of Commons 1976–83

Secretary of State for Wales under Harold Wilson, the distinguished parliamentar-
ian George Thomas was elected Speaker of the House of Commons in 1976. After
his resignation in 1983 he was created First Viscount Tonypandy and sat in the
House of Lords until his death in 1997. This extract is taken from his memoirs
Mr Speaker.

In mid-1982 the Queen gave a state banquet for the Reagans at Windsor Castle, where I renewed my acquaintance with Mrs Reagan, whom I had met at the wedding of Prince Charles and Lady Diana the year before.

The banquet itself was a considerable strain for Mrs Thatcher and those of us who knew that there had been very heavy losses in Bluff Cove as Welsh Guardsmen were being landed prior to the taking of Port Stanley on the Falklands. The news had not yet been released and that was the only time I saw Mrs Thatcher show any real sign of strain during the whole Falklands campaign.

I think that had a man been Prime Minister, he would probably have lost his nerve long before. Any man would have gone back to the United Nations to make sure he was not going to be ostracised by the world community, in much the same way as the opposition were putting themselves in the clear if things went wrong. Britain would have lost all influence in international affairs if Mrs Thatcher had submitted to the pressures and gone back to the United Nations. It would have meant that never again would Britain take any decisive action to defend her people. The Prime Minister showed remark-able courage and determination throughout the whole of the tragedy, and she knew tragedy was inevitable once the islands had been invaded by Argentina. But by her action she saved the good name of Britain.

The whole exercise showed that British youth, who never thought they would have to do that sort of thing again, could respond magnifi-cently to the challenge. The Falklands affair reinforced my belief that the British character has not really changed, despite all the troubles that we face with violence and sometimes appallingly selfish behaviour. We are still a tough little race, and now the world knows it.

Baroness Cox
Conservative Peer
———————

Caroline Cox worked as a sociologist and in nursing education before being raised to the peerage as Baroness Cox of Queensbury in 1983. She has been a Deputy Speaker of the House of Lords since 1986.

In December 1982 I received a telephone call 'out of the blue' asking me if I could spare the time to come down to Downing Street to meet the Prime Minister. With a mixture of excitement and terror, I asked if I might have some idea of the purpose of the meeting. With the prospect of meeting this formidable lady, I said that I would be very happy to come with an open mind but preferred not to come with an empty mind! I was advised that it was not possible to indicate the reason for the meeting but would I please be at Downing Street at 4.45 p.m. the next day. Knocking on the black door with the golden 10, my knees were shaking; by the time I reached the waiting room my mind was a 'white-out'. The only possible reason I could think for this invitation was a furious letter I had written to my MP about nurses' pay. At that moment I could not even remember a ward sister's annual salary!

Suddenly the doors opened and a charming man said, 'The Prime Minister will see you now.' I steered myself through the doors into 'the Presence'! Margaret Thatcher welcomed me graciously. She then said, 'Please sit down. I will come straight to the point because I believe in coming straight to the point.' I braced myself and she said, 'I am drawing up a list of names to go to Her Majesty the Queen for recommendations for life peerages. May I have your permission to put your name on that list?' It was a good thing I was sitting down or I would have fallen over backwards with astonishment.

She then said, 'In the Lords, I hope you will support us on education; I know you do not always agree with us on health. However, you always have freedom to speak and to vote according to conscience.'

She then said, 'I must ask you to treat this conversation in confidence until there is a press release next week. However, I expect all your family know you are here. You had better think of something to tell them. Why don't you just say that we had a little conversation about education?' She added, 'But you can tell your husband about the peerage, because spouses are different!'

I appreciated her thoughtfulness, thinking of the reception committee waiting for me at home. My children, their friends and neighbours all knew I had been to Downing Street and would be waiting eagerly for my return.

Lady Thatcher's anticipation of this situation enabled me to forestall the persistent questioning from my family. And by telling my husband I was able to come to terms with the shock of this offer which would transform my life.

I always profoundly respect Margaret Thatcher's principle of granting me the freedom to speak and vote according to conscience. Subsequently I took her at her word and not infrequently spoke and voted against the government's policy. I believe that this principle is essential for the effective fulfilment of the role and responsibilities of the House of Lords as a refining and a revising Chamber. Without it, it becomes merely a politicised rubber stamp for the House of Commons.

I hope that present and future Prime Ministers will follow Lady Thatcher's example and respect the principle of the spirit of independent thinking and voting, for without it the importance and fundamental significance of the second Chamber is so profoundly diminished that its *raison d'être* will be destroyed!

Lord Young
Cabinet Minister 1984–89
---

*David Young served in Margaret Thatcher's Cabinet as Minister without Portfolio,
then as Secretary of State for Employment and finally as Secretary of State for
Trade and Industry before retiring from the Cabinet in 1989.*

I first met Margaret Thatcher when she spoke at a lunch I chaired in
the late seventies. Many of the guests came up to me afterwards and
said 'If only...' None thought that she had any real chance of winning
the next election.

At that time I was already working for Keith Joseph but I did not
meet her again until some time after the 1979 election when, as Special
Adviser to the Department of Industry, I would accompany Keith to
occasional meetings at No. 10. However, observing Margaret at work
from the far end of the table was one thing, dealing directly with her
when she felt strongly about something was quite another.

Keith left Industry for the Department of Education and some time
later I went to the Manpower Services Commission. Eventually in
the autumn of 1984 she invited me into Cabinet as Minister without
Portfolio with responsibilities for employment.

I chaired a number of subcommittees, one of which was engaged
in developing a two-year YTS and in due course we agreed the terms
of a new scheme. One of the issues was the benefit of £16 per week
payable to unemployed school leavers and many of my colleagues,
myself included, thought that this early indoctrination into the welfare
state was quite wrong. I persuaded my committee that we should abolish this benefit but give the YTS entrants £25 per week, which they
would be expected to earn.

Our White Paper was due to be published just before the Easter
recess. When the Prime Minister was in Beijing the previous December
to sign the Accord on Hong Kong she announced that I was to bring
a trade delegation of some of the biggest UK companies at the beginning of March.

I was busy selecting and inviting my delegation when the bombshell dropped. I received an invitation to call on the Chief Secretary who gave me a simple message. Since the Treasury thought that many more young people would be attracted into our new scheme than collect benefit, it would cost £200 million more of public expenditure, and where was the additional money coming from? Now, I had no department, thus no budget to cut, so I was told that if I wanted this scheme, I must persuade my colleagues to find the amount for me. No one volunteered, so I went back to my committee and persuaded them to restore unemployment pay provisions once again.

Then the day came when I had to obtain the Prime Minister's agreement to our paper. As soon as the meeting started I knew that I was in trouble. She was adamant that we should stop paying school leavers benefit if they wouldn't enter the scheme, and nothing I could say would change her mind. The scheme in full, or nothing.

The following day was my last before I left for China. I asked for a meeting to raise the matter again and she met me in the morning with a small number of colleagues. Again nothing I could say would change her attitude. Paying benefit to school leavers was wrong, when they had the chance to earn more by entering YTS and that was that. I had rarely known her so adamant.

My White Paper, my first, was in ruins. I asked to see her, one-to-one, and she saw me in the middle of the afternoon. No matter what argument I used she was would not budge. The terrible thing was that I knew that she was right, but I also knew that without my White Paper, the chance for a two-year scheme was gone, probably for good.

I had to take the committee stage of a Bill in the Lords that evening and I went through the motions in the House in a deep depression. At about eight o'clock I slipped a note to my Private Secretary to see if the PM would see me later that evening. She would, and at eleven o'clock after the business in the House I went over to No. 10.

The discussion ranged back and forth for about an hour and I did not appear to be making any progress. The clock struck and I told the Prime Minister that it was now my birthday. Suddenly she changed and reluctantly, but with good grace, agreed to the amended scheme. I left as quickly as I could before she could change her mind. I still had my boxes to do, I still had to pack and we were leaving at the crack of dawn but I was happy.

We introduced the two-year YTS and the year after we were able to abolish benefit for school leavers.

Much has been said about the Falklands, but a little known fact about the Falklands is that every night during the six weeks of the campaign she would have a list of the casualties and every night, before going to bed, she would write a long, hand-written letter to the parents or partner, explaining how they lost their lives and in what a good cause it really was.

I was to experience this myself two or three years later. My younger brother, Stuart, who was Chairman of the BBC, died. On the day he died, by the time I got home, there was a three-page letter from Margaret, consoling me and talking about Stuart. An hour later, I got a phone call from Shirley, his widow. She had just received a similar letter, entirely different in content. Later on that day, my mother rang me. She had also received a letter from Margaret. How many serving Prime Ministers would take the trouble actually to do that?

One other little story shows that side of her character. After she had left office, my wife and I took her and Denis out for dinner. We were sitting at the Savoy when a waiter spilt something over my wife's dress. Margaret grabbed my wife's arm and said, 'Don't say a word. If you complain, he'll lose his job.' How many people would actually think that way? With all the talk about the Iron Lady, I pay tribute to a very human lady who accomplished so much for us all.

Major-General Julian Thompson
Brigade Commander during the Falklands Conflict

Julian Thompson served with distinction in the Royal Marine Commandos for many years, eventually rising to the rank of Major-General. He is currently a Visiting Professor of War Studies at King's College.

Following the march past of the representatives of the Falklands Task Force at the Mansion House in the City of London in autumn 1982, a luncheon was held in Guildhall, hosted by the Lord Mayor of London and attended by sailors, marines, soldiers and airmen of all ranks. After lunch, the Prime Minister, Mrs Thatcher as she was then, rose to speak. Before she began, there was a prolonged, spontaneous standing ovation, cheering and clapping for her, led by the junior ranks in Guildhall without any encouragement or lead being given by the officers present, but quickly taken up by all of us with the greatest enthusiasm; we wanted to show our affection for her. I was sitting opposite some of the members of her Cabinet, who were open-mouthed in astonishment. We adored her, and would have done anything for her. In all my years service, I have never seen anything like it. In the last hundred years, I can think of no politician except Winston Churchill who struck such a chord with servicemen, who usually have no time for politicians.

Some years later, Margaret Thatcher, still Prime Minister, attended an exercise involving the SBS boarding a 'target' ship. There was an advertisement around at the time featuring a man overcoming a series of difficult obstacles, all with the aim of carrying a box of Cadbury's Milk Tray to his lady love. I decided that the SBS would follow his example, and they entered into the plot with enthusiasm. The storming of the target was a great success, culminating in an SBS operator stepping forward, unzipping the top of his wet suit, and presenting the Prime Minister with a box of Cadbury's Milk Tray. She was surprised but delighted, and when one of her aides tried to take it off her, she rebuffed him, saying that the chocolates were for her and no one else. We all loved her for calmness in the face of one or two potentially unnerving moments on that particular exercise, her enthusiasm, and, dare one say it, because she is an extremely handsome lady. We appreciated that too.

Lord King
Conservative Peer

Tom King was Conservative for Bridgwater from 1970 to 2001. He served in the Cabinet from 1983 to 1992 in a variety of positions. He was raised to the peerage in 2001.

If I have one criticism of a great Prime Minister, it would be that in showing the leadership for that national will she worked far too hard. The one thing that I remember at Cabinet meetings – and one or two of my colleagues may recall this – was the occasional stifled yawn because it was such an extraordinary time. I remember walking out of a reception at No. 10 that she gave one evening. She was saying goodbye to various guests and just ahead of me was a BBC producer from the World Service. She said, 'I do like the World Service. I listen to Radio 4 at 11 p.m. and midnight, and then I switch to the World Service and listen to that at one o'clock, two o'clock and three o'clock.'

I came into the Cabinet at the very beginning of January 1983. My mother died two weeks later. I think that the first Cabinet meeting we had was when Parliament came back. She took me to one side and asked, 'Did your mother know, before she died, that you had come into the Cabinet?' I said that she did and she replied, 'I'm very pleased.' It was that sort of personal interest in people that made such an impact on us all.

The bomb outrage at Enniskillen shocked everybody in Northern Ireland, right across the communities. It was a really difficult time when the confidence that one needed to maintain was slightly wobbly. I said, 'The British Legion aren't going to allow their Remembrance Day service to be destroyed. We're going to have another service in two weeks' time.' I talked to the noble Lord, Lord Powell, who was then her Private Secretary, and asked, 'What is she doing on Sunday week?' He said, 'Oh, she's got a meeting with President Mitterrand in Paris.' I said, 'What time is that meeting?' He said, 'It's in the afternoon.' So I said, 'Look, if we organise it, do you think she'd come to Enniskillen to give the lead, reassurance and comfort that is so important?' Without hesitation, and in spite of the fact that she was a prime target for the terrorists all through her time, she came. It was wonderful cover. The press said, 'What's she doing on Sunday, with this big parade in Enniskillen?' We said, 'She's got a meeting with Mitterrand.' With the help of the RAF, she came in the morning and we had a great service. She got lashed and drenched with Fermanagh rain in the square of Enniskillen, but she did not let that put her off, and it was hugely appreciated.

John Blundell

Former General Director, Institute of Economic Affairs

John Blundell has been among the most prominent and influential thinkers on modern economics of recent years. He has worked for, and contributed to, numerous think tanks both in Britain and the USA.

The IEA (The Institute of Economic Affairs) archive contains an interesting exchange. On 24 October 1969 the IEA Editorial Director Arthur Seldon wrote to Geoffrey Howe as follows: 'May we hope for better things from Margaret?'

Geoffrey Howe replied: 'I am not at all sure about Margaret. Many of her economic prejudices are certainly sound. But she is inclined to be rather too dogmatic for my liking on sensitive matters like education and might actually retard the case by over-simplification. We should certainly be able to hope for something better from her – but I suspect that she will need to be exposed to the humanising side of your character as much as to the pure welfare market monger. There is much scope for her to be influenced between triumph and disaster!'

One evening in the late 1970s a group of younger members of the Conservative Party took Lady Thatcher to dinner in a private room at the Café Royal to brainstorm policy ideas. Two of us were very firmly trodden on.

First I suggested that all council housing be given away to current tenants. I was a newly elected Lambeth Borough councillor and I had figures to show we would be much better off if we could simply tell our Director of Administration and Legal Services to mail out every single deed. Just mail them out and get rid of them I argued.

'People will not value it properly unless they at least pay something for it' she observed, quickly moving on.

Next went a colleague destined for the Cabinet who said that she was putting too much emphasis on economic freedom and not enough on personal freedom.

'Take cannabis,' he said. 'It is available freely everywhere. Why not recognise reality and legalise it?'

'What do you mean by available freely everywhere?' she said in a tone of voice that should have told him to back off.

'Well, for example,' he ploughed on, 'my flat mate always has some and knows lots of places where he can get it!'

She turned her gaze on him.

'Peter (not his real name),' she said. 'My detective is standing outside that door. I want you to call him in now and give him your friend's details.'

I forget how Peter managed it, but he ducked and dived, weaved and wriggled, and she let him off the hook.

In 1990 I was living outside Washington DC. It was early summer and I was planning a trip to Munich and Moscow for early September. One day the mail brought an invitation to the Social Affairs Unit's tenth birthday party at the Reform Club. I was about to say no when I realised that I could fly Moscow to Vienna to London, go to the party and fly to DC the next day.

I turned up on time. As I walked up the steps in lounge suit I realised Sir Antony Jay, co-writer of *Yes Minister* and *Yes, Prime Minister*, was next to me in black tie. We fell into conversation and entered the event. An hour later we joined up again as Margaret Thatcher was working the room. She turned from the group next to us and spotted Tony in his DJ – the only one in the whole room.

'Ah Tony,' she said, 'you must be going somewhere important later!'

'No, Prime Minister,' he replied contritely. 'I mis-read the invitation!'

So I heard the author of *Yes, Prime Minister* say to the then Prime Minister, 'No, Prime Minister.'

When I became General Director of the IEA I found we had already published a collection of speeches by my predecessor Lord Harris under the title of *No, Minister*. So when Ralph turned seventy and I published the best of his articles, I had no hesitation in calling them *No, Prime Minister*.

When Michael Forsyth was national Chairman of the Federation of Conservative Students I was his national Vice-Chairman responsible for publicity. Mrs Thatcher's approaching birthday seemed to me to be a wonderful opportunity for us.

About a week before the big day (13 October 1976) we started brainstorming in The Marquis of Granby, just off Smith Square, as to what we could/should do. Eventually we settled on the idea of turning up at her Flood Street home with a very, very large bouquet of fifty red roses at about 7.30 a.m. Michael would present these to her against a backdrop of enthusiastic young students that I would recruit.

Everything was quickly arranged and the media alerted. On the morning of the big day I first picked up Michael and then this huge display of roses from a florist in Berkeley Square. The arrangement could barely fit in the taxi and we lost several heads en route.

When we pulled up there was a huge bank of cameras and a solitary policeman but not one student. 'Wait here,' I told Forsyth. I jumped out, scanned the street again and finally walked up to the policeman.

'I wonder if you have seen any students?' I asked.

'Oh yes, sir,' he replied. 'Mrs Thatcher saw them out here twenty minutes ago and invited them in for a cup of tea!'

'Should I say you are ready, sir?' he finished.

The students duly emerged and formed a cordon. Michael presented the roses and the photos went out all over the world.

I was at a round-table dinner of forty people with Lady Thatcher some years ago. After dinner we enjoyed remarks from a distinguished guest. Then came questions. Most present were fairly senior types from the media, the civil service, industry and politics. At forty-five I was pretty young but there was an even younger 35-year-old representing his boss. To be accurate this young man was actually the leading expert in the room on our topic for the night.

Into the vacuum of space and time immediately following the guests' remarks the young man proffered an interesting question.

The problem was nobody could hear what he was saying. 'Speak up, young man,' commanded Lady Thatcher.

He tried again but clearly did not measure up.

'SPEAK UP, YOUNG MAN,' she commanded again.

He started a third time. It still did not measure up. She glared down the table.

'Young man,' she said. 'Stand up and throw your voice. We want to hear what you have to say.'

Turning bright red he stood; he threw; they listened and at the end they applauded.

From March 1973 to March 1974 I was Chairman of the London Region of the Federation of Conservative Students.

My year finished just after the February 1974 general election with a dinner at the House of Lords sponsored by the historian Lord Blake. My guest of honour was Margaret Thatcher. She had been invited nearly a year earlier as Secretary of State for Education. Now she was appearing before us as shadow Secretary of State for the Environment.

Everything had been meticulously planned and at the appropriate moment the head table of eight trooped in. Some 200 people were standing staring at me as I thought to myself, 'We've forgotten something here. Oops, something's wrong. Why is everyone standing up. Why aren't they sitting down?'

Just as I was about to panic Lady Thatcher's left foot kicked, yes kicked, me on the outside right ankle.

'Grace, you fool,' she muttered.

Nobody had been lined up to say grace!

I stuck my head down, said grace, and we all sat down. Phew!

Over dinner she discovered that as retiring Chairman I had personally paid for the wine for the top table.

'Oh, I can't have that,' she said and quickly passed me some folded money under the table.

I was hosting a dinner once for a famous politician from overseas. Lady Thatcher's office asked if she and Sir Denis could attend and I replied yes.

On the night, Sir Denis failed to show and I faced having an empty chair at dinner.

I quickly recruited a Tory MP friend who is a generation younger than Lady Thatcher, tall, straight and, my wife tells me, handsome in a battered kind of way.

We sat down to dinner. I tapped on a glass to get attention and made a few announcements.

I concluded by saying that Sir Denis's place had been taken for the night by Mr X MP.

'Really,' said Lady Thatcher in an arch voice. 'Nobody told me,' she concluded.

Lord Deben
Conservative Peer

John Selwyn Gummer was elected MP for Lewisham West in 1970 and for Eye (later Suffolk Coastal) in 1979. He retired from Parliament in 2010 and was then raised to the peerage. He was appointed Chairman of the Conservative Party in 1983 and joined the Cabinet in 1989.

Ministers in Margaret Thatcher's governments learned there was no point in approaching her on anything if you didn't know your stuff. She would drill down immediately to the heart of the matter and would punish any loose wording or imprecise phrase unmercifully. What was less obvious was that she would change her mind, however inconvenient it was, if she were convinced of your case. She was tough-minded and determined but not obstinate or inflexible. She had the stature and the self-confidence to accept that she needed to change course.

My most dramatic memory of that was one evening when I was being briefed by the vets from the Ministry of Agriculture. They were giving me the arguments that I would have to deploy at the next day's meeting of the Council of Ministers in order to defend the British position which sought to restrict the movement of beef because of concern about animal disease. Our partners in the EU were suspicious of our arguments which they thought had more to do with protectionism than a concern with animal health.

Mrs Thatcher had weighed in publicly some weeks earlier to defend the UK position and, as was usual with her, no one could have mistaken her commitment and determination. I began the meeting with the vets with no qualms about our position. I had always taken a strong line on animal health and I was used to arguing from a minority position in the Council of Ministers. The Prime Minister had given me the backing I had wanted and so all seemed set for a good battle but one which I expected to win. Nonetheless, I followed my normal routine which was not to rely upon written submissions but to argue these detailed policies with the experts so that I was fully able to hold my own round the table. It was a procedure I had learned from Michael Heseltine who, rightly, said that it enabled a minister to ferret out weaknesses and inconsistencies much more effectively than when presented with a sanitised written brief.

On this occasion, I expected no difficulties. This was a long-standing view on which I had no doubts. Then came the shock. As we discussed the issues, the science upon which our position was based seemed less and less certain. The vets became evasive and their answers less precise. Gradually it emerged that our public posture was no longer well-grounded. Fundamental changes in the science had occurred and we had not applied them to our political position. If any one of my fellow EU ministers had been properly briefed they could have shot me down in flames.

It was 7.30 at night. I was due out on the 10.30 plane with a policy that didn't hold water but one that had been recently and publicly commended by the Prime Minister. What was more, if we were shown to be scientifically wrong, a whole raft of other positions would be undermined. Given Mrs Thatcher's position, I couldn't just change the policy. I had to get her agreement. A phone call fixed an appointment for 7.30 next morning and I set about preparing for the ordeal.

Here was a classically difficult proposition. She was on the record. She had handbagged the European Union. I was to get her to change her view, admit we were wrong and agree with the Commission. Not an enviable task! Worse, it was a very technical matter. I knew from experience that the real problem would be to get enough time to explain the issues logically before she came in with a reprise of her public position. I had to find a way to get the science across before we moved to the politics. There I was on safer ground. Mrs Thatcher was never afraid of facing up to the science even if it were politically inconvenient. I had learned that long before on climate change, where she was the first major political figure to accept the evidence of man's effect on global warming.

So I sent for one of the most astute and trustworthy of my advisers, Simon Dugdale, the Head of Information. Could we, at that time of night, produce five story boards to explain the problem and the solution sufficiently clearly to hold the Prime Minister's undivided attention on this important but very narrow issue? We worked on the wording and one of his graphic staff produced the boards.

At 7.30 next morning, I was ushered into the little study on the first floor at No. 10. The time and the urgency of the meeting meant that there was no Private Secretary. I launched into the explanation. Mrs T. liked the innovation of the story boards. She listened intently, asked some confirmatory questions, then, with a grimace, finally said, 'I'm sorry to say, John, it looks as if you're right. We'll have to change tack. It won't do to be proved factually wrong. But you better be right!' The fierce look in her eye was unmistakeable but so was the fact that she was not the obstinate and inflexible woman that her detractors portrayed. Even on a matter so sensitive, so opposite to what she wanted, so removed from her own instincts, she was willing to change if the facts demanded it. There are few in high office with the self-confidence and commitment to truth who have the guts to let the science prevail. It was that sterling quality of absolute probity that was one of the reasons that she was such a star and such a great woman to work for.

I was Chairman of the Conservative Party on that terrible night in Brighton and I was with le Lord, Lord Butler, and Margaret Thatcher at that very time. It was very late. We were writing the speech. Those occasions went on for ever. I thought I had the final bit. I knew I had not, of course, because there used sometimes to be speeches where I would be in the cellar writing on the autocue as it was moving and as she was speaking a bit that she decided she did not like. However, on this occasion, the noble Lord, Lord Butler, was finishing some work with her and I had just walked across the corridor to get the final speech photographed when there was a terrible bang. Automatically, the girls working in the office running off the speech and I all got to the floor. There was a second bang because the roof lifted off and then dropped again. It sounded like another explosion. The dust began to fall.

On my knees, I moved towards the door, opened it and put my head around it. On the other side of the corridor, the door to Mrs Thatcher's room opened and she was on her knees looking around the door. 'Tragic comedy' are the only words that I can say to describe what was happening. It was a mixture of, 'What has happened? What should we do? Don't we both look silly?' She got up, brushed herself down and said, 'Right, we had better get on with something.' But what should we get on with, because we had no idea? She knew that things had to go on. She never said, 'The party conference will continue.'

Everyone assumed that it would because we knew exactly how she would react and precisely what we would be expected to do. So we went off and organised the continuance of the conference. No one asked the question, except for the local chief of police. We soon told him that he had better not ask her that or he might be in even worse trouble than he clearly was going to be. The conference continued, although it was a harrowing and difficult time.

I was lucky enough to help write a lot of Mrs Thatcher's speeches. She kidnapped me after a speech I had made at a wedding. I was not in Parliament at the time. She said, 'Would you come and help me write speeches?' I was surprised because I did not come from the same part of the party and I would not automatically have been thought of as a natural writer. But once she knew that you were loyal and that you cared about her, the relationship was absolutely one of trust, confidence and support. Occasionally, she would say, 'Don't listen to this John, I am going to say something nasty about Europe.' She would say it and then she would say, 'You can listen again now', and we would move on.

I could not understand why I was seated next to her on the day we went with the Queen to open the Channel Tunnel. I was the Secretary of State for the Environment. We were both sitting there and I could not understand why. Then I realised that I was the foil. As we moved out of the station, she said, 'This has got nothing to do with the Germans, you know. It is entirely the French. But I do not see why we import all that food from France. Why should we buy French cheese? We have perfectly good cheese of our own.' I realised that she wanted an argument; so an argument we had. The argument went terribly well and we were halfway through before either of us recognised that we had gone into the tunnel. It was absolutely a typical part of what she loved, which was to discover where she wanted to be by saying something to which she demanded a response. Her only demand was that you were rigorous in your argument. I have watched her destroy people, although never her inferiors. She never set people down if they were in a humble position. However, she destroyed people who pretended that they knew the facts but came ill prepared. You never went ill prepared to a meeting with Margaret Thatcher.

You grew to have a very deep affection for her, even though you often disagreed. That was a very unusual ability on her part, and it was, as the noble Lord, Lord Young, said, down to her kindness to us all. If you had not had anything to eat, there were late-night meals in her flat. The first thing she would ask if you were late was, 'Have you had something to eat?' I have eaten more coronation chicken produced by Margaret Thatcher than I have at any other place or at any other time. I think that she did know how to cook other things but that was the staple diet. She also always knew about your family. She always asked about them and was interested in them. She knew their names and never forgot any of those things. When you think of the number of people she had to deal with, that was remarkable.

Of course, she could make terrible mistakes. She came to my constituency during the campaign for the 1979 election, which she won. She did so as a favour, because I was fighting a seat which the Conservatives had always won, but she made time to come. We decided that it would be very good if she went to a farm. She arrived and there was a rather ill calf, which she was not supposed to touch. We had a nice fluffy lamb for touching. However, she walked up to the calf, put her arms round it and picked it up. It was very heavy. For the photographers, it was fantastic – wonderful. Holding up the calf, she said, 'I'm going to call it Victory.' However, the calf was ill and we got every vet in Suffolk to attend to it. We hid the calf from public eye and kept it alive until after the election. We were terrified that this blooming calf would die on us.

Margaret Thatcher was a very beautiful woman. She had beautiful hands and lovely ankles, and she knew precisely how to use both. Any woman who is stupid enough to think that there is something unsuitable about using the gifts that God has given her should be ashamed of herself. She knew perfectly well that she used them not because she was not as good as men but because she was better than men, and she also wanted to have a bit of an advantage. It was a pleasure to see how she turned herself out and how she never forgot that she was a woman.

I think that history will remember a rather special thing about her. She was a very cautious woman. She did not take on things lightly and she took them on one at a time. She recognised that you could not have a whole plethora of interventions, initiatives, new ideas and headline-grabbing ideas. She knew that you won things only by taking them one by one, by fighting them through and succeeding with them one at a time. Caution is something that does not normally go with a charismatic leader, but one reason that she stayed for so long and was so successful was that she did not go ahead with the abolition of the dock labour scheme until she had dealt with the problems of the mining industry. She did not move to privatise water until she had made sure that people recognised that it was the only way to pay the bills. She had a quality of caution, which is something that very few people of her strength have ever evinced.

It was a privilege, a pleasure and enormous fun to work for her. Things were always unexpected and changed utterly all the time. You never knew what she was going to say or how she was going to receive a carefully crafted few paragraphs, but you did know that you were in the company of greatness. She was a star, and stars rarely come. When they do, we should recognise them without rancour and certainly not say, 'It is not quite as bright as we would like it to be', or that it fell in a different way than we might have liked. We should just say, 'Thank goodness that our lives have been enlivened by that star.'

David Davis

Conservative MP 1987–

David Davis was first elected to Parliament in 1987 as MP for Boothferry, later Haltemprice and Howden. He has served in the whips' office, as a junior minister in the Cabinet Office and then as Minister for Europe. He was Chairman of the Public Accounts Committee from 1997 to 2001 and was a party leadership contender in 2005.

Soon after my election to Parliament in 1987 I happened to be walking through the Members' Lobby when I suddenly observed an old friend, Michael Forsyth, a well-known Thatcherite and later to become a leading light in the No Turning Back Group.

Michael had been elected in 1983 and by now had become a junior minister. He was running, literally running. His hair was dishevelled and he was carrying not only his box, but somehow balancing a full tray of papers on his arm.

'Slow down,' I called out. 'Rome wasn't built in a day,' I added as an afterthought.

'Yes,' cried Forsyth over his shoulder, as he swept passed me. 'But Margaret wasn't the foreman on that job.'

Alan Duncan
Conservative MP 1992–

Alan Duncan has been the MP for Rutland and Melton since 1992. He joined the Conservative front bench in 1998 and is now a minister in David Cameron's government.

In June 1996, I hosted a summer drinks party in my London garden for the No Turning Back Group of Conservative MPs. Mrs T. was the guest of honour as President of the NTB Group and Michael Portillo, then Secretary of State for Defence, was among the guests.

There was much debate at the time about the review of Defence budgets and Mrs T. assailed Michael Portillo with questions about what would be left of our Defence capability.

Hoping to settle her down by assuring her of our adequate equipment in the future, Michael said: 'Don't worry, Margaret, we have lots of invitations to tender.'

She exploded: 'Invitations to tender – invitations to tender – you cannot win a war with invitations to tender!' and then she paused, quietened down and said, 'I am so sorry, Michael, I must not, I must not.' She then turned around as if to speak to someone else, the conversation having finished and, just as everyone thought that peace had broken out, she swivelled vigorously on her heels, pursed her lips, pointed her finger right at Michael Portillo and said in a determined and pointed manner: 'Michael, have you ever won a war? I have!'

Lord Forsyth
Conservative Peer

Michael Forsyth was MP for Stirling from 1983 to 1997. He served as a minister in the Scottish Office under Margaret Thatcher and later became a member of John Major's Cabinet.

From time to time I helped Lady Thatcher as she attended the House of Lords. However, it was becoming something of a burden. I found that trying to keep going with my job and being here to look after Margaret was quite difficult, so I thought that I would tackle this problem. I said, 'You know, Margaret, you've been Prime Minister and you've done a great service to our country. You don't need to come here as often as you do.' She turned to me and said, 'Michael, when we accept appointment to this place, it is our duty to attend here. How many times have you been here in the past two months?' That illustrated her love for Parliament and her devotion to it. Someone said earlier that she was scared of nothing. She was quite scared of the House of Commons. I remember seeing her knees knocking when she was making speeches. That was because she respected the House of Commons. When you were discussing policy she would often say, 'What do we do about telling Parliament?' This was always central to her, and she had great respect for our constitution.

I first met her through Keith Joseph, as a young man in my early twenties, at the Centre for Policy Studies, now so ably chaired by my noble friend Lord Saatchi, where they were trying to build the blocks to turn around our country. As a young man I was told that Britain had no future, that it was best to emigrate. Somebody wrote an editorial in *The Times* saying that it would be impossible to govern without the support of the trade unions. I thought, 'I'm going to have to get involved here.' I never wanted to be a politician, but I ended up becoming one because of Margaret Thatcher, Keith Joseph and the battle of ideas. Ideas fascinated her. Whenever you had an issue or a policy discussion, she would always start by saying, 'What are the facts?' and then you would work out how you were going to sell this particularly difficult policy.

She was quite forgiving of mistakes, and I made a few. As a young man I was involved in her leadership campaign as Chairman of the Federation of Conservative Students. We produced literature to encourage people to vote for her which was aimed at young people. I made the mistake of sticking one of the stickers on the Party Chairman's door in Central Office, and there was the most almighty row, because the slogan was 'Put a woman on top for a change'. I thought, 'She will never speak to me again', but typically, she pretended not to understand the double entendre.

It is said that you can judge people by their opponents, and that has been used in the context of the disgraceful minority of Trots and socialist workers who have behaved so badly in recent days. I will mention one thing about Gordon Brown. As Prime Minister, Gordon Brown invited Margaret to No. 10 on several occasions but on one occasion she was invited for the unveiling of a portrait – a portrait of Margaret that had been commissioned and paid for privately. In his tribute to her, Gordon Brown said that there were only three other oil portraits of Prime Ministers in No. 10 Downing Street. One is of Walpole and was the first portrait of a Prime Minister to hang in the Cabinet room; another was of Wellington, who saved us from Napoleon; and the third is of Winston Churchill, who saved Britain and Europe from the Nazis. He went on to say, 'And I think it is entirely appropriate, Lady Thatcher, given what you have done for our country, that the fourth should be of you.' I was astonished by that, and then I thought, 'Well, actually, it is possible in politics to recognise brilliance and achievements while still disagreeing.' Gordon Brown deserves considerable credit for recognising that.

The noble Lord, Lord Griffiths, mentioned Margaret's Methodism. Her religion was very important to her. However, she could be pragmatic about it. In her latter years a number of us tried to get her involved in social occasions. It is often said that she was not interested in the arts and music and so on, but that is nonsense. She was just so busy sorting out the country that she did not have time for it. I invited her to Ascot, and she said, 'Well, I was brought up as a Methodist and we're not really keen on this gambling, but I understand there are six races.' She opened her handbag and said, 'I've got £5 for each race. Is that all right?' The first race was run and she lost, and she looked extremely glum. I had seated her next to someone who was a racing expert, and I said, 'What's happened?' She said, 'We've lost.' I said to this chap, who was called Dominic Burke, 'Dominic, if you lose the next race you'll go the way of Michael Heseltine.' She said, 'That's quite right.' She won every single subsequent race. She had all this money and said, 'I'm not sure the Methodists were right about this gambling,' and was so pleased that she stood on the balcony and joined in the singing of 'Roll out the Barrel'. I thought, if only people could see the real Margaret Thatcher, and not the Margaret Thatcher that has been painted as an image.

A number of people have pointed to her having a feel and affection for, and an easy way with, ordinary folk. When I worked for Flemings investment bank, we had a fantastic collection of pictures. She asked to see the pictures, so I arranged a dinner and a number of prominent people from the City came to it. They all sat down while we finished looking at the pictures. I was taking her up and everybody was waiting for her. Then the lift door opened and a cleaning lady came face to face with Margaret Thatcher and said, 'Oh, Mrs Thatcher, I like you.' Margaret said, 'My dear, what are you doing here at this time of night?' She said, 'I'm just finishing my shift, but I'm such an admirer of yours.' They got chatting and Margaret said, 'Do you do the whole place yourself?' The cleaner said, 'No, I've got all my friends downstairs but they won't believe that I've met you.' Margaret said, 'We'll go and meet them.' I said, 'But Margaret, we've got a dinner going,' but she went down and talked to all the cleaning ladies while everybody else had to wait. That was very typical of the way in which she operated.

Since 1990, she has been supported by a magnificent team of people. Of course, Denis was her main support until his sad death but Mark Worthington, her Political Secretary, really did work seven days a week and twenty-four hours a day. He did a brilliant job and sometimes dealt with very difficult issues which came up from time to time. I would particularly like to mention Cynthia Crawford, who was with her from the start. Crawfie organised her – she was very careful about how she used her clothes and how they could be recycled.

However, Margaret always turned out absolutely immaculately, down to the last day that she was here, for a lunch just before Christmas.

I went to the last lunch that she held in No. 10 before she left as Prime Minister, when Keith Joseph paid a handsome tribute to her. He had been the architect of so many of the ideas that she, with her pragmatism and clarity of mind, had gone on to implement. He said that she was a beautiful giant who had achieved more than any of us ever dreamt would be possible. I cannot add to how he put it. He is, sadly, not with us here today but made such a tremendous contribution quietly to the Conservative Party and its philosophy.

Sir David Mitchell
Conservative MP 1964–87

David Mitchell was the MP for Basingstoke from 1964 until 1983 and MP for Hampshire North West from 1983 until 1997, serving as a minister in Margaret Thatcher's government.

I recall an elderly constituent coming to one of my 'surgeries', as UK Members of Parliament like to call their constituency advice sessions. It was a Saturday morning, he was last in my queue and stayed on to recount his wartime experiences.

He had been shot down over the Channel coastline and burned on his arms. At that time Basingstoke Hospital was the major burns unit in southern England. After some treatment there he was sent to Newcastle by train for further specialist treatment.

As the train stopped at Grantham the sirens sounded for an air raid. Shortly after the 'all clear' sounded it was announced that the train would go no further until morning. Everybody got out and organised themselves as best they could for a somewhat uncomfortable night.

An air raid warden approached my bandaged constituent asking where he was spending the night, to which he gave the reply, 'I'm OK, I've got a place on the ticket office floor.'

'No you haven't,' came the rejoinder, 'you are coming home with me.' This total stranger took him home, and he had a comfortable bed for the night.

Next morning breakfast was cooked by the blond pigtailed daughter in the house who then picked up her school satchel, kissed her parents goodbye and left.

He had had his breakfast cooked for him by a future Prime Minister – and that tells you something important about the home in which Margaret Thatcher grew up.

Lord Waldegrave
Conservative Peer

William Waldegrave was Conservative MP for Bristol West from 1979 until 1997. He was a junior minister throughout most of the Thatcher government, before being appointed Health Secretary in 1990. He served as a Cabinet minister throughout John Major's administration and was raised to the peerage in 1999.

I was her last appointment to the Cabinet. In the run-up to the first Gulf War, I was going across two or three times every day as Minister of State at the Foreign Office until she said, 'Come in, William, I want a word with you. You are to be Secretary of State for Health.' This was unexpected news to me, as it was to the rest of the country and certainly to the health service. She looked at me and said, 'I think you need a large whisky. I will have one too. Now, Kenneth has stirred them all up' – that was my right honourable friend Kenneth Clarke – 'and I want you to quieten them all down.'

She was extremely pragmatic, in the best sense, about the health service. She made it perfectly clear to me that if I thought that the reforms which had just been launched were not well based, it was up to me to stop them. As a matter of fact, I came to believe that they were the right thing to do and tried to follow them through. However, that showed that although she was often described as an ideologue, she was not. She did not fall into the mistake of thinking that there were grand theories to explain everything. She stuck to common, decent morality and then looked at the facts.

It has been said by others that her science training was crucial to her. I think that it was; she was the first and only woman to be Prime Minister and the first and only scientist to be Prime Minister. I hope that there will be more of both. She played an extremely important part in a number of crucial scientific issues, of which perhaps the most famous was the work to take action to stop the production of CFCs – chlorofluorocarbons – which were damaging the ozone layer. It did no harm, of course, that some of the crucial science which led to the proof of the damage to the ozone layer had been done by British scientists, by the British Antarctic Survey, so it was respectable science. She acted.

It was not always so successful. As a minister in the Department of the Environment, I tried to persuade her to impose flue gas desulphurisation on the power stations to stop acid rain. She did not want to do it, partly because she did not want to put the price of coal up and damage the coal industry even more, although this may sound paradoxical to some. I plotted with Horst Teltschik, who ran Chancellor Kohl's office, and said to him ahead of a bilateral summit in Bonn, 'Will you get your man to really put some pressure on over this, because I think she might move.' She obviously saw me coming a long way in advance. We arrived in Bonn in helicopters and got out. There was a local inversion – a local hot day – and therefore smog. 'Now Helmut,' she said to the cowering Chancellor – he was always a little nervous of her, as were others – 'I will tell you what you have here. You have got an inversion and a smog. If you had proper clean-air laws, like we do in England, that would have put paid to all that. I will explain the chemistry to you if you like.' He did not want to know the chemistry and no more was heard over that weekend of my plot. She was not an ideologue, she was somebody who looked at the evidence.

As another example, where she is often misinterpreted, she understood that F. W. de Klerk was something different and that all the clamour about sanctions was irrelevant. She preserved Britain's position, so that when things began to move in South Africa, well briefed by a formidable ambassador in Lord Renwick, we had leverage and she could say to de Klerk, 'We will help you do this.' That is what Mr Mandela himself recognised. He paid tribute to her role in the final transition days from apartheid in South Africa. It is a crude and completely ignorant caricature to say that she was on the wrong side in South Africa – when it came to it, she played a crucial part.

The House deserves one apology from someone like me, who is a member of the University of Oxford, which she loved. I was present once when she was at a dinner at Somerville, my mother's college, and spoke so movingly about what Somerville had meant to her, a grammar school girl coming into the world, and how passionately she supported the equality of opportunity that those colleges provided. It was a disgraceful example of the perennial ineptitude of the collectivity of the University of Oxford, which has nearly always managed to get these issues wrong – it got it wrong over Asquith and it got it wrong over her. It remains a disgrace and I only wish that there were some way of putting that right posthumously, but there is not.

In 1973, my then boss, Lord Rothschild, made a speech – or at least he gave a lecture which was then leaked – saying that in the year 2000 Britain would be half as rich per capita as France, which caused displeasure to the then government of Mr Heath. It did not happen and instead we just overtook France. What had happened in between? Lady Thatcher had happened.

Edwina Currie
Novelist, Broadcaster and Former MP

Edwina Currie was the MP for Derbyshire South from 1983 until 1997 and served as a junior minister at the Department of Health. She is a bestselling novelist, diarist and broadcaster.

I first saw Margaret Thatcher in 1975 at the party conference, her first after she had defeated Ted Heath. She was our new party leader, a pretty young (forty-nine) married woman with young children, a scientist, a brain. I was a recently elected Birmingham City councillor. I put in slip after slip to speak and was turned down. Eventually I was told, 'You're not important enough.' I went away, determined to return when I was.

Yet our paths were very similar. Some were coincidences I exploited to the full – for example, that we had the same birthday. Others were not chance. We both came from the provinces, had fathers with small businesses who loved talking politics, mothers who were quiet home-makers: our fathers were the models. We both went to state grammar schools, and on to Oxford to read chemistry. The old universities were looking for provincial girl state school scientists. It was much easier for an ambitious girl to win a place in science than in anything else.

So it meant I knew about her, and that it was possible to leap over all the barriers and become an MP like that. We were both outsiders. It also meant that I worshipped her, as did all the Young Turks of the day.

I first came across her face to face at a new MPs' tea party in her room at the Commons in the summer of 1983. My colleague Robert Jackson was at that time still an MEP and *rapporteur* of the budget committee in Brussels. Margaret turned to him sweetly. 'When will we get our rebate back, Robert?' she asked. 'Oh, Prime, Minister, it's not our money...' the unfortunate man began to explain. 'Not OUR money?' she squawked, and proceeded to demolish him, until nothing but a smoking heap of ash was left in his seat.

She turned to me. 'How are you getting on, dear?'

I decided to choose an anodyne subject. 'Fine – except with 158 new

Members, accommodation is a bit of a problem,' I began (we didn't have the spanking new parliamentary building then).

'Really?' the eyebrows shot up. 'Do you have a desk?'

'Yes, I found my predecessor's.'

'Good. And a secretary?'

'Yes, I brought one from Derbyshire.'

'And a phone?'

'Yes, we...' my voice began to falter.

'And a filing cabinet?'

'Yes, Prime Minister, I have two...'

She sat back, 'Well, you've only been six weeks, I should say you're doing rather well. When I arrived in 1959 it was six months before I had anywhere to sit...'

An important early event in that parliament was the defeat of the unions, and of Arthur Scargill's miners in particular. With a mining seat (it used to be George Brown's) I was at the coalface on this. It was a meticulously planned operation. Scargill had piqued the government by threatening strike action in 1981, before ministers were ready for him. Nick Ridley was put to the task. Soon, mountains of coal were piling up at the power stations – as we could observe daily, since five coal-fired power stations were visible from my own home. After the 1983 election, Scargill was finessed all through the winter, and bounced into calling the strike as spring started. That meant he would have to stay out at least six months to have an effect.

My miner constituents took a postal ballot. Over 90 per cent voted, with 85 per cent voting to continue working. The UDM was born. What they hated most was the use of the strike weapon to try and bring down a government – as it had Jim Callaghan's in 1979 – just after another election. It seemed anti-democratic to them, an impression reinforced by Scargill's refusal to ballot his own members, as the rule-book required. 'What's this about rolling back the tides of Thatcherism, Edwina?' one miner said to me. 'We voted for the tides of Thatcherism. That's why you're here.' The tide had turned, and washed Mr Scargill and all the strikers away with it.

It was a famous victory – more so, and more enduring, than the Falklands. With it went any hope of a union bringing this country to its knees again. The effect on our reputation abroad was dramatic and beneficial. When Toyota wanted to come to Europe in 1989, there was no question: it had to be strike-free Britain. And it was no accident that they chose a spot away from existing car factories and in the middle of a strike-free country – again, within view of my house in south Derbyshire.

The story of Margaret Thatcher's later years included both remarkable success such as the ending of the Cold War and her friendship with Gorbachev, and ignominy and failure. I voted against her in 1990, knowing full well that had she continued as party leader we would have lost my marginal seat and many others with it. By then, voters other than committed Tories had had enough.

But serving with her was a magical experience, one which could never be bettered. We are a stronger, finer country for the standards she set, and the leadership she gave.

Lord Thomas

Chairman, Centre for Policy Studies 1979–91

Hugh Thomas is a writer and historian and a former Foreign Office diplomat. He was Professor of History at the University of Reading from 1966 until 1975.

I had the pleasure and drama of being the Chairman of Margaret Thatcher's favourite think tank, the Centre for Policy Studies, for all her time in power. It was a great privilege and great fun.

When she asked me to undertake this, I said, 'But Prime Minister I do not know about economics.' She said, 'Economics doesn't matter: history matters and you know history.' I think she believed that. She thought that the historical background to events was more important than anything else. For example, when she went to the Soviet Union for the first time, she arranged a meeting of historians of the Soviet Union of great distinction such as Leonard Shapiro, Hugh Seton-Watson, Isaiah Berlin, George Urban and others to discuss the historical legacy of Russia and how far Russia could be said to be influenced by its own history even in Soviet days. The same thing was true about Argentina. She was interested in the history of the countries to which she went.

Once I summoned up my courage and wrote an analysis of the different dynasties of China, which I hoped would help her when she went to Beijing for the first time. I gave it to her and I saw the surprised eyebrows of that great Sinologue Sir Percy Cradock rising in laughter. Incidentally, Sir Percy was one of the many people in the civil service whom she greatly prized and appreciated.

It is worth mentioning her historic position on foreign policy. It was remarkable that by the late 1980s, she was on the closest possible terms with Mr Gorbachev, the General Secretary of the Soviet Union and at the same time a great personal friend and ally of President Reagan. To have been great friends with the Soviet Union and the United States was a remarkable and unique achievement. I do not think that we ever had that, even in the days of Sir Winston Churchill, when the doubts about Stalin were always present and lurking behind.

I happened to go to a dinner in Downing Street the night that the

Argentines surrendered. The historian present, Sir Michael Howard, pointed out that the victory that we had had over the Argentines had not really had an equivalent since the Battle of Agincourt in terms of number of people killed on our side as opposed to those killed on the enemy side. 'Not since Agincourt,' said Margaret Thatcher, who appreciated the allusion vigorously.

Margaret Thatcher was always concerned with things other than economics and it was a pleasure to have had such an interesting and moving time working at her disposal as I did for ten years.

Greg Knight
Conservative MP 1983–97 and 2001–

Greg Knight was MP for Derby North from 1987 to 1997 and was elected MP for East Yorkshire in 2001. He served as a whip under John Major and now serves under David Cameron.

There are two incidents that I recall that perfectly sum up Margaret. In October 1984 I was having dinner with Ian Gow, who was then Housing Minister. He told me how he had earlier in the day got a 'flea in his ear' from the Prime Minister.

He had been visiting a new housing estate and while there he had given a live radio interview. He said he had told the interviewer that he held 'very high aspirations for increasing home ownership in Britain' and went on to say that he hoped that 'one day it might be possible for it to become as high as 80 per cent'.

He then left the housing site to open a factory, before returning to Westminster. While at the factory, he was called to the site foreman's office to take a phone call and was astonished to find that it was the Prime Minister on the phone.

'Ian,' Margaret began. 'What is wrong with 100 per cent?'

The second incident took place in the mid 1980s, on an extremely hot day in one of the reception rooms at 10 Downing Street. Most of the parliamentary party was in attendance. I was circulating around the guests and found myself joining some Conservative MPs, most of them 'Knights of the Shires', who were standing near to a closed window complaining about the oppressive heat. 'Can't you get a footman to open this bloody window, Greg?' one of them enquired. Before I could respond, Margaret appeared from behind the MP standing opposite to me, jumped on a chair and opened up the window herself. At this, one of the staff serving drinks leant over my shoulder and said, 'She's bloody marvellous. She never asks anyone to do a job if she can do it quicker herself!'

Lord Denham

Government Chief Whip in the House Of Lords 1979–91

Lord Denham served under Margaret Thatcher as Chief Whip in the House of Lords throughout her time as Prime Minister. He is also a successful novelist.

Like most members of the House of Commons, Margaret Thatcher was never quite able to understand what the House of Lords was all about. Until she reached it herself, that is. But throughout her eleven years as Prime Minister, it fell to me, as her Chief Whip, to try and put this right.

'Why is it,' she asked me once, 'that you are always being defeated in the House of Lords, whereas we never are in the Commons?' The short answer was that, the House of Lords being a revising Chamber, without regular defeats of a government of whatever party, the system simply wouldn't work. But I gave the more practical one. 'Because, Prime Minister, you have an overall majority of over 140 in your House, whereas in ours we haven't got an overall majority at all.' It was absolutely true, both on paper and in practice. Even at that time, if both the official opposition and the Liberals voted against us, we still needed the support of a majority of crossbench peers if we were ever to win a division. But Margaret somehow couldn't be persuaded of that at all.

'Why,' she asked me on another occasion, 'don't you revise the procedures of the House of Lords so that you can get our business through more smoothly?'

'I can't do that, Prime Minister.'

'Why not?'

'Because next time there's a Labour government,' I said, 'we're going to need those very procedures to prevent whatever enormities they try and inflict on us.'

There was an awful silence, at the end of which I couldn't help feeling that I was lucky not to have been taken out and shot as a traitor for the very suggestion that there could be a Labour government again.

One of Margaret's great charms, however, was that she had the most beautiful manners. There was an awful occasion when a Housing Bill was going through the Lords and a memorial service for Lord Dilhorne, a highly popular former Conservative Lord Chancellor, had been scheduled for that same afternoon. It was attended by almost every backbench Tory peer. The opposition had divided the House on one of their early amendments and, much to their surprise, had inflicted a crashing defeat on the government. Highly delighted, they thereupon called division after division and won three more amendments in quick succession, before enough government peers to stop the rot had managed to filter back in.

It so happened that the Prime Minister was holding one of her periodic parties for the hired help in Downing Street that evening, and I reached the top of the stairs at No. 10 just as she had been informed of the fourth defeat. I was her guest and she gallantly contrived to make a joke of it... but anyone could see that in reality she didn't think it funny at all. My only consolation was that Reggie Dilhorne himself would have enjoyed – and I like to think indeed was enjoying – the whole thing quite enormously.

Andrew Rosindell

Conservative MP 2001–

Andrew Rosindell is a former National Chairman of the Young Conservatives and Chairman of the International Young Democratic Union. He was elected MP for Romford in 2001.

It was Margaret Thatcher who made me want to get involved in politics. Even though I was only in my early teens, somehow our new Prime Minister seemed to represent all the things that my instincts had told me were right. At last, Britain had a leader who was prepared to fight to restore our nation's confidence and pride and demonstrate the bulldog spirit that some thought we had lost.

As Prime Minister, Mrs Thatcher was first and foremost a patriot. She loved her country and believed in everything British, but knew the country had to change economically and saw it as her mission to drive forward reforms that would bring long-term prosperity for our people.

Difficult and dangerous times lay ahead of Margaret Thatcher when she entered 10 Downing Street in 1979, but nothing would deflect her from doing what she knew was her duty to the nation. Her deep sense of patriotism was always the driving force that kept Maggie going!

The 1982 party conference at Brighton was my first encounter with Mrs Thatcher. I was introduced to the PM by the late Ian Gow who was her PPS during her first term in office. As a very young YC, I watched her address the party conference with the theme of 'The Resolute Approach'. Having liberated the Falkland Islands and restored a sense of self-belief to our country, Margaret Thatcher was stronger than ever.

There was always a union flag on the platform at party conference when Margaret Thatcher was leader and we always sang the national anthem at the beginning and end of conference. She understood that patriotism was one of the Conservative Party's greatest strengths. Not for her the shallow short-termism of the politically correct and today's so-called 'modernisers'.

On the night freedom was restored to the people of the Falkland

Islands, crowds gathered outside No. 10 to cheer Mrs Thatcher and as she greeted the crowds, the spontaneous singing of 'Rule Britannia' echoed all around. It was precisely that spirit which characterised her years as Prime Minister. Standing firm for Britain is something that always came naturally to Margaret Thatcher and how we have missed that characteristic in our leaders since then.

As Chairman of the National YCs in 1993, Margaret Thatcher came to a conference I had organised for young political leaders from across Europe. This was the first YC event she attended since standing down as Prime Minister. What surprised our guests from the continent was the reaction of the UK YCs who greeted Lady Thatcher as if she was still leading the Conservative Party. She was adored by the younger generation within the party and was so much more in touch with their views, ideals and aspirations than those who had succeeded her. Central Office were horrified that I had organised an event with the former leader.

I did it again in 1996 when for EYC (European Young Conservatives) and IYDU (International Young Democrat Union), I asked Lady Thatcher to address the Freedom Dinner at the Britannia Hotel in Docklands.

This time young people came from all over the world. Many spoke passionately about why they owed so much to the Iron Lady who, together with Ronald Reagan, had led the world towards freedom. The most moving statements came from a young girl from Poland who spoke of how Margaret Thatcher had represented a beacon of hope for the people of Eastern Europe and a young leader from Argentina who thanked the former Prime Minister for standing up to dictatorship, which had led to the restoration of democracy in Argentina too.

Union Jacks were draped around the room and patriotic songs were sung by everyone. It was a truly memorable occasion, but at ten o'clock it was time for Lady T. to depart, although we had not reached the point when the national anthem was to be sung. We were way behind schedule. Lady Thatcher refused to go until we had all stood to sing it. 'I am not leaving before the national anthem,' she said to me and so, to the delight of everyone present, Lady T. remained until the end.

In 2001, Lady Thatcher made Romford her final stop of the general election campaign. Having arrived in Romford market, she was greeted by hundreds of cheering people, not just party activists, but ordinary local residents who loved her for what she had done for her country and admired her like no other.

'Spike', my Staffordshire bull terrier, was the first to welcome her, dressed in his Union Jack waistcoat and wearing his 'I love Maggie' badge. When Lady Thatcher came to Romford again in March 2005, my new dog 'Buster', also a Staffie, was there wearing his cross of St George waistcoat. It came as no surprise that Lady T. soon made friends with both Spike and Buster. Somehow, all three of them seemed to represent the true spirit of Britain, the bulldog spirit!

Sir Mark Lennox-Boyd

PPS to Margaret Thatcher 1988–90

The MP for Morecambe and Lunesdale from 1979 until 1997, Sir Mark Lennox-Boyd was Parliamentary Private Secretary to the Prime Minister from 1988 until 1990. He went on to become the Parliamentary Under Secretary of State at the Foreign and Commonwealth Office.

No one who knew Margaret will ever underestimate the extraordinary trouble she took for those who worked for her, for her friends and of course for her family.

Notwithstanding her reputation for hard work, Margaret used to get extremely tired and one of the responsibilities of her PPS was to protect her from unnecessary demands on her energy. I well remember one incident which initially caused me bafflement. She had an engagement on a Friday afternoon with the Thames Valley Police and another early morning meeting on the Saturday at Chequers. The obvious plan was to drive from the police meeting to Chequers for the night, but earlier in the week in question, she announced that she intended to return to No. 10 on the Friday evening for a quiet supper and work and to be driven to Chequers on the Saturday morning. She was, as usual, clear and firm, but provided no explanation as to why she had chosen to subject herself to an extra two or more unneeded hours in a car, some of it in rush-hour traffic. I pressed her and she realised that she must give an explanation if she was not to lose credibility with the several people who were present. 'You see Denis has a dinner in London on Friday and I wish to return to be at No. 10 with him because he likes eggs and bacon for breakfast on Saturday, and there will be nobody in the flat but me to cook.' I cannot remember if we managed to get Denis driven to Chequers after his Friday dinner, but I very much hope we did.

Lord Harris

General Director of the Institute of Economic Affairs 1957–88

Raised to the peerage in 1979, Lord Harris of High Cross was among the most respected political and economic thinkers of his time. He was a founder member of the Institute of Economic Affairs and of Buckingham University. He died in 2006.

I had met Margaret Thatcher a time or two before, in the 1960s. Once was over dinner with a bevy of businessmen including a rather self-important Arnold Weinstock – whom she made seem pretty feeble. Another occasion was over lunch with a motley bunch of back-bench Tory MPs who were lamenting the difficulty of putting across the complex case for free markets – which she resolved brusquely by suggesting they should ask their constituents whether they would rather shop at Marks & Spencer or the Co-op!

But the first personal encounter I recall more vividly was in the twilight days of Ted Heath, at the Department of Education of which she was then Secretary of State. She had agreed to meet informally with a small deputation of academics, including Sydney Caine and Max Beloff, to hear about our plan to establish an independent university – once we could raise the first million or so for start-up costs!

A sudden Cabinet crisis over the Middle East prevented her prompt arrival so she had arranged for us to be met by a junior colleague named (Bill) van Straubenzee. Not for nothing was he nicknamed 'strawberry tea'. Beautifully turned-out in suit and matching waistcoat (probably with lapels), he received us in a slightly scruffy office, but with a contrived pomp and ceremony more suited to a state occasion. He invited us to sit around him in a small semi-circle and, with appropriate solemnity launched into a discourse on the importance of higher education, periodically stretching out an elegant leg in order rather elaborately to adjust the crease in his immaculate trousers.

Suddenly, the door burst open and in rushed Margaret Thatcher, complete with handbag and a striking hat, which was allowed those days. Explaining that she might be called away again in a few minutes, she perched on the edge of a chair and told the junior minister to carry on. He had hardly completed his opening statement – to the effect that there was 'no hostility' in the department to the broad concept of an independent university – when the lady broke in: 'No, no, William, can I put that differently?' She then proceeded to declare with deliberate emphasis that there was positive enthusiasm for the idea of competition from an institution of respected academics independent of the state.

Leaving the deflated van Straubenzee with little better to do than contemplate the crease in his other trouser leg, she emphasised with a candour new to me from a politician, that we would not receive – nor should we expect – any subsidies or special favours. What she would promise was to remove any bureaucratic obstacles that discriminated against the new enterprise. (It was precisely such equal treatment which that famous social democrat, Shirley Williams, refused to grant a few years later as Secretary of State for Education. Thus when one of Buckingham's first graduates applied for an army commission under a special system of graduate entry, Mrs Williams refused to support the appeal of Max Beloff, our first Principal, for equal treatment that was automatically granted to equivalent products of state universities.)

In 1976 when the University College of Buckingham was ready to welcome its first intake of sixty students, it was Margaret Thatcher who performed the opening ceremony and in 1983 it was her government that awarded the institution its royal charter as the University of Buckingham, of which she was to become Chancellor in 1992.

My second, more personal memory of Maggie's decisive style was at Chequers just two weeks after her election victory in May 1979. My wife and I had been totally astonished to be invited for Sunday lunch and to find ourselves guests of the Thatcher family – Denis, Mark and Carol plus Douglas Hurd and wife, Lady (Janet) Young and husband, who all lived nearby.

I was further amazed to find myself at the table placed on the Prime Minister's right and almost dumbfounded when she suddenly leant across and confided her decision to put me into the House of Lords. I managed to get out the words: 'Do I have any say in the matter?' to which she answered shortly, I thought almost sharply: 'No' and with an impatient shrug of the shoulders proceeded to complain of the delays of official procedures before my name could be checked and formal marching orders issued.

I still recall the irritation, bordering on anger, with which she added: 'I sometimes think I'm the only one trying to get anything done.' I recall those exact words simply because they came into my mind so often thereafter as she struggled against Cabinet colleagues, departmental committees, civil servants, journalists and no doubt many others, in her sometimes lonely mission to subdue the trade unions, check the money supply, curb government expenditure, and resist the rising tide of mischief from Brussels. I was therefore not in the least surprised that she saw off the Argentine junta and got Peter Walker to stand firm for months against Scargill's militant miners. I can think of no previous British PM this century, Churchill always excepted, who regularly stuck to his guns and displayed in Keith Joseph's words, 'such personal, moral courage'.

I had scarcely been introduced as peer in July when her PPS, the incomparable late Ian Gow, sounded me out (at a celebration party in his Eastbourne constituency) on whether I would consider quitting the crossbenches in the Lords to accept a ministerial appointment. I did not hesitate even for one second before replying: 'I'm afraid not, in no circumstances,' adding, 'I beg you not to put our friendship at risk by ever raising that dangerous question again.' Dangerous for me because I knew if I became Maggie's political leg-man, I would never be able to refuse her anything – even when I might think the great lady was, conceivably, in the wrong. Only my immediate family should be able to call on such absolute loyalty!

A more light-hearted memory, although second-hand, was told me with a chuckle by Geoffrey Howe in the days when he still basked in Maggie's favour. At an early Cabinet meeting, he had a strong impulse to smoke. Seeing no one else had lit up, he stealthily extracted a packet of cigarettes from his pocket, followed by a box of matches, before looking round to see if anyone was noticing. The Prime Minister leant across smiling and whispered: 'Go on, Denis smokes!'

Lord Tebbit

Conservative Peer

Norman Tebbit served in Margaret Thatcher's Cabinet from 1981 until 1987, most famously as Secretary of State for Employment. In 1985 he became the Chairman of the Conservative Party, a position he held until 1987.

During Margaret Thatcher's time as Leader of the Opposition her twice-weekly clashes at Prime Minister's Questions, first with Harold Wilson, then with Jim Callaghan, often set the political agenda. It was essential in those clashes – in which the Prime Minister holds all the best cards, including the inestimable advantage of the last word – that she, not he, should emerge the winner.

Her success depended in considerable part upon briefing not only on matters of fact but on tactics to wrong-foot her adversary. I was privileged to be a member of her briefing team which consisted of Airey Neave, Michael Dobbs – then a Central Office researcher – George Gardiner and from time to time others such as Nigel Lawson. Naturally our existence became known and we were dubbed by a Labour journalist 'The Gang of Four' and the name stuck.

It was during these years that I came to know and understand Margaret Thatcher. It was a privileged position but it sometimes had its downside.

I doubt if speech-writing for anyone is all honey – certainly it was not so in her case. As in most things, Margaret Thatcher was pretty much a perfectionist about speeches and a good many drafts finished in the waste bin before she was satisfied with a script. I soon learned that holding back my preferred phrases or paragraphs improved their chances of finding their way into the speech rather than the bin, but sometimes the writing sessions went on far too late for my liking.

I well remember being approached in the division lobby at 10 p.m. 'I've just got a draft of a speech – and it's awful – would you be able to look at it for me, Norman?' she asked.

'Of course, when is it for?'

'Oh good,' she replied, 'tomorrow lunchtime – do come round to the office.' Somewhat taken aback I followed her to the office where fellow speech-writers were assembling with pads and pens in hand. We were soon at work but it was hard going to hit the right note. Somewhere about three in the morning I was beginning to wilt and was caught in the midst of a great yawn.

'You're not very bright tonight, Norman,' she commented.

'It's not tonight,' I said rather huffily, 'it's tomorrow bloody morning.' Somehow that night we got a decent draft for her and I concluded that, like me, Margaret Thatcher worked best under pressure – pressure that causes more discomfort to one's aides than oneself!

It is often said of her that she was divisive. However, there were two great influences in her life. One was her scientific training. The other, of course, was her religious belief. There is a precedent for being divisive: there are sheep and there are goats. Margaret Thatcher was aware from both her scientific training and her religious beliefs that there are things that are right and things that are wrong, technically, scientifically and morally. She pursued that which she believed to be right. I must say that as her Party Chairman I found that my life was made much easier by my understanding of the certainties of her beliefs. She never asked me to commission a focus group. Had I been asked I would have resisted manfully, I hope. What is more, if I woke in the morning, turned on the radio and heard the BBC's version of the news of the day I would know what her reaction would be to the news because of the certainty of the construct of her beliefs. It made life very much easier for me.

I should also like to say how grateful I will always be for the fact that she gave me the opportunity to serve in high office the country that she and I love. I am also grateful to her for that other side of her character, for the support that she gave to my wife and me after we were injured. No doubt somebody in this House will correct me, but I cannot think of a precedent for a Secretary of State remaining in office as Secretary of State although absent from the Cabinet for over three months. She allowed me to run my office from my hospital bed. Admittedly, I had the support of two splendid civil servants in particular who ran my private office, both of whom have appeared again in other roles: Mr Callum McCarthy, and another fellow who I believe has achieved high office somewhere more recently; he was the Secretary of State for Health not long ago. They were quality people, but it was she who backed me and allowed me to continue.

I did not always agree with her, because I have some rather strong convictions and views, too. I recollect one occasion when I left her office at No. 10, walked back to Victoria Street, got into my office and asked my Private Secretary if there had been any calls from No. 10. 'No, Secretary of State,' he said, so I knew then that I was still the Secretary of State while I was walking back.

Of course, she was brought down in the end not by the electorate but by her colleagues. Not only is it quite remarkable that she won three elections running – someone else has done that since – what was remarkable was that she polled slightly more votes on the occasion of her third victory, when she had been in office for eight years, than on her first. I regard that as a triumph for her.

My regrets? Because of the commitments that I made to my own wife, I did not feel able either to continue in government after 1987 or to return to government when she later asked me to do so. I left her, I fear, at the mercy of her friends. That I do regret.

Lord Davies
Labour Peer

Quentin Davies was Conservative MP for Stamford and Spalding from 1987 until 1997 and Grantham and Stamford from 1997 to 2010. He defected to Labour in June 2007. He was raised to the peerage in 2010.

I am not widely thought of as a Thatcherite, but I would certainly have described myself as that when I was first elected to Parliament in 1987. I regarded – and still regard – Margaret Thatcher's first two terms of government as a period of heroic achievement – the economic successes, the end of the 'British disease', the privatisations, the Right to Buy, Personal Pensions, the creation of a property-owning democracy, standing up to bullying from any quarter, and historic victories against trade union power, Argentinian invasion and the Cold War. Until the Bruges speech I never found myself in anything other than enthusiastic agreement with her. Her personal attitude to politics – conviction, consistency, unstinting and tireless conscientiousness, setting the highest standards for herself and her ministers, absolute integrity – I still regard as a model for any age. And her period of office transformed, at least temporarily, the attitude of the British electorate to politics itself. In retrospect it was a shining oasis between the Wilsonian cynicism and national decline that preceded her, and the drift and scandals that followed. One of my proudest moments was when I was made a PPS at the end of my first year – sadly for me on the eve of the shattering Bruges speech!

Two recollections – which illustrate both one of her weaknesses and one of her outstanding strengths. Six months after my election I was invited to her room in the Commons with a dozen other new arrivals. We sat around the table. She made a few introductory remarks and then asked for our comments on how things were going. Everyone said 'wonderful, Prime Minister' or words to that effect – indeed she was at her apogee and there was little enough to criticise. 'Well, come on,' she said, 'something must be less than perfect.' I thought that an admirable approach. So I plunged in. I said that I thought we ought not to fight the next election without being able to point to something we had done for the old age pensioner – it had been the one serious difficulty during the 1987 election.

I didn't make it into a second sentence. She flew at me with a string of well-remembered statistics. Didn't I know that average pensioner household incomes had increased by 50 per cent since 1979, that now two thirds instead of one third of those retiring had some income other than the National Insurance pension etc., etc.? (As it happened I knew most of this almost as pat as she did – but it didn't really meet my point.) The monologue lasted perhaps twenty minutes and began to cover the whole issue of Treasury controls and how essential they were. My colleagues sat motionless, as if paralysed, as the diatribe gathered in intensity. Some surreptitiously moved their eyes towards me, though without daring to move their heads – glances of horror or fascinated anticipation rather than of sympathy. Clearly I had committed *lèse-majesté*, and now fully deserved to be thrown to the lions. Then finally the energy of the volcano seemed spent. There was neither time, nor inclination, nor I suspect breath left to discuss anything else. We filed out in silence – I, and to a lesser extent I suspect all of us, feeling a little giddy.

Of course I had misjudged the invitation to express dissent – however respectfully or tentatively I had endeavoured to do so. I had fallen into the trap set by Mao Tse Tung when he launched his Hundred Flowers Campaign and begged loyal party members to speak up with any complaints or criticisms they had. The difference was that Mao's victims were rapidly physically liquidated. Margaret remained utterly friendly in the lobbies – and clearly did not veto my promotion to PPS. Nor was that the last occasion when I ventured some comment or suggestion. But the response was always of a predictably binary kind – either she had already thought of the point herself or it was a very silly idea. Perhaps it often was. But for all my great respect and admiration for Margaret I began to pity her Cabinet colleagues. And I started to fear that with Margaret bearing such an immense burden of work, and taking alone such a vast range of short-term and long-term decisions, some terrible mistake might one day be made.

My second recollection comes from the end. It was well known in the party that I was supporting Michael Heseltine in his bid for the leadership. I had never disguised my views from Peter Morrison,

Margaret's Private Secretary, from the whips or from anyone else in the House. But I felt it cowardly to leave it there, especially as I genuinely admired so much that she stood for, and was conscious of the historical greatness of the personage, and the somewhat awesome gravity of the decision we were about to take. So I wrote her a personal letter. I expressed the sincerest admiration but I explained why I had found it necessary to vote and campaign against her. I said I thought her European policy had split the party irredeemably, was inconsistent with her own Single European Act, and while we remained in the European Community (as it was then called) inhibited us from exercising any real influence within it, thus inevitably preventing us from optimising the national interest. I might have added that we had lost a historic opportunity to take the lead in Europe.

Of course I never expected any reply. Under the emotional stress and trauma of the moment any other political leader I feel sure would simply have flung the letter into the nearest waste-paper basket – I do not doubt I would have done so myself. But two days after the second round, when there was no conceivable political or ulterior motive in conciliating me, I received a courteous hand-written response. I recall the surprise I felt as I opened it. My conflicting emotions were I think, once again, though for rather different reasons, almost giddying. But this time, as I thought of Margaret Thatcher the human being beneath her public greatness, I could only marvel.

Lord Robertson
Labour Peer

George Robertson was Labour MP for Hamilton from 1978 to 1999. He was Tony Blair's first Defence Secretary and in 1999 became Secretary-General of NATO.

Some three years ago, I was looking after Baroness Thatcher at the annual ball for the British Forces Foundation, where she was the patron and I a trustee. I said in casual conversation, which was actually very difficult with Baroness Thatcher, 'I saw Carol on television the other night.' She said, 'Oh yes. Carol was on. She speaks too much sometimes.' I said, 'I wonder where she got that from?' and she said, 'From her father of course.'

On the day I was appointed Secretary General of NATO in 1999, I received hand-written letters from both Jim Callaghan and Margaret Thatcher congratulating me on the job that I was about to take and offering me their best wishes for what I was about to do. It was a remarkable thing to get two such letters on the same day. I had a lot of experience in foreign affairs to take with me to NATO. A lot of what I had to do in opposition was to agree with the government over the Falklands, Hong Kong and the rest of it. I also had to attend a series of functions held by the government. I used to think that Lancaster House was my works canteen. I went to one lunch in Downing Street with Russell Johnston, representing the opposition parties, in honour of the King of Tonga. He was a very large gentleman with a very small voice. Russell Johnston and I were very keen to get back to the House of Commons for Question Time at 2.30 p.m. but recognised that we could not leave before the principal guest. We waited until the last second when Mrs Thatcher walked out of the room with the King of Tonga to escort him to the lift. Russell Johnston and I shot down the stairs but were overtaken by the Prime Minister. She said, 'The king is in the lift.' Clearly, if the King of Tonga was in the lift, nobody else could get in. I said, 'Yes, he's quite a sizeable guy, but very difficult to hear at the back.' She said, 'Oh, wasn't it fascinating what he said?' Her eyes were glowing. 'He said he's probably the first Prime Minister in history to go on to become king.' Russell Johnston and I had the same thought at the same time, but neither of us had the courage to say it.

She was a remarkable person. As I travelled both as Defence Secretary and Secretary General of NATO, I realised that she was a very significant figure outside the country. As her popularity declined in this country and indeed in her own party, there was absolutely no doubt that the pioneering instinct that she had had, especially in Central and Eastern Europe, was well registered and recorded, and will be there for a long time to come. I have had a lot to do with Russia. I was the first Chairman of the NATO-Russia Council. I recognise that the Russians saw in her somebody who was strong in her beliefs and in what she stood for. They respect strength. The collapse of the Soviet Union that occurred – I remind the House – thirty months after its exit from Afghanistan was a seminal moment in world politics. However much we disagree with her in other areas, we cannot underestimate the role that she played in that tectonic shift.

That is something that we have to register and remember. She was a mixed blessing. Of that there is no doubt. I have got a feeling that some of these distasteful and disgraceful demonstrations that have taken place in the streets might well have pleased her. She was not somebody who expected acclaim and unanimity, whether it was in the European Council or in the country as a whole. I remember the night that Lord Forsyth of Drumlean organised a special dinner after 9/11 in memory of the employees of JPMorgan Chase who had died in the attacks on the World Trade Center. Margaret Thatcher was there with Denis at the table. She made some comments about me speaking at the dinner; anyway, she was quite cordial. At the end there was a toast, the loyal toast to Her Majesty the Queen, followed by a toast to the President of the United States of America. I leant in across and said, 'What if there was a toast to the President of the European Commission?' She looked at me and said, 'The words will never pass my lips.'

She was a great lady. There will be mixed feelings about her, but there is no doubt about the impact that she had on this country.

Sir Richard Body
Conservative MP 1955–2001

The veteran backbencher Sir Richard Body was Member of Parliament for Billericay from 1955 to 1959, then for Holland and Boston from 1966 to 1997, and from 1997 to 2001 for Boston and Skegness.

It was in 1949 when I first met Margaret Roberts, then with ICI at Manningtree in Essex. She came to help me as the Conservative candidate in the London County Council election when I was standing for Deptford.

Television was yet to dominate our electioneering; canvassing was limited and public meetings were held every day, indoor in the evenings and outdoor ones in the daytime.

Margaret came to speak outside New Cross Station in the rush hour to scores of commuters on their way home, and I well remember her standing with microphone in hand beside the loudspeaker car.

The memory does not fade. It may have been her first open-air meeting, but any nervousness was difficult to detect. She spoke with modesty and sincerity and observers might have thought her demure and earnest. Her speech perhaps was rather too intellectual for a transient audience, yet quite a number delayed their journey home to hear the reasoned arguments.

In those days almost any meeting had a lively amount of heckling. It was in many ways a far more democratic form of electioneering than is the case now, because the speaker had to be on the ball and if unable to get the better of the heckler the audience would soon lose interest, while in open-air meetings it would melt away. It is much to her credit that that was not the case on that evening outside New Cross Station.

I much regret that we did not invite her to speak at one of the many indoor meetings we held throughout the constituency, as she was so obviously in command of her subject I have no doubt that she would have been a match for any heckler.

I met Margaret many times in those days. We were both YCs and prospective parliamentary candidates and attended regularly the monthly meetings we used to have in the Candidates' Association. At one subsequent supper Ted Heath and she once sat beside each other. I remember he was cheerful to all while she was taciturn yet attentive to everything said around our table.

There were many other occasions too. I remember her as unfailingly considerate towards other people, whoever they were and whatever the circumstances.

We later went on to practise at the Bar and both of us became pupils to masters who were 'in crime'. In those days there were only five sets of chambers that were of criminal specialists with an aggregate membership of no more than sixty.

Now, it might be added, it is about twenty times that number.

Only four courts sat at the Old Bailey then and seldom a brief for a young barrister, so it meant going to London Sessions, by the Elephant and Castle. Going down to grubby cells to take instructions from old lags was not to her liking. What was worse were the occasions when they sought a dock-brief. This required all barristers who could not escape the court to sit in the front row of counsel benches – usually there were about a dozen of us there, for other young hopefuls would crowd in – and the old lag would emerge from the cells and shuffle to the well of the court to stand in front of counsel clutching his £2.4s. 6d. Then he would run his eye up and down the rank of newly made wigs, usually pointing his finger along the line as he looked, and then cry out 'I will 'ave 'im' or in Margaret's case it would have been 'I will 'ave 'er'.

So naturally she turned her back on that sort of life and moved to the more intellectually congenial world of tax chambers.

In obtaining a seat for the 1955 general election I had better luck than her, and when I decided to stand down from Billericay, choosing to concentrate on the Bar instead of Parliament, she applied to take my place in the constituency, despite my advice not to go there. She was one of the twelve chosen for interview, but fortunately rejected. She went on to be adopted for Finchley but had she been successful in Billericay her future might have been different, for a subsequent defeat in that seat would have been inevitable.

The Earl of Caithness
Conservative Peer

Malcolm Caithness served as a junior minister under Margaret Thatcher from 1985 and then later under John Major until 1994. He currently serves as an elected hereditary peer in the House of Lords.

It is hard to think back and picture accurately Britain twenty-one years ago. The West had lost its sense of purpose and the state dictated vast areas of our lives. We seemed to be in a quagmire from which no government could extract us. Margaret Thatcher was the first leader in Europe to stand up and say there was a better way. Her governments were pioneers in changing the role of the state and enhancing the freedom of the individual to what we, and most of the rest of the world, now take for granted. The reforms were bitterly contested, mostly by those who are now advocating the same policies. At times she was portrayed as uncaring and seeming not to listen. However, I found a different side to her.

Just after I had been appointed a whip in the early summer of 1984 she held a reception at 10 Downing Street to which I was asked. I had never been there, nor had I met my Prime Minister. She was receiving her guests at the top of the stairs and, in due turn, I was introduced to her. She stopped receiving her guests and took time to show me, the most junior member of the House and the youngest in the room, some of the pictures in the house and explain its history to me. She then went back to her other guests. That action is the mark of a very 'big' person and considerate hostess.

My first important working meeting with my Prime Minister was after about six months as Minister for Prisons in the Home Office. I thought I had a reasonable understanding of my brief by then. In our discussions it was soon apparent that she knew more of the detail and 'nitty gritty' of the policy than I did. It amazed me that someone with so many other issues to contend with had such detailed knowledge and cared so much about one aspect of a junior minister's portfolio. I realised then that if, in future, I did not know more than her at every meeting concerned with areas of my responsibility I would not last long in her government.

Some years later in 1989, as a minister in the Department of the Environment, I was due to attend a very difficult negotiation in Brussels over emissions of 'greenhouse' gases. Nick Ridley, the Secretary of State, had backed my proposals for a tightening of standards leading to a reduction in emissions, but this would be costly to our industries as expensive new equipment would be needed. We produced a paper on it and all the other departments briefed against it so a meeting was called to decide what to do. Nick was tied up in the Chamber of the House of Commons on the Housing Bill, so I had to argue the case with a serried rank of Cabinet ministers opposed to me. Against the wishes of some of her most seniors ministers she backed Nick and my proposals and that became the new government position. Rightly she then espoused the policy in typically forthright terms. Since then the standards have been tightened yet again, but at the time she was making a bold new move by backing a minority view.

Robert Key
Conservative MP 1983–2010

Robert Key served under Margaret Thatcher and John Major in a number of ministerial posts.

I first came across Margaret Thatcher when I was a master at Harrow School and her son Mark was a pupil. She was one of a galaxy of Conservative politicians whose children were entrusted to Winston Churchill's old school. In the 1970s, in addition to the Thatchers, Harrow pupils included young men bearing the names Macmillan, Heseltine, Maudling, Churchill, Onslow, Oppenheim and others. The former MP Bobby Allen (whose son served for many years in the private office at No. 10) was a Governor of the school, as was Mary Soames. To varying degrees they all encouraged and assisted the development of my political leanings.

As a House Tutor at Harrow, I had a lot of contact particularly with the senior boys and with their parents. Margaret Thatcher's son, Mark, was in Bradbys and his House Tutor, Alan Sankey, was charming, assiduous and courteous. After lunch one day he walked into the entrance hall at the house to find a woman waiting to see the Housemaster. He enquired whether she had come about the job of house matron. What a pity he did not recognise the Secretary of State for Education! This tale does say something about that generation of politicians who placed huge faith in the schools they chose and their teachers – and who expected no special favours.

I was accepted onto the Candidates List in 1975 and I fought Frank Dobson in Holborn and St Pancras South in 1979. Our long-suffering daughter Helen was born just before the general election that year and her second name is Margaret! Helen met Margaret for the first time on the day before polling day in the 1983 general election. The Liberals had declared Salisbury in their top ten target seats (as they always do!) and since I was a new candidate in my home town the powers that be at Central Office ordained that the Prime Minister should pay a flying visit to Salisbury. She landed at Old Sarum Airfield by helicopter and came by coach into the Guildhall Square where over 10,000 people were waiting for her. In the middle of the square was a Land Rover provided by my farming friend Richard Crook. On it waited the Key family including four-year-old Helen. Margaret made magnificent progress through the throng and as she climbed aboard a friend asked Helen what was special about today. 'After this, I'm going swimming,' she piped. We won the seat with a healthy majority!

In the autumn of 1984 I received a mysterious message on the Members' letterboard in the House to contact the Chief Whip urgently. What had I done? He explained that in the Tory Party there was a long tradition of an honorary PPS being provided for former Prime Ministers. Would I look after Ted? I knew the dangers of acceptance.

I took the risk. It would not be true to say I never regretted it – it was misconstrued by some of the press and it was certainly misconstrued by quite a lot of people in Salisbury! However, I learned a huge amount not only about Ted Heath and his beliefs and vision – but also about Margaret Thatcher. One of my duties was to act as go-between. On one occasion there was a confidence motion put down by Labour. Ted was in Israel, adding to the political round by conducting a major symphony orchestra in Jerusalem. The message came from the Chief Whip that I must tell Ted to return to London. The whips could not contact him.

I did! He was out in the desert and somehow I managed to speak to him. He said he would not come back. I asked if I could tell No. 10 that if he had been able to come back he would have supported the government in the no-confidence motion.

He agreed and he also let me put out an appropriate press notice. I telephoned No. 10 and spoke to Margaret's PPS. We agreed there was no alternative!

Margaret was always approachable. She would always listen to a good argument with terrifying attention and total concentration as she fixed you with her laser-beam eyes. She would listen and if she decided you were right she would back you. She did this twice for me.

On the first occasion, a group of us were absolutely convinced of the basic injustice of no financial provision to help haemophiliacs who had been infected with the HIV virus from contaminated NHS blood transfusions. A distraught mother in Salisbury came to me to tell me that her little boy at primary school had become infected this way. Other parents had found out – and they would not allow their children to attend the same school. The Head was forced to tell the mother her child must leave the school. It was absolutely terrible. I joined with a small band of Conservative MPs and we went from junior Health Minister to Secretary of State for Health – all to no avail. John Hannam persuaded us that we must go to the top. We did. Margaret met us in her small upstairs study at No. 10. She clipped her famous handbag shut, put it on the floor, and gave us her total concentration as we put the case. In spite of all the briefing from the No. 10 Policy Unit and the Department of Health, she had never seen it or thought about it in our terms. She knew we were right. The next day there was a statement in the House announcing a substantial ex-gratia payment to establish a trust fund to be administered by the Haemophilia Society. Many of us know that at heart Margaret was a compassionate woman.

On the second occasion, in the never-ending saga of what to do with Stonehenge (in my constituency) – a problem that has defeated Margaret Thatcher, John Major and Tony Blair – I was convinced that she had been given faulty briefing by the Ministry of Defence who are big landowners near the site. The location of the current English Heritage favourite for a new visitors' centre was unacceptable to local people and I had battled through the Whitehall machine and the PM had agreed to see me. We met in her room at the Commons. I came equipped with maps – and she was soon on her hands and knees on the carpet as I explained the problem. She agreed with me. The site was dropped.

That degree of access, concentration on detail and compassion was all part of the magic that made Margaret great. That was at the height of her power. Towards the end of her term she became less accessible and I am sure that led to disenchantment with her style. She had set impossibly high standards to maintain for as long as ten years. Incidentally, that degree of accessibility was never matched by her successor, John Major.

Having served Ted Heath as unofficial PPS, then Alick Buchanan-Smith and subsequently Chris Patten as PPS for four years, my moment came. In 1990 I was the lay member of the Medical Research Council. In spite of my duties to Chris Patten (who was Secretary of State for the Environment) I really had to attend a Medical Research

Council meeting in London even though it was the middle of the party conference in Bournemouth. I had caught the train up to London and arrived at the MRC in Park Crescent to be told by the receptionist to phone Chris Patten's Private Secretary immediately. He was already on the way to collect me in a government car. When he arrived, the Private Secretary bundled me straight into the car and took me to Waterloo where I caught a train back to Bournemouth. I would be met at Bournemouth by the Chief Constable who would take me straight to the Prime Minister. What on earth was all this about? The Private Secretary stayed mum. I was indeed met at Bournemouth by the Chief Constable who took me in his Jag to the Highcliffe Hotel. There I was ushered up to Margaret Thatcher's modest suite where she asked me if I would be prepared to join her government. What can a man say? 'Yes, Prime Minister. Thank you very much. I will not let you down.' Nor did I. Within a couple of months she had been challenged for the leadership of the party – and of course I voted for Margaret.

By the time I got downstairs in the hotel, slightly numb at the thought that I was now a Minister of the Crown, however humble, the world had already been informed of the appointment and I was surrounded by the press. Suddenly the sea of cameras parted and there was Ted Heath. He walked up to me, grinned broadly said, 'Congratulations – you poor sod!' and stumped off.

Lord Renton

Conservative Peer

Tim Renton was Conservative MP for Mid Sussex from 1974 to 1997. He was a member of the Thatcher government from 1984 to its end and served as Chief Whip from 1989 to 1990. He was raised to the peerage in 1997. He is the author of Chief Whip: The Role, History and Black Arts of Parliamentary Whipping.

Even in her busiest days as Prime Minister, Margaret Thatcher was outstanding in her care and concern for her friends and the tight circle of those who worked directly for her.

It was often said that one reason why Margaret was so slow to accept that interest on house mortgages should cease to be tax free was because one of her private office secretaries told her how hard it would be for her to pay her mortgage if the tax exemption was removed. From my own experience, when a newspaper reported that one of our daughters had been very badly burned on a charity journey across Africa, I received a card from the Prime Minister within hours asking after her, and this was followed by daily enquiries about her progress.

As Margaret Thatcher's last Chief Whip, I never saw this solicitude in greater evidence than on the day of the murder of Ian Gow, the Member of Parliament for Eastbourne. Ian was Margaret's Parliamentary Private Secretary from 1979 to 1983 and then a junior minister who resigned in 1985 rather than vote for the Anglo-Irish Agreement.

It was 30 July 1990. We had just completed an extensive ministerial reshuffle following the resignation from the Cabinet of Nick Ridley, one of her closest allies. His departure had already left the Prime Minister feeling isolated in her own Cabinet.

Ian and his wife, Jane, were long-time friends and neighbours in Sussex. The shortlist for the Eastbourne constituency had had just two names on it, Ian's and mine. Despite police warnings, Ian regularly parked his car overnight in the road outside his house at Hankham, near Eastbourne, and a bomb exploded when he started his car on Monday morning. I heard of his death at ten in the morning and told

No. 10 that my wife Alice and I would drive over immediately to be with Jane. We were soon joined by their son, Charles, and his fiancée, and by Father Peter, the Bishop of Lewes, and the local priest, Father Jonathan. Alice and Jane went to the local church, where Jane was the organist and Ian a churchwarden. A number of people were there and they came one after the other and hugged Jane, many of them crying, and then went out to leave her alone.

It was a two-hour journey from London and the Prime Minister arrived at Hankham in the early afternoon. She came out of the car up the steps into the garden looking pale, but wholly resolute. I felt enormously for her. Ian had not only been the Parliamentary Secretary to whom she had been closest but he had become a strong and sympathetic supporter. As she said during the course of the day, 'If I was feeling low, Ian would often say to me, "Come back and have some supper just with me and Jane." And I often did.' I took her into the house, showed her the room where Jane was and then went out and discussed arrangements with the Sussex Chief Constable, Andrew Turnbull, then the Civil Service Head of her private office, and Peter Morrison, her new Parliamentary Private Secretary.

Margaret spent the afternoon comforting and talking to Jane. An impromptu communion service was to be held at 7 p.m. but was moved forward to 6 p.m. so that the Prime Minister could attend before returning to London. The church was almost full and the Prime Minister sat in front on one side, Jane and her two sons on the other. I wrote in my diary for the day that, in church, the Prime Minister 'looked forlorn, withdrawn, quiet and cut off, not her usual vibrant dominating self but almost isolated, quietly miserable'.

The Prime Minister and her small team arrived back in London in the late evening. There were to be no cracks in her armour. Thirty-six hours later she flew to Aspen, Colorado for an International Conference and meetings with President George Bush. That night Iraq invaded Kuwait, oil prices soared, sterling plummeted and Margaret, in the words of her own autobiography, told the President 'my conclusions in the clearest and most straightforward terms'. Three months later a bad-tempered European Community summit took place in Rome. The arguments about economic and monetary union came to a head and this led to the resignation of the Deputy Prime Minister, Geoffrey Howe, on 1 November and Margaret's own, three weeks later, on 22 November.

These storms were political ones and are part of history. I have never forgotten, though, her kindness, her concern and her private resolution on that sunny July day when, amid the peace of the Sussex Downs, brutality and violence took the life of someone whose support she treasured and whose humour she enjoyed.

Alex Aiken
Conservative Party Press Officer

Alex Aiken was Chairman of the Conservative Students in 1989–90 and joined the staff of Conservative Central Office in 1993 as a press officer.

The Conservative Student National Committee had an annual meeting with the Prime Minister. I attended the meetings in 1989 and 1990. I recall two points from the 1990 meeting.

First, we had a set agenda covering various higher education issues. These were always robust discussions which usually overran their allotted time. At the start of the meeting, following the introductions, Mrs Thatcher launched into an attack on 'socialism' in higher education. As this continued, I feared that we would lose the later points on the agenda, so I intervened. I told the PM that though her views were correct we had to get through the agenda so we had better move on to the next issue. Slightly stunned to be stopped in mid-flow she said: 'Oh yes, OK – you tell us what's next.' Colleagues said afterwards that they were amazed that I had told the PM to 'shut-up'. However, we did get through the agenda.

Later in the meeting we were due to have an official photograph of the committee and the PM. The arrangement of the furniture in her office made positioning difficult for the whole group. This didn't present a problem to the PM who simply lifted the large settee up and dragged it across the room to the astonishment of the committee and officials.

During the two leadership elections of 1989 and 1990 the three Chairmen of the youth sections of the party – Young Conservatives, Students and National Association of Conservative Graduates – wrote joint letters in support of Mrs Thatcher during the leadership elections of 1989 and 1990. We received personal replies on both occasions.

The day she resigned as leader on 22 November 1990 the Conservative Student Office became a focal point for younger Conservatives. Around thirty came to the office in Artillery Row and simply sat and watched the events unfold in stunned silence. No one could believe it.

Mrs Thatcher caused panic in the party's press office in May 1990 when she rang the press office in the early morning after the elections asking to know the results in the Borough of Barnet – covering her Finchley constituency. Neither the hapless duty press officer – it was about 7 a.m. – or any other staff knew the results. Naturally there was much recrimination and the following years saw the duty officers armed with comprehensive results for all seats.

Baroness Browning
Conservative Peer

After serving as Chairman of Women into Business, Angela Browning became the MP for Tiverton and Honiton in 1992. She retired from the House of Commons in 2010 and was raised to the peerage.

As an aspiring MP in the 1980s I was fortunate enough, as Chairman of Women into Business, to host a reception at the Banqueting House in Whitehall. The Prime Minister spent the evening with us, presenting prizes and circulating among the guests, for over an hour. My husband had accompanied me and as the Prime Minister was about to leave I introduced her to him. She had never met either of us before but she immediately turned to him and said: 'Oh yes, you're an accountant, aren't you? Tell me, how are the businesses in Devon doing?'

I was quite stunned. Her attention to detail and the fact that she had done her homework for what must have really been a routine event was more than impressive.

John Whittingdale
Conservative MP 1999–2010

John Whittingdale was Margaret Thatcher's Political Secretary from 1988 until 1990 and her Private Secretary from 1990 until 1992. He has been a Member of Parliament since 1992.

I was fifteen when Margaret Thatcher became leader of my party and like so many of my generation and those that followed, I was influenced in my politically formative years by her exposition of ideas and beliefs developed with Keith Joseph and the Centre for Policy Studies. That clear articulation of an ideological philosophy attracted me to become involved in Conservative politics. Three years later, I was lucky enough to meet her for the first time when I began to work for the Conservative Party. I was in her office on the day Airey Neave was killed, and some years later I was working for her in Downing Street on the day that Ian Gow was assassinated – two terrible blows to her personally.

I first worked for Margaret Thatcher directly during the two general election campaigns of 1983 and 1987 when I accompanied her on her tour of the country. It was my first experience of her punishing work load, her extraordinary attention to detail and her occasionally somewhat unreasonable demands. I also saw at first hand her instinctive feel for the aspirations and beliefs of the people of Britain. It was her identity with those people that allowed her to articulate so clearly what they wanted and that delivered successive general election majorities for the Conservative Party of 144 and 102 – some of us might think that those were the days.

In 1988, Margaret Thatcher asked me to become her Political Secretary in Downing Street. I saw then her huge respect for Parliament itself. She occupied the position of Prime Minister, but she never forgot that she was also the Member of Parliament for Finchley and she believed that it was her duty to come here not just to speak but to vote – to go through the division lobby on behalf of her constituents. I used to help her with preparation for Prime Minister's Questions, which in those days lasted for just fifteen minutes and took place twice a week. She used to spend six or seven hours preparing for that fifteen-minute session. We used to go through briefs from every department across Whitehall, which set out the exposition of the government's policy and the line to take. Sometimes, she did not think it was very good and I would be sent to ring the minister's Private Secretary to tell him that the Prime Minister did not like a particular line. Occasionally, she strode across the study, took the phone from my hand and told the Private Secretary that not only did she not like the line to take but that she did not even like the policy either. Every now and again, she had a remarkable ability to distance herself somehow from the policies of the government of which she was also leader.

I also saw at first hand her immense personal kindness and compassion. As has been said, those were often shown to the most junior members of her staff. On the famous occasion when the waitress spilt the soup on Geoffrey Howe, it was not Geoffrey Howe whom Margaret Thatcher worried about, but the waitress. She always insisted that she could never be late – particularly to funerals, to which, sadly, I used to accompany her occasionally. We used to sit in lay-bys for fifteen or twenty minutes; we would have set off early in case there was heavy traffic because she could not allow herself to be late.

I know that both government and opposition members received personal handwritten letters from Margaret Thatcher when they experienced a tragedy in their private lives or with their families. She had enormous compassion. If ever she found out that somebody was alone at Christmas, she would always say that they should come and spend it at Chequers with her. Ronnie Millar, the playwright, told me that he would spend many months trying to think of excuses why he would be busy, because being with Margaret Thatcher at Christmas might not be the most relaxing way to spend it.

Of all the demands on the Prime Minister's time, the one that occupied the most was speech-writing. Every speech went through at least ten drafts and major speeches many more. As Margaret Thatcher's Political Secretary, my job was to coordinate the preparation of speeches to party audiences. My year was divided between fixed points: the Central Council meeting, the Scottish Conference, the Local Government Conference, the Women's Conference and most important of all, the Conservative Party Conference in October.

Work would start on the party conference speech at least a month in advance. At a preliminary meeting, the Prime Minister would set out her ideas as to the areas that the speech should cover. This was usually done in an unbroken flow of raw Thatcher thought which our in-house speech-writing team, and those that I would commission from outside, would have to turn into draft speech form. Subject areas would be allocated between speech-writers and they would then be sent off to prepare paragraphs on each topic for inclusion. Once we had collected a number of contributions, these would be tacked together in a rough structure and the process of refinement and polishing would begin.

It was an immensely time-consuming process and at least once in the preparation of every speech, the Prime Minister would lose confidence in the whole process, tell us that it was all useless and demand that we start again from the beginning. The next few hours would be spent slightly tweaking the sections and then reinserting them while assuring her that they were completely different from the original. At the early stages, we would be meeting once a week. This would then increase to every day and then the whole of the weekend before the conference would be spent working on the text at Chequers.

Once we got to Blackpool, Bournemouth or Brighton, the whole time would be spent in the Prime Minister's suite surrounded by paper, with a core team which was boosted by those drafted in to make suggestions and improvements. A single critical word at the wrong time could undo weeks of work and my job was as much to keep well-meaning but destructive critics away as it was to bring in and encourage contributors. The average length of a party conference speech is about forty minutes. I worked on three and in each case Margaret Thatcher spent at least eighty hours working on the text: two hours for each minute of the speech. Those actually writing the speech spent much more.

The hardest and most important parts of the speech to write were the jokes. Margaret Thatcher was not naturally a joke-teller although she has a dry sense of humour. However, she recognised that without jokes, a speech is flat and dull. A good joke-writer was therefore valued above all others. On our core team, we had two principle joke-writers: the late Sir Ronnie Millar and John O'Sullivan, a journalist and commentator who had been brought in to the Number 10 Policy Unit. They had very different styles and each brought a different kind of humour. However, in each case, Margaret Thatcher frequently required persuasion that what they had written was indeed funny.

In 1990, the party conference speech was particularly important. Margaret Thatcher was under heavy attack and had recently suffered the resignation of her Chancellor, Nigel Lawson. Her speech had to be as good as she had ever delivered. A few weeks earlier, the Liberal Democrats had unveiled their new party symbol. It was supposed to represent a bird taking wing, but in the mind of John O'Sullivan it immediately became a dead parrot. He decided that he would write a section of the speech devoted to mocking the Liberal Democrats and would include a section of *Monty Python*'s dead parrot sketch. To anyone familiar with *Monty Python* it was a terrific idea and very funny. Unfortunately, the Prime Minister had not even heard of *Monty Python*.

When we came to read through the draft of the speech, Mrs Thatcher paused when she reached the dead parrot section and looked at John O'Sullivan as if he were completely mad. We knew that this would happen and so had prepared our strategy in advance. 'This is,' I explained, 'one of the most famous comedy sketches ever written. It will be instantly recognisable to every person in the audience.' I was slightly less certain of this latter point, knowing Conservative audiences, but all of us present insisted to the Prime Minister that it would be the highlight of her speech.

The joke survived that read-through but I knew that she was not convinced. On each subsequent occasion, whenever we reached the parrot section, she stopped and said: 'Are you sure that this is funny?' After about the third or fourth occasion, she tried a new tack. 'I need to see the sketch,' she said. 'If I am to deliver it then I need to get the inflection absolutely right.' As it happened, I had at home a video of the Python film *And Now for Something Completely Different*, which contains the dead parrot sketch. I therefore brought it into the office the next day.

One of the more surreal moments during my time at No. 10 followed. Sitting in my office watching the dead parrot sketch were Margaret Thatcher, John O'Sullivan, Robin Harris, who was also helping with the speech, Peter Morrison, her PPS, and myself. At any time, it is a very funny sketch. But the absurdity of the situation made it all the more amusing and I and the three others found it so hilarious that we had tears rolling down our cheeks. Margaret Thatcher, on the other hand, was all the more mystified. It was not her type of humour and she found it difficult to see why we were laughing so much. However, given that we all were, she accepted that it must be funny and so, true professional that she was, she attempted to master the emphasis and inflection of John Cleese's delivery. She did so brilliantly and was soon able to deliver faultlessly the famous lines: 'This parrot is no more. It has ceased to be. It has expired and gone to meet its maker.'

In the days leading up to the conference, the Prime Minister required constant reassurance that people would find the lines funny. She was clearly still full of doubt. However, I was able to get to enough people in advance whose opinion she was likely to ask that she was eventually persuaded. Every time we ran through the speech, I found myself laughing at the passage which simply added to the Prime Minister's puzzlement.

Finally, we got to the day of the speech. The text was finished, it had been typed up on to the autocue and we had completed the final rehearsal at which she practised her delivery and the inflections of the speech. However, as we waited for her to go on to the stage to deliver the speech, she was still worrying about the passage and looking for reasons that it might not work. Just as she was about to go on, another doubt arose in her mind. She looked at me and said anxiously: 'John, Monty Python – are you sure that he is one of us?'

To try to explain to her that Monty Python did not really exist would have been to risk disaster. I therefore did not even try and instead said to her: 'Absolutely, Prime Minister. He is a very good supporter.' Thus reassured, she went on to the platform to give the speech. She did so perfectly and received the biggest laugh of all when she delivered with perfect comic timing the words of the dead parrot sketch.

After Margaret stood down as Prime Minister, she came on several occasions to support me in Essex. Essex has always been Thatcher country. When she came to my constituency of Maldon at the election in which I first stood as candidate, after she had stood down as Prime Minister, the pavements had crowds four or five deep of people who had turned out to see her. Not all were supporters of hers or of mine, but they wanted to be there because they recognised that she played such a hugely important role in their lives and the life of their country.

Even today, when I occasionally meet parliamentarians, and

sometimes even leaders, from different countries, if I say to them that I served as Margaret Thatcher's Political Secretary, that lights their interest; in many ways, it is what I am most proud of. It was a privilege to know her and an even greater privilege to have worked for someone who was one of the greatest Prime Ministers this country has ever had.

Ann Widdecombe
Conservative MP 1987–2010

Ann Widdecombe was MP for Maidstone between 1987 and 2010. She served as a junior minister in John Major's government, and joined the shadow Cabinet in 1998, where she served as shadow Health and then shadow Home Secretary. She is also a bestselling novelist.

In the 1980s when the issue of CND was still a very live one, I helped Lady Olga Maitland set up an organisation known as Women and Families for Defence. My contribution to the group was to write a booklet entitled *A Layman's Guide to Defence*. The group, deciding that it would like a photo opportunity, asked to see the Prime Minister. Margaret Thatcher agreed to see us but in her usual way it was before breakfast on an extremely dark winter's morning. We trudged along to 10 Downing Street scarcely past dawn and were received by the Prime Minister looking as if she had just walked out of a beauty salon. She was very lively and interested in what we were doing.

After we had been there about ten minutes the doorbell of No. 10 went and Edwina Currie arrived on the doorstep wearing a hat! She had never been active in the group and none of us was quite sure what she was doing there, and a very embarrassed Olga, who had had to turn several people away as the invitation limited the numbers very stringently, had the job of turning away this formidable lady from the doorstep of No. 10.

We had expected a five-minute audience but Mrs Thatcher gave us the best part of an hour.

Michael Brunson
ITN Political Editor 1986–2000

Michael Brunson is best known for being ITN's face of current affairs for fourteen years. This passage is adapted from his autobiography A Ringside Seat.

My first-ever encounter with Margaret Thatcher, a little over a year before she became Prime Minister, was explosive, and therefore memorable. I had just returned to the United Kingdom after a spell as ITN's Washington correspondent, and I had already been told that I would be the reporter assigned to cover her eventual general election campaign.

In January 1978, as Leader of the Opposition, she gave a wide-ranging television interview, during which she was asked about the issue of immigration. She replied with what she later described as some 'extremely mild remarks'. What she actually said was this: 'People are really rather afraid that this country might be rather swamped by people with a different culture.' Others immediately found her remarks, and particularly her use of the word 'swamped', as anything but mild, hearing in them an echo of Enoch Powell's notorious 'rivers of blood' speech almost exactly ten years earlier.

The following day, Mrs Thatcher was due to conduct a morning's campaigning for the Conservative candidate in a by-election in the Ilford North constituency to the east of London. I immediately suggested to the News Editor at ITN that I should go and cover it. The Conservative campaign headquarters for the by-election turned out to be an old café, the former, though still appropriately named, Seven Ways Restaurant, since it was right next to the massive Gants Hill roundabout. The news conference was to be held in a large and unusually depressing room, hung from floor to ceiling with the faded maroon curtains which had presumably once been the establishment's glory in its heyday.

The news conference was surprisingly poorly attended, with no more than five or six other journalists present. I was therefore able, at an early stage, to ask about the previous evening's interview, and

I thought it perfectly natural to ask whether she had not regretted having raised the issue.

A volcanic eruption followed. She had not raised the matter. How could I possibly say that she had raised the matter? She had simply been asked a question, and she had replied to it in a perfectly honest and straightforward manner. What on earth was I talking about? How could I possibly put such a question to her?

Stunned into silence, I left it to others among the equally astonished press corps to take up the running, and they quickly turned to local matters. The news conference drew to a close and I assumed that that was the end of the matter. But I was wrong.

During some closing remarks, the volcano erupted again. Mrs Thatcher announced that she wished to say a word or two about the media. As she did so, what President Mitterand is once said to have called 'the eyes of Caligula' swivelled menacingly in my direction. She wanted journalists to know that she always did her homework, and that if we were to be regarded as true professionals, she expected us to do ours. Of course, she wanted good relations with the media, and she was perfectly prepared to answer any and every question. She always had, and she always would, with one proviso. They had to be accurate questions, properly based on facts. Had we got that? Was that quite clear? The tirade delivered, she swept from the room.

Blimey! Was this the woman that I would have to deal with during the rigours of a general election? I soon realised, however, that it had been an exceptionally useful experience. It gave me, at our very first meeting, a clear insight into the way Margaret Thatcher operated. Above all, it showed me how strongly she believed in the old adage that the best form of defence is attack – seizing, that morning in Ilford, for example, on the tiny technicality of whether or not she had raised, or had simply responded to, an issue in order to defend herself. It was all to stand me in good stead not just during the 1979 campaign, but during the many times over the following years when we were to meet again.

Sir Edward du Cann
Conservative MP 1956–87

Sir Edward du Cann represented the constituency of Taunton for more than thirty years. During that time he served in numerous positions within the Conservative Party and on many House of Commons committees. He received his knighthood in 1995.

Having been a strong supporter of Margaret Thatcher from the moment she became leader of the Conservative Party in 1975, I have a thousand clear memories of her.

Many people, MPs and others like me, will have watched her with admiration on public and semi-public occasions – standing resolute and indomitable at the dispatch box in the House of Commons, facing down the barrackers; evoking the enthusiasm of Conservative Party members at party conferences; and (how well I remember those occasions) her presence at meetings of the 1922 Committee, the backbench Tory MPs, where *prima inter pares* she solicited, deserved and obtained their loyal support all the years that I was their Chairman.

And, in her early days as leader, and even when she won the general election in 1979 and became Prime Minister, that wasn't always easy.

Her achievements as Prime Minister were formidable. The memories of her successes, which were also our country's successes, will endure to her credit.

There are a multitude of personal memories, also, which I sometimes recall. Most are private recollections, and should remain so. But not all.

I remember when we first met, at a meeting of prospective Conservative parliamentary candidates in 1950, a dominantly male group. All of us were recently demobilised after our wartime experiences in the armed services. The late Airey Neave, fresh from his duties as a prosecutor at the Nuremberg trials, was our secretary and convenor. She was young and attractive. Naturally, she made a great impression on these lively men. And yet – she showed an exceptional keenness and capacity for self-advertisement, which was somehow daunting. Certainly it was untypical of her fellows.

Later, those of us who became MPs learned that her thrustfulness was one of her enduring strengths.

When I was a Treasury minister, she came once to my constituency to open an old peoples' home. This was when she had her first ministerial appointment. I remember how my friends in Taunton were impressed by her seriousness, and slightly in awe of it. Here was a paradox which would endure: the truth was that she cared deeply about social issues, and yet that reality was not as widely believed as it deserved to be.

When she first became leader of the Conservative Party, it took her a long while to settle into that position. The House of Commons then, like the party, was also very much a masculine society. (Blair's babes hadn't yet been invented.) I am not sure how easy it was for her to fit into the smoke room camaraderie that was the style of the Conservative parliamentary party at that time. Nor did she always find it easy in those early days to shine in the House, but her determination, her chief characteristic, carried her through. Her hard work led to an apparently easy style to fell her argumentative opponents with her oratorical handbag, full of the notes of the careful preparation that was her habit.

I remember thinking in 1975 that it would reflect well on the Conservative Party to elect a woman as leader, the first political party in Britain to do so; and even that it would be more creditable if she were to become Britain's first woman Prime Minister. (Not that the feminists in our society ever appeared to find her remarkable success attractive.) Her sex, on occasion, was an advantage to her. I have seen Tory MPs sit on their hands when Eden or Macmillan or Heath entered the room. When Margaret came in, they always stood up, to a man.

Sometimes she could be dictatorial – too often perhaps. In the end the parliamentary party revolted, following the example of one of her long term Cabinet colleagues – who owed his career to her. It was his personal attack on her in the House that marked the beginning of the end. Gratitude is not often the hallmark of politics. (I often wondered why some of her close ministerial colleagues were apparently supine under the criticisms which she never held back. She liked an argument. I suspect they found it hard to argue with a woman.)

She and her immediate predecessor, Ted Heath, were in one respect in the same mould: they could be aloof, even with their close colleagues, self-contained, in a way which their predecessors in my experience, Eden, Macmillan and Home, were not. My good friend Airey Neave, who had masterminded her election as leader of the Conservative Party and became the head of her private office before his murder in the House of Commons by the Irish, told me, to my astonishment, that he was less close to her than he had expected. Leadership can be a solitary business.

As Chairman of the 1922 Committee, I was privileged to have a close relationship with her. Never was I received with anything but courtesy. Even when I had private advice to offer on matters of concern to the Conservative parliamentary party, including advice for which she did not care, she would hear me out with attention, take note, and, more importantly, take action.

There is one of our meetings, which I have most often looked back on, our last private meeting in the House, when I told her it was my intention, after thirty-one years, to retire as an MP. Typically generous, she pressed me to change my mind. I reflected aloud that it was sensible to retire early: perhaps then one's supporters might express regret; it would be foolish to wait to be pushed. I told her that she might consider this herself in due course. That advice, I remember, seemed to upset her. Now I wish I had pressed the point harder. Had she taken it in due course, she would have been spared the pain of her, eventual, unpleasant dismissal by the electorate of Tory MPs. Matters could have been, and should have been, differently arranged.

She was badly counselled at that time. I hope that, while I had responsibility in the House of Commons, I never gave her poor advice: whenever we disagreed, which was rare, I still (after all these years) believe that I was right. Perhaps I learned that self-confidence from her. If so, it was a good lesson for a politician to absorb.

Lord Howard

Conservative Peer

Michael Howard was Conservative MP for Folkestone and Hythe from 1983 until 2010. He joined Margaret Thatcher's government in 1985 and was appointed Secretary of State for Employment in January 1990. Two years later he became Secretary of State for the Environment before being promoted to Home Secretary in 1993, a position he held until the 1997 general election. He was leader of the Conservative Party from 2003 to 2005.

I first saw Margaret Thatcher in action when, as Secretary of State for Education in the Heath government, she addressed a dinner at the Coningsby Club, a Conservative dining club of which I was Chairman. She was very impressive, in complete command of her subject and, I thought, radiating authority.

Even so, I am not sure that I then saw her as a future Prime Minister. But, following events from outside the House of Commons, I was delighted when she was elected leader of the Conservative Party in 1975.

People forget the state of the country at that time and in the years which led up to 1979. The air of defeatism which was the prevailing climate of the time was the economic and social equivalent of Munich. I remember hearing Peter Jay, then regarded as the rising guru of his generation, analyse: 'Either,' he said, 'we shall have a government determined to tackle the causes of their weakness, in which case it will have to take such unpopular measures that it will never be elected for a second term, or we shall have a government not prepared to take these measures in which case weakness and failure will continue and accelerate.'

The measures which Margaret Thatcher took were certainly unpopular. But from the beginning she displayed the resolve and determination which made her, to my mind, the peacetime counterpart of Churchill. I had relatively little contact with her after that first encounter, even after I entered Parliament in 1983.

She was then at the height of her powers with a majority of 144 and an opposition that appeared to be in terminal decline. Her encounters with

Neil Kinnock were so one-sided as to be embarrassing – in sharp contrast with the performance of the present incumbent in Downing Street.

In September 1985 I was asked to join the government. That is a moment no one forgets. I was at home in Kent at the time and was asked whether I would be free to take a telephone call from the Prime Minister. Then I received another call and was asked whether I could go to London to see her.

'Why does she want you to go to London?' asked my wife.

'Perhaps her telephone's out of order,' suggested my eight-year-old daughter.

My first job was Minister for Corporate and Consumer Affairs in the DTI. It was there that I began to have first-hand experience of the Prime Minister's interest in, passion for and mastery of detail.

We were discussing some complicated point I think related to the Financial Services Act, in her room at the House of Commons. She asked me the meaning of a reference in a footnote to the brief she had been given. I hadn't a clue. I can't pretend that I made sure that I was the master of every footnote from then on but I had certainly been given a powerful incentive to prepare very thoroughly for meetings with the Prime Minister.

It is always dangerous in politics to have very specific and particular ambitions. But I had one: I desperately wanted to enter the Cabinet while she was still Prime Minister. I only just made it. In January 1990 she made me Employment Secretary. In November of that year she was gone.

I have often been asked, and often thought, about the fateful events of that November. The advice I gave her and my thoughts and emotions have been described in full elsewhere. I told her that if she decided to fight on I would fight with her to the last ditch. But I also expressed my view that she would lose in the second ballot, possibly by a large margin.

I still think that honest advice was right though, of course, we shall never know. But I do not share the view of those who say that even if she had survived she could never have won a fourth general election. I think she would have won again and we can all speculate endlessly on the difference that might have made to the history of the last ten years.

It has been said many times that she was a divisive figure. She was. She had to be. There was no consensus on the right thing to do for our country. If she had waited for consensus, nothing would ever have happened. She saw what needed to be done and she did it with clarity, courage and conviction. It is also true that her divisiveness on occasion extended to members of her administration. On one occasion, a minister sent a paper to her that she rejected. He had the temerity to send it back with the words, 'Prime Minister, this is government policy'. She replied: 'It may be government policy but I don't agree with a word of it.'

In 1979, as we all know, Europe was divided in two. The eastern half was subjugated to the yoke of communist tyranny. The part that Margaret Thatcher played, in partnership with Ronald Reagan, in freeing those countries, has been well documented. However, there is one aspect of the story that is less well known. In 1990, as her Employment Secretary, I went to Poland. Lord Fowler, my predecessor, had set up something called the Know-How Fund to help establish small businesses in the newly free countries. My opposite number was Jacek Kuroń, who had been imprisoned for his opposition to communism. He took me to see Marshal Jaruzelski, the man whose regime had imprisoned him. Marshal Jaruzelski told me about the part Margaret Thatcher had played in the rise of Solidarity. He said: 'She visited Poland during one of Solidarity's strikes in the shipyards of Gdansk. She said to me: "You know, this isn't an ordinary strike and you ought to talk to its leaders." Until then, I had had no more intention of talking to them than I had of flying to the moon. But she persuaded me, so I began to talk to Lech Wałęsa – and you know what happened after that.'

For my part I shall always regard it as a great privilege to have served for five years, under one of – and perhaps the – greatest peacetime Prime Minister our country has seen.

Michael Cockerell
Documentary Film-Maker and Author

The award-winning documentary film-maker Michael Cockerell has been involved in the production of political television for over thirty years, most famously as chief political reporter for the BBC's Panorama. *He is the author of* Live from Number 10 – the Inside Story of Prime Ministers and Television.

The death of Britain's first woman Prime Minister received what might be called Thatcheration coverage across all media – print, digital and electronic. But relatively little attention focused on how she learned to use television to become the country's first and most formidable small-screen premier.

In the early days as leader it was not like that at all. According to *The Times*, she came over on TV 'with all the charisma of a privet hedge'. I interviewed her on the night in 1975 when she won the leadership and she seemed as fragile as porcelain as she said: 'It is like a dream – to follow in the footsteps of the great Winston, of Harold Macmillan and of Ted Heath. I almost wept when they told me – in fact I did weep.' She bit her lip and her eyes glistened.

From the outset Mrs Thatcher was concerned not to become a casualty of the cameras. She knew that her predecessor Ted Heath's unappealing TV manner had helped bring him down. And the new leader would react to the sight of a TV crew almost in the manner of a primitive tribesman faced with a white man's camera – it was as if she thought it might somehow take her soul away.

But she appointed as her television adviser a colourful character called Gordon Reece. He was a diminutive former TV producer, who looked rather like Ronnie Corbett. He ran on champagne and smoked huge Havana cigars. Mrs T. later knighted him for services to her TV image.

Under his tutelage, she underwent a complete makeover in her appearance for television. At the time she played down Reece's contribution. When I asked Mrs T. in 1979 how important he was to her, she responded wide-eyed: 'Gordon Reece? Do you know I think he comes to me for advice not the other way round. And it's always been that way.'

Mrs T. was being economical with the actualité. After she left office, Lady Thatcher was more candid: 'Gordon was absolutely terrific. He said my hair and my clothes had to be changed and we would have to do something about my voice. It was quite an education, because I hadn't thought about these things before. He was a real professional.'

And she quoted specific advice Reece had given her about what she should wear for TV: 'Avoid lots of jewellery near the face. Edges look good on television. Watch out for background colours which clash with your outfit.'

But Reece's focus group findings told him that while many voters welcomed the strength of her free-market convictions, on television she often came over as shrill, domineering and uncaring. Specifically Mrs Thatcher's voice put people off – it was perceived as too high-pitched.

Reece arranged for a voice coach from the National Theatre to teach her techniques to lower her pitch. One was to practise humming; the other was to keep repeating the word 'ngakokka'. When I asked about her new voice, she said: 'When you ask me a question, I say to myself think low.' I wasn't sure whether or not that was a comment on my interview technique.

Reece also taught her to stop worrying and love the boom micro-phone. He told her that recorded snippets of her conversation could make her sound more down-to-earth and in touch with voters. In later years she could never see a microphone without offering some seemingly spontaneous comments to people she met – whether it was another political leader or someone in a factory or hospital – knowing that TV people cannot resist 'natural sound'.

But there were some things Mrs Thatcher would never say on camera. I filmed her when she visited the British Embassy in the States in the late 1970s. Peter Jay, who was then our man in Washington, asked: 'What would you like to drink?' She made no reply but out of sight of the camera wrote a brief note to the ambassador. Later I discovered it read 'whisky and soda'. She was certainly not going to be filmed asking for one, still less drinking it.

Reece also arranged for Mrs Thatcher to appear on TV programmes that were outside the political leader's usual round of current affairs and news – like *Jim'll Fix It*, starring the late and unlamented Jimmy Savile. When Tory critics claimed her appearance on the programme was demeaning, Reece responded: 'Rubbish. I simply encourage her to appear everywhere she can to the best advantage. It's the most ludicrous intellectual snobbery to say that a politician shouldn't appear on general interest programmes because the viewers are supposed to be on a lower level of humanity than the people who watch *Panorama*. They have votes too and if she talked down to them they would soon rumble her.'

Mrs T. had become very media savvy as I saw when I filmed behind the scenes during her 1979 general election campaign. Reece had introduced the photo opportunity, beloved of American presidential hopefuls, into British elections. Until 1979 no previous aspirant to No. 10 had given an election campaign press conference clutching a two-day-old calf in a meadow.

When I asked her about it at the time, she said: 'The press said they did not want a picture of me with a load of bullocks. There was this tiny calf. The photographers have their job to do and I am very conscious of that.'

In the campaign Mrs Thatcher was determined to counter Labour's charges that she was dogmatic and uncaring. In an interview with me, she assumed a kittenish persona. I put it to her that there sometimes seemed to be two Mrs Thatchers: one toured supermarkets and factory floors, exhibiting endless fascination about the minutiae of people's lives and jobs. The other was the platform politician – full of zealous conviction.

'How many Mrs Thatchers are there?' I asked. She smiled and replied confidingly: 'Oh, there are three at least. There is the intellectual one, the intuitive one and there's the one at home.'

Her voice was so low and breathy, her manner so intimate – even coquettish – that the late Sir Robin Day, watching in the studio when the filmed interview went out, joked: 'The untold story of the election campaign: Margaret Thatcher is having an affair with Michael Cockerell.'

As a schoolgirl, Margaret Thatcher had wanted to become an actress. And as Prime Minister she was to play many different roles on television: Iron Lady, tearful mother, simple housewife, world statesman and war leader.

A favoured method of getting herself across was the big set-piece TV interview. The PM had different ways of dealing with interviewers. Some she coated with honey, while she would bite the heads off others. As she put it: 'This animal if attacked defends itself. So when I come up against somebody who is out to do a very belligerent interview, I say to myself: by God, anything you can do I can do better – and I'm belligerent back.'

By her own admission she would become very nervous before a high-profile TV appearance – and the tension inside No. 10 was palpable. When I asked Mrs Thatcher what she thought about big set-piece TV interviews, she replied: 'I hate them, I hate them, I hate them.'

The PM would rehearse for interviews with her blunt Yorkshire Press Secretary Bernard Ingham, who pulled no punches in playing the part of the interviewer. One time, as Sir Robin Day set off for one of his major *Panorama* interviews with Mrs T. in Downing Street, he said to me: 'Why don't I start the interview "Prime Minister, what's your answer to my first question?"' Sir Robin felt he knew that whatever he asked her she would come up with the sound bites she had prepared earlier. But sadly, despite my prompting, he never did begin an interview in that way.

In 1984 Margaret Thatcher became the first Prime Minister to agree to appear on a chat show. The timing was no coincidence. The miners' strike was at its height. Although the opinion polls showed that a large majority of people blamed Arthur Scargill for the violent confrontations with police that dominated the TV screens, the attacks on Mrs Thatcher as dictatorial and callous were getting through. She and her advisers calculated that she would benefit from appearing on a programme that showed her human face.

Michael Aspel asked whether both living and working at No. 10, she ever got the chance to relax. The grocer's daughter replied: 'I started life living above the shop. Do I ever relax? No, I am always on the job.' The studio audience fell about with laughter. Mrs Thatcher beamed with pleasure at the audience response without ever seeming to have understood what she had said.

Some time later I reminded the PM that when I had first filmed her as leader the TV cameras seemed to fill her with dread and she wished they would go away. 'Over the years,' she replied, 'I've learned that what you people want is a positive answer and that is what I always give you.' And in a way she always did – even when she was saying 'no, no, no'.

The last time I interviewed Mrs Thatcher as Prime Minister was when she was celebrating her tenth anniversary in No. 10. It was a pretty surreal experience. She talked to me looking into the middle distance almost as if she were Joan of Arc, hearing voices.

I had earlier asked Willie Whitelaw, her recently retired Deputy Prime Minister, how long he felt Mrs Thatcher would continue in office: 'Oh, she is very fit, very strong. I hope she'll go on for a very long time,' he replied. 'But she is not immortal,' I'd ventured to suggest. 'No she is not immortal,' responded Whitelaw, then added, 'but perhaps she is.' In No. 10, I recounted this exchange on camera to Mrs T. Reviewing the tape today is revealing.

On freezing the frame at exactly the moment she hears my intimation of her mortality, a remarkable look comes over her face for an instant: an apparent mix of alarm and blinding revelation. Within a few frames it is gone and she recovers her composure when I tell her that Whitelaw has said perhaps she was immortal: 'What a sweet thing of Willie to say – no, I am not immortal and I don't know how long I will go on – and no one does.'

The next year she was gone from No. 10. Her departure left a huge hole for political journalists. Once you had Margaret Thatcher in your viewfinder she rarely failed to produce riveting images and powerful quotes. The modern media which in any case tends to magnify personalities had for the fifteen years of her Tory leadership been faced with a giant-sized one. Disraeli, Lloyd George and Winston Churchill became Prime Ministers before the age of television. Happily the late Lady Thatcher did not.

Lord Ashdown
Liberal Democrat Peer

Paddy Ashdown was elected to Parliament as MP for Yeovil in 1983, a seat he represented for eighteen years. He was Leader of the Liberal Democrats between 1988 and 1999.

In a life that has, I suppose, had some small excitements, nothing that I have ever experienced so terrorised me as having to stand up as a young, inexperienced, wet-behind-the-ears leader of my party to question her in the House of Commons when she was at the full plenitude of her powers, with the inevitable result that I would be ritually handbagged twice a week in front of the microphones of the nation. Thank God there was no television in the Chamber then.

My wife and I had been invited to one of those Downing Street events to mark the visit of some foreign leader; I honestly cannot remember exactly who it was. Afterwards, as we came down the stairs of No. 10, we met the Prime Minister coming up. My wife, who, I should explain, is much more rampantly left-wing than I am, hated her policies with a passion. The Prime Minister stopped and talked to us for a few moments. As she moved away, my wife hissed through gritted teeth, 'She's absolutely bloody charming, damn it.' So she was – to everyone, except of course those who happened to be in her Cabinet, as that group of wholly unextinct volcanoes sitting in front of me will no doubt attest.

This was only one of her many paradoxes. She was not at all the straightforward, black-and-white, no-nonsense, unbending warrior leader that she latterly liked to portray. She knew, at least until the very end, when to compromise and did so, perhaps most significantly when, although relishing her anti-Europeanism, she nevertheless signed Britain up to the single European market.

In my view, three qualities set her apart as something different but each of them had its drawbacks. The first was a passionate commitment to freedom. As a Liberal, needless to say, I mostly welcomed that, although perhaps not as much as I should have at the time. Later, in

Bosnia, when I tried to get a stagnant economy moving, I found myself putting into practice many of the very things that I had opposed when she introduced them: aggressive liberalisation of the markets, stripping down the barriers to business and lowering taxation. In these things she was right at the time, even if today we find that, taken to excess, some of these attributes have not led to greater prosperity for all but to near ruin and a disgusting climate of greed for the few. In this, I suspect that revolution she started has perhaps somewhat run its course. Our challenge today is to find a kinder, less destructive, more balanced way of shaping our economy, but that is today. At the time when she did those things, they needed to be done.

However, her belief in freedom was, one might say, strangely partial. She did much to enhance individual economic freedom, and our country was much the better for it, but she did far less to enhance the political freedoms of, for instance, the gay community or the people of Scotland, or perhaps most markedly and paradoxically – and this has been commented on, too – the standing of women in society. She was – and arguably, given the context at the time, this was one of her very greatest achievements – Britain's first woman Prime Minister. However, her influence and power came not from the exercise of the female principles in politics but from the fact that she was far better than any man at the male ones.

Her second defining quality was her patriotism. David Cameron, the present Prime Minister, recently called her the 'patriot Prime Minister'. It is a good phrase and an apposite one. However, her patriotism too, though so powerfully held and expressed, was more about the preservation and restoration of Britain's past position than it was about preparing us for the challenges of what came next. She used her formidable talents to give our country a few more years of glory, and for that we should be eternally grateful. However, that legacy means that Britain today still finds itself uncomfortable and undecided about its true position in the world, not least in relation to Europe, where the infection that she planted still has the capacity to rip apart her party. There can be no doubt that she restored our country's position in the world but in a way that perhaps today makes us even less able to answer Dean Acheson's famous challenge that, having lost an empire, we have yet to find a role.

Her final triumphant quality was of course her courage. This, I think, is the pre-eminent quality of leadership and she had it in abundance. Yet this, too – her greatest asset – had its dangers. I used to have a principle in distant, more robust days that I would never take on operations anyone who was not at least as frightened as I was, but she was frightened of nothing. She could see the risks but she ignored them if she believed she was right and paradoxically this, in the final analysis, was what ended her long term as Prime Minister. Is it not always hubris that gets us in the end?

She was complex, extraordinary, magnificent, fallible, flawed and infuriating. One thing, however, is certain and cannot be denied except by those so sunk in bitterness that they will not see: she won great victories for what she stood for at home and huge respect for our country abroad. If politics is defined – and I think it can be – by principles, the courage to hold to them and the ability to drive them through to success, then she was without a doubt the commanding politician and the greatest Prime Minister of our age.

Julia Langdon
Political Journalist

Julia Langdon is a freelance political journalist and former Political Editor of the Daily Mirror *and the* Sunday Telegraph. *She is the author of* Mo Mowlam: The Biography.

Perhaps the most chilling moment of my relationship with Margaret Thatcher occurred at about 30,000 feet. We were in an RAF VC10 – as we so often were – en route on this occasion to Australia. I had looked with horror at the official itinerary when it had arrived shortly beforehand. It was long and characteristically busy and the worst thing was that we had one night in the air on the outward journey and then a row of one-night stopovers in a series of different Australian cities. I realised gloomily that we wouldn't be able to get any laundry done until we reached Bangkok, ten days or so into the journey. When the Prime Minister came back in the plane to rough it with the riff-raff on the first leg of the journey to somewhere in the Middle East, I politely asked her by way of conversational small talk what she had made of her programme. 'Well!' she said, clearly much exercised on the point, 'do you realise we won't even be able to get any laundry done until we reach Bangkok!'

It was, I have to report, quite alarming to discover that one's reaction in an unpredictable set of circumstances should be so completely identical to that of the Prime Minister. And not any old Prime Minister either.

We went around the world together several times, Mrs Thatcher and I. Entirely at her behest, of course. During her years as Prime Minister, I was Political Editor of this and that and instructed by my various employers always to accompany Her Nibs wherever she went. It was the most brilliant fun, although probably more particularly in retrospect because there were lots of endless days and sleepless nights. And when you did get into bed for the first time in what felt like weeks, somewhere on the other side of the world, you could always rely on the newsdesk to ring and say that a reader had rung in about some trivial fact they wished to challenge.

I was there when military bands turned out at midnight to play obscure national anthems at the other end of the interminable lengths of red carpet laid across some foreign airport tarmac. I have watched elderly despots dance attendance upon her and I have watched her dance. It isn't always quite as glamorous as it might sound. I have trailed her around building sites in the Middle East, a sewer works in Cairo, a mining operation in Namibia, a new mass transit system in Singapore. I have watched as she took tea in a trench with two African Presidents in a war zone on the Mozambique border and as she was unexpectedly presented with an Arab stallion in a Middle Eastern desert and didn't quite know how to explain that it wasn't quite her thing. I have winced in feminist sympathy as the light of the Jordanian sun cut through her dress and made it look as if she was stark naked as she inspected the honour guard lined up to salute her. I have watched strong men and women faint from heat in refugee camps in Israel and Zimbabwe and Jordan and Cambodia and wondered if she was going to make it – and, yes, whether I was too. Possibly not in that order. I was on her plane when we were shot at by guerrillas on the way to visit Malawi – not that I knew about it until her first volume of memoirs was published. 'Fortunately they missed,' she said, recounting the incident. Together we have attended the Bolshoi, a wedding in Tbilisi, a mass in Zagorsk, a riot in Melbourne, another one in the heat and dust of a Saharan harmattan as we watched a dhurbar in Kano.

It was always work. She didn't relax. There were very few opportunities for hanging around the swimming pool if there was one. She didn't like sightseeing and she wasn't really interested in culture. She didn't want anybody to think that she was pleasure-seeking or enjoying herself – except, of course, in a political sense. She was once prevailed upon to show that she had an understanding of these things, however. We had whizzed around the wonders of Luxor in a couple of hours, typically at midday with the temperature at 120 degrees or so, simply because it suited her programme to do it at this insane time of day. Someone told her that really she ought to show she was interested in the wonders of ancient Egypt for their own sake. So when we took off she ordered the pilot to take the VC10 down to 3,000 feet so we could admire the temples of Abu Simbel in the Upper Nile. On the next trip we circled Ayers Rock in Australia. Reader, I must tell you, that we did not do justice to these wonders of the world.

There were many wonderful moments of our travels together and I cherish some in particular. There was, for example, the time at the Expo in Brisbane when she was touring the site and many eager Australians had packed the area for a glimpse of the great Maggie Thatcher. It was terribly crowded and the public were penned away from the celebrity tour of the exhibits. There was, however, a middle-ranking reptile enclosure which contained the press. Mrs Thatcher was about to move among us and, seeing some small children who were eager to catch a glimpse of this legend of their lifetime, I offered to take one small child off her mother and give her a better view. I was holding her up to see the great one pass and Mrs Thatcher stopped at the sight of the little girl's excited small face. There were no other children around because this was the press area and the public were so much further away. Mrs Thatcher didn't realise this, however, and with a politician's instinct homed in. The horror on her face when she realised that I was holding the child was a wonder to behold. 'Oh!' she said with complete disgust and incomprehension. 'It's you!'

I think my favourite moment, however, was in Moscow when Mrs Thatcher was due to meet the armed service chiefs of the USSR at their equivalent of the Ministry of Defence. I had arrived somewhat latterly, behind the rest of my press colleagues but very slightly before the Prime Minister. For the purposes of this anecdote it is necessary to recognise that to someone in the Soviet Union one middle-aged West European woman looks very much like another. Anyway, I whizzed into the lift to go to the appropriate floor where Mrs T. was due to meet the top brass – literally – of the Soviet military machine and when the lift doors opened they thought she had arrived. There was music and an attendant group of military snapped to attention, saluted and clipped their heels. A man with a lot of scrambled egg on his shoulders stepped forward to greet me. 'I'm from the *Daily Mirror*,' I said, by way of explanation. 'Mrs Thatcher isn't here yet.' They were very embarrassed. I thought it was just wonderful.

William Hague
Foreign Secretary 2010–

William Hague became the leader of the Conservative Party following John Major's resignation in 1997. He had previously served as Minister of State for Social Security and Disabled People and as Secretary of State for Wales. He is Foreign Secretary in David Cameron's government.

Many people will have memories about Margaret Thatcher etched indelibly in their political consciousness. Mine has to be the final speech she made in the Commons as Prime Minister in November 1990 following her decision to stand down from the leadership of the Conservative Party.

She had been Prime Minister for eleven years and dominated British politics. She was one of my earliest political heroes and I remember sitting there, as a junior backbencher, watching with a deep sense of sorrow that she was about to bow out.

But what a way to go! Anyone expecting her to be downbeat or subdued by the experiences of recent days was sorely disappointed as she recounted how Britain had been rescued from the spiral of decline and stagnation in which decades of socialism had left it. At one stage Dennis Skinner intervened to suggest she might become Governor of the new European Central Bank. 'What a good idea,' she responded to the hilarity of the House. To Tory cheers, she went on, 'I'm enjoying this.'

It was then that the Conservative backbencher Michael Carttiss spoke for many of us when, pointing across the Chamber, he said, 'You can wipe the floor with these people.' It was a magical performance, never to be forgotten by those who saw it.

A few months later I saw her come into the Commons tearoom and fall into conversation with Dennis Skinner. On seeing her he had cried out, 'It's not the same without you, love.' Looking across at him she replied, 'How are you, dear?' before the two of them sat together for about forty-five minutes in earnest discussion, while the rest of us strained to hear what they were talking about. Whatever people's views of her policies she was held in immense respect right across the spectrum.

I saw that again in my own leadership election in 1997 when she went to the tearoom for the first time since leaving the Commons five years earlier – much to the amazement of many new Labour MPs who had never seen her in the flesh before! All the old authority, presence and conviction that she exuded as Prime Minister came back as she handbagged any wavering Conservative MPs.

They were the same qualities that had sustained her through some of her most difficult times as Prime Minister – such as the speech on 22 November 1990. It is hard now to appreciate just how difficult that speech was to make. Yet it turned out to be her grand finale as Prime Minister, worthy of everything she had achieved in eleven years. Moreover, to many of those who were privileged to be there, it was quite simply one of the greatest parliamentary performances that we had seen, or are ever likely to see.

Bernard Jenkin
Conservative MP 1992–

*Bernard Jenkin is the son of former Thatcher Cabinet minister Patrick Jenkin.
He was elected MP for Colchester North in 1992 and since 1997 has represented
Harwich and North Essex.*

My first proper meeting with Margaret Thatcher was when she
was still an MP. I learned how her passion for the truth made
her such a dangerous adversary in argument – a danger which
she harboured long into old age – and she loved a good spat. John
Whittingdale arranged for her to meet some bright young candidates
before the 1992 election – and I was included too. Two of them now
serve as senior Ministers of State. As they tried to justify UK membership of the exchange rate mechanism, she scorned the one who had
worked closely in her government. 'Oh,' and she said his name in piti-
ful tones, and then with heavy inflection and glaring eyes, 'I am so
disappointed with you.' Then she listened to the other, who argued that
the exit from the exchange rate mechanism would involve too much
loss of face for the government. She looked outraged. 'Loss of face?!
What is loss of face compared to the loss of 350,000 jobs? If you think
that, you're a fool! There's the door!' Not an easy introduction for an
aspiring candidate.

As well as enjoying a good spat, she also had a dry sense of humour,
which she demonstrated during the 1992 general election in Essex. A
junior reporter from the *Essex County Standard* breathlessly caught up with
her hectic pace in Maldon and asked, in front of 200 other journalists,
'Do you agree that the Conservative campaign is lacking in oomph?'
Mrs T. retorted, with heavy irony, 'That's what I'm here for, dear.'

Once elected to the Lords, it is simply not true that she spent her
time trying to subvert new MPs' support for John Major. On the
contrary, given how hurt she had been by her dismissal as leader and
Prime Minister, how angry she was about what the government was
or was not doing, and how appalled she was by the Maastricht Treaty,
she was incredibly restrained. It was the new MPs elected in 1992 who

wanted to see her in the days before the great vote on Maastricht of November 1992. She was holding a heavily annotated copy of the Treaty, something which Ken Clarke had already admitted he had not read at all. She was passionate in her condemnation of Maastricht. It should not be forgotten: her Bruges speech and her determination to veto such a treaty was the reason certain senior figures were determined she should have been deposed. I mentioned that three of us had been summoned by Michael Heseltine who was apparently going to try to persuade us to change our minds and I asked for her advice about the meeting. 'Take your treaty! He's no good on the detail!' she declared. That turned out to be very good advice, but only five of the new intake voted against or abstained on that crucial Maastricht vote. One, Iain Duncan Smith, subsequently became leader.

In later years, a friend of mine was wandering past a bookshop on Piccadilly a few years ago, where he spied Lady Thatcher engaged in one of her marathon book-signing sessions. He wandered in to observe the growing mêlée which surrounded her, as she rattled off one signature after another. Everyone who approached her seemed to have a little tale to tell. One chap explained that he was a friend of Cecil Parkinson. 'A true friend,' said Lady T. My friend, who had by this time joined the queue, held out his book for her to sign and said: 'I'm a friend of Bernard Jenkin.' 'Bernard,' she exclaimed, 'is a true believer.' 'Yes,' said my friend, 'a good Eurosceptic.' Lady Thatcher looked up at him and said, 'Except I call them "Defenders of Britain!"' With that, she handed the duly signed book over and looked towards a teenage girl who was next in the queue. 'I'm not a friend of anybody's,' announced the girl. Lady Thatcher apparently dissolved into fits of laughter!

What we miss from politics today is her certainty, her seriousness, her clarity of principle, her fusion of the practical with her sense of moral purpose. Those who disagreed with her undoubtedly felt that to be arrogance on her part, but she felt she was a guardian of greater truths and principles, which were far more important than her mere self. This, with her formidable intellect, gave her an extraordinary prescience about the world. How right she was about the exchange rate mechanism, and about the Maastricht Treaty and monetary union. I would caution those who try to use her name in support of the EU as it has become, as though she would ever have put her name to the Lisbon Treaty or anything like it.

As she grew older, we regarded Lady T. less and less as a former Prime Minister, more and more as a favourite aunt or grandmother. Sometimes it was hard to believe that this small, frail lady had once held the world in the palm of her hand. The whole nation will be for ever in her debt.

Andrew Riley
Archivist

Andrew Riley works at the Churchill Archives Centre in Cambridge and is responsible for the archiving of all of Margaret Thatcher's personal papers and documents.

Lady Thatcher first visited the Churchill Archives Centre, with Sir Denis, on a Sunday early in 1994. Typically, she wrote an immediate thank-you letter to our then Keeper, the historian Correlli Barnett, recording her gratitude for the archives staff 'who preserve the lessons of history for us' and for seeing a display of wartime papers which recorded 'Churchill's genius' in inspiring confidence in wartime victory.

In 1997 Lady Thatcher generously donated the bulk of her personal and political papers to the Margaret Thatcher Archive Trust on behalf of the nation. Since then, the trust has supported their cataloguing and preservation at the centre, alongside the papers of Sir Winston.

After 1997 Lady Thatcher continued to chair and support the work of the Archive Trust and was a regular visitor to college. With her help, funding was raised for a new wing to house her papers and provide expansion space for the Archives Centre. At an early meeting to report progress on the design her eyes focused intently on me as she queried the direction of air flow movements in the extension. Of course, she had alighted on the one ambiguity in the design proposal and I had a few awkward moments under her gaze.

The extension was eventually opened in 2002 by Lady Thatcher who reached towards the somewhat alarmed Director of the Archives, Allen Packwood, to relieve him of a large pair of scissors to cut the ceremonial ribbon. She asked him, perhaps unnecessarily, 'Shall I go to the left or the right?'

The Thatcher Archive contains over 3,000 boxes of papers, memos, photographs and correspondence. And one of the famous handbags, which I collected from her aide 'Crawfie' back in 2002. It felt very odd leaving her office with such an iconic and historical artefact. The bag dates from the mid-1980s, with a helpful handwritten note from Lady Thatcher recording its provenance.

In 2006 the centre co-curated an exhibition at Parliament which was opened by the then Prime Minister, Tony Blair. I stood beside Lady Thatcher as Mr Blair recounted how he had asked her at Prime Minister's Questions in 1984 about her familiarity with the famous 1944 Employment White Paper. To his horror, she had stood in Parliament and, without warning, had answered him by pulling out her own copy of the document from her handbag. The White Paper, heavily annotated and headed 'Margaret H. Roberts' is now safely in her archive.

We were privileged to work so closely with Lady Thatcher who was always generous with her time in talking to our donors and supporters. In 2009 we hosted a luncheon in London to mark the start of a conference examining the legacy of the Cold War. The then US ambassador to London was booked to give an opening address to start the lunch but was caught up in terrible traffic near the Embassy. Our guests were disappointed but had a very welcome forty-five minutes to talk to Lady Thatcher, pay their tributes and take photographs before the ambassador arrived. It was a reminder of her influence on the world stage, even in retirement.

Eric Pickles

Conservative MP 1992–

Eric Pickles was leader of Bradford City Council from 1988 to 90 before being elected to Parliament in 1992. He served successive Conservative leaders in frontbench positions and is now Secretary of State for Local Government and Communities.

Those who get their views of Margaret Thatcher from a *Spitting Image* puppet or the cartoon vitriol of a leftish stand-up comedian – all poll tax and miners' strike – don't get close to the woman's achievements. Equally unreliable is the image of flag-waving patriots – land of hope and glory and the victory over the Argentinian Junta.

Of course, Lady Thatcher was a patriot, a great war leader and a woman of enormous vision, but behind that mask stood a subtle, clever and flexible politician who was determined to save a United Kingdom on the slide. I saw her close up from the early years of her leadership right the way through to the end of her premiership and on and off during the remaining years of her life.

I listened to some of the protesters following her death, and I was struck how young they were; few would have been born while she was still PM, most of their leaders would have been infants in the latter years of her premiership. Also they seem to have no idea of what a mess this country was in the late 1970s. The fashionable view was that Britain was ungovernable. Thank goodness Mrs T. was never a dedicated follower of fashion.

I could talk about exchange controls, overbearing trade unions or public services run on a take it or leave it basis, but for a simple example of how different life was before Thatcher, consider telecommunications.

Before 1979 the state ran the telephone system, you regarded it as a special privilege if it graciously granted you the right to have a phone line, particularly if it was a line exclusively to your home and not shared by a neighbour. The model was the same but you had a choice of colour: black, red, grey or ivory; available wall mounted or free standing, but be prepared to wait for weeks for instillation. Towards the end of the decade trill phones made a tentative appearance.

In a few short years Mrs Thatcher presided over a telecommunications revolution, the effects of which are still being felt. From mobiles to super-fast broadband, none of it would have been possible with the old GPO.

I first came into regular contact with her when I was a National Officer of the Young Conservatives. I was National Chairman in her first full year as Prime Minister. She, along with other members of her Cabinet, granted enormous access to the YCs. Looking back, considering what was going on, astonishing access. So we saw close up the shifts and tensions within her first Cabinet.

There were many in my party that doubted her ability in the early years. Her position was far from secure. I watched her carefully build alliances with charm, persuasion and persistence. She loved argument and debate; anyone coming to her with a half-worked-out idea or who presented prejudice in place of facts, would be in real trouble. Those who knew their stuff and held their ground earned her respect.

Place her outside debate and it would be hard to find a kinder person. While Prime Minister, at a very busy time for her, she took time out to change my life.

I was in my mid-thirties, leader of Bradford Council at a time when most other leaders were in their mid-fifties. I was not sure I wanted to spend the next thirty years in local government defending past decisions and uncertain whether to try for Parliament.

Contemplating my future at a Central Council (spring conference) at Scarborough in the late 1980s I felt a vice-like grip on my elbow. Turning round I was face-to-face with Mrs Thatcher. Somehow she heard of my dilemma and decided to give me a push – literally a push: frogmarching me across the room to the Party Vice-Chairman with responsibility for candidates. Addressing two startled men (me and the Vice-Chairman) she said 'Mr Pickles would like to be a MP, and I think he would make a good MP. I think you should give him a form and an interview.'

I duly completed both, plus passing the selection weekend. From that point on I was on my own, granted no special favours, but knowing that she was supporting me was a great boost to my self-esteem.

The Thatcher Archives are lodged at Churchill College, Cambridge, and a few weeks ago I was given a tour. The iconic handbag, complete with contents, is there. Among the documents is a tiny piece of paper, her notes for the St Francis prayer (Where there is discord...), which she spoke before entering No. 10 for the first time. Since her death I have thought of the optimism of these words and of the destiny she would fulfil.

Margaret Thatcher is the greatest British peacetime Prime Minister of the twentieth century – I feel privileged to have known her.

Sir John Junor
Journalist

Sir John Junor was Editor of the Sunday Express *for thirty two years, from 1954 to 1986. This is an extract from his autobiography* Listening for a Midnight Tram. *He died in 1997.*

My first impressions of Margaret Thatcher were mixed. She did not seem quite as attractive as her pictures suggested. Indeed she gave me at my first meeting with her the impression of being entirely asexual. Nor was I over-impressed with her as an intellectual.

If I had thought Margaret Thatcher lacked sex appeal that first time I met her, my views were to change in time. So were those of many others. Of course there were some who had always found her sexy. Douglas Clark, when Political Editor of the *Sunday Express* attended a Tory conference at Blackpool when she was Minister of Education in Heath's government. After a night of drinking with delegates in the various hotel bars and reception rooms he retired to his bedroom in a jolly mood and still not ready for his sleep. Suddenly he found himself thinking of Margaret Thatcher and in a mad impulse picked up his bedside telephone and asked to be connected to her room. When a sleepy and utterly virtuous Margaret Thatcher answered she gave a very dusty answer indeed to his suggestion that she might care to come to his room for a nightcap.

As the years passed Margaret Thatcher's sex appeal actually increased. Jim Prior told me once how one or two ministers had, as he inelegantly put it, tried unsuccessfully to get a leg over. Which proves, I suppose, the truth of the old adage that power is the greatest aphrodisiac of all. Margaret came to the dinner given by Victor Matthews at the Ritz to celebrate my twenty-fifth anniversary as Editor of the *Sunday Express* in November 1979. Ted Heath had shared our table. Not long afterwards I asked Margaret why she would not have him in the Cabinet. I pointed out that it might lessen her difficulties enormously. She looked at me and replied: 'I couldn't. He wouldn't want to sit there as a member of the team. All the time he would be trying to take over. I have to tell you this, John. When I look at him and he looks at me I don't feel that it is a man looking at a woman. More like a woman looking at another woman.' Poor Ted.

In 1981 I was asked to broadcast a six-minute talk on any subject I pleased. I chose Margaret Thatcher. I related a few stories. It was the first Sunday after the 1979 general election. The scene was Chequers and the new Prime Minister was giving lunch to the principal members of her Cabinet, some of them accompanied by their wives. The girls who were serving at table, all of them members of the Women's Royal Naval Service, were perhaps just a little understandably nervous. The main course was a leg of lamb on a salver. As one of the Wrens was threading between the guests, catastrophe arrived. The lamb skidded off, landed on Sir Geoffrey Howe's shoulder and spattered his Sunday best suit and tie in gravy. Mrs Thatcher was instantly on her feet. She ran round the table, not to give comfort to Sir Geoffrey but to the Wren. Putting her arms around her, she said: 'Don't worry dear. Don't worry. It could happen to anyone.'

A second story concerns her driver George Newell, who had died from a heart attack at the age of sixty-two. His funeral was in Eltham on a Friday in a week that had been a crisis week for the Prime Minister. The easiest thing in the world would have been for her to send a representative. But no. She went herself. She sat in a pew comforting the widow. And she tried her damnedest to prevent the story of her kind act getting any publicity at all.

My third story concerns a young member of her staff whose wife had left him, taking their children with her. It was three days before Christmas. He was in the depths of despair at the thought of having to spend Christmas on his own. Then the telephone rang. It was the Prime Minister. 'Are you doing anything for Christmas?' she asked. 'If not, why don't you come and spend it with Denis, Carol, Mark and myself?' For she had known the desperation of his loneliness. And cared.

After making the broadcast Margaret was good enough to write and thank me. 'Bless you for all the nice things you say and they came just at the right time.' It was a warm gesture to make. But then that is the kind of gesture Margaret Thatcher always made.

Sir Gerald Howarth
Conservative MP 1983–97 and 2001–

Gerald Howarth was elected MP for Cannock in 1983 and served until 1987. He became MP for Aldershot in 2001. He was a Defence Minister from 2010 to 2012.

In February 1991, just two months after the pygmies in the Tory Party knifed her, I became *de facto* PPS to Mrs T. after her official PPS, Peter Morrison, had turned his attention to other pursuits. I lost my Staffordshire seat of Cannock and Burntwood in June 1992, but continued to call in to see Mrs T. at her new office in Chesham Place.

As is well known, she became more and more hostile to the Maastricht Treaty to which John Major ('the man from Coldharbour Lane' as she regularly called him) had signed up. One day, I enquired casually what her plans were for the forthcoming weekend. She replied that she was visiting Paris to dine with French President François Mitterrand.

She continued with that steely, emphatic determination with which so many had already become familiar, 'I am going to tell President Mitterrand that if he signs the Maastricht Treaty *"France est mort"'* – effectively meaning that as a nation state 'France is dead'. My rather limited knowledge of French emboldened me to suggest that '*La France est morte*' would be more grammatically correct and therefore more effective. She then proceeded to rehearse the line.

I was not present at the dinner, but on the following Monday the President of France announced that there would be a referendum on the Maastricht Treaty – eventually approved by a margin of less than 1 per cent. I am sure that the combination of the powerful message conveyed in Mrs T.'s best French and the deployment of that same feminine charm which won from the King of Saudi Arabia the UK's largest ever defence contract, resulted in France holding the referendum the UK should have had. This year the French people heeded La Dame de Fer's message and rejected the EU Constitution.

After losing my seat in 1992 in Cannock and Burntwood, I was told that if I did not distance myself from Margaret Thatcher, I would never get a seat again. However, I had a wonderful letter from Enoch Powell who said, 'My Dear Gerald, Hard luck but be of good cheer. Fidelity to persons or to principles is seldom unrewarded.' Thank you to the people of Aldershot who rewarded me by offering me the first seat that came up after the 1992 general election, which I think rather worried No. 10 at the time. I have not changed my principles; I have been a supporter of Margaret Thatcher from the very first time she put her name forward to be leader of our party and I do not regret that. I think she has been the salvation of the nation, and that she restored our position in the world.

None of us can forget Margaret Thatcher's extraordinary elegance. I remember coming to the Chamber during an all-night sitting. It was four o'clock in the morning, people had had a bit to drink and, for us chaps, there was a bit of stubble and it was really pretty unpleasant. I was sitting on the front bench wondering when this purgatory was going end, and then there was a frisson at the back of the Chair. All of a sudden, in walked the Prime Minister, not a hair out of place, handbag there, smiling. We sort of slid up the bench and looked at the Prime Minister, saying, 'Here I am.' She was an inspiration to us all and she inspired huge loyalty. When I asked Bob Kingston, her personal protection officer, what it was like working for her, he said, 'I would catch bullets between my teeth to save that woman.'

The soldiers whom Margaret Thatcher so admired reciprocated and admired her. I was at the Painted Hall for the twenty-fifth anniversary of the Falklands campaign. A lot of people who had been injured, either mentally or physically, were there. When Margaret Thatcher got up to leave, there was the most astonishing roar from men who had been maimed, cheering their warrior leader who had instructed them to go into battle and they wanted to pay tribute to her.

As people have said, Margaret Thatcher showed immense kindness. In my case, when Neil Hamilton and I faced extinction after we were defamed by the BBC *Panorama* programme, it took a bit of time to see the Chairman of the party – who happened to be Norman Tebbit – but only a couple of days to see the Prime Minister. She listened for twenty-five minutes and at the end she turned to the Chief Whip, John Wakeham, and said, 'These are members of our party in good standing. Please ensure that they get the necessary support.' We got that support. We won our libel action and the director general of the BBC was fired, and as a result of Margaret Thatcher's kindness, we were able to resume our political careers.

Baroness Shephard
Conservative Peer

Gillian Shephard was Conservative MP for South West Norfolk from 1987 to 2005. She served as a Social Security Minister under Margaret Thatcher and from 1992 to 1997 was a member of John Major's Cabinet. She was raised to the peerage in 2005.

It was the day of a No. 10 reception. Conservative Prime Ministers used to hold these after Buckingham Palace garden parties, when spouses were likely to be in London.

When we arrived, Tom and I became conscious of a number of meaningful glances and smiles from the Chief Whip, David Waddington. Although the air was thick with reshuffle gossip, I had no clue that his demeanour and my future were linked. Eventually, however, he came over and said, 'The Prime Minister would like a word with you,' and showed me into a small sitting room. In swept Mrs Thatcher, resplendent in party gear.

'Dear,' she said (her usual form of address when she was not quite sure of your name – always called me 'dear') 'I want to bring you into the government and you will be going into the job I began with, Under Secretary of State at the Department of Social Security. There is a lot of detail to master, it is important to do that. You will be working for Tony Newton, as John Moore is leaving the government. Now you had better get back to your husband.'

Amazed, I crept back into the reception, where I found Tom deep in conversation with Mark Thatcher. 'I just called in, only to find Ma shuffling,' he said, irreverently, I thought, in the circumstances. Within seconds the Chief Whip bounded up and within a few seconds more the whole room knew. It was a memorable way to get one's first government job – I did not realise at the time that doing it in this way merely saved the Prime Minister some time on the following day – and such was her professionalism, she gave no hint either.

However, the next day, I arrived at the office, wondering what to do next, only to find (it was 8.30 a.m.) that No. 10 had already been on to my constituency secretary, my office and my Norfolk house. Cowed, and thinking that it had been a very short ministerial career, I rang No. 10. 'Dear,' said Mrs Thatcher, 'Just to be quite clear and confirm what I said last night,' and went on to re-state her offer. She added, 'If I were you, I would get straight on round to the department – there's sure to be plenty to do.'

I did, giving officials the shock of their lives and forcing the very genial Permanent Secretary to spend the next hour with me while my predecessor packed his bags for the Home Office.

You cannot, after all, have two ministers in one job at the same time.

In the early 1980s, ministers and, in particular, the Prime Minister, were followed by demonstrators wherever they went. When Mrs Thatcher visited Norfolk County Hall, she swept in in a motorcade. The statutory demonstrators let loose all their tomatoes and eggs at the first two or three cars, only to be dumbfounded, not to say enraged, by the sight of Mrs Thatcher, unscathed and waving from the fifth car.

It seemed to me to be such a good tactic that I recommended it to Martine Aubry when she, as my opposite number, the French Employment Minister, was similarly dogged by demonstrators. She thought it a great wheeze and said she would adopt it too. History does not relate the French outcome.

Lech Wałęsa
President of Poland 1990–95

Lech Wałęsa is a Nobel Peace Prize winner and the founder of the Polish trade union, Solidarity. Following the collapse of communism he became Poland's first democratically elected President.

When I look back upon those momentous days of the late 1980s, the liberation of Eastern Europe from communism, I know that Solidarity started something at the Gdansk shipyards that triggered a domino effect of change behind the Iron Curtain.

Without Solidarity it would not have been possible. And Solidarity's strength came, quite literally, from solidarity – from the determination of Poles to stand together in a common struggle: workers and intellectuals, believers and non-believers, young and old. That was the first step to victory.

But on its own it would not have been enough. Without Solidarity's friends in Britain, the changes we wanted to achieve would not have been possible. Because for us it was also vital to know that our fight had the support of the democratic world. Margaret Thatcher's support was crucial. She had always been among our friends, and in those dark days she showed it.

In 1988 we were very weak after years of fighting under martial law. We needed help. Then Margaret Thatcher came to visit me and Solidarity's other leaders in Gdansk.

It was strange, our first meeting, because I had heard about her strong character and I rather wondered what she would make of a trade unionist like me. After all, I knew that she had had a difficult time with the unions in Britain. But what came through was her good spirit and decisiveness. Beyond any ideology, she had respect for human dignity and respect for democracy.

She knew very well what our union was all about. She knew it was more than simply a workers' rights organisation, that at its heart it was a movement to secure freedom for millions of people. In our battle this was the only thing that mattered, and so that first meeting between us was a real building block of freedom and democracy.

Back then we were serious, because the enemy was so dangerous. Now, however, I am able to look back at my ease. I am grateful for the memories of Margaret Thatcher. I will always admire her class and tenacity.

Sir Bernard Ingham
Press Secretary to Margaret Thatcher

Sir Bernard Ingham was a journalist who then served as Press Secretary to Labour Cabinet ministers including Tony Benn and Barbara Castle. In 1980 he was recruited to be the Prime Minister's official spokesman in No. 10 Downing Street.

It was one late winter's evening when Margaret Thatcher proclaimed to me the triumph of capitalism over communism. We were in a supermarket in north Moscow on her memorable 1987 trip to the Soviet Union. It was as empty as its shelves. All she could find to buy were a few tins of sardines for Wilberforce, the No. 10 cat.

If her views on communism's retail failure ever reached Mikhail Gorbachev, he certainly got his own back the next evening at the Bolshoi theatre. At the interval, they retired for a private supper and fell to arguing, their favourite pastime. They went on so long that we officials went in search of them as the audience chattered away in the dark waiting for them to return to their box.

As they emerged, bantering, Thatcher introduced me, her Press Secretary, to the Soviet leader as 'the man who keeps the British press in order'. Quick as a flash, through the interpreter, Gorbachev retorted: 'But I thought you said the British press was free and independent.' For probably the only time in her life she was lost for words. I laughingly filled the vacuum: 'Altogether too free and independent for my liking, sir.' Gorbachev chuckled. He had scored a point.

This was one of the two great diplomatic relationships Thatcher formed in her eleven years in No. 10. It was far more unlikely than her bond with Ronald Reagan. It began at Chequers in 1984 with her telling him straight: 'I hate communism.' And it was sealed a few hours later when, after an afternoon's debate with him before a log fire, she proclaimed Gorbachev to be 'a man I can do business with'.

Who would have thought that this tactless champion of freedom – this person who thought and told Gorbachev communism brought neither justice nor prosperity to the people – would enjoy such fun and reward in the Kremlin? Within five years the Iron Curtain had collapsed.

But that was Thatcher. She was a politician with the courage to follow her instincts. And she never ceased to find a way forward to a better world, not by smarm or flattery but by a fierce determination. She could, in fact, be a very uncomfortable friend, though all my memories of her are happy ones. Indeed, she thought you were not much of a friend if you were not unfailingly candid.

Reagan came to recognise, all too often, her wearing ways. She was second to none in her support for the President of the US as leader of the free world. But she gave him some handbaggings over his initial reluctance to support the UK over the Falklands, his invasion of Grenada in the Caribbean and his offer to Gorbachev to ditch nuclear weapons.

'Has he gone mad?' she asked when she heard of the nuclear offer at a Reykjavik summit. Afterwards, she flew the Atlantic 'to wash his head', as the Foreign Office put it, at a memorable Camp David summit.

Both Reagan and Gorbachev could recognise constancy and integrity when they saw it. It is one of the triumphs of her personality that this woman from a relatively small island came with Reagan, Gorbachev and, I believe, the Polish Pope, John Paul II, to play such an important role in liberating Russia from communism.

Thatcher was also blessed with an ability to exist on little sleep – four hours a night seemed to be the weekday average – a robust constitution and a loyal, ever-supportive husband, Denis, who brought a certain earthiness to her life after her strict Methodist upbringing.

When the lights kept going out in Goa during a Commonwealth conference in 1983, he charged on to the veranda of their bungalow, next to Indira Gandhi's, and addressed the Fort Aguada hotel complex in the following terms: 'This bloody place is high on the buggeration factor.'

Denis also enabled me to compile the Thatcher scale of drinks in ascending order of alcoholic potency: opener, brightener, lifter, tincture, large gin and tonic without tonic, snifter, snort, snorter and a snorterino, which more or less emptied the bottle in one go.

He was as much his own man as she was her own woman, but he knew his place. In a way he offered her the candid support that she gave to world statesmen.

I shall remember her for predominantly four things. First, her purpose – a resurgent, striving, go-ahead Britain that brought a power for good to the world. She was above all a patriot.

Second, her boundless courage in persevering for seven years with her economic policies before she felt able to say they were working; facing down the IRA; recovering the Falklands and seeking without sanctions but by sheer force of personality an end to apartheid and the release of Nelson Mandela.

Third, her indifference to criticism if she thought she was right, as she usually did. She never aspired to be loved.

The week of her death showed how she came to be respected, not least paradoxically by those celebrating her death. If she had not counted for something, they would not have bothered.

Finally, there was her personal kindness. When my wife was run over by a runaway lorry in Croydon in the middle of the Falklands campaign, she made it clear she expected to see a lot less of me until Nancy recovered.

Then I sent a pregnant press officer – Colleen Harris, a lovely girl from Guyana, who became Prince Charles's Press Secretary – on a prime ministerial visit to Bradford. When it turned wintry, Colleen ended up cosseted on the back seat of Thatcher's car for the drive back to No. 10.

Thatcher wasn't just a pretty face. She was tough as old boots with an iron will, a truly disconcerting directness and not much sense of humour. She was a remarkable human being. Complex yet as readable as a book. The Iron Lady with a heart. A one-off job.

Michael Reagan
Conservative Writer and Broadcaster

Michael Reagan is the son of former US President Ronald Reagan and is an author and commentator on conservative issues in the US.

Margaret Thatcher is most famous for teaming up with my father Ronald Reagan and Pope John Paul II to peacefully end the Cold War and bring about the collapse of the Soviet Union.

But at home, the 'Iron Lady's' intellect, political will and love of freedom and capitalism also saved Britain from its long, slow death by socialism.

Prime Minister Thatcher freed up Britain's economy by deregulating business, privatising government-owned industries and breaking the back of the powerful unions that were smothering her country to death.

I'll never forget meeting Lady Thatcher several times in London and in the United States. But my greatest memory of her occurred in 2004 when, despite being very ill, she attended my father's funeral at the Reagan Library.

The morning after the funeral, as I was eating at the hotel with my family, I greeted Lady Thatcher when she came in for breakfast.

'Oh, Michael,' she said in that great accent of hers. 'Think of how much we could have accomplished if your father had been elected in 1976, not 1980.'

'Lady Thatcher,' I said with the greatest respect, 'I think God chooses the time for many of the things that happen in the world. And 1976 wasn't that time; 1980 in fact was.'

'Why would you say that?' she said.

'Simply because I look at 1976 and I say, "Where was Margaret Thatcher? Where was Pope John Paul II? Where were Lech Wałęsa and Helmut Kohl and Mikhail Gorbachev?" In 1976 none of you were in positions of power to do anything.'

'But 1980 was the right time,' I said to Lady Thatcher.

'You were Prime Minister. Pope John Paul was Pope. And you had a man in Washington DC, who understood freedom. Because you were all in positions of power in 1980 you were all able to work for the betterment of the world.'

'Oh, Michael,' Lady Thatcher said, 'I didn't think of that. You're right.'

Because Ronald Reagan was elected in 1980, his legacy and the legacy of Margaret Thatcher will be tied together forever – thank God. And though the Iron Lady and my father have both passed away, their legends – and historic accomplishments – never will.

Cynthia Crawford
Personal Assistant to Margaret Thatcher

Cynthia Crawford, known as 'Crawfie', was Personal Assistant to Lady Thatcher from 1978 onwards. They became best friends.

I didn't meet Thatcher until the day I started work for her, which was 10 September 1978, when I went to the House of Commons as a package deal with David Wolfson. He was on the board of Great Universal Stores and was trying to help her to win the election.

Our relationship sort of built up. She won the election and we went to Downing Street. I was working in the political office, doing whatever came along. I soon started to travel with her. We built up a rapport. It probably came about because I didn't have to rush home to cook an evening meal for my husband. (He was living in Worcester. I wasn't with him during the week.) I could stay on and perhaps do something with her in the evening, chat to her or help her sort out her wardrobe. I came home every weekend and she went to Chequers. She was always very sensitive to people who had families. She used to say: 'Well, you must go home, dear.'

Mine was a supportive role. I was there to make sure her personal life went smoothly. We used to have meetings before every trip. She and I would sit down with the programme and decide what she would wear at each event.

In 1987 she was going to Russia for the first time and I had seen a wonderful coat in Aquascutum's window and I went to get it. A lot of her clothes up until that time had been homemade by a lady. She made all those dresses and blouses with bows and things. Mrs Thatcher went to Russia and she looked absolutely fabulous. I said to her: 'If you are going to fight an election in June, why don't we ask Aquascutum to make you up some working suits.' She agreed, so we ordered these suits. It was when the power shoulders were in and it just revolutionised her. She looked fantastic. She enjoyed all the new outfits and got away from the dresses. She never wears trousers. She always likes formal clothes, even at home.

Because her mother was a dressmaker she knew exactly how things should be made, how hems should be turned and how stitching should be done.

Every outfit had a name. It was mostly the name of the place where it was first worn, such as Madrid Pink or Prague Green. We might say, 'We'll take Waddesdon Navy' – because she had several suits in navy. Waddesdon was where she took Mitterrand, and they had a wonderful meal. We knew we were talking about a navy suit that had a trim of a cream collar with navy roses.

I wouldn't hesitate to say, 'You can't go out in that' or 'Your makeup isn't right' or 'Your hair looks a mess'. I wouldn't hesitate. I mean, your best mates tell you, don't they?

We had a few arguments. I usually lost. Not yelling, she didn't yell. Not about politics. It was about domestic things. She was very forthright and determined about her views.

I think she enjoyed being with her political chums more than anything. She had very few close friends; a sister, of course, but few best friends.

The Falklands War showed her in her real colours. I used to stay at Downing Street with her, and we used to sit up all night listening to the World Service. We used to sit on the bedroom floor – the heating would have gone off and there was a two-bar electric fire in the bedroom – kick our shoes off and relax. When she went up to Northwood for the briefing every day, I used to go to bed, but she didn't. She had practically no sleep for three months. Just catnapping. She was so incredibly strong and determined. Not once did she flag.

At Christmas 1988 my husband was knocked down in the road. I had to come straight home. The next day was the Lockerbie disaster. It was a horrific day. Even that night she phoned me to see how my husband was. She was always very sympathetic. I said: 'Look, you mustn't ring me because you have had such a terrible day yourself' but she said, 'No, I wanted to know how things were.' I don't think it ever came across during her premiership that she had this soft, sympathetic side. It was always that she was the Iron Lady.

When the Brighton bomb went off, everybody was in a terrible state. We were all just packing up. I think it went off at 2.50 a.m. Somebody said: 'What are we going to do with the speech that she was due to give the next day?' We decided we would put it in the handbag – that was the safest place. Anything that was highly secretive or precious, we would put in her handbag because we knew she was never parted from it.

We went to the police station first, then to the police training place at Lewes. We shared a room. I can see it now. It had an avocado bathroom suite. We said a prayer and we lay down, but we didn't sleep. And, of course, we went back to the hall and she did her speech. It was a very strange and strained night.

In 1990, when she didn't get the vote in the leadership contest, we sat up all night in Paris. She had to go to Versailles after hearing that news and she said she would fight on. When we were leaving for Paris, I had gone to see Denis and said that hopefully we would come back with the right result. But he said to me, 'She is done for now.' I went to Paris and I never whispered a word of it to anybody. When she found him to say that she hadn't got it, but she was going to fight on, he still supported her.

She used to read the odd thriller, especially on holiday. But she was always hungry for news. Whenever we travelled, we had CNN on nonstop. On Saturdays at Chequers, Denis used to insist that she sat down after dinner and they used to like to watch *Miss Marple*. She was very interested in the garden at Chequers and Downing Street. She put in some lovely rose beds. She didn't do it physically herself, but she took a great interest in it. And the art. When she became PM she brought in a lot of traditional art: Turners and a Henry Moore. She was always a very neat person, so she would always spend a little time tidying her wardrobes and cleaning her shoes. That would be relaxation for her.

Her sense of humour was very, very dry. In fact, so dry you could miss it. She wasn't known for her sense of humour. She lived a very serious life and conversation – well, there was no small talk. She loved discussing politics. She and Ronnie Reagan had this great rapport about politics. She admired him beyond words – and Gorbachev. She would always say how much she admired him and what he had done for the world, and he adored her. He had a soft voice and he used to talk to her in a wonderful way. Gorbachev was a bit of a flirt, actually, the eyes would be flashing a bit. She didn't mind that, I mean, nobody minds a bit of flattery, do they?

When I read something about her in the newspapers that I knew was incorrect, I felt very annoyed for her. She tended to take those sorts of things far more on the chin. She also never wanted somebody patting her on the back every five minutes because she knew herself that she had done her level best. I think her father instilled that in her. Do your very, very best and never follow the crowd. That was her personal policy.

I would defend her to the last because she was a complete star in my life. I learned a lot from her, and I tried to do all I could for her. She taught me lots of things, including that you should only do one job at a time and concentrate completely. Whether she was writing a speech or tidying a drawer, it had her total concentration. She taught me that.

I think she did a lot for the women of this country and I know that she worked her socks off for the country. She did her utmost for Britain. I don't think she ever got over the way in which she was deposed by her own party and her own colleagues. It still rankled, and there is no doubt that with the possible exception of Churchill, she was the greatest Prime Minister of the last century. In my book, she was the greatest Prime Minister.

Baroness Warsi
Conservative Peer

Sayeeda Warsi stood for Parliament in Dewsbury in 2005. She was raised to the peerage in 2007. She was Conservative Party Co-Chairman from 2010 to 2012 and is now a minister in the Foreign Office.

My personal memories of Baroness Thatcher began in a living room in West Yorkshire and ended on the benches of the House of Lords.

I was born in the early 1970s. It was a time of unrest and instability. And I remember, quite clearly, watching a woman on TV come to No. 10 to, quite simply, sort things out.

My mother actually voted for Mrs Thatcher – a real leap of faith for someone from a minority community living in the north of England, and therefore not your traditional Tory.

But Mum's faith in Mrs T. paid off for our family. As Prime Minister, she unleashed enterprise, enabling my father to quit his job as a cabbie and bus driver and start his own business.

Mrs Thatcher said in a 1985 speech that 'a new resilience derived from diversity can only strengthen Britain'. Her policies certainly backed that belief, with her emphasis on hard work, fairness, responsibility and opportunity helping people like my family to get on in life.

By the 1990s, when her days at No. 10 were over, I recall Mrs Thatcher for another reason: her stance on the war in Bosnia. While the world dithered, there was one decisive voice: that of our former Prime Minister, entreating the international community to 'act now'. In 1992, she foresaw a brutal massacre. Three years later, when Bosnian Serbs committed genocide in Srebrenica, she was proved correct. This, for me was a defining, if overlooked, moment in her career.

In the late 2000s I was appointed to the House of Lords, where I had the honour of sitting on the red benches alongside Baroness Thatcher. But it wasn't the fearsome, forthright Iron Lady I came across; it was a gentle and kind figure who enjoyed chatting with me about the shalwar kameez I was wearing. I wonder if she truly knew that I was only there because of the opportunity she had given Britons, and the inspiration she had given me.

Kate Adie
Journalist

Kate Adie was chief news correspondent for the BBC and has reported from war zones all over the world. This is an extract from her autobiography The Kindness of Strangers.

We spent days camped outside various chateaux during summit meetings, and lived in fear of having to interview Mrs Thatcher, mainly because none of us understood the intricacies of EU funding, and our diffident questions were lawnmowered as she raced over the ungrateful ground of Europe. Trevor McDonald and I were waiting in line when she devoured a young reporter from independent radio, who'd had his daisy-head chopped off in the first answer so proceeded to what he thought was safer territory.

'It's Easter this weekend.'

'Yes?' said Mrs Thatcher, challengingly.

'Will you be taking a holiday?'

'Holiday? Holiday?!' The reporter cringed. The Prime Minister looked as if she'd been asked if she'd be spending a few days in a brothel.

'WHAT'S THE POINT OF A HOLIDAY?' she bellowed to anyone who cared to listen. Silence followed, and Trevor and I edged out of the room, unwilling to be masticated.

Francis Maude

Conservative MP 1983–92 and 1997–

Francis Maude was Conservative MP for North Warwickshire from 1983 until 1992 and then re-entered Parliament in 1997 as MP for Horsham. He was Minister for Europe at the end of the Thatcher government. He now serves in David Cameron's government as Cabinet Office minister.

Margaret Thatcher dominated my early political life. My father had been one of her first adherents, worked very closely with her in opposition, and served in her first Cabinet. So it was a special thrill for me to be asked to serve as one of her ministers when I was a young MP in my thirties.

She was exciting to work for. She usually had complete mastery of her brief, and was fierce with people who didn't. Always much more pragmatic than the ideological caricature suggests, she liked a discussion and relished a debate. What she demanded was for her colleagues to be on top of their brief, and to make things happen. I recall a vigorous meeting on electricity privatisation, when I, to my horror, as a 33-year-old found myself alone in a meeting with the Prime Minister, Chancellor and the Energy and Scottish Secretaries. I had the temerity to challenge what she and Cecil Parkinson were proposing and promptly got handbagged for my pains. I recall to this day the swift inner debate – do I subside in a quivering heap, or get up and get stuck in? Luckily I did the latter, and earned her respect as a result. (And ultimately on the specific issue I was proved right...)

Being in her favour could result in irritating one's colleagues. I remember a Commons speech on Europe that disappeared into the famous handbag to be pulled out at regular intervals, waved at ministers with the words: 'THIS is what you should be saying! Read Francis's speech!' Unlikely to make me popular with my colleagues.

In British politics she was a Titan, eclipsing all the rest. As a Prime Minister she was quite literally world-changing. Alongside Reagan she stood up to the forces of communism, determined to see liberty return across Europe. At home she was tough, decisive and passionate. Yet she was also kind and compassionate, despite her iron image. When my baby son was taken frighteningly ill she took the time to write to me and my wife by hand, later remembered and always asked after him. It was a touching example of how much she genuinely cared for the welfare of those around her.. And she did this while she was leading the country at a time of great stress.

She transformed Britain from a basket case to a world-leader. The 'Sick Man of Europe', brought low by the 'British disease', became the destination of choice for investors keen to put their ideas and money to work. Under Thatcher, a divided country learned to stand proud again.

To this day I remain a passionate Thatcherite: sensibly Eurosceptic, a fiscal conservative believing fiercely in sound money, an economic liberal committed to free markets, believing we're a stronger country when we have a big society and a small state. I've become more socially liberal since then, as Britain itself has. But she, while believing strongly in the importance of the family, was never censorious about people's private lives.

Politics is often called the art of the impossible. Yet Margaret Thatcher never accepted that. She would not listen to naysayers and those who said 'it can't be done'. She wanted to know how it can be done. The lesson for us? Do what you believe in. Don't take no for an answer. Press ahead. Argue your case. Believe in ourselves and our country; and the British people will believe in themselves and in their country.

And for me at the end? Relief that the funeral arrangements which I coordinated came together. Pride in a very British ceremony that did full justice to one of Britain's very greatest Prime Ministers ever. And a tearful farewell to a world-changing statesman, a force of nature and a wonderful lady who shaped my political life.

Sue Cameron
Journalist

Sue Cameron is a former presenter of Channel Four's A Week in Politics. *She writes for the* Daily Telegraph.

A story about Margaret Thatcher's innocence is told by Charles Powell, her long-time friend and foreign affairs adviser. Lord Powell says she was most indignant when a colleague was accused of having 'Ugandan relations'. Unaware that this was a euphemism for bonking, she said she knew for a fact that the man had never been to Uganda in his life.

Her naivety could be embarrassing. As Leader of the Opposition she was up against Jim Callaghan, and at one shadow Cabinet meeting she launched a tirade against the Labour PM. 'Jim Callaghan couldn't organise pussy!' she cried. The men around the table looked at each other, some rolling their eyes and one or two sniggering behind their hands. But there was an unspoken agreement to let the matter rest.

To their consternation she repeated the phrase – word for word – the following week and her shadow ministers realised that unless they stopped her she would come out with it in public. Explaining why she couldn't use it was not easy. I'm told the conversation went like this:

'Margaret, you really mustn't say that about Callaghan – it could be misinterpreted.'

'Misinterpreted?' she asked in puzzled tones. 'How misinterpreted?'

'Well, the word pussy has more than one meaning – it's a double entendre.'

'Double entendre? What double entendre?'

'Well, it can be taken to refer to the anatomy.'

'Anatomy? Whose anatomy?'

'Part of the female anatomy.'

'Part? What part?'

'An unmentionable part!'

Keith Simpson
Conservative MP for Broadland 1997–

Keith Simpson was elected MP for Mid Norfolk in 1997 and is now PPS to the
Foreign Secretary, William Hague. He is also a military historian and sits on the
Commonwealth War Graves Commission.

I was appointed Special Adviser to George Younger, Secretary of
State for Defence, in May 1988. In July, John Whittingdale, Margaret
Thatcher's Political Secretary, wrote to all the Spads inviting them to a
meeting with her in Downing Street on 3 October just before the party
conference. In John's words, 'It is a three-line whip with no bisques!'

The previous meeting between Margaret Thatcher and the Spads
had been a year before and when I asked them what it was like, it
became apparent that it was something that filled them with both
apprehension – because she really grilled them over policy – and
expectation – because it was a privilege to have such an opportunity
with a very busy Prime Minister.

I took advice from Andrew Dunlop, my predecessor at the MoD and
then in the Policy Unit, and Archie Hamilton, who had been her PPS
and was now Minister of State for the Armed Forces. Both emphasised
that you had to be on top of your brief, to expect to be interrupted
and challenged and under no circumstances to be overwhelmed by her
questions and sheer verbal firepower.

The civil servants in George Younger's private office were filled with
foreboding. I was told that while she admired the armed forces and
placed a high priority on defence of the realm, she believed the MoD
was profligate, incompetent and hopeless at procuring weapons and
equipment. I was told that on my shoulders rested the reputation of
my Secretary of State, the MoD and not least my own future. Gulp!

Classically, George Younger was relatively relaxed about the meeting and said he assumed I would be well briefed and would know how
to deal with her – 'Good luck.'

I knew that the Prime Minister would quiz me about defence budget
overruns and the cost of a new weapon including a replacement main

battle tank for the army where the choice was between the German Leopold, the American Abrahams and the British Challenger. I had read a note by Charles Powell from her private office about her recent meeting with the Chairman of Vickers, who was lobbying for Challenger. She told him she was fed up buying British equipment that didn't work. He replied that his tanks were made under warranty.

Cometh the day, cometh the trial. Late on the afternoon of 3 October all the Spads, about a dozen of us, gathered in the Cabinet room with John Whittingdale, her Political Secretary, and Robin Harris, Director of the Conservative Research Department. Charles Powell moved in the wings. The Prime Minister came in and my immediate reaction was to think she looked tired, frail and somewhat bowed. She fiddled with her necklace and the neck of her jacket all the time. But any first impression of frailty and tiredness was soon swept away as the meeting began. She told us that she wanted to hear what we were putting into our ministers' speeches for the party conference, what were the main issues in our departments, and what ideas we had for the future. She emphasised the need to control public expenditure and emphasised the role of the individual as against the state. She was quite pessimistic about public borrowing and credit, and in a swipe at the Treasury said if we were a Labour government critics would have a field day.

Then the inquisition began as she went round the table questioning Spad after Spad about ministerial plans and policies. I was fascinated to observe how my colleagues dealt with her aggressive line of questions and continual interruptions. The Treasury Spads were over-confident and rather arrogant initially, but soon retired hurt. Despite their valiant efforts Spads at Transport, Health and Social Services were brushed aside. Patrick Rock at Environment and Anthony Teasdale at the FCO argued their corner and were not overwhelmed by her questioning. The Cabinet table began to resemble a casualty clearing station.

Finally she came to me, and said 'You are Keith Simpson at Defence, what have you got to say for yourself?'

Perhaps with more bravura than common sense, I replied like Oliver Twist: 'We'd like some more money.'

There was a split second of total silence, then the Prime Minister in that well-known raised voice said 'MORE MONEY!' For about two minutes, although it appeared longer, she worked herself up to a splendid fury and, without pausing for breath, launched a violent attack on the MoD and all its failings – extravagant budgets, over-spends, procurement failures.

Out of the corner of my eye I could see my fellow Spads looking either very apprehensive at me having raised a whirlwind or gleeful that I was the object of so much focused fury. It was impossible to get a word in edgeways, and later I said to my wife Pepi that I'd learned in our marriage to let exhaustion come into play, and then attempt to explain my case. Briefly, I was able to point out that government policy was strong defence, she had agreed on new equipment, including a replacement tank, and that the MoD under George Younger, who had replaced Michael Heseltine – at that point a stabling glint appeared in her eye – was getting to grips with MoD failures. She merely nodded and passed on to the next Spad. The meeting ended with neither tea nor a real drink.

I left thinking that I had been well and truly chewed over. But at the door the Prime Minister stopped me, and to my surprise said I had argued my case very well and that she valued robust debate.

It took about ten minutes to get back to the ministerial floor in the MoD opposite Downing Street. I was greeted by members of the private office all waiting and tearing their clothes, saying how could I have got into an argument with the Prime Minister, what was I thinking of, the reputation for the MoD was irreparably damaged. It was fascinating to think that all over Whitehall, private offices had been in contact with No. 10 to find out what had happened at the Spads meeting.

Later I told George Younger about what had happened and he roared with laughter, saying it was a good learning experience, and now I realised what Cabinet ministers went through. Looking back on the meeting I thought what a formidable and remarkable Prime Minister she was, who after nearly ten years had command over so much policy and had clear, if at times rigid, objectives and prejudices. Certainly I had learned a lesson about 'going over the top' in the face of such a formidable politician. Perhaps I should have followed the example of Peter Luff, the Spad at the DTI, who had managed to sit in such a position that Margaret Thatcher couldn't see him and was thus never questioned. His minister, David Young, congratulated him on this achievement!

Margaret Thatcher stands with the six editions of *Time* magazine that bear her face, September 1983.

MT stands solemnly at the San Carlos cemetery remembering servicemen lost during the Falklands conflict, June 1992.

Former Tory Prime Ministers Ted Heath and MT sit impatiently at the Bournemouth party conference in October 1998.

LEFT MT gazes up at a marble statue of herself standing in the Guildhall, May 2002.

RIGHT MT with her beloved husband Denis after he had been released from hospital following heart bypass surgery, February 2003.

MT, flanked by her daughter Carol and son Mark, at Denis's funeral, June 2003.

LEFT MT sitting alone in the Lords awaiting the State Opening of Parliament, November 2003.

BELOW MT halts at the coffin of former President Ronald Reagan at his state funeral on Capitol Hill in June 2004.

LEFT MT greets the Queen as she arrives at the Mandarin Oriental in Knightsbridge to celebrate the former PM's 80th birthday, October 2005.

BELOW MT in the Royal Box watching the ladies' singles final at Wimbledon in July 2006.

LEFT MT stands beside a bronze statue of herself inside the Palace of Westminster. The statue was created by Antony Dufort, February 2007.

RIGHT MT, with then Prime Minister Gordon Brown and his wife Sarah, steps out of her old official home at 10 Downing Street, September 2007.

BELOW MT, Cherie Blair and Tony Blair at a church service to mark the 25th anniversary of the Falkland Islands' liberation at the Falkland Islands Memorial Chapel, Pangbourne College, Berkshire, June 2007.

MT with Anne
Jenkin (later
Baroness Jenkin) at
a Christmas party
in 2007.

MT meets Chelsea
Pensioners during
a visit to the Royal
Hospital Chelsea,
February 2008.

Conservative leader
David Cameron
unveils a new bust
of his predecessor,
February 2008.

LEFT MT attending the service for the Most Noble Order of the Garter at St George's Chapel, Windsor, when Prince William joined other members of the Royal Family as a Knight of the Garter, June 2008.

RIGHT MT and David Cameron meet for dinner at the Goring Hotel in Belgravia, February 2009.

MT, seated between John Major and William Hague, waits for Pope Benedict XVI to deliver a speech at Westminster Hall during the second day of his state visit, September 2010.

ABOVE MT chats intently with Conservative MP Conor Burns at Speaker's House, 2011.

LEFT MT watches schoolchildren playing football in Battersea Park. Her carer and housekeeper Kate sits next to her, March 2012.

Peter Lilley
Conservative MP 1983–

Peter Lilley entered Parliament in 1983 as MP for St Albans. He was a founder member of the No Turning Back Group of Thatcherite MPs. After a succession of junior ministerial jobs he was appointed to Margaret Thatcher's Cabinet. He remained in the Cabinet until the general election defeat in May 1997.

I first worked for Mrs Thatcher as a humble speech-writer, long before I entered Parliament or became a minister and eventually joined her Cabinet. My most personal memories conflict with the caricature that has been built up over time, as much by her friends as by her opponents. First, she was immensely kind. The less important someone was, the kinder she was to them. She gave her ministers a pretty hard time, and quite right too. I remember an occasion on which she had returned from three days abroad, having had little sleep. I had been summoned, in my role as a minor cog in her speech-writing machine, to help with some speech. She tore a strip off the Chancellor of the Exchequer before noticing me. She saw that I was wearing a black tie and deduced that I had been to a funeral, and was immediately full of solicitude for me – in marked contrast to her tearing a strip off her senior minister.

Mrs Thatcher could also be remarkably diplomatic, not least in how she handled those who worked for her. As a junior Treasury minister, I once ventured to disagree with a policy of a Secretary of State, and we were both summoned to appear before her to argue our respective cases. I thought my arguments were overwhelmingly the better ones, but she summed up in favour of the Secretary of State. Subsequently, she sent me a private message saying, 'Peter, I was impressed by your arguments but it would have been quite wrong for me to overrule a senior minister in favour of a junior minister on a matter that was not of paramount importance.' She was right.

One of the greatest myths about Mrs Thatcher is that she didn't listen. People jumped to that conclusion because she did not respond to their ideas with some bland remark like, 'How very interesting.'

Instead, she argued with people to test their ideas to destruction. But if the ideas could withstand her assault she took them on board. I remember the Thatcherite No Turning Back Group of MPs inviting her to discuss our draft plans for schools. She tore them to pieces; we counter-argued and she laid into those arguments too. When she left, even some of her strongest devotees were saying, 'It is true, she doesn't listen. Our arguments were much more convincing than hers.' Those of us who knew her said, 'Don't worry, we won the argument. She knows we won so she will be giving hell to whoever briefed her.' Sure enough, she took most of our proposals on board in the manifesto and implemented them. She had listened.

Mrs Thatcher was also very cautious, again in contrast to the legend that she recklessly took on all comers. At the expense of a humiliating settlement with Arthur Scargill in her first parliament, she deferred a confrontation in order to allow Nigel Lawson to build up coal stocks so that, should another confrontation arise – as indeed it did – the nation would not be held to ransom. Her trade union reforms were implemented progressively, step by step, and whenever she felt that she had bitten off enough for one parliament, she would politely reject proposals for further reform, however much they appealed to her. However, once she was convinced that a policy was right in principle and workable in practice, and that it had been elaborated in detail – of which she had a masterly grasp while maintaining a focus on the central issues – she would push it through with unswerving tenacity.

Lord Wilson
Civil Servant

Richard Wilson was a career civil servant and was head of the Downing Street Economic Secretariat in the late 1980s. He eventually rose to become Cabinet Secretary under Tony Blair.

I served Mrs Thatcher, for three years, from 1987 to 1990, as head of her domestic and economic secretariat under Lord Armstrong, and then under Lord Butler. It was a period of extraordinary and rapid change in so many areas: local government, with the community charge – I still cannot call it the poll tax; we were trained not to – the National Health Service, privatisation, education, with the introduction of the curriculum, the inner cities, and so on. The list felt endless.

Mrs Thatcher depended very heavily on briefing. She would use it once she came to the conclusion that she could rely upon you, and she did so very intensively so you had to get it right. There were occasions when she would disagree with one of her colleagues in a meeting. She would challenge them as to whether they were right or not on the strength of a brief. I can tell you, you learn things about the human body – your pores open in moments of stress – which I will not forget.

The other side of the coin was that she worked enormously hard; this, I am sure, is well known. We delivered lots of briefs to her in the evenings, and by the morning she would have mastered and be ready to use them to challenge with enormous skill. I remember saying to her on one occasion, 'You must have worked very late to get all this into your mind.' She said, 'Well, I find midnight is the worst. By 12.30 I get a second wind.' That, for me, captures it.

She was also very generous in the way in which she treated people who worked for her. She attributed to you qualities which you certainly did not have. I remember sitting down next to her at one meeting. She was deep in thought, and turned to me and said, 'Now, can you explain to me what a put option is?' That is quite a difficult question cold, when a lot of other ministers are coming in. On another occasion, when ministers were discussing the national curriculum, she was passionate about the importance of schoolchildren learning poetry by heart. She launched unexpectedly into some Robert Browning, which she quoted at some length. Then she could not remember what came next, and turned to me as the secretary and said, 'Now what happens?' Of course, I had not the faintest notion what happens next. It was very generous of her to think that one might know, but of course I did not.

She was also very kind, sometimes in a rather clumsy way. I was summoned on a Saturday to Chequers to explain to her a very complicated submission which I had put to her on the Friday night about how we might make the poll tax work or avoid some of the more difficult consequences which it seemed likely to have. It was really, really technically difficult. I was shown in to see her and she gave me a cup of tea. I had that in one hand and in the other she put an enormous cream bun, so covered in icing sugar that when we spoke there were clouds of it. We then had this very difficult and serious discussion while I held these two objects in my hands. It was a good meeting but it was slightly unusual.

We have heard about her caution. There were all sorts of sides to that quality. I used to be astonished by the certainty with which she felt that she knew and understood what the British people were feeling and thinking, and where they stood, whatever everyone else among her colleagues was saying or thinking.

One example which comes to mind was that a decision had been taken that the National Dock Labour Scheme should be abolished. That was being planned in great secrecy and we had reached the point where ministers were in a position to give the go-ahead. There was fear of a strike, and so on. When we met the Prime Minister, Mrs Thatcher said, 'I can see that all the plans are ready but I should say that we are not going to go ahead with this decision today. We are not going to make the announcement. It is January and it is cold and foggy. The public are depressed and have had enough bad news. This is not the right time. We will wait until the spring, when the sun and the daffodils are out, and it will be all right.' I found myself thinking, 'How do we record this?' but we recorded it and, lo and behold, the government waited until the spring and the decision went exactly as she said. It was fine, but there was a sense in which she was certain about the timing. It was all going on in her head and it was very impressive.

The other side of Mrs Thatcher, which I hope does not get overlooked, was her interest in science. I remember No. 10 organising groups of PhD or post-doctoral researchers to come and meet her. She would grill them for an afternoon and they would emerge looking exhausted, while she would look hugely refreshed by the experience of having cross-examined them on their science.

I think it was in the autumn of 1988 that, having read over the summer about climate change, she decided that it was a really big problem which people had underestimated. I am not sure that the world remembers it but she made a speech to the Royal Society – way ahead of international opinion, or opinion in this country – in which she very clearly set the problem out in scientific terms. She drew attention to the threats that it presented for future generations and the moral imperative that she felt governments had to act on it. That was a very important landmark in people realising that it was a problem. It illustrates the limitations of the power of even a great Prime Minister such as Mrs Thatcher that very little happened immediately because of it, but it is interesting that her scientific background led her to that insight.

Lord Butler, when she had finally surrendered her office to Her Majesty the Queen, gave a small impromptu party to enable some of us who had worked for her to say farewell. I remember two things about that occasion. One was that she was going round saying very intense things. I am not even sure that she entirely knew what she was saying to everyone. I remember her coming up and saying to me, 'What I always feel about problems in government is that the important thing is to work out what is the right thing to do. You may not be able to achieve it, or not immediately, but that has to be your starting point. That has to be your goal.' For me, that is what marks her out as an outstanding and extraordinary leader, perhaps above all.

The other thing I remember is the noble Lord, Lord Butler, himself saying in his speech to her, 'Prime Minister, when we are old and retired the only really interesting thing about us will be that we worked for you.' That was a lovely compliment. I certainly feel hugely privileged for having worked for her. Those are three years that I would not have missed for all the world.

Patrick Nicholls
Conservative MP 1983–2001

Patrick Nicholls served as a Parliamentary Under Secretary of State at the Department of Employment and later at the Department of the Environment. He held the seat of Teignbridge from 1983 to 2001.

On the Monday following the general election in 1987, the Under Secretaries were being appointed. Having been told I was to be responsible for trade union reform, apparently on the basis that I had been a successful divorce lawyer, I was invited to a drinks party that evening at Downing Street.

All the new Under Secretaries arrived and were standing ramrod straight with a glass of sherry waiting for the Prime Minister to come in. Uncharacteristically she was slightly late. She bustled in some ten minutes later and said, 'I have just had a meeting of the Cabinet. What a load of moaning minnies. They all said they were tired but I told them they weren't.'

A number of us saw the possibilities in this statement. Only I was rash enough to follow them up by asking, 'And when you told them they weren't tired, did they believe you Prime Minister?'

Without a trace of irony or humour she looked straight at me and said, 'Patrick, if I told them they are not tired, they are not tired.'

She was like that, Mrs Thatcher. She is sadly missed.

Baroness Miller

Conservative Peer

Doreen Miller was raised to the peerage in 1993 after serving as the Chairman of the Women into Public Life Campaign and the Chairman of Barnet Family Health Services Authority.

It is sometimes said that Margaret Thatcher did not do enough to promote the interests of women in political and public life – especially in regard to appointments to her government.

However, her attitude to women in both spheres was entirely consistent with her general political philosophy: people as well as businesses make progress according to ability; no special favours, no quotas. Market forces, if you wish.

My own personal experiences of her were quite different.

In 1979, just prior to the election, I was given the opportunity of playing a major part in the production of a pamphlet for her constituency, in the form of a newspaper called the *Finchley Leader*, one edition of which had the prescient front-page headline WE SHALL BE THE NEXT GOVERNMENT.

Time moved on, and while Prime Minister she took time to encourage the work of the 300 Group, an all-party organisation dedicated to getting more women into the House of Commons of which I was Chairman – not, you will notice, Chair or Chairwoman or Chairperson! In 1991, at the invitation of David Astor and the 300 Group she unveiled a plaque at the house where Nancy Astor lived while she was an MP.

In 1990, it was at her special request in her capacity, not as Prime Minister, but as a local MP, and with the concurrence of the other local MPs, that I became the Chairman of the Barnet Family Health Services Authority because, as she explained, since its area included her own constituency of Finchley, she regarded it as a politically sensitive appointment which was likely to be targeted by pressure groups and required someone with experience in politics as well as the organisational ability to perform the task.

This was the first of three public appointments which I have no doubt contributed to my CV coming to the notice of 'the powers that be', contributing to my elevation to the House of Lords, so I shall always be grateful for that particular nomination.

As a whip in the House of Lords, I was not responsible for the group of peers that included her. Ex-Prime Ministers get someone far more senior than the absolutely lowest office holder in the government hierarchy (because that is where government whips in the Lords stand on the organisation chart – and for a long time I was the most junior of them).

Nevertheless, as someone who had the unique opportunity of being both in touch with the government on the one side and the grass roots on the other I sometimes wanted to remind her of the contents of the current hymn sheet when, as sometimes happened, she departed from it. But how?

There is a riddle which asks, 'How does a porcupine make love?' The answer is 'Very gingerly.'

I have to say that when I tactfully and as casually as I could 'had a word', explaining what the activists in the field were thinking, she listened carefully, nodded, and continued to go about her own way. The point is that there was never any suggestion of 'Who do you think you are talking to?'

Perhaps that says something about her character and what made her the great Prime Minister that she was. There was time to hear a different opinion, but in the end it would be she who made up her own mind and her own decision.

Fortunately for this country her instincts were many more times often right than wrong.

I have no doubt that many other contributors to this collection of anecdotes, with a far closer connection to Margaret Thatcher, will be able to give a detailed picture of her in her high office.

All I can do is to speak of her as a colleague in local politics, in her little publicised capacity as a supporter of women's interests and as a member of the greatest legislative Chamber in the world that anyone can have the privilege of belonging to.

I believe that when she is judged by history – history that will be written far removed from the hurly-burly of current politics and political disputes – her many achievements for the benefit of our country will outlive the 'little local difficulties' in which she was still occasionally involved.

Nicholas Finney
Businessman

Nicholas Finney was director of the British Ports Federation and National Association of Port Employers in the late 1980s and masterminded the campaign to persuade Margaret Thatcher to abolish the Dock Labour Scheme.

In March 1984 at the start of the dispute with the National Union of Mineworkers, Margaret Thatcher was invited to the International Press Centre to receive the Aims of Industry 'National Free Enterprise Award'. In her speech thanking Aims for the award, she used the opportunity to make it clear that she was not going to bend in the event of the miners striking. She made one of her iconic statements after reminding the audience that the coal industry received over £1.3 billion in subsidies each year and that uneconomic pits must close. 'I sometimes wonder if everyone is to demand subsidies and demand even bigger subsidies, unlimited subsidies, if everyone wants to be kept, who is there to do the keeping? Who is to keep the kept?'

It is said that she had no sense of humour, but wit she certainly had. On the same occasion, right at the end, she asked to see the actual award which was the usual glass obelisk with a design on it. Peering at it she said, 'This award is a private enterprise award, but it has one sphere up here and quite a few trapped in a cage down here. That was 1975. Don't you think you could untrap a few now?' She brought the house down!

The second occasion I recall comes much later indeed, when she was no longer Prime Minister. Iain Dale and I had been invited to Australia in 1991 after the successful campaign to get rid of the National Dock Labour Scheme which was finally repealed in July 1989. The Australian Waterfront was notoriously militant and senior members of the Liberal Party, who were in opposition, wanted to see if they could devise a blueprint to implement dock work reforms when they returned to power. Our job was to help devise such a plan.

In the course of this work and during an earlier lecture tour which I had carried out, we came to know Ian McLachlan well.

Ian had previously been the President of the Australian National Farmers Federation. He was, in 1992, part of John Howard's shadow Cabinet. He was dedicated to labour reforms and much admired Margaret Thatcher.

I was rung by Ian early in 1992. He said that he was arriving in the UK in two weeks' time and he asked if Iain Dale and I could arrange for him to meet Margaret Thatcher. We desperately searched around for any opportunity that might exist before settling on an event held by Aims of Industry (them again!) at which Margaret was speaking as the principal guest.

Ian duly arrived and as usual the meeting was packed and we despaired. How would or could we reach her after her speech? Well, sheer determination and some sharp elbow work led us eventually to a spot right in front of Mrs Thatcher. 'Er, this is Ian MacLachlan. He is in the Australian opposition party who hope to form the next government.' Before Ian could say anything, Mrs Thatcher looked at him with her piercing blue eyes and said, 'Quite. And when are you going to get rid of those crooks who are running your country?' Ian was so stunned that he could barely utter a word before she was whisked away. As we led him back to the exit, it seems that his admiration for the great lady may have become slightly tarnished as he could be heard muttering, 'Bloody rude woman.'

After the successful repeal of the National Dock Labour Scheme in 1989 and the recognition that this signalled the end of dock labour's threats to the national economy, several large port authorities, classified as trust ports, wanted to complete the privatisation that had begun with the sale of the British Transport Docks Board and Sealink in the early 1980s. Two authorities, Clydeport and Tees and Hartlepool managed to promote private Bills to allow them to go private but there seemed little prospect of the government finding time for the necessary primary legislation.

Iain Dale and I were commissioned by a group of major port authorities to see if the government could be persuaded to change their mind. With four other transport measures proposed, it looked like 'Mission Impossible'. Then, out of the blue, Woodrow Wyatt rang me up and said he wanted to write an article in *The Times* which urged the government to finish off privatising the ports. I was summoned to his house in St John's Wood to give him a briefing. The article duly appeared entitled 'Harbouring a reservation'. The removal of the Dock Labour Scheme wasn't enough, he argued. The PM should push the other ports into the private sector. We were pleased but not overly optimistic. Even when Woodrow rang me after the article had been published to tell me that he had spoken to Margaret Thatcher to push the content of it – 'I ring her every Sunday morning to have a chat about the latest story' – we still didn't fancy our chances. How wrong we were.

A few weeks later in April 1990, a breathless and very excited Elizabeth Buchanan, who was then Special Adviser to Cecil Parkinson, the Secretary of State for Transport, said on the phone, 'You've done it, you've done it. You've got your Ports Bill.' After we had recovered our senses we asked her what had happened.

It seems that the Prime Minister was presiding over a Cabinet committee examining Scottish legislation. It was hard going and it was clear that Margaret Thatcher was in an irascible mood. Suddenly she put down her papers with a flourish and said, 'I have had enough of this Scottish tedium. Cecil, I want a Ports Bill!' And so that is how the further transformation of Britain's ports industry was achieved.

Michael York
Downing Street Messenger

Mrs Thatcher was very generous to the staff and made sure we were all looked after. Sometimes if it had been a very long day she asked us to eat with her. We called her the 'Mother Hen'.

When she used to walk into the private office everyone always used to stand up for her. That sort of thing doesn't happen these days.

One of my favourite memories of Mrs Thatcher came in the 1980s when I was polishing brass before Queen Elizabeth II came for a special meeting of heads of the Commonwealth at Downing Street. A figure (Mrs Thatcher's) appeared above me and I said, 'What a nice pair of legs.'

'Thank you very much Michael,' she said, and walked down the corridor laughing to herself.

Lord Renwick
Diplomat

Lord Renwick served in the Diplomatic Service in a number of ambassadorial posts including South Africa and Washington. His memoir A Journey with Margaret Thatcher: Foreign Policy Under the Iron Lady *was published in spring 2013.*

A few weeks after his release, I received a message from Nelson Mandela asking me to see him in a small private clinic in Johannesburg, where he had been admitted suffering from exhaustion. It was by then my umpteenth meeting with him. At the end of each one of these, he would urge me to consider joining the ANC. It was, he contended, a broad church and 'you think like us'. This was a debatable proposition. Each time I reminded him that, as Mrs Thatcher's envoy, I would not be able to accept his invitation. He kept insisting that I was his adviser and by now I realised that, just as he had co-opted his warder, who ended up as his batman, and the Minister of Justice, who had kept asking me to help get him released, so I too was being co-opted on to the Mandela team.

His next target for co-option was more ambitious. It was in fact the Prime Minister. The rest of the ANC held against Margaret Thatcher her opposition to further sanctions. They wanted to fight with her. Mandela held the opposite view. She was, he said, a very powerful lady, 'one I would much rather have on my side'. He wanted to know: how was he going to get her there?

The world since then has chosen to regard Mandela as a saint and he has indeed some saintly characteristics. I was no less impressed, however, by his extraordinary political cunning and adroitness in seeking to ensure that even, apparently, his most determined potential adversaries were brought over to his side.

He was about to leave on his first visit to the United States, to be followed by a meeting in London with Margaret Thatcher. I told him that we were extremely worried about his schedule in the US, where he was expected to visit seven cities in ten days. If he allowed his US hosts to do so, they would end up killing him. To give him some rest beforehand, we were arranging for him and Oliver Tambo (the ANC President) to spend a quiet weekend together in the English countryside on his way to America, a gesture enormously appreciated by Mandela.

Amid much hilarity, we then agreed to conduct a dress rehearsal for his meeting in Downing Street, with Mandela playing the role of Mandela and me that of Mrs Thatcher – one I had by then got to know quite well. 'You must stop at once all this nonsense about nationalising the banks and the mines,' I told him, on her behalf. 'But it was your idea,' Mandela replied, referring to the influence of the London School of Economics and others on budding African politicians in the 1950s. 'It was fashionable then,' he added with a smile. I replied that it definitely was not fashionable now. This was not a policy he should try defending in Downing Street. Mandela thanked me warmly for these 'tips' for his meeting with the Prime Minister.

Once in England, Mandela telephoned Mrs Thatcher before departing for the United States to thank us for arranging the weekend with Tambo, only to receive a stern lecture about his programme.

Mandela arrived back in London, as I had feared, with a chest infection and utterly exhausted. I saw Mrs Thatcher before the meeting. Mandela, I told her, was no Marxist and it was the regime that had forced him to threaten violence. His own activities in that regard had been limited to trying to blow up a few electricity pylons. He was, I told her, very different in character to any other political leader I had ever encountered. Asked if he bore any resemblance to Mugabe, I was able to assure her that I had never met two political leaders who bore less resemblance to each other than Nelson Mandela and Robert Mugabe. I reminded her that he had waited twenty-seven years for the chance to tell her and other heads of government his story. 'You mean I mustn't interrupt him?' she enquired.

Mandela was accompanied by his deputy, Thabo Mbeki. The meeting lasted three hours, with the Prime Minister very concerned about Mandela's state of health, and attempting to revive him with a small glass of port. As he put it, 'She chided me like a school-marm for not taking her advice and cutting down on my schedule.' Displaying, for once, exemplary patience she listened, asking no more than a couple of questions, for over an hour as he explained to her the history of the ANC and the difficulties he was facing in negotiations. He thanked her for the support he was receiving from us, but made no headway with a half-hearted plea for more sanctions.

Over lunch, there was an intense discussion of the sort of constitution which ought to emerge and which we could support. She found him 'supremely courteous, with a genuine nobility of bearing' and, to her amazement as well as that of others, devoid of any trace of bitterness. But she also found him very outdated in his attitudes, 'stuck in a kind of socialist time-warp', which was hardly surprising, she acknowledged, given the three decades he had spent in prison. Her attempts to correct this resulted in a hilarious exchange on basic economics.

The meeting lasted so long that members of the press waiting outside began to chant, 'Free Nelson Mandela!' Mandela felt that it had gone very well and, to the dismay of her domestic opponents, emerged on the doorstep of 10 Downing Street to pay tribute to the Prime Minister for the role she had played in helping to secure his release. Margaret Thatcher, for her part, had proved no less susceptible than others to Mandela's courtliness and charm. Her insistence that the ANC should announce an end to the 'armed struggle' was answered by Mandela when they did so four weeks later.

Jerry Hayes
Conservative MP 1983–97

Jerry Hayes introduced a number of Acts including the Sexual Offences Act, the Nurse Prescribing Act and the Video Recordings Act. He held the seat of Harlow from 1983 to 1997.

I'm on the independent left of the Conservative Party. During the Thatcher years I was regarded as a rebel. Heaven knows why, I just believed in social justice and pragmatism. But in those days that was about as popular as a rat sandwich. On one occasion I reduced our majority from 140 to 4. I was not always popular with the right.

The truth of the matter is that Thatcher was not an ogre who despised the poor and ground their faces into the mud as she slashed public expenditure to the bone. And nor was she some sainted figure who could do no wrong. She was a determined, single-minded woman who tapped directly into the aspirations of ordinary people. People who did not want the country run by the unions. People who were fed up with Soviet exchange control laws that only allowed them to take £100 out of the country. People who wanted to better themselves and wanted their children to have equality of opportunity. People who wanted to buy the council houses that they had lived in all their lives. In short, people who were fed up by being told by the state how to run their lives.

To her credit Margaret Thatcher stuck up two fingers to two shibboleths: the class system and ratchet socialism. And the cosy political elite did not like that one little bit.

If you think that Cameron is having a bit of a rough time with his backbenchers, it was nothing compared to the venom that was poured upon her by not just her backbenchers but by her Cabinet. In the early days she would be seen sobbing in the whips' office. Even during the Falklands War there were those both in Cabinet and the back benches praying she would fail.

Her real legacy is that she changed the way Britain thought about itself and the way the world thought about us.

So let me explode some of the most popular myths. She did not cut back public expenditure. It increased in real terms by approximately 30 per cent except for Transport and Defence which were cut by 3 per cent. Nor did she expand the armed services. She cut them to the bone so much that there were ministerial resignations.

And Europe? She was not anti-European at all, merely wanting a just settlement for the UK. Ironically, Thatcher gave away more powers to Brussels in the Single European Act than ever before.

To be honest, although I admired her single-minded determination I always found her difficult, probably because she was devoid of any sense of humour. In the 1979 campaign ITN's Mike Brunson interviewed her in a hardware shop where she picked up an enormous drill and said, without any understanding of why the camera crew were in hysterics, 'This is the largest tool I have ever had in my hand.' And then, sitting astride a large field gun after the Falklands War she turned to the crew enquiring, 'Do you think this will jerk me off?'

I remember when I was first elected in 1983 I was asked to join her with a crowd in her office behind the Speaker's Chair. As we all trooped in she put us at our ease by shouting, 'Whatever you do, don't queue up,' and going over to Giles Shaw, who was Minister of State at the Home Office, and asking how things were in Environment, to which he replied that he was actually in charge of the police. She gave him a glare and in full Lady Bracknell mode exclaimed, 'Don't be ridiculous,' and moved on.

And once when I had been called into No. 10 for a bollocking she rolled up ten minutes late. This was the time when there were thoughts that we would allow the USA to bomb Libya using our airbases. The party line was that this was not an option. So, in an effort to ameliorate the handbagging that was to come I towed the party line (for once). The lady gave me a steely stare and informed me that the reason she was late was because she'd just given the bombers the order to head for Tripoli. Oh, dear.

My favourite story was when I was on a boat with her, organised by the City of London for her to light up the newly cleaned up Tower Bridge. The champagne was flowing and the Remembrancer sidled up to me in a terrible state. 'She's in a foul mood, positively spitting tacks. What should I do?' When I asked him what he was offering her to drink and his reply was champagne I came up with a solution. 'At this time of night she prefers to drink whisky. Get a police launch to head for the nearest Bottoms Up and get a bottle of J&B.' He did, and the rest of the evening was sweetness and light.

Poor Margaret, life without the wonderful Denis must have been unbearable. We have witnessed the passing of a phenomenon within a whirlwind.

It was a privilege to have known her although I won't pretend that it was always easy.

Richard Kaye
Public Affairs Manager

As a boy, I was a chorister at Winchester Cathedral. John Wakeham's sons were at the school at the same time. We sang the Lloyd Webber requiem at the abbey for the people who were killed at Brighton. We went to No. 12 afterwards. Mrs T. arrived, ignored the adults, gathered us boys together and gave us a tour of No. 10. She congratulated me on a little solo, and I was astonished that she remembered, and then I asked her why her photograph wasn't on the staircase. She said, 'My dear boy, one's photograph is only there when one is a... *has been*.' It never seemed possible that she would be one of those.

Deborah Slattery
Conservative Party Agent

Deborah Slattery was Conservative Party agent in the marginal seat of Norwich North from 1988 until 1993.

I was fortunate to meet with Margaret Thatcher on many occasions due to my work as a party agent. The first time was when she was invited to Wramplingham Hall in Norfolk to meet party workers and professional agents. It was with some trepidation but also with a knowledge that I was hugely privileged that I went off to the venue with four association members to meet the great lady.

Patrick Thomson (sitting MP) introduced our members to her before finally introducing me as his agent. I was so surprised at how her manner of casual pleasantries with the others changed. She took my hand, placed her other hand on top and drew me into her space so that we were very, very close. 'My dear how very nice to meet you,' she said, 'Do tell me, are you getting our message across?' And then she said, 'Deborah, you have a VERY, VERY difficult task in Norwich North (serious voice, steely stare), believe me, I know!'

Two others occasions spring to mind. We were in Blackpool at the party conference and my friend and I were at the Imperial Hotel because she desperately wanted to see Maggie up close and have an opportunity to take a photo. MT swept down the staircase with Kenneth Baker by her side; she was an absolute vision in a shimmering black-and-white gown and jacket and looked stunning and vibrant. The press took photos and my friend was desperately trying to get a good shot. MT was about to turn to leave with her entourage when she spotted us both. She pulled away from her group and said, 'I hope you are enjoying conference.' My friend Charlotte shook her hand and I took some lovely pictures. It was a lovely gesture and Charlotte was absolutely thrilled.

When the East of England agents were invited to Downing Street to a reception, she spoke to us all individually and spent a lot of time with agents from marginal or difficult seats, encouraging and thanking us for our hard work.

Finally, when she had left Downing Street, she was invited to Norwich to a book-signing dinner. The time came for us to queue to get her book signed. We were told not to ask for it to be personalised, as this would take too much time. She signed my book and when she was told that I was the former Norwich North agent, she asked me, 'Why former?' I replied, 'I was not needed after the 1992 election.' She said, 'Indeed, indeed, I know how that feels.' (These may not have been her exact words, but it is what she implied and I knew the irony of it!)

Paul Schooling
Downing Street Gardener

Mrs Thatcher loved the garden, and after she left office she came to a reception at No. 10. She was walking in the garden by the roses with then Prime Minister Tony Blair and I introduced myself to her.

With her keen eye for detail, the first thing she said to me was, 'What have you done with my roses?' This was because after she had left we replaced the roses with the hardier David Austin variety.

She loved roses, so much so that a former gardener picked a rose for her every day to go in her study. She also liked Downing Street to be decorated with house plants.

When she left office I remember us all clapping her out and her crying. She then composed herself and walked out.

Piers Morgan
Journalist and Broadcaster

Piers Morgan is a former Editor of the News of the World *and* Daily Mirror.

Margaret Thatcher came to power in 1979 when I was fourteen, and was the first person (and to date, the only Tory leader) I ever voted for, in 1983 – inspired by her extraordinary courage over the Falklands War.

As a highly opinionated (I know, hard to believe) and politically strident student in Lewes, Sussex, I wrote to her after winning a glorious victory in a college debate on nuclear disarmament against some CND supporters.

Thatcher replied, congratulating me on my win, and sending a signed photograph.

I wasn't a fan of her pitiless treatment of the miners, her betrayal of the Hillsborough victims and their families, or the repulsive poll tax.

But she inherited a Britain in decay, turned us into a nation of entrepreneurs and house buyers, smashed the unions' stranglehold on many industries and gave us great stature on the world stage – not least here in America, where people still revere the Iron Lady.

I first met Thatcher at a drinks party in London thrown by Rupert Murdoch in 1994, soon after I'd become Editor of the *News of the World*.

She was clutching, and drinking liberally from, a vast tumbler of whisky, and was in splendidly bombastic mood, haranguing me loudly for daring to suggest that interest rate rises were hurting ordinary people.

'What a load of nonsense!' she said. 'It's much better for them because they'll have a lasting, smooth recovery without inflation coming back again, which it was tending to do.'

I replied that this wasn't going to help families with mortgages – the same families she'd encouraged to buy homes in the first place – especially if house prices collapsed.

She stared at me for several seconds, then began jabbing me hard in the chest with her firm, bony fingers.

'You don't know what on earth you're talking about, young man! And I suggest you think very carefully before putting any of that rubbish in your newspaper!'

The lady was not for turning, but my ribcage was about to.

Murdoch, who'd heard all this, laughed, saying, 'I wouldn't tangle with Margaret if I were you, Piers – there'll only be one winner.'

Love her or loathe her, Margaret Thatcher was the most trans-formative, domineering, dominant, bold and unique Prime Minister of my lifetime.

Barbara Taylor Bradford
Novelist

Barbara Taylor Bradford is a bestselling author who has sold more than thirty
million books. She has written twenty-eight novels.

The grocer's daughter from Grantham, who lived above the shop
yet aspired to great things, has passed away. But she will never
be forgotten.

Margaret Thatcher, who was made a baroness for her services to
her country by the Queen, was the greatest peacetime Prime Minister
of the twentieth century. She was also the most powerful woman in the
world during her reign at No. 10.

And what a reign it was. When she became Prime Minister, Britain
was at its lowest ebb, on the edge of a precipice, and in economic
ruins. It was certainly no longer considered a world power.

She managed, through extraordinary intelligence, foresight, logic,
brilliance, force of personality and self-belief to bring it back from the
edge, and to safety and success. Such enormous success that she was
adored by her admirers, and hated by those who didn't 'get it' and
were envious and jealous of her amazing triumphs and popularity.

She herself rose above all that nonsense, as she called it, and never
lost sight of her goal: saving her beloved country and its everyday
average people from disaster, bringing the land back to a prosperity
it had not known for many years. She was able to do this because
she had a true understanding of economics, the tyrannical unions and
their domination, inefficient nationalised industries, and city councils.
Blessed with a quantity of female practicality and common sense, she
put it to good use. Most of all, she was a true visionary, who saw the
future and what Britain could become. Patriotic, humane and compassionate, she came from the middle class and so understood the middle
class, and all of their problems, dreams, desires and needs.

Eventually she made London the financial capital of the world
because of the Big Bang. This was the name given to her deregulation
of the City in 1986.

She fought the idea of abandoning the pound sterling for the euro, and won. How right she was, and we should be grateful to her for that foresight and for her dogged insistence. She also fought the idea of a federal European state, and did not want Britain to become a member of the Union. But nobody listened, sadly.

Maggie, as the populace loved to call her, brought Britain back to centre stage. We loved her for it, and so did the rest of the world. She was a star... today they would call her a ROCK STAR! I rather think she was exactly that.

Let's not forget her closeness to President Ronald Reagan. She helped him to end the Cold War and bring down the Berlin Wall, and fought a war to keep the Falklands British and free of Argentinian control.

It was a Russian journalist who called her the Iron Lady, a title she rather enjoyed. And in a way, I think she was tough, but in an elegant way. She was one of the most feminine women I have ever met. She loved clothes, shoes, handbags and jewellery. I've always admired her for that, and for owning up to it. Power in a lovely dress... A woman of substance indeed.

She became Prime Minister in 1979, which was when my now famous novel was published. We met through Irwin Bellow, who was Chairman of Leeds City Council and in charge of housing. He was brought in by Mrs Thatcher to advise her about the selling of council houses to their tenants, not only in Leeds, but throughout the country. It was because of his help that she was able to bring in a Bill in Parliament enabling this to finally happen. He was her right-hand man in her endeavours, and she elevated him to the peerage for his hard work. He became Lord Bellwin.

It was Irwin who arranged for Bob and me to go out to our first event at No. 10. It was an evening cocktail party given by Mrs Thatcher for those in the arts. Bob and I were thrilled to attend. I recall being at the end of a long reception room, talking to a small group of people, when I noticed that I was facing an open door. I stepped to one side, and caught a glimpse of an oil painting of my great hero, Winston Churchill. Edging away from the group, I went and peeped around the door. This opened onto a small landing, and hanging over a spiralling staircase was that huge portrait of the great man.

Naturally, it was too tempting to resist. I stepped onto the landing, and went to get a better look at the portrait. A moment later I heard that inimitable voice, asking cordially, 'Are you all right, Mrs Bradford?'

I swung around to face Margaret Thatcher. 'I am, thank you, Prime Minister,' I said. 'I was just standing here, thinking that as a little girl growing up I could never have imagined that one day I would come to No. 10 and stand here looking at the portrait of Winston Churchill.'

'I know what you mean, Mrs Bradford, neither did I,' she answered me with a twinkle in her eyes. As we walked back into the reception, she told me how much she had enjoyed my book, and I congratulated her on being the first woman to become Prime Minister.

Margaret Thatcher saved Britain in the post-war years, just as Churchill had saved the country in the Second World War, not to mention Western civilisation as well.

Sir Winston had a state funeral, and so did she. She certainly deserved it.

Paul Elliott

Former Flight Lieutenant, Royal Air Force Police

For one or two years, I was privileged to be one of the numerous people who are needed to support the busy schedule of the Prime Minister. I was a serving Flight Lieutenant in the Royal Air Force police. My role was to implement the aviation security arrangements for senior government ministers whenever they travelled overseas on official engagements, Prime Minister Thatcher especially. Some of these trips were highly publicised, notably when we carried a large contingent of the press as well as the official party on the aircraft. Others were much less well written up, on occasions when it became necessary at very short notice for the Prime Minister to engage in a one-to-one meeting with her foreign counterparts.

Except on one long flight from Ascension Island to the Falklands, when Margaret and Denis Thatcher travelled in a caravan which was anchored firmly to the floor of a Hercules VC10 freighter (and the rest did their best to be comfortable in the cargo bay), we all invariably flew in the relative luxury of a VC10, the pride of RAF Support Command. My work was only made difficult by the few 'VIP' (and middle-ranking) passengers whose arrogance forbade them from obeying simple security instructions such as those appertaining to items which were unacceptable for carriage in the aircraft. We searched everyone's personal luggage each time it was loaded and I remember worrying about how I was going to achieve this in the case of the Iron Lady, on the first occasion I flew with her.

I need not have feared. Margaret Thatcher was the most understanding of all the passengers and that was my experience on every occasion that my team dealt with her. It was my responsibility to be the first down the aircraft steps whenever we arrived at a destination. Depending on the security climate, there were different procedures for the way in which I, followed by the Prime Minister, would descend towards the inevitable red carpet and the rows of host foreign dignitaries who waited to greet her. Each time, I briefed Mrs Thatcher immediately before we left the safety of the aircraft, and on every occasion she listened attentively and did exactly the right thing. Other senior people who I escorted for similar reasons were often flippant and reckless. The Prime Minister was never like that; of course, she did not suffer fools but to me and the other junior people who did our best to get things right, she was always most understanding.

Between the ceremonial duties and the pressure of events on the ground, the aircraft often acted as a place of sanctuary for our VIP passengers. It was inevitable that everyone on board relaxed after take-off; the cabin was not enormous and offered little individual privacy. Obviously there were many private moments shared and these should never be discussed in public. However, some VIPs were especially distant, verging on pomposity, but Mrs Thatcher was never the 'icicle' in these circumstances which I know that many people imagine her to have been. She did also engage in pleasant small talk during long-duration flights, always accepting that the majority of her time was consumed by the affairs of state, punctuated by catnapping from which she had an amazing ability to awake without a call according to the timetable of events. Impeccable timing and very tight schedules were a feature of these journeys across the world; it was always our aim to arrive and depart exactly on time, but sometimes political negotiations were extended and we had to wait on the tarmac for several hours longer than anticipated for the principal passenger to board the aircraft. I remember this happening in the stifling heat of a Middle Eastern country and again in the intense cold of winter in Norway. On both occasions the Prime Minister apologised to us all on her late arrival – something that none of her male ministers ever did when we were transporting them in similar circumstances.

We did not always bother the Prime Minister with the understandable operational difficulties which were experienced from time to time and I remember wondering if she would be annoyed if this were to be revealed. I got my answer. We had taken off from London one lunchtime in the autumn of 1992, en route to Tokyo (and thence to Beijing for the purpose of Mrs Thatcher signing the agreement to release Hong Kong to the Chinese). A couple of hours later we were cruising towards the North Pole, with Mrs Thatcher enjoying a break in the captain's seat on the flight deck, when the navigator was notified that the authorities in London had received a claim that we had a bomb on the aircraft. This was most disconcerting, although I was convinced that our tight security arrangements made the probability highly unlikely. Nevertheless the aircraft captain (a fellow RAF Flight Lieutenant) decided that we should make an unscheduled landing to check. He told the passengers that we needed to refuel due to unexpected head winds. We landed at a remote United States Air Force base in Alaska, offloaded everyone and surrounded the aircraft with service vehicles so that no one could see what we were doing from the terminal building. I am assured that Mrs Thatcher spent the time being perfectly charming to a USAF major who was the senior officer at the base and was in a blind panic having received such an unexpected visitor.

In the event, we experienced no explosions but I remained unsure as to whether or not the Prime Minister would explode if she found that we had not revealed the real reason for our unscheduled fuel stop to her. It was left to me to tell her some five weeks later, long after we had returned safely to London and were being entertained at a reception in No. 10 Downing Street. She listened carefully to my story and simply said 'thank you'. I am sure that her calm reaction was absolutely genuine. I reflected again how worrying it must be for people in public life whose lives are under constant threat. If she felt the danger, Mrs Thatcher did not show it.

In September 1983, I was in Germany with Mrs Thatcher's party on another state visit. The aircraft captain received the message that my mother had died suddenly in England. I was of course distressed and unable to return home to see my family as quickly as I would have liked. I did not expect any of the senior party to learn of my loss and was extremely surprised when Mrs Thatcher sought me out and spoke to me with great kindness. From a personal point of view I shall never remember Margaret Thatcher as an Iron Lady; I think that she had a remarkable ability to blend ordinary human qualities with the need to represent herself as the boss whenever that was required.

Lord Mawhinney
Conservative Peer

Brian Mawhinney was the Member for Peterborough from 1979 until 1997 and for North West Cambridgeshire from 1997 to 2005. He served as a Northern Ireland minister from 1986 to 1992. He served as Transport Secretary and Party Chairman under John Major. His memoirs, Just a Simple Belfast Boy, *were published in spring 2013.*

Backbenchers have little personal exposure to any Prime Minister, but one day was memorable. I was on the 1985 Finance Bill committee, which sat for ten weeks. We started about 4 p.m. every Tuesday, worked through the night until lunchtime next day, reconvened on Thursday afternoons and worked until late at night. We all became pretty exhausted.

One Wednesday morning we went down to the tearoom for a breakfast break to find the Prime Minister waiting for us. Someone had advised her of our long hours and thought we would all appreciate a visit from her to say thank you.

Full of vim and vigour, looking immaculate, she sat at the middle of a long table. I found myself sitting opposite.

She was at her argumentative best. No matter what anyone said about anything, she argued. She was, or seemed to me to be, loud and dominating. She made no allowance for the fact that we had just missed yet another night's sleep in defence of her government. If she did say thank you, I do not remember. What I do remember was the argumentativeness. It was both wearing and irritating to my sleep-starved mind.

Finally, I could take it no longer. I knew I had to move, for otherwise I would say something that definitely would not be career-enhancing. 'Please excuse me, Prime Minister, I have one or two things I must do before the committee reconvenes.' I left the table, the first to do so, in what seemed even to my exhausted sensibilities to be a stunned silence. Too bad. She was driving me nuts.

It so happened that on the day of this particular Thatcher breakfast, my wife Betty and I were going to Buckingham Palace for a garden party and then on to No. 10 for a drinks reception. Betty arrived at the Commons to find me in very bad form.

In my exhaustion I was still fed up with Margaret and her insensitivity, no matter how well-meaning she had intended to be. In my view her ill-judged behaviour well reflected one aspect of Margaret's personality – on occasions she was simply a steamroller.

I knew that at her receptions Margaret greeted guests with Denis beside her. She would hold out her hand and, when you took it, abruptly whip you across to Denis.

As I contemplated our No. 10 visit, a befuddled plan emerged.

When I shook hands I would plant my feet and refuse to move when she sought to whip me across to Denis. If she broke her wrist in the process – too bad! How irrational could anyone get?

As we mounted that famous staircase I could see Margaret in the doorway of the state reception room. Betty gave me a warning look. I stopped myself in front of Margaret as she took my hand.

Instead of moving it along to Denis she held it with a gentleness that was real and clearly meant to feel so. She leant towards me and looked into my eyes.

'Did you get any sleep last night, Brian?'

'I got enough, Prime Minister, thank you.'

'Yes,' she said and nodded, 'you got enough.'

She then handed me on to Denis with what I can only describe as tenderness. What a remarkable, sensitive woman.

In the space of less than half a day all the personality traits that made Margaret such a formidable leader and so loved and admired were on display. She was tough, fully briefed and strong-willed and had a well-developed instinct to try to stiffen the resolve of colleagues and others. She was thoughtful in her kindness and, sometimes, tender and caring towards those who worked closely with her. She could come across as dominating, irritating and beyond correction. Yet most of the time most people thought that handling those aspects of her personality was an acceptable price to pay for all her many strengths and virtues. Thatcherism's place in history already seems to support that analysis.

Dominic Prince
Journalist

Dominic Price is a journalist with The Independent.

As an eight-year-old schoolboy, I had a somewhat quirky desire to visit Big Ben and I wanted to look out through the clock face over London. There was only one problem: it wasn't open to the public.

I was told by my mother to write to our local MP, one Mrs Thatcher, then on the back benches of the opposition. My mother's political affiliations were clear. She was not a supporter, and her sympathies were with the Labour Party, a position she made no secret of.

With not a great deal of hope, I wrote to Mrs Thatcher, who swiftly replied saying that she would be delighted to arrange a visit for me, my brother and a phalanx of friends, all under the age of nine. After further correspondence, a date and a time were arrived at and we were told to present ourselves to an official at Westminster one morning during the Easter holidays.

It was a joyful affair, with us wide-eyed children climbing the 334 steps to the top of the building and being deafened by Big Ben in action. The panoramic view had us glued; we had photographs taken in the clock face. Aged eight, none of us really had much of an idea what an MP was. All we knew was that Mrs Thatcher had fixed it for all of us and that she was frightfully important because she had very posh writing paper.

That might have been that, but when we arrived home my mother sat us all down and told us to write to Mrs Thatcher and thank her for arranging our trip.

We were of no use to her electorally. Did she perhaps think that she could sway our parents to vote for her the following year? I doubt that very much, and anyway she could have had little doubt about my mother's political leanings.

We all regarded the chapter as having come to an end. But a few days later, I received a hand-written note from her on House of Commons notepaper thanking me for thanking her. It read:

Dear Dominic,

Thank you for your letter. It was very nice of you to write to me. I am so glad that you enjoyed seeing Big Ben. It is much bigger than it looks, isn't it? My children have always enjoyed walking round it – except for the climb up the stairs.

Yours sincerely, Margaret Thatcher (Mrs).

She wrote similar letters to all my friends. I say similar because they were all different, telling a different story to each of us. I often wondered about her motivation and, as a low-minded journalist, I am still wondering.

In a similarly sceptical vein, I had some nagging doubt about her children having visited Big Ben, but as I had no way of establishing the truth it went to the back of my mind. Nevertheless I treasured the letter, and in my teens I had it framed, and now it peers down at me in my office.

Several years ago, I wrote to our local Labour MP, Martin Linton, telling him how much I had enjoyed my trip and enquiring whether he could arrange the same for my children. I didn't even receive a reply. And about a year ago, for some bizarre reason, I found myself at a lunch with Mark Thatcher. I asked if it were true that he and his sister, Carol, used to visit Big Ben. In a sort of sullen, graceless way, he confirmed that it was, but went on to say, 'But of course you couldn't visit nowadays; it's been banned by the bloody Health and Safety.'

He was nearly right. Visits are still undertaken, but you have to be over eleven to attend.

I don't know what the story tells us, except that maybe people don't always fit into the boxes it is convenient to place them in. There is, though, one final act to the story. According to collectors of Thatcher memorabilia, the letter is now worth around £1,000.

George Osborne
Chancellor of the Exchequer 2010–

George Osborne has been Conservative MP for Tatton since 2001. He has been Chancellor of the Exchequer since 2010.

I hardly knew Margaret Thatcher. I watched her eviction from office by her fellow Conservative MPs from my room at university, bemused like the rest of the country. I met her a few times as a young MP.

But there remains the powerful impression of the only long one-to-one meeting I had with her, when I was shadow Chancellor. She was already unwell and unengaged with contemporary issues. Various attempts to bring up issues from her period as Prime Minister led to stilted exchanges. Then I brought up the tactics we were using to oppose the Finance Bill then going through Parliament, and I said that I drew my inspiration from the aggressive approach that Iain Macleod took when he was shadow Chancellor in the 1960s. She lit up. Suddenly the words flowed. She had been a junior member of Macleod's Treasury team, she said; Macleod had divided the team into relay legs to keep the governing MPs of the Labour Party up through the night, and she had led for the opposition in various successful assaults.

And she was flowing with advice to me: 'You can't spend what your country hasn't got; strong defence rests on a strong economy; in Parliament, if you're not on the attack you're in retreat.' Wow! I saw for myself for the first and only time why she had been such a force of political nature throughout my whole life.

Michael Brown
Journalist and Conservative MP 1979–97

Michael Brown was Conservative MP for Brigg and Scunthorpe, later Brigg and Cleethorpes, from 1979 to 1997. He is now sketchwriter for The Independent.

I first met Margaret Thatcher shortly before the 1979 general election when she made a flying visit to my Brigg and Scunthorpe constituency. It was a grim industrial area employing 20,000 steelworkers at the nationalised British Steel Corporation and had returned a Labour MP for decades. I was selected as the candidate, at the age of twenty-four, for this safe Labour seat in 1976 – on the day Harold Wilson resigned as Prime Minister.

I was identified by Mrs Thatcher's minders as 'one of us' and the constituency was rewarded with 'critical seat' status. Mrs Thatcher's twenty-minute whistle-stop was a whirlwind. I merely introduced her to Tory supporters as 'our next Prime Minister', having been told she did not like listening to other people's speeches. Although she asked me how the campaign was going, she did not allow me to reply – a pattern I was to experience many times during my encounters with her over the following years. Answering her own question, she told me, 'You've got to get the message out on the doorstep in fifty words and in less than a minute' – campaign advice I found invaluable. I was miffed at her brusqueness but the *Scunthorpe Evening Telegraph* headline and photo IRON LADY IN STEEL TOWN was a candidate's dream publicity.

The constituency count began on the morning of Friday 4 May. We already knew that Mrs Thatcher would be Prime Minister but it took three recounts before my election, with a wafer-thin majority of 486, was confirmed after lunch.

I received a telegram (no mobile phones or emails in those days) from the Chief Whip: 'Congratulations. House will meet 9 May. Your attendance essential.' It was underlined three times. The excitement of taking my seat that day – at twenty-seven, the youngest MP – and witnessing the first woman Prime Minister speaking at the dispatch box was probably the greatest moment of my life. It is hard to convey just what an extraordinary event the election of a woman as Prime Minister was to be. Years later during a school visit a ten-year-old asked me whether it was possible for men to rule in Buckingham Palace and Downing Street.

Shortly after the election I went to a victory reception at No. 10. This was my first encounter with Denis. 'Can I smoke?' I enquired as he puffed on an un-tipped Senior Service. 'Good God, boy, yes – and get a large G&T for us both off that waitress.' Anxious to show off how well I had done in becoming the first Tory MP for Scunthorpe since Sir Berkeley Sheffield (Samantha Cameron's great-grandfather), I wanted to impress Mrs Thatcher. She asked about the result. 'I got 31,500 and a majority of 486.' She glowered at me like an errant son. 'No, Michael, I got 31,000 – you got 486.'

The honeymoon was short-lived. First the new Chancellor doubled VAT in his June 1979 Budget. By December steelworkers embarked on a futile three month all-out strike. This led to the government withdrawing the subsidy to the loss-making BSC and the devastation of the Scunthorpe steelworks. On one day 10,000 constituents were made redundant and unemployment was to rise to 25 per cent. But I was certain 'there was no alternative' and spoke vigorously in the Commons in support of the government's economic and industrial policies. Late one night, Ian Gow, the Prime Minister's Parliamentary Private Secretary – with whom I shared a Commons office – sought me out. 'The Prime Minister knows how busy you must be, but wonders if you could spare a few minutes to give her some advice on the steel industry.'

Mrs Thatcher was marvellous on these occasions (often about 12 a.m. in her Commons office during the regular pattern of late-night sittings when she was usually present), sitting with her shoes off and her feet on the sofa, tucking into a box of chocolates, and generous with the measures of whisky. But, as to listening to anything I had to say, it was often a waste of time. Ian would ask me if there was anything on my mind the Prime Minister needed to know. She must have thought he was addressing his remarks to her as the midnight monologue would begin.

Occasionally, however, I would get a word in and something would stick. I complained about the government's slowness in making progress on trade union reform. I wanted the closed shop abolished and union ballots introduced. In return she expressed her own exasperation. 'I can't understand why this government isn't doing enough.' It was extraordinary to hear the Prime Minister frustrated at the lack of progress the administration, over which she presided, was making.

It was only then that I fully realised just what a battle Mrs Thatcher had in making her economic case inside the Cabinet. For the first two years, until the 1981 ministerial reshuffle, she had to plot and scheme, with the few Cabinet allies she had, to defeat the 'wets' – led by Jim Prior, Peter Walker, Ian Gilmour and Norman St John-Stevas. John Nott, the former Trade Secretary, details in his autobiography how he, Geoffrey Howe, Keith Joseph and John Biffen would meet most weeks with Mrs Thatcher in the Downing Street flat to plan how they would overcome Cabinet opposition. His account suggests that Mrs Thatcher was the Leader of the Opposition to the majority against her inside the Cabinet. She was, frankly, in a very precarious position.

My tiny majority and surprise win meant that I assumed, by the end of 1981, I would lose my seat and the Tories would probably lose the election. But the Falklands conflict changed all that. Only then did Mrs Thatcher become mistress of all she surveyed. With a little help from the Labour split, the newly formed SDP and Michael Foot, the golden age of Thatcherism was about to begin. And my own ringside seat was to outlast Mrs Thatcher until 1997.

Francesca Makins
Conservative Party Activist

We were at a Buckingham Palace tea party in 1989 and following our presentation to Prince Philip in the line-up, we moved away to look at the lake. While standing there looking, I turned back to take in the vista when I saw Mrs T., Denis and her protection officer walking towards the Queen's marquee between the lake and the palace.

I said to my husband Bill: 'There's Mrs T., I'm going to go over and speak to her.'

'You can't do that,' exclaimed Bill. 'Just watch me,' I replied. 'They'll never let you near her,' he reckoned. 'Of course they will, it's Buckingham Palace for heaven's sake. She *must* be safe here!'

Off I trotted and fronted up to her saying: 'Prime Minister I am *very* pleased to meet you.' The Prime Minister smiled with her lips, but not her eyes and stretched out her hand. Before she had time to say anything I launched in with: 'Although it is a great pleasure to meet you, I would really like to shake the hand of your husband, as I think he is a such a gentleman and a wonderful support to you.'

With that she clasped my hand (now smiling hugely) and turned me towards Denis as she said: 'Oh Denis, this young lady wishes to meet you and shake your hand.' And with that she stood aside for Denis and me to shake hands and for me to say my piece. Then she said quietly: 'I am sorry, my dear, but we have to go as we cannot keep Her Majesty waiting.' With smiles all round they walked off to Her Majesty's marquee.

I'll never forget it – their lovely smiles and her pure pleasure in someone acknowledging Denis.

Lord Saatchi

Conservative Peer

Maurice Saatchi is the co-founder of M&C Saatchi and chairs the Centre for Policy Studies.

After she was deposed, the view arose in our party that it would be a good thing, as there was much tension in the party at the time, obviously, if the former Prime Minister was invited to our party conference. It would be cathartic. She would not speak – that would be too dangerous – but she would go on to the stage to receive the applause of the party and that would be a cathartic moment. That was the idea.

I was with her in the green room in Blackpool and, in the course of making the kind of conversation that one does in the green room at party conferences, she said, 'What did you do last night, Maurice?' I said, 'I had a lovely dinner with Professor Anthony King,' whom she knew. She said, 'Where did you go?' I replied, 'We went to a lovely restaurant, but a funny thing happened.' She asked what. I explained that we were upstairs; the downstairs was absolutely packed, as all restaurants in Blackpool are during party conference week. I explained that upstairs, there was only our table for two and the rest of the room was empty. A long table was laid out for dinner for about sixteen people. Professor King and I had the room to ourselves. I also explained to her that when it was time to pay the bill, I asked the woman who owned the restaurant, 'What happened to those people?' It was a shocking moment and I remember it vividly. I have never described it before, but I am doing so now. She said, 'You did this. Your party did this. Don't you realise that my husband and I can't keep this place running? Party conference week is the most important week of our lives. Without the money from party conference week, this restaurant would close.' I said that I was very sorry; I paid the bill and we left. It was very upsetting. She was in tears.

I explained all that to Margaret and then – this is exactly what happened – she said, 'Maurice, pass me my handbag.' I did not know what she was talking about. I passed her handbag to her and she started to rummage inside and took out her pen. She continued to rummage inside and took out a cheque book. She said, 'Maurice, what was the name of the restaurant you went to last night?' I said, 'I think it was the Blackpool Brasserie.' She wrote the words Blackpool Brasserie on the cheque and said, 'How much do you think they lost as a result of those people not coming?' I replied, 'I don't know, £300 or £350.' She made out the cheque; she signed it 'Margaret Thatcher'. She tore it out of her cheque book, gave it to me and said, 'I want you, Maurice, to take this cheque to the restaurant, give it to the man or the woman who owns it and tell them, "Conservatives don't behave like that."' What a woman.

Nicholas Bennett
Conservative MP 1987–1992

Nicholas Bennett served as a Welsh Office minister in the Major government and held the seat of Pembrokeshire from 1987 to 1992.

If you visit the house of any former Conservative parliamentary candidate from the 1970s and 1980s, the likelihood is that there will be a picture, in pride of place, of the occupant and Mrs Thatcher. My house is no exception to the rule; indeed I have two. The first shows a fresh-faced young man sitting awkwardly with her in the Leader of the Opposition's room in the summer of 1978. The second shows the same people eight years older against a bland backdrop at a specially organised photograph session for candidates. Across Britain there must be several dozen almost identical photographs in every one of which Mrs Thatcher's pearl necklace is shown with the clasp slipped down to the side of her neck.

On the Conservative back benches at the start of Margaret Thatcher's third term I saw her at the height of her power. The first two terms had seen the Right to Buy, victory in the Falkland's War, the rebate of our European contribution, trade union reform and the privatisation programme. Further privatisations were to follow in what proved to be the final years of her administration; these were accompanied by the creation of NHS Trusts, the Education Reform Act and cuts in income tax.

By the time I arrived in the Commons she had been Prime Minister for eight years. She faced her third Labour leader Neil Kinnock and at the twice-weekly Question Time she dominated the exchanges. Her famous ability to survive on four hours' sleep a night (was this later to be the cause of the strokes?) meant that she had an unrivalled knowledge not only of strategy but also of the detail of policy in every government department.

Frequently, after Question Time, she would be found in the tearoom talking to backbenchers and gauging the political temperature.

Invited to join the No Turning Back Group in 1988 I found myself a member of what the press called 'the keepers of the Thatcherite flame', and at the time of the two leadership challenges in 1989 and 1990, 'Mrs Thatcher's Praetorian Guard'.

In the spring of 1990 I was invited to lunch at No. 10 and found myself placed next to the Prime Minister. I remember discussing with her my recent motoring holiday through the still communist-controlled East Germany and Poland. I'm not sure she entirely approved as she was not a fan of the Germans; however, shortly afterwards I was appointed Parliamentary Private Secretary to Roger Freeman MP, newly promoted to Transport Minister of State. Clearly the lunch placement had followed a whip's recommendation and I must have passed the interview! Cecil Parkinson, one of Mrs Thatcher's closest political soulmates, headed the Department of Transport at that time. I recall being in his office, along with several members of the Conservative constitution committee, when Geoffrey Howe's resignation statement was carried live from the House of Commons on 13 November 1990. Cecil appreciated at once the serious damage that the statement would cause with its call to arms for a challenge to Mrs Thatcher's leadership.

The following week was a maelstrom of plotting and lobbying in an attempt to ensure that she won the ballot against the Heseltine challenge. The No Turning Back Group met three nights in a row. Mrs Thatcher's re-election campaign was a shambles. Her indolent and complacent PPS Peter Morrison assured her it was 'in the bag'. After she narrowly failed to get the required majority on Tuesday 20 April we met the following night downstairs in the Commons. We learned from NTB Cabinet members that they and the other members of the Cabinet were being summoned one by one to see her. During the discussion I made it clear that although I would fight in the last ditch for her, I felt that her support was likely to ebb away rather than flow backwards. Peter Lilley supported my assessment in the face of accusations of defeatism by Neil Hamilton and some others.

Margaret Thatcher decided late the same evening not to stand in the second ballot. I heard the rumours around 11.30 p.m. The next morning I drove to the *TV-am* studios to appear as a Thatcher supporter on the morning show. I spoke on my car phone to a sleepy Peter Morrison at Downing Street during the journey. I told him I would not disclose what I knew but would play a straight bat and say that she would be fighting on. After the broadcast I arrived at the Commons Norman Shaw North building at about 8.30 a.m. and after parking my car I met Teresa Gorman, the MP for Billericay and gave her the news that Mrs Thatcher was going. I then made my way to the regular ministerial meeting (known as 'Prayers') at the Department of Transport. Cecil Parkinson confirmed that Cabinet had been brought forward to 9 a.m. and after a brief discussion he went off to the meeting. John Butterfill MP, his PPS, and I went to the Commons. As we entered the Members' cloakroom the teleprinter spat out the resignation announcement. We both decided that we would support John Major if he stood for the leadership. Shortly afterwards we went back to the resumed ministerial meeting at Marsham Street and Cecil Parkinson gave a blow-by-blow account of what occurred in the short Cabinet meeting.

The following week, Margaret Thatcher held a final lunch at Downing Street for her closest supporters. John Redwood and I were the only two members of the 1987 intake invited. During drinks several of the NTB including Edward Leigh and Michael Brown indicated they were going to support Heseltine. Mrs Thatcher was horrified. 'You can't vote for the regicide, you must support John!' she exclaimed.

During her final speech as PM I was seated in my usual place two rows behind her. The performance was one of her best, so much so that I called out 'take back the resignation', a cry taken up by Michael Carttiss (Great Yarmouth) who was sitting next to me – he was the one who yelled out, 'you can wipe the floor with these people' – but of course the die was cast.

The loss of office hit her hard. I recall talking to her in a division one night a couple of months later. She stared out into the darkness through the windows of the Aye lobby and it was clear that she was suffering from a minor breakdown. Such was her resilience that within a few months she recovered her balance.

From time to time after leaving Parliament we would meet and I was always greeted with a warm 'hello dear'. My final memory, which I captured with my camera, was a Christmas NTB in the late 1990s. It was the tradition that former members were invited back as 'country members' to the celebrations at the Institute of Economic Affairs in Lord North Street. The House of Commons and Lords were engaged that night in a parliamentary 'ping pong' over a piece of contentious legislation and divisions were called in quick succession in both Houses. We ex-MPs stayed on drinking in the Lord North Headquarters. Eventually David Davis returned from the vote and a few minutes later Margaret returned without Denis. She kicked off her shoes, accepted the proffered whisky and our small band entertained her for another hour. Freed from the cares of office, she relaxed with a group of her younger supporters, putting the world to rights.

Steve Nallon
Actor and Comedian

Actor, writer and voice artist who provided the voice for Margaret Thatcher on the 1980s satirical puppet series Spitting Image.

Technically the voice isn't that difficult to do. It's formed with a slight tightening of the larynx and is shaped mainly at the front of the mouth around the lips. The pitch, lower than most women's, is well within my range. But none of this matters. What really matters in creating any voice is *attitude*. You know a voice is ready when you have somehow captured and illustrated the way a character is thinking. And in creating Margaret Thatcher I had the huge advantage of being brought up by my grandmother, a direct speaking 'tell 'em like it is' working-class Tory.

My social background is the sort most modern Labour MPs would die for. It comes with tin bath, cobbled streets and outside toilet – I have distinct memories of all three. My father was a caretaker, his mum and dad a cleaner and a miner. My mother died young and her parents were a seamstress and a man who earned his living selling newspapers from his front door. Bringing up two children alone became too much for my father and eventually my maternal grandmother took on the duty. A child of ten in the middle of the First World War and mother of three kids with a husband away fighting in the Second World War, she had faced hardships that I can't imagine; but the result was she instilled in me self-reliance, a discipline for hard work and the importance of saving before you can spend. Sound familiar? She believed that the unions were the cause of most of Britain's economic woes and that socialists were hypocrites with a 'don't do as I do, do as I say' attitude. This was exemplified by Barbara Castle, who wanted to get rid of private beds in the NHS but stayed in one herself; if a Labour supporter had the misfortune to confront my grandmother on her views, her name was often brought into the argument.

The point of all this is that I understood instinctively where Mrs T. was coming from and I realised that this had to some extent helped with the voice when I did some coaching with actresses playing Thatcher in *Thatcher: The Musical*. Most were *Guardian*-reading liberal lefties, and the problem was that they simply couldn't make the voice believable. So I had an idea. I made them write out what they believed politically and got them to say it in their Thatcher voices. Now hearing Thatcher support nuclear disarmament, back a wealth tax and advocate inflicting unmentionable atrocities upon Michael Portillo's nether regions was a little odd, but it worked. They at last sounded convincing for as I said to them, 'If you don't believe what you're saying, I can't begin to believe you!'

So, did I believe everything Thatcher believed or said? No: there was quite a bit of acting going on but at least I understood where that belief came from. The mistake I think many impressionists made was to do her in a slow and sometimes patronising drawl, speaking as if she'd just heard your dog had died. I always took the opposite approach. I spoke quickly, instinctively, combatively, without fear of what was being said. Of all the voices I do, hers is the most energising. I used to get dizzy after twenty minutes; God knows how she did it for a lifetime.

There is a story told by Roger Law of *Spitting Image* that when Thatcher was visiting a Docklands TV studio above which the *Spitting Image* puppets were made, she walked into the workshop and shouted, 'Stop work immediately!' Everyone was suddenly shocked into silence and down tooled. Thatcher, so the story went, was really Steve Nallon dressed up! Personally I don't remember the dressing up bit, but in a choice between legend and fact always print the legend. The version of Thatcher's voice I did on *Spitting Image* had little to do with how she actually spoke or sounded but more how people *thought* she sounded, the image of the sound in our heads, as it were. Plus it of course had to match the grotesqueness of the puppet, and so to do that I injected more of her steely House of Commons tones into the voice. We once even did her as a subservient poodle, licking Ronnie Reagan where poodles sometimes like to lick themselves, with Ronnie saying, 'Gee, it's a shame I'm only screwing her country!' The one sketch when I began to realise that *Spitting Image* was on balance doing her more good than harm was a sketch where a scientist was examining her blood through a microscope. 'The DNA structure is indescribable. The defence system is impenetrable. She's the perfect winning machine. It's almost as if...

she were an alien!' Thatcher's shadow then appeared, but on seeing her full on she had the head of the alien from the Ridley Scott movie, together with extending dripping jaws that promptly devoured the said scientist. A note to future satirists: don't try to bring down a political system by suggesting its creator is indestructible!

So, what was my political attitude to the lady? In truth she wasn't really a Tory at all but a nineteenth-century laissez-faire Liberal. ('That which thy fathers bequeath thee, earn it anew if thou wouldst possess it,' she said in one speech.) The argument I always had with my grandmother and the one I would have with Thatcher is that life is never quite as neat or simple as that, and what's lacking in Gladstonian economics is any counter balance. I have never been a socialist nor even a sympathiser but I have been shaped morally by the modern social philosopher John Rawls, who, as a 'thought experiment', asked us to imagine what sort of society we would choose to create and live in if at birth we were ignorant of our place in it. 'Airy-fairy nonsense! You've got to live life as it is, love, not in a dream world,' my grandmother would have said. I suspect Baroness Thatcher would have agreed with her.

Esther Rantzen
Broadcaster

Esther Rantzen is the founder of ChildLine and former presenter of the BBC show, That's Life!

Mrs Thatcher and I are both products of the same Oxford college, Somerville. When she went there, and when I did, it was for women only, and we were taught by generations of pioneering women scholars. But I have never believed Mrs Thatcher should be judged, first woman Prime Minister though she was, as a woman. We at Somerville were encouraged to think rationally, using our minds, not our gender, and for me Mrs T. thought like a scientist. She wanted to put forward policies that worked and were successful. She felt the same about people, encouraging those who worked and were successful. But there was one area in which it seemed to me that she thought and acted like a woman. And that was the absolute priority she placed on child protection.

I came up with the idea for ChildLine in 1986 (0800 1111, free, confidential, open 24/7) and there were plenty of people at the time who were horrified by the concept that abused children could be encouraged to ask for help themselves, on their own initiative. But Mrs Thatcher understood immediately that an anonymous helpline was the only way abused or neglected children could be helped. Child abuse, especially sexual abuse, is a secret crime. It usually goes undetected by any helping agency. ChildLine offers abused children their one safe way to seek protection.

Given the controversy around the idea, it was a thrill for the ChildLine team when very soon after our launch she hosted a reception at No. 10 for us. There is a picture of her with some of the stars that came, including Frank Bruno, David Frost and Susan Hampshire. But even more important than the celebrities we were able to invite were the philanthropists and the government ministers to whom we were able to describe our work. I stood in the receiving line next to the Prime Minister, pinching myself because I couldn't believe I was in such distinguished company, as the rich, famous and powerful shook our hands. There was a momentary lull in the line of guests, and Mrs Thatcher turned to me.

'Miss Rantzen,' she said, 'What are the long-term effects of child abuse?'

It was a big question, and I answered carefully. 'Well, Prime Minister,' I replied, 'everything we learn as children about love, trust, and loyalty, we learn first of all from our parents, and if instead we learn from them shame, fear, and betrayal, it's not surprising that abuse victims often end up with broken marriages or in addiction units, psychiatric hospitals, or prison.' By the time I had finished Mrs Thatcher's famous blue eyes had glazed over, and I thought, 'Dammit, I've bored her. I've spent a lifetime boring my family, and decades boring the viewers; now I've bored the Prime Minister.'

The guests began arriving again, and we continued shaking hands. Then Mrs Thatcher brought out the embroidered footstool she always stood on so as to be seen and heard by everyone, and started her speech. She talked about the NSPCC (of which she was a constant supporter) and of Christmas time (which was approaching) as a time to think about children. Then she said, 'You know, if everything we learn as children about love and trust and loyalty we learn first of all from our parents, and if instead we learn from them shame and fear and betrayal...' and she went on, word perfect, exactly as I had inadvertently briefed her. I stood next to her, with two thoughts in my head. Firstly, I felt relief that I had not intended this to be my speech, because I was speaking second. And then, awe, at how brilliantly she had taken a brief, recognised information she could use, and used it, perfectly.

I spoke next, nervously reading every word, describing the suffering of the children who were ringing ChildLine. The third speaker was a survivor who was fundraising for us. She took my place on the footstool and looked around the grand stateroom, filled with distinguished guests. 'My father,' she began, 'was a Mason and a policeman, and I tell you that because I want you to understand how respected he was in our community. But nobody knew what he did to us children, once the front door had closed behind him.' And then the memories and the occasion overwhelmed her, and she broke down in tears.

She got down and disappeared into the crowd, and I took her place on the footstool and explained that it was too late to do anything to protect yesterday's children like her. However, she had told me that she was determined to do everything she could to save today's and tomorrow's children, like her own daughters, and that was why she was raising money for ChildLine. Then I got off the footstool, and went to look for her. Someone said, 'She's in the Prime Minister's private study.'

So I followed her, and found myself in a room with comfortable sofas; our fundraiser was sitting on one of them, while the Prime Minister bustled around filling a glass of water for her, and finding a towel for her to dry her eyes with. As I arrived, Mrs Thatcher was saying 'Now, my dear, you can stay here as long as you want. And cry if you want to, it's better to let your feelings out; don't try and bottle them up. That will only make you feel worse.' I watched, hugely impressed. Was this really the Iron Lady? This was an empathetic woman, instinctively saying and doing the simple, right, comforting and supportive things. I said, 'Don't worry, Prime Minister. I'll stay here, you go back to the reception,' and when she was sure we didn't need any more help from her, she went back to the party.

But that wasn't quite the end of the story. On my way home with my husband, Desmond, we stopped to buy an evening paper, and there on the front page in a huge headline was the report, PRIME MINISTER COMFORTS SOBBING VICTIM OF ABUSE IN NO. 10 AT A CHILDLINE RECEPTION TODAY... So her team had spotted what I had seen – the Iron Lady showing a compassionate heart – and had decided to use it. ChildLine also gained helpful publicity.

So I treasured the memory of the consummate politician who could take a brief, show instinctive compassion, with a highly professional team to support her, and use the whole event to support the work of an important new charity.

Later she came to visit our offices and said, 'You call ChildLine a helpline, I call it a life line.' And quietly, pausing in one of our corridors, she pulled out of her iconic handbag a personal cheque, and made a generous donation to ChildLine.

Towards the end of her life, Lady Thatcher attended a 'Women of the Year' lunch. She had been advised not to make any more public speeches, but typically she had ignored the advice, and spoke eloquently about history and her feelings about her country. Afterwards I went up to her and said, 'Lady Thatcher, I want to thank you for the wonderful support you gave ChildLine in our earliest days. We could not possibly have launched so successfully without your help.' She looked at me, and once again I have a memory of those bright blue eyes, focused on me. 'Nothing,' she said slowly, 'is more important than protecting children from abuse. Nothing.'

And I knew that came from the Iron Lady's heart.

Andrew MacKay
Conservative MP 1983–2010

Andrew MacKay won the 1977 Stechford by-election but lost the seat in 1979. He re-entered Parliament in 1983. He was Deputy Chief Whip in the Major government.

There is a tradition at the Conservative end of the Commons Members' dining room that MPs make up tables as they come in – in other words take the next available space without rank or favour. Imagine my surprise when on a busy three-line running whip night a few days after Margaret's resignation I looked up and there she was sitting next to me! Anxious to avoid platitudes or appear sycophantic I asked her what she was missing most. She immediately fished her diary out of the famous handbag and painfully turned the empty pages.

The cruelty of our political system was graphically illustrated – one moment, a diary crammed with meetings and decision-making, the next, nothing. My thoughts went back to our first meeting in March 1977 when as a young candidate in the Stechford by-election she, as the new Leader of the Opposition, successfully campaigned for my election. As a framed, signed photograph on our wall shows she was in the thick of a large crowd at the Fox and Goose Shopping Centre, immaculate and energised as always, while the then trendily, long-haired candidate looked on with admiration!

It was truly an end to a magnificent era.

Henry Kissinger
International Statesman

Dr Henry Kissinger served as National Security Adviser and Secretary of State during the Nixon and Ford administrations. He is a prolific writer and broadcaster.

The ultimate task of a leader is to guide a society's transition from where it is to where it has never been. Conventional wisdom understands best what has already been experienced. But societies flourish by testing possibilities rather than celebrating achievements or wallowing in frustrations. To walk this lonely road requires, above all, courage and character. Great leaders inspire their people to discover and to explore their potential. Margaret Thatcher is such a person.

It is impossible for me to think of Lady Thatcher in terms of birthdays. To me, she is timeless; she will always be in my mind as she was the day I first met her, over thirty years ago. Just elected Leader of the Opposition, she called on me at Claridge's Hotel. Jaunty, exuding vitality and assurance, she proceeded to explain her philosophy of leadership. She disdainfully dismissed the conventional wisdom that political contests were about winning the centre. In such a political system, the parties would look vapid and, what was worse, indistinguishable. The public would soon tire of electoral uniformity and, in time, despise leaders avoiding their responsibility of charting the future. Her faith in democracy based on drawing sharp distinctions would leave the ventre in play, but it would have to choose between sharply defined alternatives. She was confident she would win the next election and govern on that basis.

History vindicated that vision. Lady Thatcher was elected and re-elected twice.

I saw her often in the years of her incumbency as well as in her retirement. Her buoyancy has never flagged and her faith in her verities has remained constant: resistance to tyranny, alliance with America, insistence on a society shaped by free decisions and not the state, and suspicion of supra-nationalism.

In 1981, I visited London during the Falklands crisis to celebrate the

200th anniversary of the founding of the Foreign Office. At a lunch at the Admiralty, various senior officials outlined possible compromises based on a mediation proposal by Alexander Haig, then US Secretary of State. At tea with Lady Thatcher, I tried to explore her views on these schemes. She refused even to discuss compromise. She was, in fact, so irate at the very idea of it that I protected my lunchtime interlocutors by assuming responsibility for their ideas.

Lady Thatcher has had her prejudices. One of these was the possible ambition of Germany to achieve domination on the continent. At a dinner, I was quoting Bismarck to the effect that the best a statesman could do was to grasp the hem of God's cloak and walk with Him a few steps. Lady Thatcher, who had not been paying full attention, asked what hem of what cloak I proposed grasping. I said that it was not meant literally; it was a famous quote from Bismarck. 'Bismarck, the German?' asked Lady Thatcher. When she heard the affirmative reply, she ended the conversation with, 'Time to go home.'

But German leaders told me after unification that when they examined the files of the defunct East German foreign ministry, they found that Lady Thatcher had said nothing behind their backs that she had not said to their faces – an assertion they could not make of some other allies.

So I will conclude by emphasising how much I have learned from Lady Thatcher, including that greatness must not be confused with complexity. She has been inspirational, above all, because she incarnated unshakeable faith in the power of free people to shape their future. It has been an honour to be her contemporary.

Tim Quint
Conservative Activist

On a handful of occasions, I was lucky enough to meet the late Baroness Thatcher (then simply Mrs T.). Curiously, one of my enduring memories is of an occasion when I did not meet her!

In 1982 I was a law student at the University of East Anglia and a member of the Conservative Association formed by my good friend Iain Dale.

In January 1983, Iain attended a reception for chairmen of the various university associations at Downing Street. The event was, of course, hosted by Mrs Thatcher herself, and Iain has recounted elsewhere his recollections of that evening.

The following year I succeeded Iain as Chairman of the Association. Dared I hope for a similar invitation?

I remember not whether it was in December 1983 or perhaps January 1984 but indeed the formal invitation duly arrived. I was to be off to London in mid-February to meet the Prime Minister.

Imagine then my dismay when just a couple of days before the scheduled appointment, the Russian leader Yuri Andropov passed away and it was announced that Mrs Thatcher would be attending his funeral in Moscow.

Of course, the reception proceeded as planned. I seem to remember a clutch of Cabinet ministers (ably assisted by Denis) ensuring the evening was still one to remember. However, I couldn't help feeling someone was missing.

As a true blue Thatcherite, I must confess to feeling rather cheated at having been deprived of what would then have been my first meeting with the Great Lady by the death of a man who would certainly not have held her in the same high esteem.

I also remember that fateful day in 1990 – the day on which such a wonderful woman was betrayed by a clutch of weak-willed men.

Shortly after the news broke, I received a call from another of my good UEA pals, Mike Norris. We had worked together for many hours during the 1983 campaign. We must have visited every single street in the Norwich North constituency. The one thing that sticks in my mind is the mixture of complete surprise and utter joy on the faces of a number of lifelong (but obviously long-forgotten) supporters we unearthed in the most unlikely of locations. They were overjoyed, not only that we had actually bothered to canvass their opinion, but also to have the opportunity to express their support for the cause or their gratitude at perhaps being enabled to purchase their council house. On many occasions, they jumped at the chance to display a Conservative poster or board even within areas that were otherwise a sea of red. To suggest that Margaret Thatcher appealed only to the well heeled or those enjoying a public school education misses the point entirely. One of her great attributes was that she appealed to such a broad cross-section of society. Indeed, this above all is, I think, what annoyed the opposition so much. She was encroaching upon what they believed to be their own sacred territory.

When I took that call from Mike Norris on 28 November 1990, I remember very well him saying, 'Our country will never be the same. This will change things forever.' How right he was – and in so many ways.

I fear we may never see her like again. Steadfast leaders exhibiting such passion and conviction are rare indeed. I consider it a privilege to have lived through the Thatcher years and as a child of the 1960s, I suppose it is compensation for having missed Churchill!

Christopher Collins
Margaret Thatcher Foundation

Christopher Collins works for the Margaret Thatcher Foundation and curates its website, www.MargaretThatcher.org.

When we were working on *The Path to Power*, we struggled to find good material on her years in opposition and so Lady Thatcher agreed to invite in some colleagues from that time for a chat. One afternoon there arrived at her Belgravia office a man we shall call 'Norman'. It is sometimes said, nobly, that 'Margaret Thatcher had no use for yes men'. But that is untrue. She found them very useful indeed, because they did what she wanted most of the time, and there was such an abundant supply of them. In fact, if she hadn't found them useful, what could have been done with half her parliamentary party?

'Norman' was an excellent yes man and the conversation dedicated to extracting his reminiscences actually consisted almost entirely of her telling him what *she* remembered, which of course we already knew. He would occasionally interject, 'Yes, Margaret,' 'No, Margaret,' 'Absolutely, Margaret,' in a manner evidently familiar to her. As he was leaving, he came over to me and said, 'You know I have some notes I took at the time, and I wonder if you...' But before I could grab hold of this gift, the only remotely useful thing to come out of the whole exercise, his former boss came between us and firmly closed the meeting, 'So *good* of you to come, Norman. Love to Miffy. *Bye.*' And off he went. Undoubtedly she hadn't wanted him to tell us anything.

She waited a few seconds, then padded to her office door in stockinged feet. In exaggerated, almost pantomime style she peered down the corridor to make sure he was gone, gently closed it, then leant forward and said to us in a stage whisper, twinkle-eyed and triumphant, 'Nice guy, Norman. *But a bit of an old smoothie.*'

Crispin Blunt
Conservative MP 1997–

Crispin Blunt has been MP for Reigate since 1997. Prior to that, he was Special Adviser to the Foreign Secretary, Malcolm Rifkind. He was Prisons Minister from 2010 until 2012.

I first came into personal contact with Margaret Thatcher in 1994. I was accompanying Malcolm Rifkind as his Special Adviser; he was giving her a private advance briefing on the Front Line First changes to the armed forces. It was an hour's worth of rich political entertainment, and one began to appreciate how much her style depended on ministers who were prepared to stand up to her.

Front Line First was an uncomfortable exercise in budget cuts driven by the government's wider need to put the UK's finances back on track after the 1990–91 recession. It came on the back of the reductions already in train following the end of the Cold War. Plainly a number of senior Defence figures, past and present, had already been to see her to raise their concerns over the state of our defences.

As warm-up training for making the announcement to the House of Commons a week later it could not have been bettered. As a briefing it lasted less than thirty seconds before the avalanche of opinions and questions began to be delivered from Lady Thatcher, who was supposed to be receiving the briefing. She ranged over the whole Defence Portfolio, from the strategic relationship with the USA, to points of detail over infantry overstretch in Northern Ireland, to the highly charged emotional ties that accompany much of the politics of Defence – in this case on the decision to move the Royal Marines musical training from Deal where they had been bombed by the IRA some years before.

Gradually over the course of an hour her position moved from the inquisitorial, as she satisfied herself that Malcolm's position was sound, to one of offering help. The cost savings achieved had more than met their objective; indeed to our surprise, we found ourselves able to add to the front line capability of the armed forces, and the major capability increase we were after was to place cruise missiles on our hunter killer nuclear-powered submarines. She was well briefed and aware we were having difficulty convincing the Foreign Office of the requirement. The FCO's attitude came as no surprise to the great lady, 'They're not wet, they're drenched.'

Anthony Seldon
Contemporary Historian

Dr Anthony Seldon is Master of Wellington College and the author of many books about various Prime Ministers, including Brown at 10.

My parents were waiting for Mrs Thatcher all their lives. Throughout my teenage years, they would endlessly complain about the Labour and Conservative governments, particularly the latter, which they thought useless. The talk was all about Hayek and Friedman, Robbins and Tullock; they were the heroes, and Wilson and Heath the villains.

The world brightened with the defeat of Heath in the election of February 1974. They started to talk in hushed tones about a new body called the 'Centre for Policy Studies' and they encouraged me to work for it in my first summer holiday from university. At its HQ, I suddenly found myself face to face with this apparition in blue. I have no idea what I said or did in my weeks there, though I do have a distant memory of getting figures wrong for Keith Joseph, who was a far more regular attender than she.

My parents had come from such different places. My father: the child of Jewish immigrants who died in the Spanish influenza plague and brought up in the East End as the stepson of a cobbler. My mother: from aristocratic parents, but whose father had gone bad and become a communist. Both parents were ardent believers in self-help and in the free market, and they both loathed the state, which they saw as paternalistic and destructive of individual initiative and enterprise. My father found his intellectual home in the Institute of Economic Affairs, my mother in her long campaign for the education voucher.

The new-style Thatcher, who emerged from the Heath government disillusioned with corporatism, was their woman. They began to talk more and more about her, especially after she took the leadership from Heath. Then, in the summer of 1977, the phone rang at our home in Kent; it was the maverick *eminence grise* Patrick Cosgrave to say, could he bring the blessed lady to a garden party my parents were holding?

The news got out and it suddenly became a much bigger party. She breezed around among the rhododendrons, blue on pink, listening attentively to everyone. The next morning, I was alone at home and she phoned up from Scotney Castle in Lamberhurst with a heartfelt message of thanks.

I never shared my parents' fervour for the free market, so I did not share their mounting disappointment that Mrs Thatcher failed to live up to the high expectations of her. They liked what she did on inflation and the trade unions, but thought she failed on welfare. In her last conference speech, the candle flared one final time before going out when she talked about education vouchers and parental choice in schooling. A month later she was gone.

I was never more excited about Mrs Thatcher myself than when she stood on the doorstep of Downing Street and quoted from St Francis of Assisi on her very first day as Prime Minister. That was the high point, and from then on it was downhill all the way. I hated the triumphalism of her saying 'Rejoice' on the recapture of South Georgia in the Falklands, and I passionately wished that the concern that she showed when her son Mark was lost in the Sahara during the Paris-Dakar Rally could have also been displayed to all those who lost their jobs and way of life as a direct result of her policies. She would have been a greater leader if she had engaged more with those who were losing out from her policies, and if she had done more to come up with practical plans to give them fresh hope.

What a shame it was, I felt, that in her latter years in Downing Street she was surrounding herself with an ever-narrowing coterie of right-wing admirers, who were telling her what she wanted to hear rather than what was right. Great leaders welcome divergent viewpoints; she increasingly didn't. I regret that she didn't do more to follow up the concern she had expressed about the damage to the global environment. She could have done so much more as Prime Minister in so many areas. I admire her for her great achievements but for me, the Thatcher governments were as much about lost opportunities as those great achievements.

In the last four years of her premiership, I was running the Institute for Contemporary British History where we tried to assess her as a historical figure, with writers such as Robert Skidelsky, John Campbell, Ben Pimlott and John Vincent. The work bore fruit in the volume I edited for the Oxford University Press on her tenth anniversary, *The Thatcher Effect.*

After her fall from power, I was one of many brought in to advise on the writing of her memoirs. At one point we were watching television when the news broke of Robert Maxwell's death. 'He never would have committed suicide,' she said. I was pleased to help, but I could not admire the way she conducted herself towards her successor, whose authorised biography I was writing, and whose time at No. 10 she did so much to damage with her 'noises off'.

The last time I saw her was at my father's memorial service in 2006. Geoffrey Howe gave the main address. She didn't seem to react. When we spoke to her afterwards to thank her for coming, we understood why. The woman my parents had so eagerly waited for was only half there.

Dame Ann Leslie
Journalist

Dame Ann Leslie is an award-winning foreign correspondent who writes for the Daily Mail.

My note at a 1973 Tory Party Conference read, 'Met a frightful woman called Margaret Hilda Thatcher.' I made copious notes about the assorted Grand Old Gents who then wielded power in the party – along with their old school ties, champagne flutes and brandy balloons – but about that 'frightful woman'? Nothing further, because I assumed that she'd never get anywhere.

Indeed, it was not until February 1977, standing with her on the Great Wall of China, that I first grasped the fact that Mrs Thatcher was more than an over-elocuted bottle blonde who had, improbably and (many believed) temporarily, managed to become Tory leader. In that role she was making an official visit to China.

It wasn't just the Grand Old Gents who didn't take her very seriously. Even Fleet Street editors thought of her as a bit of a suburban housewife joke. It might have been only four months since the death of Chairman Mao and two months after the arrest of the Gang of Four – seminal geopolitical events – but the press party on the trip were mostly chosen from the fluffy end of journalism: female columnists who could be relied upon to indulge in girl-talk about Carmen rollers with her, sniggering gossip columnists, plus two or three earnest China specialists. I still thought of her as 'that frightful woman', but now that the Cultural Revolution was over I could at last visit the enclosed land where my father was born and where my grandparents got married.

I knew that the Chinese routinely subjected their visiting 'Distinguished Foreign Friends' to what I called the 'Great Wall Stakes'. I warned Mrs T. that I'd learned the section of the wall we would be visiting at Badaling was extremely steep and slithery and, er, her high-heeled court shoes were wholly unsuitable for the challenge. She blithely assured me, 'Oh, I don't intend to be athletic, my dear!'

But then the Chinese, doubtless secretly tittering at her forthcoming humiliation, told her, 'Chairman Mao said "he who does not reach the top of the Great Wall is no great man."' Big mistake. She retorted briskly, 'That should be changed to: no great *leader*!' And off she shot up along the wall like a Blue Streak rocket and, in no time at all, she and her Rotary-wife suit, carefully coiffed helmet of hair and those 'unsuitable' shoes were mere specks on the Badaling horizon.

Her insatiable gluttony for facts – dreary swot stuff which the grand old gents tended to believe was somewhat beneath them – soon became exhaustingly evident.

Time and again on that Chinese trip, her then 23-year-old daughter Carol would moan, 'Oh, Mum, *come on!*' when it looked as if Mum had fastened onto yet another hapless Chinese official and was about to grill him about the *exact* make-up of revolutionary committees, and could he please explain *exactly* what happened to surplus grain profits, if there were any, and was the basic unit accounting method *really* the most efficient method of running an agricultural commune? While the eyes of the 'Gang of Nineteen' (as we in the press party dubbed ourselves) were glazing over at yet another baffling recitation of the *mus* and *catties* of Chinese rice production, Mrs T.'s were shining like stars.

At the end of yet another gruelling day touring communes and eating jellyfish, tree fungus and ducks' feet at yet another banquet in the Great Hall of the People, the entire Thatcher party and our 'Gang of Nineteen' were hollow-eyed with jet lag and lack of sleep. She, on the other hand, was fresh as a daisy and, turning to me, said brightly, 'Oh dear, these evening do's end so early. I wish we could go round the factories that are open all night.'

In her heart of hearts, she still belonged to the thrifty suburbs of her youth: on glimpsing cheap but neatly bundled vegetables in a Beijing market stall she cried happily, 'How wonderful – they're just like Sainsbury's stewpacks!'

Two years later I found myself once again scuttling in her blue-suited wake during the 1979 election which brought her to power, and once again marvelled at her stamina and her capacity for absorbing facts and regurgitating them with stunning accuracy. There seemed nothing on which she was not, by now, an expert – from false kneecaps to chocolate-making to types of ironing board covers. Interrupting a woman ironing a garment in a factory, she enthused, 'Oh, those ironing board covers are marvellous! Do you know, they come in two sizes, a big one and a little one, I have one of the little ones at home and you know compared to...' 'Is your wife good at ironing?' I asked Denis. 'My wife is good at *everything* she does!' he harrumphed.

Including (as he did not say) flirting. She liked men – preferably tall, young and handsome ones, like Cecil Parkinson and Michael Portillo. Frankly she did not much like most other women, especially not beady-eyed women journalists like me. I think she thought we were a bunch of wimps.

On that 1979 campaign, tour buses were not routinely fitted with onboard loos, and having given birth the previous year my bladder was not entirely stoic about having to spend hours out of reach of a public lavatory. I pleaded with her, 'Mrs Thatcher, please can we have more potty stops? I sometimes wonder whether you vaporise the stuff, like astronauts. But I can't.' The iron-bladdered Iron Lady looked at me witheringly, 'No one needs to go more than twice a day. I go first thing in the morning and last thing at night – and that's *quite* enough!'

She would always, over the years, comment on my not very remarkable clothes – 'What a lovely colour your jacket is, I've got one just like that!' – but she never wasted her high octane flirtatious charms on the likes of me, perhaps not least because she suspected that we women knew her little tricks.

Especially her use of hand-on-the-elbow body language. One victim of the latter told me how it worked. 'First she plays the role of the tough, terrifying warrior queen and then, when you are truly intimidated, she suddenly cups your elbow, gazes up at you with those china-blue eyes and breathes "My *dear*", and makes you feel you're the one man in the room who can bring out the feminine "little woman" in her. Believe me, it works!'

Indeed it did. Over the years I'd watched her deploy her hand-on-the-elbow weapon on dozens of initially recalcitrant men, ranging from the Zambian President Kenneth Kaunda, to Mikhail Gorbachev, to my own husband, who heartily disliked her public image but who, at a party at No. 10, received the hand-on-the-elbow treatment and was almost instantly seduced.

She was a nightmare to interview, as I once told her: 'You are the worst interviewee I've ever had, bar perhaps Imelda Marcos; asking Imelda or you a question is like chucking a pebble into Niagara – it's instantly swept away.' On one occasion she said, 'My dear, please don't cut in until I've explained the *whole situation* to you!' Fine – except I'd asked her about the poll tax, and its unenforceability, and she insisted on explaining the *whole situation* about Toronto's rubbish collection system instead.

No wonder her feeble Cabinet colleagues couldn't stand it anymore. But, despite myself, I adored her – and knew that the Tory Party had committed hara-kiri by turfing her out so cruelly. The Tories are still paying for that matricide today.

Sir Nicholas Winterton
Conservative MP 1971–2010

Sir Nicholas Winterton was elected to Parliament in a by-election in 1971 and served as MP for Macclesfield until 2010.

I was part of the campaign group of thirty-three under the inspired leadership of Airey Neave, Norman St John-Stevas and Sir Keith Joseph and others which campaigned passionately to achieve the leadership of the Conservative and Unionist Party for Margaret Thatcher in 1975.

It was a truly exciting time and everyone was fully committed because of Margaret's vision, not only for the future of the Conservative Party, but also for the future of our country. The commitment to this campaign was total; victory was the sole objective and it was achieved.

I never regretted my involvement as a junior member of the team, having come into the House of Commons at a by-election in the autumn of 1971. This is because there is no doubt that Margaret Thatcher's determination and philosophy changed the culture of our country and inspired confidence for the future.

In the early 1980s I became involved in the saga of the DeLorean motor car company in Northern Ireland when I outlined my concerns about the use of the public money provided to the company. My comments were made outside the House as it was in recess at the time. I was subsequently sued by DeLorean through his solicitors for $250 million, the equivalent at the time of £133 million, slightly more than petty cash I have to say. Because of the situation I requested and was granted a meeting with the Prime Minister at Downing Street. I attended the meeting on my own, despite the request I had made to bring my solicitor, and at the meeting I was faced not only by the Prime Minister but also the Attorney General, Sir Michael Havers and her Parliamentary Private Secretary, Ian Gow MP, and her Private Secretary. It was a difficult and uncomfortable meeting and it was one of the few occasions when Margaret gave way to a ministerial colleague to deal with all the matters that I raised, although I suspect and felt that she was not unsympathetic to my situation. In those days backbenchers were exceedingly vulnerable to any comments made outside the Chamber, while government ministers were covered by the full resources of the state. This was a time also when there was no House of Commons insurance cover for such matters as there is today.

For me a memorable event was when Margaret Thatcher, accompanied by Denis, visited my constituency shortly after she resigned the leadership of the Conservative Party. I believe it was the first Conservative Association function she attended after she stepped down. It was a dinner held at Titherington Golf and Country Club to the north of Macclesfield and the event was heavily oversubscribed. In fact, the club had to erect a tent extension in order to accommodate the huge number of people. It was an occasion I will remember for the rest of my life. She made an inspired speech to over 350 people and you could hear a pin drop in the room as everyone listened intently to every word she uttered.

The way that she dealt with questions was amazing, and everyone present admired her knowledge and authority. Denis Thatcher's presence added hugely to the occasion and his humour and total support of Margaret were always to be admired.

A particularly inspiring experience for me was when, during the country-wide launch of her first book, *The Downing Street Years*, I was asked by the publishers to chair and act as Master of Ceremonies at a launch in the North West in the Gateway Theatre in the heart of the city of Chester. It was an amazing occasion. There were queues to get into the theatre, and when the doors opened the theatre filled to capacity and there were people standing around the walls. All came to meet Mrs Thatcher despite the fact that she was no longer Prime Minister. I was, in addition, the lead-in speaker and it was an honour to have been asked to undertake this responsibility. She was cheered to the proverbial rafters.

Many people believe that Margaret Thatcher's decision to step down from the leadership of the party at the time when she did was a great error and the party has in a way been paying the price ever since.

Adam Afriyie
Conservative MP 2005–

Adam Afriyie entered Parliament in 2005 in the seat of Windsor. In 2007 he was
appointed Conservative shadow Minister for Innovation, Universities and Skills.

Margaret Thatcher gave this country back to the hard-working people of Britain. Her devotion to her country, her conviction, vision and determination shone through in everything she did and everything she achieved. Margaret Thatcher transformed a downtrodden, broken country into a thriving, exciting, modern nation.

I admire strong, intelligent women. I'm intrigued by them. On the one hand, I'm drawn to them and on the other hand, I'm terrified by them. I know I'm not the only man who feels this way. Margaret Thatcher was the ultimate strong, intelligent woman. She attracted and terrified in equal measure.

When I joined the Conservative Party and became active in politics in the late 1980s, it was to support Mrs Thatcher as she began to face increasing troubles from fellow MPs. Coming from a poor background, living in social housing in Peckham, I never dreamt I'd actually meet her, but it's funny how life turns out.

I had been a regional Chairman of Business for Sterling, the 'No (to) the Euro' campaign, and a spokesman for the 'No to the EU Constitution' movement. I felt that my credentials as a Eurosceptic were impeccable. So when I arrived at a small do in Finchley at which Margaret Thatcher was the guest of honour, I couldn't wait to share a word or two of empathy on all things European.

Just as she approached me to make small talk, a chap behind me said, 'There are some benefits to the euro you know.' She thought it was me! I was terrified to see that fiery glint spark in her eye. She'd spotted a damnable wet! Grabbing my left forearm, she leant forward, fixed me with a steely glare and began the opening salvo with, 'Adam, there is a reason [why] we're an island...' The tirade lasted several minutes and I was forced to stand and simply nod like a naughty schoolboy. I just didn't have the courage to say I hadn't made the comment.

Thankfully, years later, I got to know the lady better at various dinner parties and events, and my wife and I were immensely privileged to host her at our home on more than one occasion. I quickly learned that she enjoyed socialising, debating and had a truly generous spirit.

Today, I feel blessed to have known one of the greatest Prime Ministers and leaders in the history of the world. She will never be forgotten.

Brian Monteith
Journalist and Former MSP

Brian Monteith was a Member of the Scottish Parliament from 1999 to 2007 and was a leading member of the Federation of Conservative Students in the early 1980s.

Leadership is something that you either have in you or you don't. To be a good leader of men or women, you need to have a natural empathy with those that will take your commands, and an understanding of the effort and sacrifices being asked of them, no matter how small. You need to be decisive – it instils confidence that you know what you are doing and are not just making it up as you go along – while being open to different approaches and new ideas before you come to your decision, strengthening the bond with your charges.

If you have such qualities, and in many regards they can only come in life from witnessing or experiencing disappointments, from facing adversity or overcoming injustice, you will have the opportunity to inspire people to join with you and go beyond what is normally asked of anyone or might be expected of them.

Margaret Thatcher had such leadership qualities in spades, both for the nation and her parliamentary party – but also, we should never forget, for the Conservative Party. If we take a small step back and consider for a moment those people who were young enough to be her foot soldiers at the time of, first, her leadership of the party from 1975, and then her premiership from 1979, we can see the impact that she made and conclude that the party owes her a great debt.

I must admit, I did not take to Mrs Thatcher (as she then was) immediately. As a raw young teenager in 1975, not yet able to vote and with an underdeveloped knowledge of economics or philosophy, the world was very black or white to me, or should I say blue or red. I certainly had no sense of nuance about the layers within political parties. My mixture of Scottish chippyness and bravado made me dismissive and suspicious of Margaret Thatcher, whose voice I found grating in a way that I had not when Ted Heath spoke.

What had, until then, led me to be a Conservative was my patriotism for Britain born of our nation's history, and my revulsion at both
fascism and communism which I had studied at school through the
writings of Churchill. Thanks, though, to the weekend political seminars for young people held by Margaret Thatcher's Centre for Policy
Studies, I developed my political thinking, mixed with people beyond
my parochial upbringing and began to admire and believe in what
Margaret Thatcher and Keith Joseph were saying. I was hooked. And
I was not alone.

For the next twelve years I was either a Conservative student hack
or a rapidly ageing YC losing my hair. The 1970s were not only a time
of industrial strife, economic failure and regular national humiliation.
They were also the apogee of the hairy demonstrating student. It
seemed a week rarely passed by without some student union somewhere
chartering a bus to a demo here or occupying an admin building there.

To be a Tory student and speak at a union general meeting was to
stand up and be counted – and Margaret Thatcher gave many of us
the ideological steel and the cast-iron faith that we were in the right,
and could justifiably take on the intimidating odds. That she had a
developed philosophy was especially appealing to young people, who
tend to enjoy politics with a passion and can see every issue as a great
wrong to be righted or social injustice to be reformed.

Younger Conservatives gathered round Margaret Thatcher's banner
and were willing to throw themselves at the political enemy. Crucially
though, she appealed to everyone: there were no class barriers, no
advantages for some, no discrimination in Thatcher's battalions. Many
like me, whose parents had voted Labour all their lives, saw no difficulty, no contradiction in joining Margaret Thatcher's Conservatives.

The keynote speeches of Thatcher, Joseph and Howe were supplied
in pamphlet form for us young disciples to devour. Papers by MPs
with articulate reasoned arguments showing the positive future of
free markets and a strong defence were produced by the Conservative
Political Centre, while statements from CCO press office came through
my mum's letterbox daily.

The Institute of Economic Affairs and Adam Smith Institute gave
us further succour and support, arming us with the intellectual weapons and creative ideas that were to form the backbone of Margaret
Thatcher's governments. It was to become common for many of us to

pass through their doors and work for them. Some, like Philip Booth, are still doing great work there.

The growing threat of the Soviet Empire that had proxy wars, coups or revolutions in nearly every continent, and the apparent self-doubt in the West's response presented a worrying international scene, while the violent mass picketing of the Grunwick dispute and the growth of the left within the Labour Party provided a dark shadow over our own democracy. These challenges were meat and drink to Margaret Thatcher – and her resolute support for the rule of law at home and abroad inspired young Tories to put our own case and take the socialists on.

Margaret Thatcher's party was fed and watered on what our nation's problems were and what we were going to do about it. But still, there was a niggling doubt: if given the honour of leading the country would she crumble under the weight of the forces against her? Would she buckle, like Ted Heath?

Then she was elected and she never let us down. We didn't always agree (nor did we always agree among ourselves), but when the chips were down we would fall into line and fight shoulder to shoulder with her for our cause. When Kenny Everett said 'Let's bomb Russia', we all got the joke, but behind his ad-lib was the realisation that in Margaret Thatcher we had a Prime Minister who could lead the country against the gravest of perils and most desperate of situations.

Membership of both the Conservative students and YCs blossomed, no longer were student groups the out-of-season ski-club or a rival marriage bureau to the Young Farmers – they were up for politics and started winning their own small battles.

Soon I was hearing the rhetorical flourish of Des Swayne in his red St Andrew's gown, witnessing Eleanor Laing becoming the first Union President at Edinburgh University while Alex Sherbrooke (now parish priest at St Patrick's, Soho Square) and Charles Hendry campaigned there with success too. I saw William Hague make that speech at my first Blackpool conference and John Whittingdale was never out of his leather jacket. Simon Richards, now running the Freedom Association, organised his students union to disaffiliate from NUS and around the country many more of us rose up to try the same.

Dundee pulled out, then my own gaff, Heriot Watt; there were campaigns at Durham run by Nick Gibb; others at Reading by Alan

Griffiths; Leicester by Rachel Daniels, Newcastle Poly by Martin Callanan – and many, many more. The left were on the back foot. Many of these people went on to become Members of Parliament, councillors or leaders in their chosen field, such as Peter Bingle. This article cannot begin to capture them all or include everyone – but they know they were there fighting Margaret Thatcher's corner.

The greatest campaign of the time was to challenge the growth of CND and, with help from Julian Lewis and our own Mark Prisk, we saw to it young people had the materials to do it. And we won that argument.

Margaret Thatcher was an inspiration to them all.

Most noticeable in this period was how the Conservative students' membership expanded beyond the traditional Ivory Towers – and even beyond the red brick unis and into the polytechnics and small colleges. Although many students in small institutions might be part-time we just had to turn up with a folding table, set up our stall with 'Support the cuts' posters, 'Cruise on' badges and Solidarnosc T-shirts, and people would sign up. Margaret Thatcher was often fighting another battle, be it the Falklands, a steel strike, then the miners' strike – but these and other challenges and how she rose to them put the Great back in Britain and young people flocked to the YC and student groups. Combined membership must have been over 100,000.

Of course with such passion and devotion came great internal arguments about what was the right approach to this question or that; there were some who openly doubted our Prime Minister, some who wanted a little moderation here or there and others who felt she was not going quick enough or cutting deep enough. But these were the problems of electoral success and the opportunities that those created for us. We all wanted the Conservatives to win, were nervous that we might lose when there was still so much to be done – and impatient to make the changes our country needed.

Chairmen of the time such as Peter Young and Tim Linacre, Marc Glendenning and Mark MacGregor carried a torch for Margaret Thatcher deep into enemy territory, a young chap called Paul Goodman and another named John Bercow took that torch all the way into the Commons. Others such as Harry Phibbs, Gary Ling and Donal Blaney came through the ranks cutting their teeth on the ideological clash with colour and impact. Iain Dale had long hair and big ideas while Jonathan Isaby and others saw their future in the media,

PR and law. Aeroflot offices would be occupied, leaflets handed out in Red Square, Afghan freedom fighters and Solidarity trade unionists would address our conferences.

The first time I was in her company was when, as a Conservative student leader, I attended our national committee's annual meeting with the Prime Minister in Downing Street. She came into the drawing room and was astonished to find that the Education Secretary William Waldegrave was not there to take part. She told an aide to summon him immediately and twenty minutes later a heavily perspiring, quivering jelly of a man rushed in thinking he was about to be sacked. The relief on his face when he realised it was to meet Tory students made us all laugh, with Margaret Thatcher enjoying the joke she knew she had inadvertently set up.

Being a student or Young Conservative under Margaret Thatcher's leadership gave you a cause and we were happy to take the socialists on. In 1983, the 50th anniversary of the Conservative Students, our work was recognised by Mrs T. who hosted a reception at Downing Street while every year she took the first dance at the YC ball at party conference. She mixed, she listened, she laughed, but most of all she led us from the front.

We responded in kind, organising counter demonstrations so that she could see that along with the Trots there were others willing to turn up, take the heat and shout our support. 'Maggie, Maggie, Maggie; in, in, in!' we would chant, followed by a round of 'More police pay, more police pay' – which always got a knowing smile from the bobbies keeping us apart. At one counter demo ten brave souls, myself included, marched into the heart of the 300 Trots waiting to greet her as she arrived at the General Assembly of the Church of Scotland. They were demonstrating about nuclear weapons so we had placards supporting Trident. The police were concerned about us being attacked and moved us next to the demonstrators opposing the forthcoming visit of the Pope. All of a sudden the Trots lunged at us and fists flew but none of us bore a mark – the followers of Pastor Jack Glass had fancied a square go themselves and dived into the melee with the police trying to keep them apart. Thatcher drove in and waved and we made a tactical retreat to the pub, laughing over our rounds of foaming ales and thinking we must repeat the exercise the next time Mrs T. came to town. (We did, but none were ever as much a laugh as the first.)

The Conservative Party became a truly open, democratic and revitalised party under Margaret Thatcher. After having suffered two demoralising electoral defeats, she attracted many into politics that would never previously have given it a thought and she laid the foundations for future electoral success and, for those outside politics, professional achievement.

I am now in my fifties, an old bufty like those that used to tell me I was too brash, too pushy, too rebellious – but I rejoice in the knowledge that I was fortunate to be one of Thatcher's legionaries, and that because she had a philosophical and intellectual backbone, as well as great courage and fortitude, her work will be carried on by today's younger Conservatives and hope they will be as strident and outspoken as we were. Trotsky was right, the revolution must and will be permanent – he just didn't realise it would be a Conservative revolution, a Thatcherite one.

Alistair Burt

Conservative MP 1983–97 and 2001–

Alistair Burt was MP for Bury North from 1983 until 1997. He returned to Parliament as the Member for North East Bedfordshire in 2001. He is now a Foreign Office minister.

In 1986 I went to South Africa, in the depths of apartheid. Visits were not easy unless you were a regime supporter, so first-hand political accounts of what was really going on were rare.

But there was safety in numbers. When an invitation came to Parliament from Christians working for peaceful change there, Liberal Simon Hughes, Labour's Peter Pike and I were prepared to go. We resolved that on return we would see our respective party leaders.

Which was how I came to be with Mrs Thatcher, one-to-one, for half an hour. I must have spoken for twenty-five of the thirty minutes. She listened intently as I described meetings from senior government members to township leaders and a country of greater complexity and agonising introspection of all its peoples than was commonly depicted.

South Africa was incredibly toxic. Sanctions were the touchstone, and the PM was against them. But I asked her what she intended to do. She was quiet for some moments, then said, 'I just don't know, Alistair.'

I was rather stunned. Here was the PM, outwardly sure of every-thing, confessing to a truly junior sprog a newsworthy position – that she really did not know what to do about one of the world's biggest international challenges. I have always cherished the time she gave me, and the honesty of her reply.

I would not claim that I was then or became one of her closest confidants. I'm afraid I could never be counted 'one of us', for I was simply a Tory from my home town of Bury, elected at the age of twenty-eight, calling it as best I could during difficult times. Of course I agreed with the prescription of Britain's ills, which had swept me into the Commons in 1983. The north of England was already changing – and Mrs Thatcher accelerated it.

But it did hurt. I made a Commons speech and wrote of the pain of unemployment with which, to my crimson-eared panic, I heard Neil Kinnock taunt the PM at Question Time.

The South African story above reveals what a number of recollections of Mrs Thatcher appear to confirm – that in private, on the one hand, she could play absolutely to type, while on the other confound the caricature of her. While her indecision on such a topic might therefore be a mild surprise, as her hatred of apartheid conflicted with her acute concern for black workers who might be affected by sanctions, her obstinacy in not supporting sanctions when it seemed the easy course is not.

Such obstinacy added to the caricature as opponents rushed to misinterpret her position as somehow supporting the regime. These wilful distortions we see passed into leftist history, as revealed in the bile and hatred that has accompanied the synthetic posturing following her death. From a journalist who should know better – 'I grew up knowing that Mrs Thatcher would hate me' (really?) – to the contrived histrionics of Glenda Jackson, all the abuse does is mask the realisation of socialists that in a hundred years they have never produced any comparable figure in public and international esteem to be given such a send-off.

These juvenile rantings should not obscure serious examination of her, warts and all. I won't be the only one to make the Shakespearian comparison, that the very qualities which made her the leader for her times – her belief and certainty in herself and her identification with 'our people' – would be among those which contributed to her political downfall.

I think part of the anger of the left today is because, if they were around and honest in their memories, they would recall that they failed to translate the rage of the few into the votes of the many. I know Mrs Thatcher won plenty of Tory votes in Bury North and similar northern marginal seats, not because they all liked her, and not because they were all Conservatives, but because they respected her. I heard that so many times in the humblest parts of town where my father was the family doctor. They could remember the Bury of the recent past, and did not want it back. They had been divided not by her but by the union warfare against the public that 1974–79 had become.

But if I'm honest I also remember a sense that the votes were lent, and that once there was a credible alternative, once the gains of Mrs

Thatcher had been secured by John Major, the sky would fall in. And it did.

The legacy to the country was immense. To our party, just that bit more difficult.

Two final vignettes illustrate again the predictable Mrs T. and the surprising.

It's true she struggled a bit with humour and small talk. I once mentioned to her that I had run the London Marathon the weekend before. She had seen it on television. 'Marvellous,' she breathed in that unmistakeable voice. I then made the mistake of trying to gain still more credit by telling her I had run dressed as a pink elephant.

There was sheer puzzlement. An MP running a marathon was understandable. Running as a pink elephant was beyond her envelope.

She came to Bury North in the election of 1987, on course for her massive win. We toured a factory, and then rode the battle bus together to the site of an open-air rally. I asked her how the campaign was going elsewhere. She said she wasn't sure she would win, expressing a wobble herself. I looked out of the bus window. The news that she was in town had spread, and from the bus window I could see people emerging from houses and shops, and waving. 'Look out of the window, Prime Minister,' I said. 'People in Bury don't do that every day. They have come just to look at you, and tell their friends they've seen you. You'll be fine.'

And she was. Very fine indeed.

Steven Norris
Conservative MP 1983–97

Steven Norris was PPS to Nicholas Ridley and went on to be a Transport Minister in John Major's government, while holding his seat in Epping Forest. This is an edited extract from his autobiography Changing Trains.

Like most political explosions, Nicholas Ridley's resignation originated from humble beginnings. Dominic Lawson, Editor of *The Spectator*, had asked Nick for an interview. Young Lawson had earned a reputation for stitching colleagues up. A recent interview with Chris Patten had not portrayed him in a particularly flattering light. Nick, however, was intrigued. He had privately been irritated when, after the 1983 general election, it had been Nigel Lawson whom Margaret chose as Chancellor, leaving Nick outside the Cabinet as Financial Secretary. Their rivalry was as personal as it was ideological, and Nick saw the opportunity to discuss Lawson 'pere' as too great a temptation to resist.

Dominic Lawson has his own account of their meeting, but Nick himself told me that it had been part on, part off the record. Lawson produced a piece which portrayed Nick as violently anti-German, complete with a number of intemperate quotations and a lethal front-page Nicholas Garland cartoon in which Nick was seen running away from a poster of the German Chancellor Helmut Kohl on which he had apparently just daubed the hair and moustache of Adolf Hitler.

The way Lawson printed the story left Nick in a desperately vulnerable situation. He was on a trade mission to Budapest when the story broke. Camera crews jetted out to find him. He was hounded by the ratpack at every turn. The opposition predictably condemned him and called for his head. Even Charles Powell, privately a friend of Nick's, told Margaret that Ridley was becoming a liability.

It was clear Margaret felt under real pressure. On so many occasions, Nick had been her bulwark against the wets, and she was personally fond of him. I know that because she agonised for some time about his fate, not only because she liked him, but also because she realised that part of the attack on Nick was directed at her.

I spent most of the Saturday on the phone to John Cole and others trying to desperately counter the stories running on the BBC during the morning that Nick's resignation was imminent. I was not yet prepared to see him fall – not least because I believe Margaret would personally have wanted him to stay. By four o'clock in the afternoon it all came to nought. Margaret and Nick spoke; she told him that, much as she valued and trusted him, she simply could not keep him and he, a gentleman to the last, resigned.

I was devastated by the injustice of it all. It was clear to anyone who knew the man that Nick had been traduced. It was equally clear that Margaret had been forced to lose a valued ally. I was angry with Lawson and his fellow bloodsuckers, angry with those colleagues who had taken advantage of Nick's weakness and angry with Margaret for not standing up to them in the way I always assumed she would.

Sir John Nott
Conservative MP 1966–83

Sir John Nott served as first Trade and then Defence Secretary during Margaret Thatcher's first term. This extract is taken from his 2002 autobiography Here Today, Gone Tomorrow.

Men and women do behave differently. Why try to hide it? To me, Margaret Thatcher was always charming and considerate, except when we had a fierce disagreement on a policy issue – and then of course I read about it, with appropriate canards, in the press. As a person I always liked her very much, but I think that I might have been, among her Cabinet colleagues, in a minority.

Her attitude towards her colleagues, and her behaviour towards them in meetings, was dominated by her passion to get her own way. Often, she was dismissive and aggressive if someone's reasoning was different from her own. She would constantly interrupt and challenge. But if the victim did not hold his corner intellectually, she could be scathing. This did not endear her to her more timid – or should I say more gentlemanly? – colleagues. Privately, outside the processes of government, I believe that she treated even her most dedicated opponents with considerable courtesy and friendliness. She had many admirable qualities.

Those outside the world of politics often do not understand that it is a passionate profession. Most people who enter politics feel deeply, often emotionally, about key issues. That passion for politics, and belief in its primacy, was the motive force of Margaret Thatcher's great achievement

On 12 June 1982 HMS *Glamorgan* was hit by an Exocet missile. It was the morning of the trooping of the colour on Horse Guards Parade, so it was not an auspicious start to the day. I joined Margaret Thatcher on the stand, with my young son, William, to watch the parade, and afterwards we adjourned to No. 10 for lunch. Margaret had asked Rex Hunt and his wife, but really made it an occasion to entertain the children of her staff in the large dining room upstairs. I asked Margaret who had prepared the lunch 'Oh, I did,' she said. 'Mary and I stayed up late last night to put a meal together.' I recall it so well because here was the Prime Minister in the middle of a war, provided with no staff whatsoever, and yet she had found time personally to prepare a meal late at night for the children. Her image as a ruthless, uncaring harridan was misplaced; no one took more care of her staff and she was always scrupulous in showing her concern for both the health and well-being of her friends. It was strange how she could be so cruel and unreasonable to her ministers, but so kind and thoughtful to her immediate circle. Margaret had a warm and generous heart – and yet she presided over an unhappy Cabinet, continually undermined by gossip and malicious, unattributable briefing.

In her relationships with a male-dominated Cabinet – and one that had traditional attitudes to the place of women in society – she often behaved in ways which it would have been unacceptable for any man to do so. Above all, she had a woman's courage. A different type of courage from a man's. She had more courage and more obstinacy than a man. She really did believe that all men were 'wet', and in particular the species called 'gentlemen'. Of all the men that I knew in my time in politics, I cannot think of any who would not have sought an honourable settlement. I am sure Margaret never meant to do so, but she went along with the diplomatic game – because 'to win' she had to do so. She was confronted with a crisis for her government and she shut her mind to the risks of conducting such an adventure 8,000 miles away. It was a woman's war – and the woman in her won.

In the last resort, one can only judge oneself as people see you; just as one can only judge other people as you see them. Margaret Thatcher, after I resigned and retired to business (one of the few senior Members ever to do so voluntarily), ever since behaved towards me as if she was a deserted wife – in her memoirs she called me a mixture of 'gold, dross and mercury'. Some compliment!

Elizabeth Cotterell
Special Adviser to Gillian Shephard

The Centre for Policy Studies, founded by Margaret Thatcher and Sir Keith Joseph in 1974, was known in the press as 'Margaret Thatcher's Private Think Tank'. By 1980, she was its patron. We worked closely with the No. 10 Policy Unit, but the Prime Minister herself had naturally become somewhat distanced from our day-to-day activities. However, Alfred saw her regularly, often on Sundays, and would ring me in the evening with any relevant details from their meeting. On Sunday 18 July 1982 the usual call came through, this time with a difference: 'Alfred Sherman here: I'm speaking from No. 10. The Prime Minister would like to talk to you. She hopes you can help her with a difficult speech. Here she is.' As I trembled with shock and fear, the familiar voice took over. It was an interesting assignment. Dame Margery Corbett Ashby, the co-founder of the Townswomen's Guild, had died in 1981, aged ninety-nine. The Guild had established an Annual Memorial Lecture in her memory and invited the Prime Minister to deliver the first one, on Monday 26 July. Dame Margery, born in 1882, had been a suffragette and a pioneer of social and educational reform – not what popular opinion would have called a 'Thatcherite'.

Mrs Thatcher explained, clearly and crisply, what she wanted – a consideration of the century covered by Dame Margery's life – the changes it had seen and the underlying verities which had not changed.

I saw that a great plus in working for her would be that she seemed to know exactly what she wanted. Her concluding remarks explained why I had received this surprising request. 'Alfred tells me that you're an authority on the nineteenth century.' A gross exaggeration, but my PhD had involved a study of Victorian social reform. 'None of the drafts I have had so far have quite caught the right tone. Could you produce one for me? I'll have all the papers sent round in the morning and I would like the draft here by Tuesday the twentieth please.'

And that was that. I found the papers on my desk the next morning, and worked frantically. The draft went in as requested and I was summoned to see the Prime Minister on Friday 23 at 3 p.m. This was a good sign, I was assured by Ian Gow, Mrs Thatcher's Parliamentary Private Secretary: she wouldn't even be seeing me if the draft was impossible. I arrived promptly to begin one of the most amazing twenty-four hours of my life. The Prime Minister was moderate in her praise: 'You've worked very hard. You've done what I asked you to do. As a skeleton, this has possibilities. I think we can build on it.' She fingered another draft on the table and tossed it aside contemptuously. 'Not like this effort from the Research Department. Do they really think that I can preach party propaganda on an occasion like this?' My spirits lifted. This suggested that I had got the right tone, but I prepared myself for similar trenchant criticism.

To my surprise, there was none.

From the moment we set to work it was a joint effort, two people engaged in a common quest to perfect this speech. Mrs Thatcher obviously had a well-tried way of working. Each of us had a copy of the draft, while another was laid out, page by page, on the floor. It was to be a lecture, so was longer than most speeches. There were, at this stage, about thirty sheets. The Prime Minister had already marked where she wanted transpositions, expansions or contractions, or facts and figures to be checked. As amendments were made, a Garden Girl was summoned to take the pages down, section by section, for typing and re-typing. Mrs Thatcher gave her attention to every detail, yet was always keen to ensure that the main theme, constant change occurring against the background of eternal truth, ran consistently through the speech. She would read and re-read to make sure that each page achieved that balance. Her painstaking approach was tinged with an unexpected dry wit.

There was considerable trouble from the IRA in 1982 and I had mentioned the fact that in 1882 the Chief Secretary for Ireland had been assassinated in Phoenix Park, Dublin. 'I'd better not say that,' she said. 'It would sound as if I want something to happen to Jim Prior.' (Jim Prior was at that time Secretary of State for Ireland, and a leading 'wet'.) Even though some of my favourite references were taken out, Mrs Thatcher was genuinely interested in them. There was a hymn by John Addington Symonds: 'I haven't seen that since Sunday school, however do you know it?' she exclaimed.

The Prime Minister's intellect showed itself in her appreciation of the research and her insistence on factual accuracy. There was nothing shallow in her approach – not a whiff of 'the line to take' so dear to many, lesser, politicians. Then there was her Flaubertian concern for the '*mot juste*'. The thesaurus was much in use. I saw how she moulded the text into her own style, using, for example, the technique of repetition. When read cold, this can seem banal, but in oration it makes the words memorable. This meticulous process took a very long time.

In those days I lived in Huntingdon and, by around seven o'clock, I began to wonder if and how I was going to get home. Clearly, this was not something with which to bother the Prime Minister. At some convenient moment, I thought, I would suggest that I went across to the Horseguards Hotel to book a bed. I was forestalled. With a sigh of satisfaction, after finishing a difficult page, Mrs Thatcher said, 'You're not going to be able to get home tonight. You must stay here.' My feeble protests about the hotel were summarily dealt with. 'Nonsense! We've still a lot to do and I need you.' Apart from the Garden Girls, we had seen no one for about four hours.

Now staff started to come in to say goodnight. One was asked to make sure that towels were put out for me, another to get something out of the fridge for our dinner. I assumed that there was a housekeeper, lurking somewhere, to prepare the meal. But at around eight o'clock, it was the Prime Minister who went into the kitchen to cook the chicken supreme. Afterwards we washed up together. Conversation was surprisingly easy. We talked mostly about books and poetry and interesting aspects of the nineteenth century that had arisen from the speech. Then it was back to work.

At some point Carol dropped in and was asked to make sure that her room was tidy, because I would be sleeping in it. Mark, who was staying at No. 10, came in to say goodnight. On we went, draft following draft. We were both now in stockinged feet, with a drink to sip: whisky for her, gin for me. The tireless Garden Girls came and went. Finally, at 3 a.m., Mrs Thatcher decided that we should stop – until the next day. But she had to be sure that I was comfortable. So at three o'clock in the morning, the Prime Minister of the United Kingdom was running a bath for me, bringing me a night dress and toothbrush, popping a hot-water bottle into the bed just in case it was cold! Nothing was too much trouble for her – it was incredible.

The cold light of morning did not diminish her kindness. She was at my bedside at 7 a.m. with a cup of tea. At around eight, a maid appeared to cook breakfast. Then it was back to work. When I left at noon, the speech was some 3,500 words long and almost finalised, in good time to be delivered on Monday. The Prime Minister said that she would polish it over the weekend at Chequers. My extraordinary twenty-four hours was over. I went home, exhausted but elated. The lecture was duly delivered at the Institute of Electrical Engineers on Monday 26 July. Mrs Thatcher's thank-you letter followed promptly. 'It went down rather well, although I say so myself,' she wrote, 'I hope you know how grateful I am.' I felt that I was the one who should be expressing gratitude for a unique and unforgettable experience.

Nigel Fletcher
Conservative Activist

Nigel Fletcher is Founder of the Centre for Opposition Studies and Deputy Leader of the Greenwich Conservatives.

One of my first encounters with Margaret Thatcher was at the Conservative Party Conference in 1998. I was talking to a friend at the Conservative Way Forward stand, when the media scrum surrounding Lady T.'s tour of the exhibition descended on us. 'We're getting lots of interest from younger people, particularly about Europe,' I heard someone tell her. With that, she turned to me: 'What you have to remember about Europe,' she insisted, 'is that we've beaten most of them at some point in their history, and they've never forgotten it. You *have* to remember that when you're negotiating with them.' With that, she sailed majestically on, surrounded by cameras, leaving Denis trailing in her wake.

In the years since then, I encountered her again on various occasions – mostly at big dinners and receptions. Her presence electrified the room at such events, as devotees old and young were drawn into her orbit, desperate to shake her hand, say a few words and grab a picture with her. I was no different, however blasé I tried to appear. Once the lady was there, everyone wanted their moment with her.

Sometimes, it was more than a moment. In 2007, I was delighted when she accepted an invitation to view an exhibition I had organised on the history of the shadow Cabinet room – which a certain Mrs Thatcher had been the first Leader of the Opposition to use. David Cameron, William Hague, Michael Howard and Iain Duncan Smith also agreed to attend. I was delighted, but somewhat daunted at the prospect.

On the night, she arrived looking immaculate in a bright blue dress, escorted by David Cameron, who had met her at his office beforehand. We took her first to the office she had used when Leader of the Opposition, and she recalled meeting Ronald Reagan there ('Oh, he was such a great man'). Then we went through to the shadow Cabinet room itself, where she viewed the exhibition and posed with her four successors, sitting together at the table amid much laughter.

At the reception afterwards, I spent an hour escorting her around the room, introducing her to guests including my partner and my parents. It was a relaxed occasion, and she was on terrific form – displaying several flashes of vintage Thatcher. Some were unexpectedly ironic. A former colleague who had recently left the Research Department told her he was having trouble adjusting to life outside, and kept calling his successor to ask what was happening. 'Oh no, you mustn't do that,' she told him, 'because it's his job now, and you mustn't interfere.'

Near the end of the evening, I asked whether returning to the rooms had brought back memories of her time working in them. 'Well, you see so many rooms in politics, it's difficult to remember,' she replied. Then she thought for a moment, and continued emphatically: 'I remember No. 10 much better – but, of course, we were there for *such* a long time.'

Hartley Booth
Conservative MP 1992–97

Hartley Booth succeeded Margaret Thatcher as the MP for Finchley in 1992.

A t the end of July 1991, I was selected to be Margaret's successor. Technically, of course, I was selected to be the prospective
parliamentary candidate for the constituency of Finchley. It was all
over the world press and I urgently needed to liaise with her, the
sitting MP, to ensure that I did not make any politically unsound statements to the media, who were literally queuing up to discover what
it was like to follow the great lady. She came on the phone and said,
'Congratulations.' Then she said, 'Can you afford it?'

As with so many areas, Margaret was concerned about matters of
detail and so often thought of the people around her, sometimes in the
most disarming way, like this. It was one of the reasons I could never
abide the mindless hectoring she suffered, and that I too received from
the left, that she did not believe in Society. She believed in society
with a small 's', which meant the Christian principle of loving your
neighbour, and she certainly believed in community, not leaving it all
to those who provided from the great height of Whitehall, but as the
neighbourly actions of getting involved in the nearest charity or in
voluntary work to help people around you. She did not believe in the
individual as a selfish autonomous unit, either. She saw the individual
as a person with dignity and responsibilities towards neighbours.
'Selfish greed' was the mindless accusation against Margaret and her
policies. Nothing was further from the truth. These conclusions came
from my encounters with her over the two stages of my work with
her. I was overwhelmed by the evidence of the love and care she had
shown to constituents over the years, extending from the local special
school for children with autism to the many dozens of constituents
I met.

Before the election, Margaret briefed me on the needs of the Greek
Cypriots and the Jewish community. She took a judicious stand on the
latter group, very properly avoiding backing any one political party in

Israel, and stressing that the country should observe UN rulings with regard to its neighbouring states.

The constituency party members revered her. One man was papering a wall in his house with her written replies to his questions. (He continued with mine until I put a stop to it.) People told me how she would organise her arrivals to be exactly on time. They would say, 'Prime Minister Thatcher was a wonderful MP. We could always rely on her punctuality. If the car bringing her was early, we would see it go round the block, and park. Then on the dot, her driver would stop outside the hall or wherever, and out she would step. We thought she was royalty really.'

Lord Plumb
Conservative Peer

Henry Plumb was President of the National Farmers' Union in the 1970s. He served as a Conservative MEP from 1979 until 1999 and President of the European Parliament from 1987 until 1989.

On one occasion we met late at night following a successful vote in the Commons, to discuss the European issues of the day. She greeted me very warmly and we had an extremely amicable conversation, accompanied by three large whiskies. As I was leaving, her mood suddenly changed, and she said, quite belligerently, 'Henry, we must discuss the Common Agricultural Policy. I am not going to put any more money into the pockets of these peasant farmers in France, and elsewhere in Europe.'

I must have been emboldened by the three whiskies and I found myself saying, 'If you will just shut up for one minute, I will tell you about the CAP.' Not surprisingly, she looked a little startled at my less than tactful words, and said, 'You'd better come back in.' So we went back into her room, more whisky was provided, and I said, 'Those peasants as you call them, the small farmers, get nothing out of the CAP. It is big farmers like your brother-in-law, on his farm in Essex, who are getting the money from the intervention payments they receive on their surplus wheat, £50 a tonne, while we still have a wheat mountain. Yes, the CAP wants changing, but surpluses are not the fault of the so-called European peasants, their problem is social, not economic.'

Her jaw dropped. 'How do you know my brother-in-law?' she asked. 'I was on his farm only last week,' I said, 'and I can tell you that what I said is right. You can ask him yourself if you want.' I never again heard her blame 'European peasants' for the problems of the Common Agricultural Policy, but I always wondered what kind of conversation she might have had when she next saw her sister and brother-in-law. I left without being handbagged.

Sir Richard Parsons
Diplomat

Sir Richard Parsons served as ambassador to Hungary, Spain and Sweden.

I served in the Madrid embassy for four-and-a-half busy years from 1980 to 1984. This period encompassed the Falklands conflict. The Spanish Prime Minister, the able Calvo-Sotelo, had the sense to see that Mrs Thatcher could be an ally in getting Spain into the European Union and NATO, and thus into democratic Europe. He helped us in various discreet ways which made a favourable impression. The time was right to try and make progress over Gibraltar. The trouble was that the Franco regime had closed the frontier between Gibraltar and the Spanish mainland. This was a great handicap to our side. If we could get the barriers removed, it would be much easier for Britain to support the return of Spain to the modern world. The advantage would be to both sides and under the leadership of our excellent Foreign Secretary, Lord Carrington, we agreed to draw up and submit to ministers a draft agreement which should do the trick. Calvo-Sotelo was to visit Downing Street for this purpose.

On the morning of the day itself, I flew to London and arrived at No. 10 to find Mrs T. holding a briefing meeting with Lord Carrington and his officials from the FCO. I slipped into a modest place at the end of the table. The PM was saying that she was very unhappy about the draft agreement. It gave too much away, she thought, and would not be acceptable to the Conservative Party.

I cleared my throat noisily. 'What's that noise you are making, ambassador?' snapped the Prime Minister. 'I was trying to control my amusement, Prime Minister.' 'Amusement?' echoed Mrs T. in a voice worthy of Lady Bracknell. 'Perhaps you would care to explain.' 'The truth is, Prime Minister,' I replied, 'that this morning I saw off the Prime Minister of Spain at the airport in Madrid on his way to London. I heard him telling his officials the same thing as you. The draft would not be acceptable to his party.' 'The Spanish Prime Minister is worried too, is he?' responded the Prime Minister, with marked satisfaction. 'That's the first piece of good news I have heard today.'

Everything was then smoothly agreed on our side. Afterwards Lord Carrington said to me very kindly, 'You arrived just in time.' I learned something from this episode. Mrs T. had the reputation for being bossy and opinionated and averse to listening to both sides. But it was more complicated than that. She liked to hear both sides of an argument, properly explained to her. She would listen carefully if you knew your facts and were not afraid of deploying them. Heaven help you, though, if you tried a fudge. Then she would come out firmly on the winning side and present it to the world as if it were the only possible option. The Iron Lady was privately amenable to reason. How else could she have remained Prime Minister for so many years? But the public never quite spotted that and imagined that she became a kind of dictator.

Baroness Chalker
Conservative Peer

Lynda Chalker was Conservative MP for Wallasey from 1974 to 1992. She served in the Thatcher government as a minister at the Department of Transport, the DHSS and the Foreign Office. She was raised to the peerage in 1992.

When Mrs Thatcher became our leader, like so many other women in the Conservative Party, I was excited and determined to help her make it to Prime Minister. Having long been a keen European, I was well aware that there would be some difference of opinion and approach, but having always seen the Conservative Party as having a broad spectrum of views, I was determined to do my bit. The first chance came when she appointed me a junior opposition spokesman on Health and Social Security in November 1976. Getting to grips with pensions and social security was a formidable task, which she well knew.

It was thus always heartening to have her quiet enquiries, and later, when I was a minister, her remarkable support. Once we were in government in that department, we all worked the ministerial machine to try to turn round MPs' enquiries and also to reform policy so as to keep the ever-spiralling budget under control and to rid the system of the incredible contradictions in entitlements. It was in 1982, when we were legislating to remove strikers' benefits, that I knew of her full support.

The Minister of State on the Social Security Bill Committee, Hugh Rossi, had a heart condition, and could not work after 1830 hours, so when debates went on, first in the Commons until 2200 hours and then in committee through the night, with a timetable motion in force to deter the Labour opposition from their continual filibustering, I was on my own leading the government team. The most controversial part of the Bill was the removal of strikers' entitlement to social security. The opposition put down a wrecking amendment and we began to debate it at two in the morning! Within minutes of the start of the debate, the public gallery door opened, and in came the Prime Minister with a Private Secretary to listen. She remained with us for the full two hours the debate took, and wrote me a very kind note once we had defeated the opposition amendment.

There were many times when I was Minister of State for Transport when the Prime Minister gave quiet but firm encouragement, such as the battle to have seat belts made compulsory to save lives. Many backbenchers thought that this was anti-libertarian and so opposed the law change, but the Prime Minister gave me her full support to introduce the government-agreed measure, which has since saved many thousands of lives and prevented much injury in road accidents.

From the day I went to the Foreign Office in 1986 to work on Europe and Africa, I knew that my real political battles would increase. In fact, the Single European Bill to get rid of trade barriers and establish much improved working with our European Community neighbours was exactly in line with our manifesto commitments, but it was at about the time when some outrageous statements from M. Delors of France and Signor Andreotti of Italy began to inflame the anti-European fever among a proportion of our backbenchers. Throughout the passage of the Bill, I had nothing but active support from Margaret.

Later, our views on Europe diverged, but there was rarely a time when I felt I would not be supported, and Margaret was the very person who had given me the real chance in politics to focus on Africa, the development of which has been my interest and concern since I helped two girls from Botswana back in 1955. While I was still Minister of Transport, I was encouraged by her to develop transport exports in Africa, and work in West Africa had encouraged me to sharpen up my conversational French. Thus as Minister for Africa from 1986 onwards, I had the chance to expand my interest and to help to resolve many issues, thanks to Margaret Thatcher. Our views may have differed, but many discussions allowed me to learn a great deal from her and her colleagues in committees and Cabinet when I attended in the Foreign Secretary's absence overseas. The early years of Margaret's premiership were very tough at times, but that was the time when the foundations of many reforms were laid. Even if we differed, as our experiences in life were so changed by our exposure to the very challenges we had been elected to solve, I shall always be grateful for her advice and friendly guidance, so often given quite unexpectedly.

Janice Richards
Downing Street Secretary

Before I joined No. 10, I worked at the Department of Education and Science, as it was then named, in Curzon Street, as it was then named. Mrs Thatcher was the Secretary of State and, even now, I remember there was a buzz with her at the helm. Little did I know that I would be working for her again in the future, in very different circumstances. As a Garden Room secretary (so called because the secretaries' rooms overlooked the rear garden at ground level), I, with other colleagues, performed the ritualistic welcoming party for incoming Prime Ministers in the front hall of No. 10.

May 1979 was the start of a very special welcoming, and we all felt that we were going to experience not only history being made, but different and exciting times ahead. We were proved right, and those memorable years while Mrs Thatcher was in No. 10 proved to be very special times for those privileged to work there. I was one of twelve secretaries who worked closely with the private office and travelled with the Prime Minister wherever she went, either in the UK or overseas. Especially at Chequers, there was an opportunity to see a more relaxed and less pressured side to Mrs Thatcher. I recall conversations about food, clothes, family and so on.

I recall the visit to Lusaka in 1979, for the Commonwealth Heads of Government meeting – Mrs Thatcher's first of many – where the heads of state and government were accommodated in Mulungushi, a sort of tribal village complex which Kenneth Kaunda had had specially built some time earlier. However, the bungalows allocated were, to say the least, below standard, and a colleague recalled someone describing them as 'glorified mud huts'. Horizon House was the accommodation for the support staff – far superior to Mrs Thatcher's own, though she joined the staff there after a few days.

There were some memorable meals there, all the support staff sitting at a large round table with her. Clive Whitmore, at that time Principal Private Secretary to Mrs T.; Brian Cartledge, Private Secretary for Overseas Affairs at No. 10; and Sir John Hunt, the Cabinet Secretary, were there too. I also remember that Mrs Thatcher was unwell for a time during the Lusaka visit, but just had to get on with the business of the day. All marvelled at her ability to keep going. I became Head of the Garden Rooms in 1985 when my travelling days came to an end. This allowed me to work more closely with Mrs Thatcher again, but in a different way.

There were decisions to be made on gifts which were to be given, and caretaking the gifts that Mrs Thatcher received. Since she had come to power, the correspondence received had risen to 5,000 letters a week, and one needed to be selective about which should be shown to the private office and the Prime Minister. It was important that she saw a wide range of letters and learned of the personal difficulties and problems experienced by the general public, and thereby the issues that most concerned them. She took a great interest in these letters and would often add manuscript sentences in her responses.

Long-serving staff were permitted to hold their leaving parties in No. 10. Mrs Thatcher's government driver, Ken Godber, was one of these, and I remember at that party that some of those attending could not hear Mrs Thatcher's speech clearly, so she whipped off her shoes and stood on a table! When her resignation was announced in 1990, No. 10 received many sacks of mail, which entailed asking the whole office to help to open. The support she received from the general public was quite overwhelming, and one could see just how touched she was when she sat on the floor with me and my staff, opening and reading just some of those letters. It wasn't only going to be her staff who would miss her.

I feel so very fortunate to have worked at No. 10 and especially while Mrs Thatcher was there. Those who worked with and for Mrs Thatcher felt very privileged, and the admiration and respect they held for her was unquestionable. It was one of those periods when all – political staff, civil servants, protection officers – worked together in the most wonderful family atmosphere in my time in Downing Street, not repeated either before or after Mrs Thatcher's time as Prime Minister. I was one of those who lined up to welcome Mrs Thatcher in 1979 and again lined up to say farewell in 1990. It was the end of over eleven years of history, eleven happy years, and a sad end to an extraordinary period, her years in Downing Street.

Lord Cormack

Conservative Peer

Patrick Cormack was Member of Parliament for Cannock and then South Staffordshire from 1970 to 2010. He was raised to the peerage in 2010.

At the time of the Poulson scandal, a number of Members came in for severe criticism in a rather damning report. One of these was John Cordle, the Member for Bournemouth East. A group of us met with him on the Thursday before the report was due to be debated on the following Monday. We told him that there really was a chance that the House would expel him and that it would be far better if he were to seize the high ground and resign, by applying for the Chiltern Hundreds and making a statement in the House before doing so. Convinced of his own innocence, very probably rightly, but conscious of the witch-hunt atmosphere that was developing, he reluctantly took this advice and on the Friday morning made his statement. The late Sir Peter Mills, Member for Devon West, and I sat on either side of him as he did so. Peter then had to dash back to his constituency and so I had the task of looking after John Cordle and taking him to the Chief Whip's office. We were joined there by Margaret, who had sat on the front bench with him, talking to him and even holding his hand. There was nothing synthetic about this. This was genuine human warmth and real kindness. And that remained part of her make-up, even throughout her premiership.

In 1982, my then agent, a young man of twenty-five, had one of the very first heart transplants in the country. Initially, it was a great success (sadly, he died a couple of years later), and I took him, apparently miraculously restored, to the party conference in Brighton, where on the eve of her conference speech, Margaret Thatcher devoted a couple of hours to seeing Andrew in her room, feeding him cake and biscuits, and talking fondly, knowledgeably and sympathetically, as if she had been a combination of family doctor and favourite aunt. It was truly remarkable to witness.

Petronella Wyatt
Journalist

I first met Margaret Thatcher when I was nine and she was on the point of winning her first election victory. My father, Woodrow Wyatt, a former Labour politician who had become disenchanted with his old party, had come to view her as Britain's only hope of recovery. They had met at a lunch a few years before and formed a firm friendship. When he announced one Saturday that she would be paying us a visit, he spoke with reverence. 'Mrs Thatcher,' he declared, 'will be our saviour.'

What was one to expect? An icy, imperial goddess? A sly termagant? Or a respectable middle-class lady quietly pouring out the tea? At five o'clock I presented myself in my father's study. Margaret Thatcher had her face turned towards the wall. How she confounded my expectations and yet, in a strange and remarkable way, fulfilled them. Her face, which in those days was lightly made-up, had the stamp of command and also the mark of the ordinary.

Her features were regular and her suit, which was yellow, gave them a golden glow. Her gaze was both sharp and soft. 'Soah, you-ah ah Petronahlla.' At least that is an approximation of what she sounded like. (She had begun, in secret, to take vocal lessons from Harold Macmillan; the result being that she sounded a little like a Home Counties Scarlett O'Hara.) 'Cahm here, dear.' A plump apple-white finger alighted on a badge I had been given at school, which bore the words 'British Smile Day'.

'That's right,' she said. 'Keep smahling.' I was fourteen when I met her again. The woman I had sipped tea with was now the first female incumbent of 10 Downing Street. 'The Prime Minister is coming for a drink,' said my father. 'Could you made her a whisky and soda?' Trembling, I handed her a glass. Then my father did a terrible thing. 'I'm going upstairs to fetch a book. Please entertain Mrs Thatcher while I'm gone.'

I stood petrified. Perhaps because of her office, she seemed less suburban and more supreme. She had the seductive smile of Ingrid

Bergman, but there was a visible majesty of a sort that would terrify her enemies. Eventually she spoke and her divine stamp took on a surprising benevolence. 'You're not smiling any more, dear,' she said, all the affectation wiped from her now cello-contralto voice.

Her powers of recall were astonishing. I simpered. 'Which of your school subjects do you like best?' she enquired. 'History, Prime Minister.' I searched my brain for great Conservatives and blurted out the name of the reforming Victorian Prime Minister Robert Peel. There was a terrifying silence. Finally she said in a tone of pure horror. 'Robert Peel! Too many U-turns.'

Sometimes I thought my father entertained a fondness for Thatcher that balanced precariously on the edge of love. My suspicions were aroused when his thoughts turned from economic figures to her own. He compared her legs to those of Cyd Charisse and her eyes to Elizabeth Taylor's. I noticed my mother becoming increasingly annoyed as he finished one peroration with, 'Margaret is what Napoleon said about Josephine. She is all woman.'

It was true that Thatcher had a surprising susceptibility to men. Not to all men, but, like Elizabeth I, to those with a sort of gaudy glamour and an insinuating flirtatiousness: Jeffrey Archer, Richard Branson, whom she adored, and Cecil Parkinson.

She was an amalgam of strength and vulnerability. She could be jealous of other women and took praise like attar of roses: she sucked it into her skin. Once, when I impudently complimented her on her knowledge of history, she thanked me almost shyly. 'Those Tory grandees think I'm ignorant, but I have read the great Dean Swift.'

My mother admired Thatcher but was cautious of embracing her with my father's wholehearted *bonté*. She had discovered, by listening at the door, that her husband spoke to the Prime Minister every morning before breakfast. When she and Denis next came for dinner, my mother was baleful. The discussion turned to the economy and my mother decided to vouchsafe an opinion. 'You know, Woodrow, I think that...' At once she was interrupted by the Prime Minister. 'Be quiet, dear,' she said. 'Your turn will come.'

As a dinner guest she displayed a sense of humour of which the public knew nothing. My father adhered to the Edwardian habit of asking the women to leave the room after pudding, so that the men could enjoy cigars and 'serious conversation'. 'But you can't send me out of the room,' she protested, 'I'm the Prime Minister!' She also enjoyed a risqué joke. I remember mentioning the notorious, orgiastic activities of the eighteenth-century Hellfire Club. 'Shut up,' hissed my father. 'No, don't!' rejoined Thatcher.

In time, however, my mother warmed to what her detractors fail to comprehend – Margaret Thatcher's essential humanity. Her natural instincts were unselfish and compassionate. She was genuinely distressed by the misfortune of others. Her eyes would soften with tears at tales of privation. She worriedly intervened when anyone she knew was ill. When I mentioned to her, during the height of the Westland affair, that my mother was undergoing an eye operation, she was aghast. 'But why didn't you tell me at once?' The following day, my mother's hospital room was inundated with flowers and exotic hampers of fruit.

To me, she showed immense kindness and took an unwarranted interest in my activities. She encouraged me when I sat my A levels. She was with me when I decided to leave Oxford University, taking my part against my father. 'Don't be a snob, Woodrow. Those Oxford dons are unspeakable. She knows what she's doing.'

I often thought she was anxious for me to find a husband. It was not that she disliked feminism. Rather, she believed a stable home life was a prerequisite for a successful career. 'Everyone needs to be cherished,' she told me. 'Without Denis I would never have reached the starting blocks.'

It was touchingly evident how much they loved each other; and they didn't require photographs to be released to the newspapers to prove it. Thatcher had an old-fashioned view of publicity from which present politicians could benefit. Never was her family to be used to further her political career. 'If you can't manage a political crisis,' she once said, 'it is morally wrong to involve civilians.'

As I grew up, she became a fixed point in my life. It was impossible to imagine any premier but her. But it was not to be. Power failed to corrupt Thatcher, but eventually she became isolated and complacent. The Romans kept their leaders on their toes by employing someone to run behind a man during a triumph, whispering, 'You are only a mortal.' Slowly and anxiously I watched as Thatcher's once infallible antennae began to fail her.

Disaffected members of the Tory Party threw out barbs and squibs. Thatcher seemed exhausted by her travails. The results of the first ballot came in. Michael Heseltine had deprived her of an overall victory. At 6.30 the following morning, my father received a telephone call from No. 10. It was his beloved Margaret. She spoke slowly and painfully, 'I have decided to resign. I wanted to tell you before I made the announcement.'

It was the only time I saw my father cry. I, too, began to weep as he railed against 'Tory traitors – the Labour Party would never have behaved like this to any of its leaders'. I felt as if I had lost my Earth Mother, the symbol of my youth.

When my father died in 1997, her letter was the longest and most comforting I received. Then Denis followed and she seemed to diminish physically. She spoke to me of her terrible loneliness. 'Look after your mother. It's a terrible thing, to be alone.' She was becoming ill and losing her train of thought. It was anguish to watch. I saw her less and less, though occasionally she would overcome her frailty to attend parties given by friends and, for a few fleeting moments, her brilliance would emerge.

One of Lady Thatcher's least publicised qualities, which raised her above any other politician I have known, was a complete absence of schadenfreude or triumphalism. In 1992, I was fortunate enough to be asked by Alistair McAlpine, Lady Thatcher's former Treasurer and close friend, to spend election night with the recently deposed premier and her family at his London home. Denis and Mark Thatcher were understandably bitter. When Tory wet Chris Patten, whose vitriol towards her had known no bounds, lost his seat, they leapt to their feet and whooped like Watusi chieftains. I shall never forget the majesty on her features as she reprimanded them: 'Sit down at once! The misfortune of others is never a cause for celebration.'

I can hear her now, sensible and eminently kind. She was the best and wisest person I have ever known. Countless tributes will be made and countless books will call her one of the greatest figures in British history. But now I am remembering the woman who made a shy girl feel important, and the touch of her cool hand. Margaret Thatcher is dead, but I don't have to believe it if I don't want to.

Sir John Stanley
Conservative MP 1974–

Sir John Stanley MP was Parliamentary Private Secretary to Margaret Thatcher from 1976 until 1979. He was subsequently Minister of State for Housing and Construction, the Armed Forces and Northern Ireland.

Contrary to her handbag-wielding image, Margaret was the best boss I have ever had.

Know your boss by your bad days, not by your good ones. My nadir came during a weekend tour in East Anglia, deep in the Fens. At midday on the Saturday, Margaret was due to give her weekend speech for the Sunday papers in a town hall in the Isle of Ely constituency, then represented by Clement Freud. Shortly before noon we set up camp at an adjacent hotel so that Margaret could have a final page-by-page run-through of her speech.

Suddenly she looked up and said: 'John, my page seven is missing.' My blood chilled. 'I'm sure it's here Margaret,' I replied with misplaced confidence. Frantic searches through everybody's briefcases produced no trace of the delinquent page seven. 'I'm terribly sorry Margaret,' I blabbered pitiably, 'page seven seems to have been left behind in London.' 'In that case,' Margaret replied, not unkindly but changing gear effortlessly into the royal 'we', 'We will have to remember it then, won't we?'

Minutes later we were off to the town hall. I slunk in behind Margaret feeling pinhead high. She launched into her speech with customary confidence and fluency, but my trepidation mounted as she strode purposefully towards the yawning abyss of the missing page seven. Of course, I need not have worried. Without a glimmer of hesitation or faintest change of delivery, page seven was perfectly recalled from Margaret's extraordinary, computer-like memory and, in moments, she had reached the terra firma of page eight and beyond.

I awaited my sentence, fully deserved. Summary dispatch to the back benches perhaps – the equivalent in British politics to being shot at dawn. But no shot rang out and Margaret never once mentioned my

Fenland incompetence that weekend, nor at any time subsequently – true magnanimity indeed.

For those of us who were privileged to be the Leader of the Opposition's staff, it was Margaret's personal kindness and consideration, as well as her inspirational political abilities, that impelled us to work for her night and day until that unforgettable moment came in May 1979 when, already inside No. 10, we were able to welcome her back from the Palace and greet her for the first time as 'Prime Minister'.

Christopher Chope
Conservative MP 1983–92 and 1997–

Christopher Chope was MP for Southampton Itchen from 1983 until 1992 and has been MP for Christchurch since 1997. He served as an Environment Minister in the last year of the Thatcher government.

Margaret Thatcher was a passionate Conservative, but she was also a compassionate Conservative. When I first met her in 1976 – I was then Chairman of Putney Conservatives – she visited an old people's day centre in Putney, where I saw her in action. She spoke to every single person in the day centre sitting room. She, as leader of the Conservative Party, knelt down in order to be able to converse meaningfully with those who could not speak to her easily. That, for me, was a demonstration of her humility and compassion.

People have spoken about the way in which Margaret Thatcher would write letters to colleagues who had been bereaved and so on. A few years ago, my wife was in hospital. The flowers from Margaret Thatcher arrived before my own, which was rather embarrassing. That was the extent to which she was on the ball with her generosity and kindness not only to colleagues, but to their wives.

I agreed with Margaret Thatcher on almost everything. The only big issue on which I disagreed with her fundamentally was her decision not to stand in the second ballot in 1990. If she had stood, I think that she would have won and that the course of history would have been different. I am sad that those of us who went into her study that evening to persuade her to change her mind were unsuccessful. It was typical of her that she sent special notes to all of us who had tried to persuade her to stay on. It was a humiliating experience for that fantastic Prime Minister. Having been in that study and seen her condition, I would not wish it on anybody. Somebody who had served her country with such distinction and who had been a global leader in bringing freedom to much of Eastern Europe was humiliated by people whom she thought were her friends and colleagues. I thought and still think that that was intolerable. May that sort of thing never happen again.

In 1997, Margaret came and supported my election campaign in Christchurch, where we were trying to overturn the majority of about 16,000 that the Liberal Democrats had won in the 1993 by-election. That was her first outing in the campaign. She was confronted by the press because one of our colleagues who was standing in Tatton had suddenly hit the headlines. Margaret demonstrated her ability to deal with the press with a phrase or, as in this case, a very short sentence that could not result in any follow-up. When asked about Neil Hamilton, she said, 'Nobody is perfect.' In those three words, she closed down the conversation, because she was not passing judgement on his case, but saying something that applies to all of us. That is an example of how she was able to deal with the press and choose words that were effective.

Later on the same visit, we went on a private visit to the Priory primary school in Christchurch, where Margaret demonstrated other attributes: the ability to listen and the ability to speak her mind. She said to a nine-year-old, 'What do you want to do when you grow up?' He said, 'I want to be a musician.' She paused and stared with her wonderful eyes at this young man and said, 'And what else do you want to be?' That demonstrated that she did nothing for effect. When she asked somebody a question, she was willing to listen to the answer and make a comment. She gave that person the benefit of her views, whether they liked it or not. I hope that that individual is now a successful musician. If he is not, I hope that he has a back-up, which is what she was saying he ought to have.

It is a fantastic privilege to have this opportunity to pay tribute to, in my view, the greatest Prime Minister of all time.

Nancy Reagan
First Lady

Nancy Reagan was First Lady of the United States from 1981 until 1989.

About a year after Ronnie died, I returned to London for the first time in many years. I had so many great plans for all the people and places I would visit and the events I would attend. But the one appointment I looked forward to the most was with Baroness Thatcher. I wouldn't have missed seeing Margaret for the world. We had the most wonderful afternoon, talking of old times.

Most people are aware of the very special relationship between my husband and Margaret Thatcher as leaders of their respective countries during one of the most difficult periods in modern history. In fact, my husband once said that we were living in a time when 'the survival of our nations and the peace of the world are threatened by forces which are willing to exert any pressure, test any will and destroy any freedom'. He admired Margaret's strength, determination and courage, and called her 'a world leader in every meaning of the word'.

Ronnie and Margaret were political soulmates, united in their commitment to freedom and resolution to end communism. When Ronnie entered the White House, he inherited similar problems to those Margaret inherited as Prime Minister: a troubled economy, high inflation and diminished national pride. To overcome this, Ronnie said she demonstrated two great qualities. The first was that she had thought seriously about how to revive the British economy and entered office with a clear set of policies to do so. And she said her second great quality was the true grit of a true Brit.

Generous with compliments and always positive, Margaret spoke very highly of my husband's leadership. I will never forget when she credited him with 'ending the Cold War without firing a shot', and I know it meant much to Ronnie to receive that kind of praise from her.

For eight years as President, my husband never had a closer ally than Margaret Thatcher. But Margaret was not just an ally; she was also a dear and trusted friend. She and Ronnie shared the same values and beliefs, not only with regard to politics but also on a personal level. We were fortunate to see Margaret and her husband, Denis, in an official capacity, and also enjoyed spending time with them as friends on many visits together.

Throughout the final years of my husband's life, Margaret was a constant source of support and inspiration to me. She defied her doctor's orders and insisted on travelling to Washington to attend Ronnie's funeral service, and remained at my side as we flew back across the country to California for the burial ceremony at the Ronald Reagan Presidential Library. Her magnificent eulogy was one of the most heart-warming tributes my husband ever received.

Laurence Robertson
Conservative MP 1997–

Laurence Robertson became the MP for Tewkesbury in 1997. He had previously been an industrial consultant and a charity fundraising consultant.

Margaret Thatcher changed attitudes. That was her greatest achievement. Without that accomplished, none of her other achievements would have been possible.

She changed hearts and minds. When she came to office, the country had just struggled through the winter of discontent. The snow had been deep on the ground; everyone, from lorry drivers to industrial workers to hospital staff had been on strike; even the dead were left unburied. Industrial strife had been a dominant influence in the 1970s. Management had lost the will and the confidence to manage.

But worst of all was the fact that few people actually believed things could be changed or could be any different. Margaret Thatcher believed differently. She believed in the intrinsic determination and spirit of the British people, but she realised that it had to be reawakened, just as it was in 1939.

Achieving this was no mean task, but achieve it she did. She had the courage to introduce tough Budgets which set the country's finances right. She had the courage to tackle the trade union barons and hand the unions back to their members. She had the courage to set free the ailing nationalised industries. She trusted the people and sold them the homes they were living in.

People began to believe in Britain once again and the rest is history. It sounds simple but the confidence we now have in our country is down to her. To her foresight and her courage. It was difficult to understand exactly what was needed in Britain in the 1970s, though a few people did realise. But she was unique in that she was the only person who was prepared to actually do what was necessary; to have the ability to do it; and have the courage to refuse to turn back.

Now, attitudes have changed and the country is one of the leaders of the world again. What a transformation. What a Prime Minister. I only wish I could have served under her!

Lord Naseby

Conservative Peer

Michael Morris was Conservative MP for Northampton South from 1974 until 1997. He was raised to the peerage in 1997.

I was Airey Neave's unofficial PPS in 1975 and chief bag-carrier. My job was to help him organise the future leader of the Conservative Party. In the initial stages, we met in Room J3 in the House of Commons; it was my job to book it etc. The first person that the Neave team supported was not Margaret Thatcher; it was Edward du Cann. That campaign produced eighty or eighty-five supporters; it was around those sorts of numbers. However, Edward came to that group and made it clear that he did not wish to stand as the future leader, because he had recently married and he and his wife had discussed the situation and he was withdrawing his candidature.

We had an immediate meeting of the group and went through the others forecast to be running, and the consensus was that we should ask Margaret to join us. At that point, the information was that Margaret had precisely two supporters. I was asked to make contact, which I did, and Margaret came to address our meeting in Room J3. It was clear from the way that she addressed that meeting that this was a woman of considerable potential. She had a very clear strategy at that meeting and had sensed what the party wanted in a new leader. Airey turned to me when Margaret had finished and said, 'We'll have no questions now. Would you be kind enough, Michael, to take Margaret to the room next door and come back?' which I did. We had a fairly lengthy discussion. The unanimous view of the people present, except for three, was that we should support Margaret Thatcher. Most of the rest is history, other than that I was in charge of trying to persuade the 1974 intake to support Margaret.

The second example I give of Margaret and her ability and understanding of people and countries was after we took over in 1979 and I was on the back benches as a PPS in Northern Ireland. Even then, I had an interest in Sri Lanka. Judith Hart had commissioned something called the Victoria Dam in Sri Lanka. I knew about the dam – it would cost about £100 million – and I asked to see the Prime Minister to suggest to her that the project should go ahead. I had an audience with her, and with the then Overseas Development Secretary of State, and Margaret said, 'Michael, there are two points I make to you: first, that if we as a country have an agreement with another country – as the noble and learned Lord, Lord Mackay, said earlier today – we stick to it. So the agreement is that the project will go ahead. Not only will it go ahead but, secondly, I wish to be there at the opening.'

Some years later I was pleased to be there with Margaret and Denis, and we had a garden party before the formal opening at the dam. The big thing in Sri Lanka in those days was the President's elephant named Raja. Denis was asked whether he wished to give bananas to the elephant, and of course accepted. Unfortunately for Denis, he was not too good on the anatomy of an elephant. Denis decided that elephants took bananas through their trunks. Just as Margaret was about to tell him, 'No, don't put it in his trunk,' it was too late. Denis put half a dozen bananas in the trunk of the elephant, which then did a typical elephant snort and the rest of us were covered by bananas. Margaret said, 'I thought I told you early on, "Put it in his mouth, not in his trunk." Did you not hear me?'

Eleanor Laing
Conservative MP 1997–

Eleanor Laing was elected MP for Epping Forest in 1997. She had previously worked as Special Adviser to John MacGregor.

Attending a Conservative Women's Conference just before I fought my first, unwinnable, parliamentary seat as a very young, inexperienced and shy candidate, I was introduced to Margaret Thatcher and dared to make a comment about a particular matter of government policy. On hearing my comment the Prime Minister swung round, caught me in her gaze and said with her inimitable authority, 'You are absolutely right.' At that time I thought it was the greatest compliment that anyone had ever paid me – and I still think that now.

Lord Parkinson
Chairman of the Conservative Party 1981–83

Cecil Parkinson was a Conservative MP from 1970 to 1992, and served in Margaret Thatcher's Falklands War Cabinet. He was Trade and Industry Secretary in 1983 and served again in the Cabinet from 1987 to 1990.

The final hours
Thursday 22 November 1990

At about 7 a.m. the telephone rang in my London flat. I was surprised to hear the voice of Chris Chope, one of my junior ministers at the Department of Transport. He had some appalling news for me. Margaret Thatcher was almost certain to announce that she would not be a candidate in the second ballot for the leadership of the Conservative Party and would be resigning as Prime Minister. He was telephoning to ask me to make a last-minute appeal to her to change her mind. I was stunned. I had seen her the previous evening at about 6 p.m. At that time she was full of enthusiasm and determined to win on the second ballot. I therefore went out to dinner with my wife and a group of friends feeling sure that with the full and active support of the Cabinet, and with better organisation than in the first ballot, she would win well.

We had a very relaxed dinner and got home about midnight. I went straight to bed, and was soon in such a deep sleep that I did not hear the telephone when it rang about 12.45 a.m. My wife answered. It was Trevor Kavanagh, the Political Editor of *The Sun*. He had heard a strong rumour that Margaret was resigning and he wanted to talk to me about it. Ann said that I was asleep, needed the rest and she would not disturb me. She told me about this the next morning after my conversation with Chris Chope.

By 7.10 a.m. I was on the telephone to No. 10 and asked to speak to the Prime Minister. The operator asked me to wait. She came back to tell me that the PM was at the moment under the hair dryer and suggested that I telephone again in about half an hour.

I then rang Norman Tebbit to find out what he knew. As usual, he knew a lot. He had been with her until late the night before, working on her speech for the Censure Debate that afternoon, and he was sure that she would be resigning. We agreed that it would be pointless for me to telephone her again.

I left for the office where I was due to meet my ministerial colleagues in Transport for one of our regular early morning prayers. We held them on Tuesdays and Thursdays. Tuesday was 'departmental' and included the Permanent Secretary. Thursday was political and only ministers, my Special Adviser, Elizabeth Buchanan, and the desk officer from the Conservative Research Department, Perry Miller, attended. We met at 8.30, but before that Chris Chope and Elizabeth Buchanan came in and we pieced together a clear picture of the events of the previous evening and discussed the likely outcome of Cabinet. We were a sombre group.

As a departmental team we had been totally committed to Margaret Thatcher and we were still unanimous in wishing her to carry on as leader. By then, it was becoming clear that a group of younger Cabinet ministers had played a decisive role in persuading her to change her mind. For my part, I did not feel that they were particularly well qualified to interpret the mood of either the parliamentary party or the party in the country to her.

Cabinet had been called for 9.00 a.m. and we adjourned our meeting at about 8.50 so that I could get there. We arranged to meet again at 10.30 so that I could report back to them the outcome of Cabinet.

I left Marsham Street with Elizabeth Buchanan. She was on her way to the meeting of special advisers which took place each week at the same time as Cabinet. It was jokingly called the shadow cabinet and those present liked to think that the standard of discussion was of higher quality, possibly than the Cabinet, and certainly than the other shadow Cabinet.

We were both in a gloomy and angry frame of mind. I arrived at No. 10 unusually early, to find that a number of Cabinet colleagues were already waiting in the anteroom outside the Cabinet room. Most of them were looking grim and saying little. Ken Clarke was the exception. He was telling anybody who cared to listen that if the PM did not resign he would resign before noon that day. He was adamant that she had to go. James Mackay, the Lord Chancellor, was quiet and looked preoccupied. The reason for that became clear a few minutes later.

It was not unusual for the Cabinet to start a few minutes late and it did that day. The waiting was almost unbearable and the atmosphere became more tense by the minute. At about 9.10 the door of the Cabinet was opened and we went in. The Prime Minister was already there, sitting in her usual place, with Sir Robin Butler, the Cabinet Secretary next to her. She had been crying, her eyes were red and swollen and she looked deeply distressed. As we came in I noticed that a carton of tissues had been placed next to her on the Cabinet table. She picked one from the box and wiped away the tears that had welled up into her eyes. There was a deathly silence in the room. In a halting voice she said that she wished to make a statement, following which we would return to normal Cabinet business. She started to read but broke down after a few words. She started a second time and again, she broke down. At this point I spoke, saying, 'For God's sake, James, you read it.' This broke the tension. Various colleagues disagreed with me, and in the few seconds this took, the Prime Minister regained her composure and read out the statement. It was the one made public later.

I glanced at my colleagues. Most of them could not bring themselves to look at her. They sat staring at the Cabinet table so intently that they looked as if they were trying to drill holes in it with their eyes. Two or three were in tears. I felt deep anger and bitterness that the Prime Minister, who had led us to three election victories, and who only two days earlier had been a pivotal figure at a great international conference in Paris to mark the end of the Cold War, should have been treated so shabbily by her parliamentary colleagues.

James Mackay had obviously been warned in advance and had prepared a statement of his own in which he thanked the Prime Minister on behalf of the Cabinet for her outstanding service to the nation over such a long period. One or two people added their own tributes, but the Prime Minister brought this to an early halt with a characteristic remark that she found business easier to cope with than sympathy. By this time she was totally in control of herself and the Cabinet, and we moved on to our normal weekly business.

Cabinet business was dispatched quickly that morning and by ten o'clock we had finished. We all realised that this would probably be the last Cabinet meeting over which she would preside, and nobody wanted to be the first to leave. She clearly wanted to talk and suggested that we had coffee. Officials then left the Cabinet room and a rather desultory conversation began. I remember very little of what was said but three things stuck in my mind. The first was a general agreement that the next leader must come from the Cabinet. It should not be Michael Heseltine. The second was that the Cabinet felt both John Major and Douglas Hurd should be put up as candidates in the second ballot since it was not possible to know with any degree of certainty, nor was it possible to find out in the time available, which of them was the preferred candidate. The third and most memorable moment came when a colleague said, 'We are going to pin regicide on Heseltine.' The Prime Minister looked puzzled for a moment, and then came the devastating riposte: 'Oh no, it wasn't Heseltine, it was the Cabinet.' It was all the more telling because it was said without the slightest rancour. It was, to her, a simple statement of fact.

David Amess
Conservative MP 1983–

David Amess was elected MP for Basildon in 1983, a seat he held until 1997, when he became MP for Southend West.

Politically I owe everything to Margaret Thatcher. If it had not been for her leadership, I would never have won my seat in Basildon for the first time in 1983 and then retained it in 1987.

For me, Margaret Thatcher was the consummate politician. She had those unique qualities of charisma, enormous courage and determination. She was blessed with first-class skills of leadership and undoubtedly not only changed this country but the world for the better. No one, including myself, had expected to win for the first time in 1983 but all of that was due to the momentum that Margaret Thatcher brought with her in terms of encouraging ordinary working people to support Conservative Party policies. This was yet another great quality she had – common sense and a realisation of the aspirations that ordinary people had for a better life, not only for themselves but also for their children and grandchildren.

I was overwhelmed when I first entered the House as a Conservative Member of Parliament and to support a government led by Margaret Thatcher. She was truly magnificent at Question Time in the House of Commons. When she swept through the lobbies each time we voted, it was as if there was a sort of electric glow round her. She seemed to overshadow everyone.

Throughout those two Parliaments, 1983–1987 and then the one that followed, she faced many crises but never ducked a difficult issue. Debates that she was involved in were very great occasions with magnificent speeches – in stark contrast to the way things are today. I became sickened and disgusted by the whispering campaign that eventually undermined her. I kept thinking to myself, if she really was so awful, what's wrong with these chaps actually not standing up to her. I certainly wouldn't allow myself to be treated as they claimed that they were. Where was their backbone? I am sure Margaret Thatcher had greater respect for those who stood up to her, than those who – as if often described – were walked all over by her and then just complained behind her back. Pathetic. I was appalled when I listened to some of my colleagues, who had everything to thank her for, seemingly becoming concerned about our opinion poll ratings. If anyone should have been concerned, it should have been me. But I would have much preferred to have lost under Margaret Thatcher's leadership, and I don't believe that would have happened, than to have changed horses midway through a Parliament.

I was angry and inconsolable when the end finally came. And have never really entirely got over the treachery of a number of my colleagues. I actually wrote to one or two and told them what I thought of them. Conservatives should never ever air their dirty linen in public. At the very last minute I and others were drafted in to try and stiffen the resolve of colleagues but it was too late. I recall being with a number of Margaret's supporters in the room in the Lower Committee corridor thinking that if this was the way the campaign had been run so far, was it any wonder that she was in such a dire position. The effort seemed both complacent and half-hearted.

As I sat round the table going through lists of names of who was going to support who, I just thought it was so amateurish and that we shouldn't have to do it at all. That evening, I walked to 10 Downing Street and personally handed a letter in and asked that the Prime Minister be given it. Whether or not she ever received it I don't know, but it was basically telling her not to resign because she still had great support among colleagues. As I walked along the road to 10 Downing Street, down Whitehall, there was an air of sick excitement really among some of the crowds. Those were mainly the people who had been protesting in Trafalgar Square about the community charge. I kept thinking to myself that these are the very people who my colleagues are going to give pleasure to by forcing Margaret to stand down.

The next morning when I left home, I was listening to the radio and I can recall Pete Murray saying, 'This news is awful' and then he announced that Margaret Thatcher had resigned as Prime Minister. I was absolutely devastated. I could hardly concentrate on anything. When I arrived at the Commons, I bumped into a colleague who I think was one of the people who had been difficult and when he said to me, 'David, what are you looking so upset about?' I told him why, he said, 'Silly woman, I can't understand why she has resigned,' which for me, basically said it all.

I was inconsolable. I bumped into another colleague, who felt exactly as I did and we both went for a lunchtime drink. I found myself becoming increasingly angry with people. I told the whips exactly what I thought of them. Just as I told the architect of her defeat exactly what I thought of him – although he certainly showed some guts writing to me directly a few days later.

When I saw Mrs Thatcher behind the Chair, walking to her room, I just said how sorry I was about everything and she put her fingers up indicating just four votes, which is all it was. Absolutely crazy. And I was also sitting behind her when she gave her last performance at Prime Minister's Questions and she made that fantastic speech. Incredible.

When she left office, it never really seemed the same again. There was the woman who had brought the Conservatives to power, done so much to change the country for the better, now completely cast aside and humiliated on the back benches. I won a ballot to introduce a topic for debate on a Friday and I chose to do it on Margaret Thatcher's time as Leader of the Conservative Party and Prime Minister.

I am not sure that we will ever see the likes of her again.

Liam Fox
Conservative MP 1992–

Liam Fox was a Foreign Office Minister under John Major and was David Cameron's first Secretary of State for Defence. In 2005 he contested the Conservative Party leadership.

The first time I remember physically seeing Margaret Thatcher was at a speech she gave in Scotland while still Leader of the Opposition. As a Young Conservative it was not only the first time that I had ever seen a major politician speak live but it was particularly exciting as it was Margaret Thatcher who had drawn me into the Conservative Party. Coming from a very ordinary background in the west of Scotland, you didn't join the Conservative Party because you were a political careerist! It was the stark differences between the language and imagery of Margaret Thatcher and other politicians of the day which first grabbed my attention. Up till that point, in gloomy and failing Britain, there was still too much of a feeling that whatever pigeonhole you had been born into was where you should stay. It was Margaret Thatcher's liberating views on social mobility that made me a Conservative and I remember, to this day, that it was the conviction and energy that she brought to her arguments that impressed me just as much as the political messages themselves.

Almost a decade later, when I was the prospective Conservative candidate in the constituency of Roxburgh and Berwickshire, I had the first opportunity to have a one-to-one conversation with a woman who was now at the height of her political power. She had just had surgery on her hand for a Dupuytren's contracture and as a trainee GP I made sure I had swotted up on all the details in case it came up in conversation. As it turned out, it would be the cause of me receiving the Thatcher grip on the wrist, so beautifully described by the Bishop of London at her funeral service. I explained to her that there was some belief that the papal blessing, with the last two fingers drawn into the palm, was the result of a mediaeval Pope having the same medical condition and being unable to extend his fingers as had traditionally been done up to that point. She looked at me and said, 'Really?' Not understanding the significance of the question I simply nodded back. She turned the full Thatcher-ray straight at me and said, 'Really.' At this point the prime-ministerial grip was brought into full force as she put down my cutlery and asked me – more of a command than a question – for the third time, 'Really?' Realising that she was either genuinely interested or suspected me of pulling a fast one, I said with all the sincerity I could muster, 'Yes, Prime Minister – really.'

Momentous political and personal events were already dissolving into history when I spent an evening with Margaret Thatcher in New York in the new millennium. We were attending a reception for the Anglo-American group the Atlantic Bridge, where the guests included both Michael Ancram and Michael Howard. It was a very special occasion because we all knew it might be the last time she would speak to an audience in America – particularly poignant as she had such a high regard for the United States, believing it to be a flagship in the battle for liberty and the rule of law. It was difficult for her as she had recently lost Denis and had suffered a number of minor strokes. I had the pleasure of introducing her and said, 'For most of us we get to hear about history or to read about history. Seldom do any of us have the honour of meeting with history.' Those who have never known Margaret Thatcher well might be surprised at the humility she genuinely possessed and she went quite misty-eyed, saying 'no, no, not at all – that is just too kind'. She had a short prepared text to read and we wondered if she would be able to deliver it, yet within minutes not only had she recovered her full Thatcher poise but had gone off the text to give us a short, impromptu lecture on the importance of the relationship between Britain and the United States. It was the last time that I was to see the echoes that I had heard as a Young Conservative in Glasgow – and it was magnificent. An hour or so later, we were sitting together in the back of her official car as we waited to go off to the dinner we were attending. She suddenly turned and asked me, 'Remind me, dear, of the name of our host.' I replied, 'His name is Mr Mallory Factor.' Inexplicably, she then added, 'Is he related to Max Factor?' 'Why on earth would you ask a question like that?' I replied. 'I just wondered,' she said with a smile 'if he might have any free samples for an old lady.' I didn't know what to say. One of her long-serving bodyguards sitting at the front looked in the rear-view mirror and said, in what can only be described as astonishment, 'She told a joke!' We all laughed, perhaps all for different reasons.

The last time I had the pleasure of spending any time with her was when she did me the honour of attending my fiftieth birthday party at Admiralty House in London in September 2011. Being in poor health by this time, it was suggested that she should only attend for twenty to thirty minutes as she would be too tired. She was having none of it. Surrounded by many people that she had known well and many more who simply wanted to have the chance of a fleeting encounter with her, and bolstered by more glasses of white wine than those accompanying her would have liked, she played the room like the old trooper she was. To his great credit, Prime Minister David Cameron, who was also present, simply melted into the background leaving the field clear as she swept all before her. The last conversation about politics that I had with her was as we walked through the room. 'You must be feeling quite vindicated about the euro,' I said. 'Why so?' she replied. 'Well, it's looking pretty shaky.' She stopped. 'Is it really?' 'Well, it's not looking too healthy,' I suggested. Slowly moving off, she added, 'Well dear, we'll not be too sad, shall we?'

As I sat, like so many, in the crypt Chapel of the House of Commons where her coffin was resting and again at her funeral in St Paul's I couldn't help but think about all the politicians, commentators and pundits who constantly ask, 'Who will be the next Thatcher?' Their search is in vain. They will not find one.

Also available from Biteback

MARGARET THATCHER IN HER OWN WORDS
EDITED BY IAIN DALE

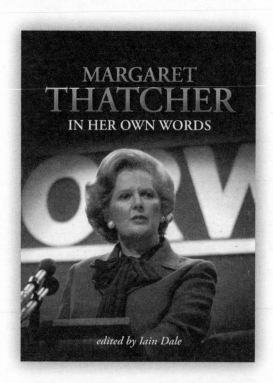

Margaret Thatcher is one of the towering politicians of the twentieth century. In terms of influence and recognition, she ranks with Winston Churchill, and remains probably the most important British leader for fifty years. A formidable and largely self-trained orator, this volume collects her greatest and most famous speeches, as well as the cream of her interviews, alongside other biographical material.

440pp paperback, £14.99
Available from all good bookshops or order from
www.bitebackpublishing.com

Also available from Biteback

THE REAL IRON LADY
GILLIAN SHEPHARD

288pp hardback, £16.99
Available from all good bookshops or order from
www.bitebackpublishing.com

A JOURNEY WITH
MARGARET THATCHER
ROBIN RENWICK

336pp hardback, £20
Available from all good bookshops or order from
www.bitebackpublishing.com